DING
CILLARY
nd SUPPORT
EPARTMENTS
o HIGHER
PERFORMANCE

LEADING ANCILLARY *and* SUPPORT DEPARTMENTS *to* HIGHER PERFORMANCE

The New Service Imperative for Patient Care

FRANK R. TORTORELLA, Editor

ACHE Management Series

Your board, staff, or clients may also benefit from this book's insight. For information on quantity discounts, contact the Health Administration Press Marketing Manager at (312) 424-9450.

This publication is intended to provide accurate and authoritative information in regard to the subject matter covered. It is sold, or otherwise provided, with the understanding that the publisher is not engaged in rendering professional services. If professional advice or other expert assistance is required, the services of a competent professional should be sought.

The statements and opinions contained in this book are strictly those of the authors and do not represent the official positions of the American College of Healthcare Executives or the Foundation of the American College of Healthcare Executives.

25   24   23   22   21   5   4   3   2   1

Library of Congress Cataloging-in-Publication Data

Names: Tortorella, Frank R., editor.
Title: Leading ancillary and support departments to higher performance : the new service imperative for patient care / Frank R. Tortorella, editor.
Other titles: Management series (Ann Arbor, Mich.)
Description: Chicago, IL : Health Administration Press, [2021] | Series: HAP/ACHE management series | Includes bibliographical references and index. | Summary: "Ancillary and support departments are essential partners in ensuring that a healthcare organization achieves its patient safety and experience goals. To be successful, healthcare leaders must understand these departments and how to optimize their performance. This book examines the key principles for effectively and efficiently leading ancillary and support teams throughout a healthcare system and shares best practices from direct patient care as well as from diagnostic, therapeutic, and nonclinical services"—Provided by publisher.
Identifiers: LCCN 2020047910 (print) | LCCN 2020047911 (ebook) | ISBN 9781640552401 (paperback) | ISBN 9781640552371 (epub) | ISBN 9781640552388 (mobi)
Subjects: MESH: Ancillary Services, Hospital—organization & administration | Delivery of Health Care—organization & administration | Quality Assurance, Health Care—organization & administration | Patient Care
Classification: LCC RA971 (print) | LCC RA971 (ebook) | NLM WX 150.1 | DDC 362.1068—dc23
LC record available at https://lccn.loc.gov/2020047910
LC ebook record available at https://lccn.loc.gov/2020047911

The paper used in this publication meets the minimum requirements of American National Standard for Information Sciences—Permanence of Paper for Printed Library Materials, ANSI Z39.48-1984. ♾™

Acquisitions editor: Jennette McClain; Manuscript editor: James Fraleigh; Project manager: Andrew Baumann; Cover design: Brad Norr; Layout: Integra

Found an error or a typo? We want to know! Please e-mail it to hapbooks@ache.org, mentioning the book's title and putting "Book Error" in the subject line.

For photocopying and copyright information, please contact Copyright Clearance Center at www.copyright.com or at (978) 750-8400.

Health Administration Press
A division of the Foundation of the American
    College of Healthcare Executives
300 S. Riverside Plaza, Suite 1900
Chicago, IL 60606-6698
(312) 424-2800

To Millie and Frank Tortorella Jr.

Contents

INSTRUCTOR RESOURCES

A test bank for this book is available to instructors who adopt the book for use in their course.

For access information, please email hapbooks@ache.org.

Acknowledgments

I would like to acknowledge all of the heroes in ancillary and support departments during the COVID-19 pandemic doing their part to care for patients. I would also like to thank the contributing authors as experts in their fields sharing best practices to improve healthcare for patients. Finally, my appreciation goes to Leonora, John, Jonathan, Michelina, Millie, Larry, Frank, Charlie, Nina, Robert, Aidan, Paul, Anthony, Amy, Edson, Nathaniel, Emilee, Ellen, Tita, Nicolle, and Maximiano for being in my life.

PART I

Leading Ancillary and Support Departments

CHAPTER 1

Introduction to Ancillary and Support Departments

Frank R. Tortorella

THIS BOOK OFFERS knowledge about ancillary and support departments from experts with years of field experience. Given the range of services these departments provide, there has been no single source for their leaders or for students of healthcare administration to learn the intricacies and best practices needed to lead these departments. This chapter presents an overview for the reader, identifies the ancillary and support departments featured in the book, highlights the integral roles that these departments play in patient safety and experience, and stresses the valuable benefits to leaders of building their network from their professional associations.

Part I, "Leading Ancillary and Support Departments," consists of chapters 1 to 3 and provides approaches for leading ancillary and support departments using the Baldrige framework and for building a culture of performance improvement (National Institute of Standards and Technology 2019). Chapter 2 describes how leaders can use the Baldrige framework for performance excellence to foster an ethic of learning and excellence. The chapter will outline best practices in leadership, including the development and communication of a department's mission, vision, and values aligned with the institution. It summarizes the key components of creating and deploying a departmental strategic plan. The chapter discusses the importance of identifying a department's key customers and their requirements for its services. It provides insight into how high-performing organizations measure, analyze, and improve performance. Chapter 2 also lists essential practices for building an engaged workforce, notes key workforce measures, and reviews key dimensions of operational excellence. Last, the chapter offers advice on how to get started with Baldrige.

Chapter 3 outlines the necessary components for implementing a culture of continuous improvement, which requires strong leadership buy-in and support. Along with describing how to meet quality, safety, and service-level expectations, the chapter explains how ancillary and support department directors seeking excellence look for ways to continuously improve their department's performance. Learning from one's failures and colleagues and from organizations using best practices is one continuous-improvement technique, as is leadership and staff development. The chapter offers an innovative framework for performance improvement (PI). It presents an infrastructure used to build a PI culture, an annual planning process, and a PI development model. Approaches include educating leaders and staff on PI methodologies, such as Plan, Do, Study, Act; setting both performance expectations for conducting PI projects and a process to hold staff accountable; and establishing a reward system to recognize PI and reinforce a culture of performance excellence. It also presents two examples of PI projects and the key elements to build a culture of PI.

Part II, "Best Practices in Ancillary and Support Departments," consists of chapters 4 to 20. Each chapter is devoted to a particular ancillary or support department, with authors sharing their leadership knowledge on the key topics listed in exhibit 1.1. Some leaders may find their first attempts to identify key units of work and performance metrics difficult to monitor; others may struggle to measure productivity. These chapters therefore will provide helpful insights on such potential issues. Each chapter ends with department-specific key terms for reference.

Exhibit 1.1: Chapter Topics

Department Description

Key Department Services

Department Organizational Structures

Key Customers and Their Performance Expectations

Key Process Flows

Key Units of Work and Volume Statistics to Monitor

Key Metrics to Monitor: People, Service, Quality/Safety, Financial

Key Informatics Issues

Staffing Models

Productivity Models, Including Work-to-Staff Ratios and Industry Performance Targets

Strategies to Improve Recruitment and Retention

Key Regulatory Issues

WHAT ARE THE ANCILLARY AND SUPPORT DEPARTMENTS?

The wide range of ancillary and support services for patients, their family members, other hospital staff, and physicians are essential in care delivery processes. Most people associate hospitals with physicians and nurses but do not realize the myriad ancillary and support departments that affect patient safety and experience. The literature defines ancillary and support departments in several ways. Typically, *ancillary departments* provide direct patient care, diagnostic services, or therapeutic services. *Support departments* provide a wide variety of nonclinical services, including but not limited to transporting patients to locations to receive care, interpreting for patients with limited English proficiency, providing health information management services, supplying retail food, and many other necessary services to provide care for patients in a safe and clean environment.

Exhibit 1.2 categorizes the ancillary and support departments discussed in this book; however, some organizations may define ancillary and support departments differently. Also, there are other ancillary and support departments not represented in exhibit 1.2. Ancillary and support services are closely integrated into patient treatment processes, requiring close collaboration with other clinical team members to build and maintain a culture of safety. Ancillary and support department employees also have direct and indirect contact with patients and their families that significantly influences their experience. Although some ancillary services produce significant revenue for their institution, many support departments

Exhibit 1.2: Ancillary and Support Departments

Ancillary	Support
Admissions	Environmental Services
Case Management	Facilities
Clinical Nutrition	Dining Services and Room Services in Food and Nutrition Services
Pathology and Laboratory Medicine	
Pharmacy	Health Information Management
Radiology and Imaging Services	Language Assistance
Rehabilitation Services	Patient Advocacy
Respiratory Care	Patient Transportation
Social Work	
Spiritual Care	

do not generate revenue. This book will provide approaches and tools to manage these departments effectively and efficiently so they can contribute to the financial health of the institution.

HOW ARE ANCILLARY AND SUPPORT DEPARTMENTS ORGANIZED IN HOSPITALS?

There is no standard approach to how hospitals organize their ancillary and support departments. Unlike colleagues in other hospital departments such as nursing or ambulatory care, where a hospital will have a vice president of nursing/ chief nursing officer and a vice president of ambulatory care, there is no standard title for the heads of ancillary and support departments. Hospitals may have a vice president of clinical support services, vice president of ancillary services, vice president of inpatient services, or another title. Alternatively, some ancillary and support departments may report to Nursing, Facilities, clinical departments, or Finance, to name some of the possibilities. Each ancillary and support department provides a specialized service but is also susceptible to becoming an organizational silo in which an organizational unit defends its own interests. To benefit from a network of professional colleagues who can collaborate and share different perspectives and best practices, hospital leadership must consider their organizational culture and structure to decide where ancillary and support departments fit best in the organization.

ROLE IN PATIENT SAFETY

Ancillary and support departments play a major role in patient safety. Some examples include an environmental services employee cleaning a patient's room, preventing a patient infection; a patient transporter finding an error on a patient's wristband, preventing a patient identification error; or a social worker on call, preventing a patient suicide. Ancillary and support staff serve on nursing, medical staff, and other multidisciplinary committees working on patient safety initiatives, where they provide valuable insights and feedback in robust discussions to identify and implement the best solutions. Educating staff on the importance of reporting safety incidents and providing consistent management support sends a clear message to staff and builds a solid foundation for a culture of patient safety. Ancillary and support department employees are essential partners with the clinical and administrative team in achieving safety goals. For example, exhibit 1.3 outlines some of the 2020 National Patient Safety Goals and shows which ancillary and support departments can influence them (Joint Commission 2020).

Exhibit 1.3: Selected 2020 Joint Commission National Patient Safety Goals

Goal	Departments that can influence goal outcome
Identify patients correctly	Admissions, Case Management, Clinical Nutrition, Health Information Management, Language Assistance, Pathology and Laboratory Medicine, Radiology and Imaging Services, Rehabilitation Services, Respiratory Care, Social Work, Spiritual Care
Improve staff communication	All ancillary and support departments
Use medicines safely	Pharmacy working with providers
Prevent infection	All ancillary and support department staff washing hands, and Environmental Services cleaning surfaces
Identify patient safety risks	All ancillary and support department staff reporting safety incidents

Source: Adapted from Joint Commission (2020).

ROLE IN PATIENT EXPERIENCE

Ancillary and support department employees' interactions with patients and their families significantly shape the quality of the patient experience. This fact is illustrated by the important roles that ancillary and support departments play in addressing the eight principles of patient-centered care (Picker Institute Europe 2020). Exhibit 1.4 lists the notable ways ancillary and support departments contribute to the patient experience. Readers may not know how integral improving the patient experience is to the core functions of ancillary and support departments, so examples for each principle follow.

All of the ancillary departments listed in exhibit 1.2 contribute to *Principle #1, Fast access to reliable health advice,* as do some support departments like Patient Transportation and Health Information Management. For example, Patient Transportation brings patients to their care location in a timely fashion, and Health Information Management maintains the electronic medical record so providers have ready access to vital health information. All of the ancillary departments are involved in *Principle #2, Effective treatment delivered by trusted professionals.* The key functions of Case Management, Rehabilitation Services, and Social Work, just to mention a few departments, are directly aligned with delivering *Principle #3, Continuity of care and smooth transitions.* Case managers work with the patient and their family and caregivers in the transition from acute inpatient care to skilled nursing facilities and/or home health, coordinating with Rehabilitation Services for home care to provide the appropriate durable medical equipment. Social

Exhibit 1.4: Eight Principles of Person-Centered Care

Principle	Selected ancillary and support department(s) supporting the principle
1. Fast access to reliable health advice	Clinical Nutrition, Health Information Management, Language Assistance, Pathology and Laboratory Medicine, Patient Advocacy, Patient Transportation, Pharmacy, Radiology and Imaging Services, Rehabilitation Services, Respiratory Care, Social Work, Spiritual Care
2. Effective treatment delivered by trusted professionals	Clinical Nutrition, Pathology and Laboratory Medicine, Pharmacy, Radiology and Imaging Services, Rehabilitation Services, Respiratory Care, Social Work, Spiritual Care
3. Continuity of care and smooth transitions	Admissions, Case Management, Rehabilitation Services, Social Work
4. Involvement and support for family and caregivers	Case Management, Patient Advocacy, Social Work, Spiritual Care
5. Clear information, communication, and support for self-care	Clinical Nutrition, Language Assistance, Pharmacy, Rehabilitation Services, Social Work, Spiritual Care
6. Involvement in decisions and respect for preferences	Case Management, Patient Advocacy, Social Work
7. Emotional support, empathy, and respect	Patient Advocacy, Social Work, Spiritual Care
8. Attention to physical and environmental needs	Case Management, Environmental Services, Facilities, Rehabilitation Services

Source: Adapted from Picker Institute Europe (2020).

workers assist patients with discharge planning for a smooth transition. Although many of the ancillary and support departments contribute to *Principle #4, Involvement and support for family and caregivers*, the staff in Case Management, Patient Advocacy, Social Work, and Spiritual Care devote most of their time to working with patients, families, and caregivers, keeping family members and caregivers involved in the patient's care plan as needed.

Principle #5, Clear information, communication, and support for self-care also requires the work of multiple ancillary and support departments (e.g., Clinical Nutrition, Pharmacy, Rehabilitation Services, Social Work, and Spiritual Care). Along with departments that provide direct care, Language Assistance is a key contributor to achieve Principle #5 for patients with limited English proficiency.

The pharmacist also speaks directly with patients to provide clear instructions on their medications. *Principle #6, Involvement in decisions and respect for preferences,* and *Principle #7, Emotional support, empathy, and respect,* are essential components of service delivery for all patient-facing staff in ancillary and support departments. Patient Advocacy ensures patient rights are followed, including patients' decisions and preferences. Spiritual Care chaplains are available 24/7 to advise and comfort patients, family members, and caregivers during their healthcare journey. Last, *Principle #8, Attention to physical and environmental needs,* involves a spectrum of departments, ranging from Case Management staff ensuring safe transitions between levels of care to Environmental Services and Facilities staff ensuring a clean and safe environment. Also, therapists in Rehabilitation Services work directly with patients to make sure they can safely function in the home environment after discharge. These examples illustrate how ancillary and support departments are integral in the many dimensions that make up a patient's healthcare experience.

BUILDING A NETWORK OF COLLEAGUES

Ancillary and support departments represent numerous diverse professions, each with unique operational and staffing challenges. Department leaders are the experts in their fields and often must focus on their daily operations, making it difficult to learn about best practices from other organizations or industry benchmarks to compare their performance against key metrics. Also, the director of an ancillary and support department may have no routine contact with other colleagues in their discipline at their leadership level. Many ancillary and support department leaders address this reality by joining a professional association to build their professional network, take advantage of professional development opportunities, and learn best practices from other organizations.

Collaborating with other leaders in one's profession can bring many valuable benefits. For example, one director of case management became a founding board member for her professional association. After the association completed a national survey of nurses and social workers to identify a core body of knowledge for hospital case managers, the professional association board used these findings to create and implement a national certification examination for nurse and social work case managers. Another example is from a support department where the director of patient transportation, through her professional association, partnered with a vendor to conduct a national survey to establish best practice turnaround-time standards in patient transportation; these were then shared with the association's members. These examples illustrate how involvement with professional associations can provide opportunities for directors to stay on the cutting edge and contribute to their field by developing a professional network and sharing best practices.

REFERENCES

Joint Commission. 2020. "2020 National Patient Safety Goals." Accessed August 19. www.jointcommission.org/standards/national-patient-safety-goals/.

National Institute of Standards and Technology. 2019. "Baldrige Criteria Commentary." Updated November 15. www.nist.gov/baldrige/baldrige-criteria-commentary.

Picker Institute Europe. 2020. "Picker Impact Report 2018–2019." Accessed August 19. www.picker.org/picker-impact-report-2018-2019/.

CHAPTER 2

Leadership of Ancillary and Support Departments Using Baldrige

Cynthia St. John

TODAY'S HEALTHCARE LEADERS find themselves in one of the world's most complex industries, at one of the most complicated times in history. Change is coming from every direction: regulatory, political, social, financial, and others. The most effective leaders seek a systematic approach to running and changing their organization—one that balances stability and agility. In their search, many healthcare leaders have found Baldrige and its Criteria for Performance Excellence useful for creating this balance and establishing a framework for the organization's approach to achieving higher quality at lower cost.

For more than thirty years, the national Baldrige Performance Excellence Program (BPEP) and its criteria-based framework have offered a systems approach to help organizations improve (and often transform) their performance. The framework helps leaders answer three questions: Is your organization doing as well as it could? How do you know? What and how should you improve or change (BPEP 2019a)? Most of the organizations pursuing Baldrige are in healthcare, but it has proven useful for other economic sectors, including business (manufacturing, service, nonprofits, government) and education.

Although awareness and use of Baldrige have increased during the 2010s, less commonly known is the revelation that Baldrige is entirely scalable and does not need to be as laborious as you may have heard or experienced. This chapter first describes three major implications for scalability and practicality that can work in a leader's favor. The remainder of the chapter then takes a deeper look at the Baldrige framework and its content, and describes how to get started. Consider this a primer for healthcare executives looking to survive and thrive in today's challenging environment.

LEADERSHIP COMMITMENT IS KEY

If a department, division, or entire organization is serious about improving, and understands the only way to get different results is to do things differently, its first question should be, "Is the top leader fully committed and willing to push forward even when it's difficult?" Notice the question is not about whether he or she is generally in favor of change, or willing to persevere through difficulty. The leader needs to be out front leading the charge, even when it is hard. But here is the good news: Scalability means the framework can be used at any or all levels of the organization. For example, the Baldrige approach has been effective for a CEO leading an entire 14-hospital system through a performance excellence journey as a way to create what he called "systemness." The healthcare system had been formed when three smaller systems merged, and each hospital had had its own unique culture, processes, and results. The CEO wanted one system with multiple locations. One culture. One set of core processes. One set of results, with all locations achieving the same high standards and contributing to the system's excellence. By contrast, other organizations apply Baldrige principles one entity at a time (e.g., by hospital or business unit). Still others take it all the way down to one division or department (e.g., Clinical Support Services) as per the focus of this book. As a result, "top leader" becomes relative, and organizations can achieve incredible outcomes at either a macro (system/hospital) or micro (division/department) level. To set your starting point, search as far up the organization as possible until you reach a key leader—in this context, the top leader for a defined level such as a system, entity, division, or department—who is not yet fully committed to the framework or the disciplined approach required for its success. If that leader is not ready or willing to be the front person for a Baldrige-based journey to excellence, the next highest leader who clearly is ready is your best choice for an initial partner. Look for the early adopters, generate early wins, and then spread the effort as additional opportunities arise.

SYSTEMATIC AND ADAPTABLE ARE NOT OPPOSITES

The second way leaders can make scalability and practicality work in their favor is by recognizing that "systematic and disciplined" is not the opposite of "adaptable and innovative." Many leaders initially perceive these as conflicting but later appreciate them as complementary. For example, when organizations first adopt Baldrige, this seeming conflict can provoke raised eyebrows. The first and easiest way to alienate large groups of people is by allowing them to believe their local flexibility is going away. At the same time, the fastest way to sink the entire effort is to let these same leaders believe their way of doing business will be fully independent with no consistency or accountability. As with most everything else, it is about balance, which is a both–and (not an either–or) proposition.

Scalability and practicality become relevant when thinking about creating the right balance at the right level. The reality is there will be some key processes, generally referred to as your *core processes*, that will need to be consistent. Core processes will be covered in more detail later in the chapter, but briefly, they relate to strategic planning, customer and workforce focus, operations, measurement, and improvement. There will be high-level process steps that are important for every entity, division, or department to use consistently. Using an ice cream metaphor, chocolate ice cream requires a standard set of ingredients to achieve a consistent flavor. That said, entities, divisions, and departments have unique aspects, such as the specific customer or patient segments served and their related requirements. Although the high-level "chocolate" process steps cannot be skipped, local needs can be addressed by personalizing that process—the equivalent of adding chocolate chips and calling it double chocolate, or adding marshmallows and nuts to get rocky road. This customization allows for adaptability as needed. Tracking key performance indicators also may reveal that certain ingredients work better than others, which can help refine processes and enable better or best practices to be spread across the division, entity, or system, in turn raising the performance of all. These process improvements become the new consistent standard until the next intentional incremental or transformational process change.

IT DOESN'T HAVE TO TAKE FOREVER TO GET TRACTION

In addition to selecting the right level where you have solid leadership commitment, and striking the right balance with systematic yet adaptable core processes, a third way to leverage the often overlooked scalable and practical aspects of Baldrige is to create traction by using the right criteria. If change agents are new to Baldrige, consider the level of criteria that makes the most sense as a starting place—whether that means the full award criteria (BPEP 2019a), the condensed question set in the Baldrige Excellence Builder (BPEP 2019b), or one of the other "stepping stone" levels provided by many of the state programs (e.g., the Texas program; Quality Texas Foundation 2020). Regardless of the level, they all have three components in common: an organizational profile (OP), the processes categories, and results. The OP is your starting point, and where traction begins. An OP is considered a snapshot of your organization; it describes what matters most to you and sets the context for everything that follows. Your leaders initially may not have all the answers to the questions covered by the OP, such as organizational and competitive environment, key relationships, strategic context, and performance improvement system. Answer the questions as a leadership team, at the organizational level where you are using the Baldrige framework. For example, if you are focusing your Baldrige effort on the organization's division of ancillary and support services, the division leader and all her department leaders should develop the OP to reflect the entire division. This step alone gets everyone on the same page, so you can start moving in a single direction.

LEADING WITH BALDRIGE

The Baldrige framework is a set of criteria, in the form of questions, derived from the practices of high-performing organizations. The questions are broken down into seven categories: (1) Leadership, (2) Strategy, (3) Customers, (4) Measurement, Analysis, and Knowledge Management, (5) Workforce, (6) Operations, and (7) Results (exhibit 2.1).

The questions are nonprescriptive in the sense that they do not dictate how to perform each of the high-performing practices (such as listening to patients and other customers to obtain actionable information, which is an area to address in Category 3: Customers). Rather, they ask how you currently do each

Exhibit 2.1: Baldrige Excellence Framework

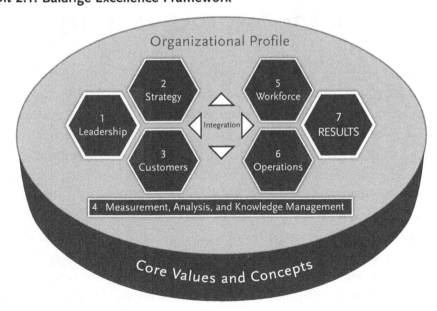

Source: BPEP (2019b).

of the things that high-performing organizations do. An additional component that bases the framework on criteria is that responses to all *process* questions (Categories 1–6) are evaluated against four factors: Approach, Deployment, Learning, and Integration (ADLI). *Results* (Category 7) are also evaluated, using a different set of factors: Levels, Trends, Comparisons, and Integration (LeTCI). Exhibit 2.2 describes the evaluation factors Baldrige uses to assess an organization's current performance (BPEP 2019a, iii–iv). Processes and results both include integration, underscoring the importance of treating the organization, division, or department as an integrated whole (i.e., a system) as per priorities identified and defined in the OP.

In the following section, OP questions have been aligned with the most relevant process category and results item(s) (exhibit 2.3), although many will have relevance across multiple categories. Although it is presented this way to help show the logical connection between Baldrige components, understand that the OP questions should be completed first. Doing so provides context for processes and results.

Exhibit 2.2: Baldrige Evaluation Factors

Process Evaluation Factors (Categories 1–6)	
APPROACH	How do you accomplish your organization's work? How systematic and effective are your key approaches?
DEPLOYMENT	How consistently are your key approaches used in relevant parts of your organization?
LEARNING	How well have you evaluated and improved your key approaches? How well have improvements been shared in your organization? Has new knowledge led to innovation?
INTEGRATION	How well do your approaches reflect your current and future organizational needs? How well are processes and operations harmonized across your organization to achieve key goals?
Results Evaluation Factors (Category 7)	
LEVELS	What is your current performance on a meaningful measurement scale?
TRENDS	Are the results improving, staying the same, or getting worse?
COMPARISONS	How does your performance compare with that of competitors or with benchmarks or industry leaders?
INTEGRATION	Are you tracking results that are important to your organization? Are you using the results in decision-making?

Source: BPAP (2019b).

Exhibit 2.3: Alignment of Organizational Profile, Processes, and Results

Organizational profile content	Process categories	Results items
Mission, Vision, and Values; Organizational Structure	Leadership	Leadership and Governance Results
Competitive Position; Competitiveness Changes; Strategic Context	Strategy	Strategy Implementation Results; Market Results
Patients, Other Customers, and Stakeholders	Customers	Customer Results
Comparative Data; Performance Improvement System	Measurement, Analysis, and Knowledge Management	All
Workforce Profile	Workforce	Workforce Results
Health Care Service Offerings; Regulatory Requirements; Suppliers and Partners; Assets	Operations	Health Care and Process Results; Financial Results

THE PRACTICES OF HIGH-PERFORMING ORGANIZATIONS

Because Baldrige is based on the things high-performing organizations systematically do to create world-class results, we can use the set of questions contained in the criteria to describe what all organizations can do to improve. If organizations, business units, and departments routinely apply these questions, they can transform themselves over time from average (or below average) to good, to great, to world class. I will specifically reference departments throughout this section, to show how these practices can relate directly to ancillary and support services in their journey to excellence.

Category 1: Leadership

High-performing departments have high-performing leaders. It is difficult, if not impossible, to have one without the other. So what do high-performing leaders do differently from their less effective counterparts? According to the Baldrige Excellence Framework, a lot. First, they set and deploy the Mission, Vision, and Values (MVV), which are core to creating an intentional and inspirational culture. They also consistently model those values, along with legal and ethical behavior.

In other words, they are worthy of being followed. Keep in mind that when you are transforming a department, you are part of something larger. Everything you do must align with the broader organization, including its MVV. As a result, your values are likely to be the same. Yet the way they translate to specific day-to-day behaviors may look a little different. If your organization does not share a set of values-based behavioral standards, create one for your department. Also, determine how to best translate your department's MVV into language or imagery that, while honoring and aligning with the organization's MVV, sets a clear and inspiring course for department staff and shows how their work advances the achievement of organizational aims.

In addition to setting and consistently communicating the MVV, high-performing leadership teams have well-defined and deployed processes for communicating with and engaging the workforce, patients, and other key customers, including opportunities for two-way exchanges and the timely communication of key decisions. They also create an environment for success, which includes building a culture defined by customer focus, high performance, learning, and innovation. These successful leaders have a strong action orientation, demonstrate personal accountability, and focus the department consistently on improving its performance and achieving the organization's mission.

Senior leaders in particular are expected to ensure an effective and responsible governance system by establishing structure, operating transparently, protecting customer and stakeholder interests, evaluating leadership performance, and planning for succession. In addition to personally demonstrating legal and ethical behavior, senior leaders should build systems for anticipating and addressing the department's legal, ethical, and regulatory compliance.

A final aspect of high-performance leadership is a commitment to the community. This commitment is about looking beyond the walls of the organization and includes societal well-being and community support. Think about what you do, what you are really good at, and find a way to identify relevant (often underserved) community groups that can benefit. Then contribute to building community health through service.

Common across all the high-performing practices is a recurring focus on results. Management by Fact is a Baldrige core value, and, as exhibit 2.3 shows, each Baldrige process category has a corresponding results item. For instance, the Leadership process category corresponds with leadership, governance, and societal responsibility results. Key metrics of senior leader effectiveness include communication and engagement with the workforce, patients, and other customers; governance accountability; legal, regulatory, and accreditation compliance; ethical behavior; and societal well-being and support of your key communities.

Category 2: Strategy

As noted, effective leaders develop and deploy their MVV, engage their work-force and customers, focus on action, and create an environment for success. The remaining categories can be thought of as the building blocks that enable leaders and their organizations to excel. Strategy is about establishing direction to ensure the department or organization delivers on its mission and advances its vision. The Baldrige Strategy category focuses on two actions critical to high performance: the systematic development and deployment of strategic plans.

Establishing direction for the department begins with thoughtfully develop-ing a strategic plan that sets the course for short- and long-term success. The plan should be based on, and directly address, relevant key factors from the OP. These factors include the MVV developed in Practice 1, along with three others: Stra-tegic Context (your key strategic challenges and advantages, similar to a SWOT analysis), Competitiveness Changes (the key changes most affecting your ability to compete), and Competitive Position (your key competitors, your relative size and growth in the markets you serve, and what you want your size and growth to be in the future). Also, factor your responses to other OP questions into your planning process, such as key customers and their requirements, key suppliers/partners/collaborators, and key service offerings. Deciding all these things up front as a leadership team will ensure you stay focused on what matters most to you now and in the future.

So how do high-performing departments and organizations develop strategy? The short answer is they develop a consistent approach that includes key process steps and participants, sets short- and long-term planning horizons, identifies strategic objectives, prioritizes change initiatives, and retains the agility to correct course midway. One of the greatest benefits of Baldrige is that it enables you to learn from organizations that have successful records of developing, deploying, reviewing, and refining their processes, and are now delivering desirable results. You can access the practices of award recipient organizations by visiting the Bald-rige website (https://www.nist.gov/baldrige/award-recipients). Consider reviewing the strategic planning processes of a few organizations, noticing the common ele-ments of each, and then adopt or adapt a process to serve as your starting point. As you apply ADLI to your process, particularly through disciplined cycles of deploy-ment and learning, it will evolve to become more effective and efficient. As noted, if you are applying Baldrige principles at the department level, every effort should be made to align your approaches with those of the broader organization. If there is a planning process in place, cascade it to the department level and enhance where needed to ensure it addresses the criteria for performance excellence. At the same time, keep it simple. Start small and then build as you mature with Baldrige by using the criteria over multiple years through iterative cycles of describing your approach (try flow-charting it), evaluating it using the ADLI factors, and improving it to more fully address the criteria.

It is not enough to develop strategy. Many leaders and organizations have created a strategic plan, only to get caught up again in the day-to-day demands of running the business while the plan ends up on a shelf. High-performing departments have an approach to properly deploy the strategy over time without straying or losing traction. The key elements of effective implementation include crafting short- and longer-term action plans to address the identified strategic objectives, deploying these action plans to your workforce (and key suppliers, partners, and collaborators as appropriate), allocating appropriate resources (e.g., financial, human) to support the action plans, identifying and using measures to track the achievement and results of action plans (including performance projections), and modifying action plans as changing circumstances indicate.

The results related to strategy (exhibit 2.3) include measures of strategy implementation such as achieving your organizational strategy and action plans. Another key indicator is marketplace performance, including market share or position, market and market share growth, and new markets entered, as appropriate. All results across all practices are evaluated through the four LeTCI factors.

Category 3: Customers

Focusing on the customer may seem obvious for any organization that needs customers to stay in business (i.e., all organizations), yet few intentionally and consistently focus on developing, reviewing, and refining their customer-related processes. By responding to the related OP questions, leaders and staff will have a clearer understanding of who their key customers and stakeholder groups are, what each of these groups expects or requires from their services and operations, and the key differences in requirements and expectations between the groups. When an organization is still early in its journey to excellence, the answers to these questions may be more subjective than objective. However, as the organization matures its processes and corresponding results, the responses will become data based and more usefully inform decision-making and action. High-performing organizations and departments have systematic approaches in two key areas: voice of the customer and customer engagement.

Voice of the customer (VOC) is about listening. Consider whether you have a well-defined, well-deployed approach for listening to patients and other customers—current and potential. Such an approach requires a systematic process for capturing patient and other customers' stated, unstated, and anticipated requirements, expectations, and desires. If you already do this well, you should have no problem answering the customer-related OP questions and knowing that your responses are completely valid, given the customer data for each of your key customer segments. Clarity regarding your key customers' requirements might come from the aggregation and analysis of survey data, focus groups, social media, complaints, rounding, and the like. Another part of listening to VOC and identifying requirements is knowing how you are doing relative to those requirements. Understanding your performance on key customer requirements is the ability to determine patient and other customer satisfaction, dissatisfaction, and engagement (relative to what they said matters most), to understand what is working and what is not.

With approaches in place to listen to and understand customer needs and requirements, and to gauge how well requirements are being met, you can engage customers more effectively. Enhancing engagement of patients and customers requires a disciplined approach to build and manage relationships across all stages of these constituents' journeys, identify and adapt services offerings to meet their requirements, and identify and resolve complaints while preventing their future occurrence. Consider also how you determine patient and other customer segments, and how you use them to understand and address their key differences.

If these processes are effective, the results should be favorable. Customer-focused results consider the current levels and trends in key measures of patient and other customer satisfaction, dissatisfaction, and engagement. In addition to levels and trends, high-performing organizations track how these results compare with those of their competitors and other organizations providing similar services. They also consider how these results differ by service offerings, patient/customer group, or stage of relationship.

Category 4: Measurement, Analysis, and Knowledge Management

For each of the practices thus far there have been key OP questions to be answered, processes to be addressed, and results to be tracked. The OP responses describe what's important; the process categories ensure there are systematic approaches for addressing what's important; and the results provide objective information about how you're doing relative to what's important (enabling learning and ongoing refinement so performance systematically improves over time). Practice 4 provides insight into what high-performing organizations do to measure, analyze, and improve performance. Also addressed is information and knowledge management, which allows best practices to be spread and organizational learning to occur. The Baldrige framework (exhibit 2.1) demonstrates how Measurement, Analysis, and Knowledge Management forms the foundation for all the other categories.

The OP asks about comparative data—specifically, what key sources of comparative and competitive data are available from inside and outside the healthcare industry. The Results section of exhibit 2.3 associated with each category asks you to put your data in perspective by showing your performance relative to these comparisons, which in turn gives organizations a more informed view of their results and enables better decision-making. For example, how are you performing relative to other similar organizations? What about direct competitors? What about benchmark organizations inside and outside of the industry? Having this information enables you to identify strengths and opportunities for improvement (OFIs), consider them through the lens of what is most important to you (your OP), and then best prioritize where to spend energy and resources.

The other relevant OP question associated with this practice asks leaders to describe the organization's performance improvement (PI) system—in other words, the essential elements of the PI approach you use to evaluate and improve key processes and projects. Organizations commonly include a PI methodology such as Plan, Do, Study, Act; additional tools such as Lean Six Sigma; and an annual Baldrige assessment.

So how do high-performing organizations effectively perform Measurement, Analysis, and Improvement? They have a well-defined, systematic approach to select key measures, collect data, and track progress relative to daily operations and strategic objectives. They also conduct appropriate analyses to ensure conclusions are valid, then report and review performance (including the use of comparisons) so leaders can make informed decisions and respond rapidly to challenges or changing needs. The outcome of the performance review process serves as its own input (i.e., integration) by allowing organizations to prioritize and act on opportunities for continuous improvement and innovation, and to cascade these priorities to relevant work groups, suppliers, partners, and collaborators when appropriate.

The other item in this category is information and knowledge management. Mature organizations have processes to ensure the quality (accuracy, validity, integrity, reliability) and availability (timely and user-friendly format) of data and information. They also know how to manage knowledge by collecting and transferring workforce and other relevant knowledge from and to patients, other customers, suppliers, partners, and collaborators. They identify best practices for sharing and implementing across the organization where fitting, and use knowledge to embed learning in the way the organization operates.

Although the Baldrige results items (collectively, Category 7) have been distributed throughout the Practices of High-Performing Organizations section in an effort to best demonstrate the critical alignment between processes and results, a few general comments on results are relevant here. The performance measurement system just described is what supplies the needed data and information for

Exhibit 2.4: Comparison of Three Results-Focused Frameworks

Baldrige Results (Category 7)	Studer Pillars	Balanced Scorecard Perspectives
Leadership and Governance; Workforce	People	Organizational Capacity (Learning/Innovation)
Customer	Service	Customer
Health Care and Process	Quality	Business Process
Financial; Market; Strategy	Finance	Financial/Stewardship
	Growth	

tracking and reporting the results asked for in Category 7. As with any organization or business unit, the ancillary and support departments' results must be measured across each of the other categories. It is only possible to know how effective processes are by the results they produce. The Baldrige results items (Category 7) address all the key process items (Categories 1–6) and align well with other popular frameworks, including Studer Pillars. Exhibit 2.4 compares Baldrige and Studer, along with the traditional Balanced Scorecard approach, to demonstrate how they work well together.

Category 5: Workforce

Similar to Category 3, this one is also about people—in this case, engaging the workforce and ensuring an effective and supportive environment so they can succeed.

The OP asks for a description of your workforce relative to key employee groups and segments, their different educational requirements, and the key drivers that engage your workforce as they achieve the organization's mission and vision (which may vary by segment).

The Baldrige process category then asks about your practices for establishing a supportive environment, which begins by ensuring the organization has the right people with the right skills. Baldrige refers to *workforce capacity* as the organization's ability to ensure sufficient staffing levels to accomplish its work processes and deliver services to patients and other customers (i.e., the right number and type of people). *Workforce capability* is the organization's ability to accomplish its work processes through its people's knowledge, skills, abilities, and competencies (i.e., the right skills). Both are necessary, and high-performing departments have well-defined approaches in place to address capacity and capability. Specifically, they

- assess their current and future capability and capacity needs;
- recruit, hire, place, and retain new employees;

- organize and manage their workforce to accomplish the organization's work and meet or exceed customer requirements; and
- prepare the workforce for increases or decreases in capacity and changes in capability.

They also ensure workplace health, security, accessibility, benefits, and policies support high performance.

With approaches in place to create an environment where staff can succeed, it becomes possible to engage your workforce more effectively. Workforce engagement is the extent of workforce members' emotional and intellectual commitment to accomplishing your organization's work, mission, and vision. High-performing organizations develop and implement beneficial practices to address the Baldrige criteria in this area, focused on building an engaged workforce. The first practice is similar to what was described earlier for customers: determining their key requirements and measuring how you are doing relative to those requirements. In the case of employees, you determine the drivers of workforce engagement and then assess how you are doing relative to those drivers. Some of the methods you use for customers (e.g., surveys, focus groups, rounding) are often appropriate here too. Another approach is to create an organizational culture characterized by open communication and high performance. This approach was also identified in the Leadership discussion. Creating this culture is a key responsibility of leadership. Yet another driver is to ensure your performance management system supports high performance and high engagement by focusing on the right things (i.e., healthcare outcomes, patient/customer service, completing action plans, and the like) and then aligning reward, recognition, compensation, and incentive practices accordingly. The final driver is learning and development. High-performing departments create a learning and development system that supports the organization's needs (operational and strategic) and the individual development of its leaders and workforce. The system is continuously evaluated for effectiveness and efficiency, and includes ways to manage career progression and succession.

Workforce results should include measures that address each of the practices just listed, providing a gauge of how they are performing and where OFIs exist. Workforce results include measures of capability and capacity, such as levels and trends in key indicators for appropriate skills and staffing levels. Workforce environment results include health, security, accessibility, services, and benefits. Workforce engagement results include satisfaction and engagement for each key workforce segment. Last, workforce development results address the development and progression of employees and leaders, which also demonstrates increasing organizational capability.

Category 6: Operations

High-performing organizations engage in practices that allow them to run the business effectively and efficiently. Whereas *strategy* is about changing the business, *operations* is about running the business. Both are essential for success, and both are relevant to any level of the organization, including ancillary and support departments.

Operations focuses on the things organizations and their departments do to create operational excellence. The OP asks four types of questions directly related to operations. The first requires leaders to define their main service offerings, the mechanisms used to deliver those services, and the relative importance of each service to their success. Second is defining the assets of the organization or department—what are the major facilities, technologies, and equipment that enable you to deliver your services? Third is defining the regulatory requirements under which you operate and need to remain compliant. Fourth is identifying the key types of suppliers, partners, and collaborators that play a role in producing and delivering your services. The answers to these questions are likely to change over time as you refine your offerings and approaches to meet and exceed customer requirements, although completing the OP first provides focus for the early work on your journey to excellence.

The Operations category is divided into two items: work processes, and operational effectiveness and efficiency. Work processes are about how you design, manage, and improve your key services and related processes. High-performing departments have a systematic, repeatable approach to designing their services and processes. This approach includes determining key service and work process requirements, and then designing (or redesigning) the services and work processes to meet those requirements (to address patient/customer and organizational needs). It may be helpful to visit the Baldrige website and view a few recipient responses to the Operations category requirements to get a sense of the practices others have used.

Additional considerations for work processes include their management and improvement. Management means implementing the processes and ensuring their day-to-day execution is meeting or exceeding key process requirements and patient/customer expectations and preferences. It also considers how you manage the supply chain, including selecting, measuring, and evaluating key suppliers. Improving work processes calls for a systematic approach to continuously improve services and outcomes, demonstrated by an increase in performance, a decrease in variability, and pursuit of opportunities for innovation.

The second item in the Operations category is operational effectiveness and efficiency. This item looks at how the total costs of the operation are controlled (e.g., productivity, cycle time), how errors and rework are prevented (including medical errors), and how the need for cost control is balanced with the needs of patients/customers when they differ. Operational effectiveness also considers the reliability and security of information systems so they are managed in a manner that controls access to and confidentiality of electronic and physical data and information. A final area to address relative to operational effectiveness is safety and continuity. High-performing departments have practices in place to provide a safe operating environment. Robust safety systems address accident prevention, inspection, root-cause analysis of failures, and recovery. Business continuity during disasters or emergencies is also fully addressed.

To ensure processes are useful, high-performing organizations track key indicators or measures of healthcare and customer-focused service results (i.e., healthcare outcomes and the performance of key services), process effectiveness and efficiency results (i.e., productivity, cycle time, other appropriate measures of process effectiveness and efficiency, security and cybersecurity, and innovation), safety and emergency preparedness, and supply-chain management results.

GETTING STARTED

The chapter began by describing Baldrige as a criteria-based framework offering a systems approach to help organizations improve (and in many cases transform) their performance. This transformation develops through continuous cycles of answering the Baldrige criteria questions, evaluating your responses using ADLI and LeTCI, identifying and prioritizing your organization's strengths and OFIs, and acting intentionally in the prioritized areas to improve processes and results. Repeating this approach (exhibit 2.5) increases process maturity and performance over time. Most organizations will repeat this cycle on an annual basis.

Exhibit 2.5: Journey to Excellence Process

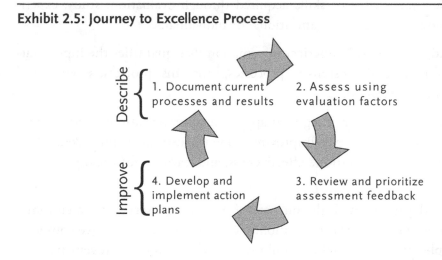

Describe
{
1. Document current processes and results

2. Assess using evaluation factors

Improve
{
4. Develop and implement action plans

3. Review and prioritize assessment feedback

To get started, pick up a copy of the criteria for performance excellence (health-care version: www.nist.gov/baldrige/publications/baldrige-excellence-framework/health-care) and begin by answering the organizational profile questions. Do not rush the process; use it to generate valuable leadership team discussions and get everyone on the same page. Once your OP is complete, move on to the process and results questions using either the full award level criteria, the Baldrige Excellence Builder, or one of the stepping-stone versions offered by many state-level programs.

Throughout your journey, visit the Baldrige website to learn from award-recipient organizations. Review their processes and results to see how high-performing organizations respond to the Baldrige criteria and what they measure to gauge performance. You will often find practices to adopt or adapt—use them. Also, reach out for support to those experienced with the Baldrige approach, including those represented in the subsequent chapters of this book. Enjoy the journey!

KEY TERMS FOR LEADERSHIP USING BALDRIGE

Approach: The methods your organization uses to carry out its processes.

Deployment: The extent to which your organization applies an approach in addressing criteria questions (how broadly and deeply the approach is applied in relevant work units throughout your organization).

Integration: The harmonization of plans, processes, information, resource decisions, workforce capability and capacity, actions, results, and analyses to support key organization-wide goals.

Learning: New knowledge or skills acquired through evaluation, study, experience, and innovation; can be organizational or individual.

Measures and indicators: Numerical information that quantifies the input, output, and performance dimensions of processes, programs, projects, services, and the organization (outcomes).

Performance excellence: An integrated approach to organizational performance management that results in ever-improving value to customers and stakeholders, improvement of the organization's effectiveness, and learning for the organization and its workforce.

Process: Linked activities with the purpose of producing a service for a customer (user) within or outside your organization. Generally, processes involve combinations of people, machines, tools, techniques, materials, and improvements in a defined series of steps or actions.

Results: Outputs and outcomes achieved by your organization. Results are evaluated from current performance (i.e., current levels); the rate and direction of change over time (trends); performance relative to similar others, competitors, and benchmarks (comparisons); and the relationship of results measures to key organizational performance requirements (integration).

REFERENCES

Baldrige Performance Excellence Program (BPEP). 2019a. *2019–2020 Baldrige Excellence Framework (Health Care)*: *Proven Leadership and Management Practices for High Performance*. Gaithersburg, MD: US Department of Commerce, National Institute of Standards and Technology.

———. 2019b. *Baldrige Excellence Builder*. Published January. https://www.nist.gov/system/files/documents/2019/02/06/2019-2020-baldrige-excellence-builder.pdf.

Quality Texas Foundation. 2020. "Application Levels Information." Accessed August 21. https://quality-texas.org/application-levels-information/.

Results: Outputs and outcomes achieved by your organization. Results are evaluated from current performance (i.e., current levels); the rate and direction of change over time (trend); performance relative to similar others, competitors, and benchmarks (comparisons); and the relationship of results measures to key organizational performance requirements (an alignment).

REFERENCES

Building a Culture of Performance Improvement in Ancillary and Support Departments

Cynthia St. John, Frank R. Tortorella, and Gayle Harper

IN BUSINESS AND INDUSTRY, continuous improvement is what sets the competition apart and determines long-term success. In healthcare, however, high levels of sustained performance not only determine success but also contribute to saving lives. Therefore, for ancillary and support departments, performance improvement and sustainability are imperative. Many reports have been published on the status of healthcare in the United States. The common theme among these reports is the unacceptable performance level on the part of healthcare entities and the need for increased quality (Commonwealth Fund Task Force 2003; Institute of Medicine 2001; Syed et al. 2018). In response to this "quality chasm," the Institute of Medicine (2001) set six aims for focused improvement: safety, effectiveness, patient-centeredness, timeliness, efficiency, and equitable care. To achieve these aims, and create the needed change in individual healthcare institutions and the industry as a whole, a commitment to the rigorous pursuit of continuous quality improvement is essential. This chapter presents an approach that ancillary and support departments can implement to rigorously and systematically improve quality. The key elements of this approach can be adopted by any entity desiring to refine its strategy for continuous improvement.

Although healthcare operations often have an internal performance improvement (PI) function, integrated and systematic approaches to improvement are less common. The recommended approach for ancillary and support departments combines three primary functions, or steps, for a "built for quality" approach (exhibit 3.1):

1. *Assessment* using the Baldrige Criteria for Performance Excellence and a scorecard as the foundation (see chapter 2)

2. An annual *planning* process
3. The *Plan, Do, Study, Act (PDSA) model* for performance improvement

---

Exhibit 3.1: Core Process for Continuous Cycles of Learning and Improvement

STEP 1: ASSESS CURRENT PROCESSES AND RESULTS

The Baldrige Criteria for Performance Excellence, developed by the Baldrige National Quality Program in 1987, is one of the dominant frameworks for examining quality in the United States (for the most recent criteria, see Baldrige Performance Excellence Program 2019). Considered by many quality-improvement experts as the single most influential document in the modern history of American business, the Baldrige criteria provide a framework for both evaluating and improving organizational performance. The criteria, and a set of underlying principles upon which they are based, are consistent with the principles and practices promoted by the "founding fathers" and leading authorities of the quality movement (Chaffee and Sherr 1992; Comesky et al. 1991; Crosby 1979; Deming 1986; Juran 1989; Marchese 1991, 1993; Schmidt and Finnigan 1992). In more recent work, the framework continues to provide empirical evidence for its effectiveness in improving quality and delivering a variety of desirable results (Link and Scott 2019; Mellat Parast and Golmohammadi 2019).

On an organizational level, the Baldrige framework is used to identify current strengths and opportunities for improvement within the seven Baldrige categories: Leadership; Strategy; Customers; Measurement, Analysis, and Knowledge Management; Workforce; Operations; and Results (refer to chapter 2 for additional information and application of this framework). The opportunities for improvement are then prioritized and used to develop annual goals. An ancillary or support department assessment process can also use a Baldrige-based approach to identify department-specific opportunities for improvement (OFIs). Exhibit 3.2 presents the key information sources (inputs) and the core processes and outputs for the assessment of customer and operational needs (see column 1: Assess). Exhibit 3.3 shows the key inputs and processes from exhibit 3.2 on a 12-month timeline, beginning with the collection of customer data via the use of multiple listening posts.

Exhibit 3.2: Infrastructure Used to Build a PI Culture

	Core process element		
	1: Assess	2: Plan	3: Improve
External: customer focus	Input: • Customer listening posts (ongoing interactions, interviews, surveys) • Department information (interviews, management meetings, environmental scanning, document review) Processes: • Analyze and synthesize customer input for key themes • Develop/revise Baldrige profiles (OP) for each department and the division Output: • Customer requirements (what our customers want or expect) • Strategic challenges and key success factors	Input: • Customer requirements • Key success factors Processes: • Scorecard review and refinement • Identification of key areas for improvement Output: • Core metrics to address customer requirements (organized by the key success factors) • List of key areas for improvement	Input: • Core metrics and current progress toward metrics • Key areas identified for improvement Process: • PDSA Output: • Demonstrable improvement on identified measures, or refinement of improvement plan to achieve desired outcomes
Example	Customer interviews led to the identification of *efficiency* as a key requirement; department profiles identified *service* as a key success factor.	For the Case Management department, one measure of service is the efficiency with which O_2 is ordered and delivered to patients ready for discharge (a cycle time measure).	See the Case Management example in the section titled "Two Examples of Performance Improvement Projects" later in this chapter.

(continued)

Exhibit 3.2: Infrastructure Used to Build a PI Culture *(continued)*

	Core process element		
	1: Assess	**2: Plan**	**3: Improve**
Internal: operational focus	Input: • Department interviews, focus groups, surveys, and document review Processes: • Analyze and synthesize input using the Baldrige framework and Criteria for Performance Excellence Output: • Self-assessment document • Strengths and OFIs	Input: • Strategic challenges • Key success factors • Strengths and OFIs Process: • Annual Planning Retreat (see exhibit 3.4) Output: • 3–4 prioritized gaps (OFIs), translated into annual goals	Input: • Annual division goals (aligned to institutional goals) • Department goals (aligned to division goals) Process: • PDSA Output: • Demonstrable improvement on identified aim statements or refinement of improvement plan to achieve desired outcomes
Example	The self-assessment identified a need to systematically "review and refine key processes to continuously improve effectiveness" as an OFI.	The identified gap is aligned with a broader goal focused on improving patient safety and quality.	See the Health Information Management example in the section titled "Two Examples of Performance Improvement Projects" later in this chapter.

Note: OFIs = opportunities for improvement; OP = organizational profile; PDSA = Plan, Do, Study, Act.

Exhibit 3.3: Annual Planning Process (for Fiscal Year September to August)

Sept.	Oct.	Nov.	Dec.	Jan.	Feb.	Mar.	Apr.	May	Jun.	Jul.	Aug.

Customer surveys/feedback (listening posts) →

Scorecards completed and monitored each month →

Complete employee surveys →

Ancillary or support department self-assessment process (Baldrige-based) →

Align scorecard with goals → (Jul.)

Ancillary or support department director retreat: Identify and prioritize department goals in alignment with assessment results; submit preliminary operating and capital expense budget (May)

Ancillary or support department: Communicate goals (Jun.)

Identify department goals aligned with institution and division goals (Jul.)

Submit final operating and capital expense budget (Jul.)

Finalize budget, aligned with any resources needed for goals (Aug.)

ASSESS ——— ——— PLAN

Patients are continuously surveyed using an organization-level satisfaction survey. Some ancillary and support departments have items on this survey that measure and provide feedback regarding patient perception of their services. Departments that do not must use other methods to receive feedback from their customers (including department-specific surveys, interviews, or direct contact). This information is used to identify key customer requirements—their needs and expectations of services. Along with patients and other customers, staff are also considered important stakeholders in ancillary and support departments.

The link between staff engagement and patient satisfaction is compelling, and employees are key partners in delivering or supporting quality care. Staff input can take the form of employee opinion surveys in January and February, as noted in exhibit 3.3. The various customer, employee, and departmental inputs provide the information on which the annual self-assessment is based. Integrating these inputs enables a comprehensive view of customer requirements, strategic challenges, key success factors, and current performance relative to these factors, as monitored by patterns in survey results over time and by key scorecard metrics.

The outputs of the Assess stage include a Baldrige-based self-assessment document (describing current processes and results relative to the seven Baldrige categories) and a list of resulting strengths and OFIs related to the identified customer requirements, strategic challenges, and key success factors. The full assessment provides a broad-based view of the ancillary or support department, and an invaluable insight into its key gaps. The review and prioritization of these gaps, or OFIs, is the focus of the next step. The prioritized OFIs are translated into the division or department's short- (one-year) and long-term (three-year) goals and projects.

STEP 2: PLAN FOR SHORT- AND LONG-TERM SUCCESS

Although identifying OFIs is a critical component in the quality cycle, not all opportunities can or should be addressed. These gaps require thoughtful consideration relative to cost and benefit. With limited resources, particularly financial and human, departments should focus improvement efforts on the critical few gaps that will yield the greatest return on selected priorities (e.g., safe, effective, efficient care). To best identify the critical few OFIs, the ancillary or support department should develop an annual planning process (exhibit 3.3). A core element in this process is a planning retreat with department-leadership participation. Exhibit 3.4 represents what happens before, during, and after the planning retreat to facilitate goal selection and refinement.

The output of the planning process is a short list of prioritized gaps and strengths with associated goals. These outputs serve as the input to department

Exhibit 3.4: Annual Planning Retreat

Before retreat:

- Department leaders receive and review:
  - Key sections from the department profile (including the department's vision and current strategic challenges and advantages)
  - Patient satisfaction survey, employee opinion survey, and department focus group feedback
  - A list of identified gaps derived from all sources of customer and self-assessment input (including survey and focus group feedback)
- Initial input on the importance of the identified gaps is collected from management and staff through a survey collection process

During retreat:

- Summarize and review the following for each category (Leadership; Strategy; Customers; Measurement, Analysis, and Knowledge Management; Workforce; and Operations):
  - Baldrige criteria
  - Survey and focus group feedback
  - Associated gaps (OFIs) and strengths
  - Initial prioritization by management and staff (pre-retreat input regarding importance), both for areas to improve (OFIs) and areas to leverage (strengths)
- Leadership team discusses and finalizes the prioritization of OFIs and strengths (rank order) for each category
- After completing the preceding process for all categories, the leadership team reviews and discusses the top priorities for each category and segments short-term (one-year) and long-term (three-year) goals
- Leadership team prioritizes across categories (top three)

After retreat:

- Translate prioritized OFIs (and strengths) into goal statements and department plans
- Determine metrics and targets
- Identify initiatives and develop action plans
- Use the scorecard to track progress

---

performance-improvement projects and initiatives, resulting in focused and integrated effort toward achieving operationally and strategically important goals. The planning and prioritization process occurs before budget finalization to gauge the financial resources needed to accomplish the top priority goals. The Operational Focus cell of exhibit 3.2, column 2 (Plan) outlines the connection among inputs, processes, and outputs relative to this core step. A parallel yet related process is the annual revision of the department scorecard to ensure customer requirements are being addressed (customer focus). The operationally focused planning process identifies the department's goals, whereas identifying key customer requirements enables each department to develop scorecard measures that track how they are performing relative to these requirements. The identified customer requirements become a way for the department to develop targeted improvement projects (discussed later in Step 3).

The scorecard serves as a means to promote balance between the needs of what might at times appear to be competing priorities. Captured on the scorecard are measures related to People, Service, Quality, Finance, and Growth (Studer 2003); these categories reflect the department's key success factors and align well with the Baldrige framework. The scorecard is reviewed annually and aligned with department goals as a part of the planning process (exhibit 3.3). Exhibit 3.5 presents sample measures for all five categories. Examining trends over time can reveal operational performance themes for the department, both strengths and OFIs.

Exhibit 3.5: Sample Scorecard Measures

Category	Sample measure	Department
People	% merit by performance level (pay for performance)	All
	% turnover (total, voluntary, first year)	All
Service	% "excellent" for taste and temperature	Dining/Room Services
	% "excellent" on support group evaluations	Social Work
Quality	Response time to transportation requests	Patient Transportation
	Coding accuracy for inpatient records	Health Information Management
Finance	Operating margin variance (actual vs. budget)	All
	Productivity	All
Growth	Develop a business plan to advance clinical pastoral education	Spiritual Care
	Reengineer medical record audit workflow and reporting	Health Information Management

STEP 3: IMPROVE PERFORMANCE WITH PLAN, DO, STUDY, ACT

Departments are advised to adopt a PDSA approach to performance improvement and develop an education program to equip staff with the necessary quality tools. Exhibit 3.6 presents a sample multiphase approach.

Exhibit 3.6: PI Model Development

Phase 1: Year 1	
Aim	**Approach**
Adopt a model or framework as the standard department approach to performance improvement. Develop PI knowledge and skill among leaders to support their mentor role and embed PI philosophy and practices from the top down.	• Select the PDSA methodology and associated quality tools as the foundation of department improvement efforts. • Require all leaders to participate in quality improvement education. • Establish the performance expectation that leaders participate in ongoing process improvement and continuing education activities.

Phase 2: Year 2	
Aim	**Approach**
Provide department managers and supervisors with a basic understanding of the PDSA methodology and further embed the PI philosophy and practices. Provide department managers and supervisors specific training and education on building team leadership skills.	• Develop and deliver education sessions for managers and supervisors to (1) increase understanding of PDSA and its associated tools, (2) standardize the department's approach to performance improvement, and (3) improve teamwork through additional training in effective facilitation skills. • Establish the performance expectation that managers and supervisors lead, or participate in, at least one performance improvement project per year. The project and its outcomes will be (1) presented to the leader's department and the director and (2) discussed during the annual performance evaluation process. • Training sessions will be provided on how to lead or mentor an effective team and what specific tools and practices are used in this role.

Phase 3: Year 3	
Include frontline staff in improvement initiatives.	• Continue to require annual manager and supervisor PI projects and encourage the inclusion of staff in these projects (managers and supervisors now become PI project mentors). • Add the employee opinion-survey results as a key input for the selection of PI projects.

(continued)

Exhibit 3.6: PI Model Development *(continued)*

Phase 3: Year 3	
Sustain the development and application of PI knowledge and skills within the department. Capture learnings and best practices; reward and recognize PI project teams.	• PDSA training is repeated annually for new managers and supervisors. The sessions are also open to any leader to attend as a refresher. • Each project is entered into a knowledge management database. The improvement projects are evaluated and awards are provided annually.

Note: PDSA = Plan, Do, Study, Act; PI = performance improvement.

The PI education sessions should train all managers and supervisors to:

- develop a project aim statement with measurable outcomes,
- facilitate effective team meetings,
- identify the factors contributing to key issues,
- collect baseline data,
- take steps to address an issue,
- measure the improvement, and
- adjust their action steps accordingly to reach their target outcome.

Each manager and supervisor is advised to lead or participate in at least one annual performance improvement project. Project selection is influenced by the department self-assessment and scorecard results, which allow managers and supervisors to identify relevant projects by reviewing the identified gaps and aligning them with division and department goals (Steps 1 and 2 in exhibit 3.2). The department should use an annual performance-management process to align staff goals with key department, division, and institution goals, and to track progress. By hardwiring the system in this manner, goal alignment and achievement increase.

TWO EXAMPLES OF PERFORMANCE IMPROVEMENT PROJECTS

Example 1 is a PI project in the Health Information Management Department. Phase I of the project focused on an organizational opportunity for improvement: decreasing incomplete scanned medical records available at discharge from 80 percent to 40 percent. Phase I results exceeded the goal by reaching 36 percent. Further exploration of the data illustrated that one particular inpatient unit had consistently higher individual percentages for incomplete inpatient scanned medical records. Therefore, Phase II of the project focused on decreasing the percentage of incomplete scanned medical records at discharge on this specific inpatient unit from 36 percent to 20 percent. Various PI tools were used to help identify causes and aid development of corresponding solutions. The Phase II project exceeded the 20 percent goal by reaching 12 percent. To maximize these favorable outcomes, Phase II solutions were rolled out systematically to all inpatient units. Ongoing monitoring of the project indicates all inpatient units were below the 20 percent goal, also averaging 12 percent. The inpatient unit that once had one of the highest individual percentages of incomplete inpatient scanned medical records continues to maintain its gains and has periodically achieved the ideal result of zero percent.

Example 2 is a PI project from the Case Management Department, where a staff member wanted to reduce the average time it takes from completion of a written discharge home oxygen evaluation to when the patient receives the oxygen at the bedside, with a goal of reducing the time from 15.5 hours to 8 hours. The team used PI tools to identify the main causes of the problem. From these causes, the team identified and implemented solutions and measured the resulting cycle time over four months. As a result, the average time from order placed to oxygen received declined from 15.5 hours to 4.5 hours, exceeding the goal of 8 hours. Time between placement of order and receipt of bedside oxygen was tracked for six months after this improvement, then tracked quarterly, with real-time intervention as needed. The improvement resulted in oxygen being received at the bedside about 11 hours earlier than pre-intervention, increased patient satisfaction, and provided a more streamlined and effective process.

Both projects directly affect patient safety and quality. The availability of the medical record at discharge and the prompt delivery of discharge equipment ensure better continuity of care. Also, medical information is readily available for return visits and appointments and for the transfer of care to receiving physicians and facilities. Timely discharges and the availability of the medical record at discharge also influence the bottom line through the availability of beds and services for other patients. These examples illustrate the many PI projects ancillary and support departments can perform to move toward a culture of continuous performance improvement.

DISCUSSION

The core process of Assess, Plan, and Improve is key to ensuring a systematic, repeatable approach is in place; one with well-defined steps, timelines, and accountabilities. The following elements are important for success.

People, Knowledge, and Skills

First, the process requires resources in the form of people with the right knowledge and skills. These resources do not need to be above and beyond current resources. If the knowledge and skills do not already exist in the department, develop high-potential employees who have an interest and tendency toward quality by sending them to your state Baldrige organization, or national Baldrige, to become examiners. The training and practical application that examiners receive become the foundation of your organizational effort. Equally important for the success of performance improvement projects is having a specialist in performance improvement as a resource for staff to consult about their projects, and to educate staff on how to use quality tools such as brainstorming, fishbone diagrams, team building, process flowcharting, meeting facilitation, and prioritization. Consider making this training mandatory for all managers and supervisors.

Systems

The process also requires key systems for managing and improving performance. Each organization already has a *performance management* system in place to evaluate and provide feedback to staff. Review it and ensure it has a built-in mechanism to align individual goals with department/division and organizational goals. One of the challenges is to help staff gain an understanding of how their work contributes to the organization's goals. Consider providing a badge card with the organizational and department/division goals for staff to include their individual goals as a quick reminder and to reinforce goal alignment. Given the importance of goal alignment to employee engagement, also consider having brown-bag educational sessions on goal alignment.

Most institutions are likely to have a *performance improvement* system (such as PDSA) in place. If not, select one and provide performance improvement training for staff. To account for normal turnover and the various educational levels in the workforce, continue to have brown-bag educational sessions to provide a solid understanding of the performance improvement process and tools.

Transparency and Accountability

Because the approach is goal focused and data driven, it's both important and easier to create an environment of transparency and accountability, which in turn supports an improvement culture. In this environment, people know what their goals are and how success will be measured. They are held accountable. It's a "tight, loose, tight" approach (relative to objectives, methods, and results). The main tool to provide accountability and transparency is the department/division scorecard. Some departments may have a challenge identifying scorecard metrics, given that this approach to quantifying performance may be new, but do not give up. Refine the scorecard during each annual cycle. The scorecard format will evolve incrementally each year as a result of feedback, making it more intuitive and easier to understand.

Proactive Versus Reactive

Having a systematic process to identify challenges and opportunities for improvement and translate them into goals promotes the proactive (versus the reactive) identification of issues and solutions. From a competitiveness standpoint, this is imperative. As part of building a culture of improvement, try to purposefully ingrain a more proactive and data-driven decision-making approach to spend less time in a crisis mode putting out fires. Create and communicate an annual planning process that you will refine each year. The planning process chronologically outlines each step, so leadership and staff have a common understanding of the big picture and what's next, and can see how the employee opinion survey and department self-assessment fit into the process of identifying goals and projects. Also, consider categorizing the key functions on department leaders' position descriptions using the categories of People, Service, Quality, Finance, and Growth. This shift in mind-set will require leaders to balance their time between strategy and operational responsibilities.

Integrated Versus Add-On

Finally, to ensure success, make the performance improvement process a part of "how we do our work" rather than an add-on. Staff may already be identifying opportunities and making improvements, but not necessarily in a robust and data-driven way. This approach provides a "conduit" in the form of a strategic and systematic approach to performance improvement. Although staff may report through feedback that they do not have time for performance improvement projects, they usually feel gratified after completing their project and seeing the impact on quality, safety, and service delivery while eliminating waste. With this performance improvement approach, staff selects meaningful projects that will improve quality, safety, and satisfaction for our patients and staff. After all, this *is* our job, not an add-on to our job. Another component of integrating performance improvement into day-to-day work relates to monitoring outcomes to ensure sustainability. Monitoring is usually most successful when the data collection is electronic, gathered and provided to departments from a division or institutional source, or built into the work process.

Cycles of Improvement

Be ready to refine the assessment, planning, and performance improvement processes over the years, starting with an operational approach and transitioning to a more strategic methodology. You may also need to fine-tune the timing of the annual planning process so the major steps occur in the right order, at the right time of year, to line up with the budget cycle. These refinements in the planning processes and performance improvement will shift from operational to strategic, giving the department leadership a longer range and more focused view. This model and the examples and lessons learned highlight several of the building blocks associated with the three components of Assess, Plan, and Improve to take departments on a journey of continuous improvement.

KEY TERMS FOR PERFORMANCE IMPROVEMENT

Assess: Evaluate or estimate the nature, ability, or quality of something.

Fishbone diagram: Sometimes called an Ishikawa diagram; identifies possible causes for an effect or problem.

Flowchart: A diagram that represents a process.

PDSA: Plan, Do, Study, Act; a model for performance improvement.

Performance improvement: An approach for continuous improvement whose basic tenets include management by fact, a focus on results and creating value, and a systems perspective.

Plan: An intention or decision about what one is going to do; a detailed proposal for doing or achieving something.

Quality: The standard of something as measured against other things of a similar kind; the degree of excellence of something.

Voice of the customer: Your process for capturing patient- and other customer-related information to understand their requirements, expectations, and satisfaction/engagement.

REFERENCES

Baldrige Performance Excellence Program. 2019. *2019–2020 Baldrige Excellence Framework (Health Care): Proven Leadership and Management Practices for High Performance.* Gaithersburg, MD: US Department of Commerce, National Institute of Standards and Technology.

Chaffee, E. E., and L. A. Sherr. 1992. *Quality: Transforming Postsecondary Education* (ASHE-ERIC Higher Education Report No. 3). Washington, DC: George Washington University.

Comesky, R., S. McGool, L. Byrnes, and R. Weber. 1991. *Implementing Total Quality Management in Higher Education.* Madison, WI: Mana Publications.

Commonwealth Fund Task Force. 2003. *Envisioning the Future of Academic Health Centers.* New York: The Commonwealth Fund.

Crosby, P. B. 1979. *Quality Is Free.* London: Penguin Books.

Deming, W. E. 1986. *Out of the Crisis.* Cambridge, MA: MIT Press.

Institute of Medicine. 2001. *Crossing the Quality Chasm: A New Health System for the 21st Century.* Washington, DC: National Academies Press.

Juran, J. M. 1989. *Juran on Leadership for Quality.* New York: Free Press.

Link, A. N., and J. T. Scott. 2019. "An Economic Evaluation of the Baldrige National Quality Program." In *The Social Value of New Technology*, edited by A. N. Link and J. T. Scott, 43–60. Northampton, MA: Elgar.

Marchese, T. 1993. "TQM: A Time for Ideas." *Change* 25: 10–13.

———. 1991. "TQM Reaches the Academy." *American Association for Higher Education Bulletin*, November, 13–18.

Mellat Parast, M., and D. Golmohammadi. 2019. "Quality Management in Healthcare Organizations: Empirical Evidence from the Baldrige Data." *International Journal of Production Economics* 216: 133–44.

Schmidt, W. H., and J. P. Finnigan. 1992. *The Race Without a Finish Line.* San Francisco: Jossey-Bass.

Studer, Q. 2003. *Hardwiring Excellence.* Gulf Breeze, FL: Fire Starter Publishing.

Syed, S. B., S. Leatherman, N. Mensah-Abrampah, M. Neilson, and E. Kelley. 2018. "Improving the Quality of Health Care Across the Health System." *Bulletin of the World Health Organization* 96 (12): 799.

PART II

Best Practices in Ancillary and Support Departments

CHAPTER 4

Admissions

Pamela Douglas-Ntagha and Pamela E. Brooks

DEPARTMENT DESCRIPTION

The term *Admissions Department* has many meanings throughout the healthcare industry. This area may be referred to as Bed Management, Patient Access, or Patient Placement. It may encompass one or more of these departments and offer several processes to place a patient into an inpatient bed. The Admissions Department usually has the responsibility of registering patients for inpatient services and emergency room visits. However, at some hospitals, Admissions functions more as a Bed Management Department, and registration functions are centralized in a Patient Access Department. Whatever name the institution chooses, they all refer to an area with a primary focus of admitting a patient into an inpatient setting through a range of access points.

The goal of an Admissions Department is always safe, correct placement of a patient into an inpatient bed. Such a patient must medically require inpatient services, meet acute care criteria for an inpatient bed, and have inpatient admission orders from a physician. Common access points for planned admissions are a physician's office (scheduled admits), operating room (postsurgery), and postprocedure areas such as interventional radiology. Common access points for unplanned admissions are the Emergency Center, the Transfer Center, unscheduled clinic admissions, and ambulatory treatment areas. The Admissions Department is responsible for fulfilling an inpatient bed request and ensuring that inpatient orders have been entered into the electronic health record (EHR). The patient is assigned an inpatient bed after the admitting physician completes these tasks. The process of assigning a bed in the electronic bed-management system (EBMS) follows specific guidelines provided by institutional leadership. These guidelines place a specific inpatient service (e.g., general internal medicine) into a specific inpatient location (e.g., Floor 20), often referred to as the "right patient, right bed" process.

The Admissions Department's clerical staff assigns the patient to an inpatient bed in the EBMS. The Admissions team uses the bed-assignment guidelines as a roadmap for patient placement. These guidelines will include a primary and secondary inpatient locations to ensure appropriate placement. However, if neither the primary nor the secondary inpatient location is available, additional assistance for such placement will be required from the Admissions clinical team, most often a registered nurse. A robust Admissions Department operates 24 hours a day, every day of the year, including holidays. These hours provide uninterrupted service for the institution.

KEY DEPARTMENT SERVICES

A key service of the Admissions Department is to maintain a continuous global view of institutional patient flow. The Admissions clinical team will guide the Admissions clerical team in bed assignments. This directional bed assignment is triaged throughout the day and can frequently change focus depending on the needs of the institution and any areas experiencing a high census. For example, the institution may experience an immediate need to decompress the Emergency Center. When beds are emptied, these beds are set to a priority clean and assigned to patients boarding in the Emergency Center.

Part of maintaining a global view of patient flow is the ability to see bed requests from all EBMS access points. This information is critical for the Admissions Department's workflow. The EBMS permits the Admissions team to determine how long patients have been waiting for a bed, their reason for admission, and what service or floor the admitting physician is requesting. The goal is timely patient placement that provides a seamless entry into an inpatient bed. When assigning beds, the Admissions team will watch for pain points at access locations where their census rises and operations slow down, then triage open beds to these areas to improve patient flow.

Another key Admissions workflow service is handling requests for inpatient-to-inpatient room transfers. Physicians make these requests for on-service placement, changes in level of care, and patient safety concerns, and as courtesy moves. The bed assignment clerical team works with the Admissions nurse to determine the priority for these moves.

DEPARTMENT ORGANIZATIONAL STRUCTURES

The Admissions Department organizational structure (exhibit 4.1 shows a sample) will depend largely on the size and the needs of the institution. The Admissions Department can be divided into two areas: clerical and clinical. Both teams have different designated tasks but operate with the same goal of safe patient

Exhibit 4.1: Sample Organizational Structure

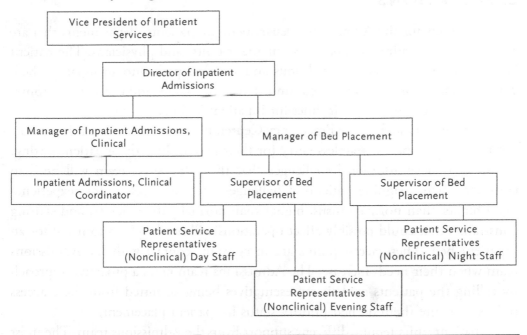

placement. The clerical side of the Admissions team should include clerical staff responsible for direct bed assignments into the EBMS. The clerical team has direct support from supervisors who cover day, evening, night, and weekend shifts, and the supervisors report to a clerical manager. The clinical team requires a registered nurse to oversee the clinical concerns with patient placement. To provide constant oversight, clinical staff ideally should be scheduled to work the same hours as the Admissions Department clerical team. If this is not an option, the clinical team should be present during the peak hours for inpatient admissions.

The clerical and clinical teams share a director who is a member of the larger institutional inpatient operations team. This larger team is usually composed of inpatient physician leadership, nurse leadership, hospital administrators, and directors for key ancillary services that focus on patient flow. These institutional leaders work with the Admissions leadership team to provide guidance and direction for inpatient flow. This direction is especially needed during high-census times when the demand for inpatient beds exceeds institutional capacity.

Another possible arm in the Admissions Department organizational structure is a Transfer Center. Some institutions will have an in-house Transfer Center, whereas others choose to contract this function out to agencies that deal exclusively with hospital-to-hospital transfers. Either way, the Transfer Center will work closely with the Admissions Department for correct, safe, and appropriate placement of all transfers to an inpatient bed at the receiving institution.

KEY CUSTOMERS AND THEIR PERFORMANCE EXPECTATIONS

Key customers for the Admissions Department are patients, departments that are access points for admitting patients, inpatient units, and physicians. The patient being admitted expects an expeditious and seamless path into an inpatient bed. The admissions process must focus on the patient's safety and excellent customer service while minimizing wait times for inpatient bed placement.

Access points such as the Emergency Center, physician clinics, and the operating room also expect a seamless entry for their patient into the inpatient setting. These areas have additional challenges that the Admissions team will need to consider when assigning patients. Challenges such as access points experiencing a higher than normal census, higher than normal patient acuity, and staffing constraints that could possibly affect operations will need to be prioritized for an inpatient bed. These access points are in constant contact with the Admissions team when their needs increase. The Admissions team takes a proactive approach by calling the patients or their representatives being admitted from these access points to assure them of their priority status for patient placement.

Inpatient units require different support from the Admissions team. The most frequent Admissions request from an inpatient unit is to arrange an inpatient-to-inpatient transfer. A physician enters the internal transfer request into the EHR when the inpatient requires a change in level of care. For example, a patient may need to be transferred from an inpatient unit serving general medicine patients to the intensive care unit. A request can also come from inpatient unit leadership requesting courtesy moves for inpatients, such as a larger corner room. Inpatient-to-inpatient moves are coordinated with the Admissions clinical team and accommodated on a case-by-case basis. The patient's safety is the top priority, and a change in level of care (e.g., a sudden need for a cardiac-monitored bed) will be prioritized over courtesy moves.

Providing direct physician support comprises another function for Admissions. Physicians will confirm Admissions is aware of specific needs for their patients. Physicians will also contact Admissions when triaging their unanticipated admissions from the clinic. The physician will determine the best mode of entry for their patient depending on bed availability. Then the physician and the Admissions clinical team will have a discussion to determine the immediate needs of the patient being admitted.

KEY PROCESS FLOWS

The key customer groups of the Admissions Department are patients (primarily inpatients), admission access-point staff, inpatient unit staff, and physicians (internal and external). Exhibit 4.2 shows that the Admissions Department's key services

Exhibit 4.2: Key Services and Process Flows

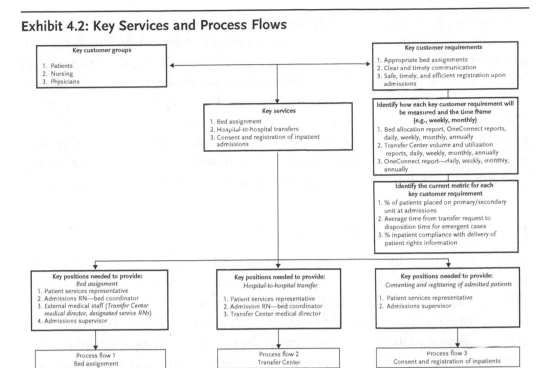

are bed assignments, hospital-to-hospital transfers, and consent and registration of patients. Each customer group has specific requirements, and Admissions should identify ways to measure each requirement against appropriate metrics to determine if requirements are being met, as shown in exhibit 4.2. In smaller Admissions departments, the clerical team should be cross-trained to work in various areas of the department (e.g., bed assignment, Transfer Center, consent and registration). Exhibit 4.2 also shows the key positions each function requires.

Bed Assignment

Hospitals across the United States are challenged with meeting the need for inpatient beds as hospital occupancy nears or exceeds 100 percent (Schäfer, Walther, and Hübner 2017). The process of allocating beds is under great scrutiny in healthcare organizations because the exact times of patient arrivals and discharges are often unknown (Schäfer et al. 2019). Bed assignments for new admissions, inpatient-to-inpatient transfers, and hospital-to-hospital transfers account for most of the Admissions clerical team's daily work. Although many EBMSs can recommend an appropriate bed assignment for a patient, the clerical team manages the process and must consider patient compatibility, unit staffing levels, patient arrival time, and special considerations such as COVID-19 and other pandemics.

Admissions departments should also create a business continuity plan with downtime procedures for bed assignments amid planned and unplanned events. Processes and preparation to promote continuity of care during downtime should include printing copies of the inpatient census and the unit census. Admissions staff should follow up with inpatient areas to validate inpatient census, pending discharges, and vacant rooms. Specific downtime procedure plans should be developed in anticipation of the EBMS, email system, phone system, and all systems going down. A robust recovery plan should be developed to operate after systems are restored including reconciling printed census with the downtime logs.

Hospital-to-Hospital Transfers

Neither the process by which hospital-to-hospital transfers occur, nor the national trends or best practices for this process, are clearly defined in the literature (Herrigel et al. 2016). However, the key steps in the process include the following. The Transfer Center initiates the Transfer Request Intake Form. The Admissions clerical team requests and evaluates pertinent supporting clinical documentation submitted by the transferring hospital. The clerical team then establishes communication among the transferring medical staff, internal accepting physician, and Transfer Center medical director. All telephone calls should be recorded in the Transfer Center including three-way physician-to-physician conversations. Raeisi, Rarani, and Soltani (2019) found lack of communication as the main handover challenge occurring during a hospital-to-hospital transfer. To ease this safety and quality concern, other relevant healthcare specialists such as critical care physicians, pediatric physicians, and others should be consulted and added to the telephone conversation to establish medical appropriateness for an emergent transfer request. Exhibit 4.3 lists the various physicians that may be added to such a conference.

Additional Transfer Center practices include daily status report on pending transfers, clinical status update before departure from transferring hospital, and real-time Transfer Center documentation in the patient's EHR. Once medical appropriateness is determined, the receiving hospital's capacity and capability to treat the patient should be assessed. Inquiries about the patient's financial resources should not be made before accepting the request for transfer if the patient has an emergency medical condition as determined by the transferring physician. If the transfer request is routine or urgent, a financial assessment and clearance can be made. Admissions departments should be aware of the average number of work hours to complete a transfer request from initial request to final decision. This information is extremely important because the volume of hospital-to-hospital transfers may be low, but the required time to complete the transfer request may

Exhibit 4.3: MD Notification for an Emergent Transfer Request

TRANSFER CENTER PROCESS
EMERGENT TRANSFERS MD NOTIFICATION
Inpatient Unit Capacity

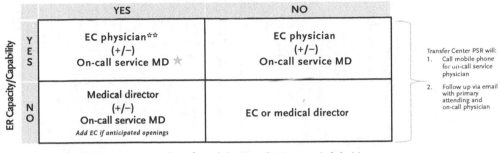

		YES	NO	
ER Capacity/Capability	**YES**	EC physician** (+/–) On-call service MD ★	EC physician (+/–) On-call service MD	Transfer Center PSR will: 1. Call mobile phone for on-call service physician 2. Follow up via email with primary attending and on-call physician
	NO	Medical director (+/–) On-call service MD *Add EC if anticipated openings*	EC or medical director	

** If ICU/pediatric/surgical transfer: Include ICU, pediatric, or surgical physician.
★ If no response from on-call service attending within five minutes, EC and MD director will make decision and notify on-call MD.

Note: PSR = patient services representative.

be high because a bed shortage has resulted in hospital-to-hospital transfers being placed on a pending list. Depending on how long a request remains on the pending list, the clerical team should work this list daily, providing the transferring hospital with updates on bed status and checking on the patient's current medical status.

Consent and Patient Registration

Checking into a hospital can be overwhelming. To shorten the consent and registration process, electronic versions of many forms can be completed online before admission. To protect patient privacy, all online forms should be encrypted and stored in a secure location. At many hospitals, patients are existing or recurrent customers. Policies may be developed where a Consent to Treat may be valid for a specific number of years, so long as the patient is treated within the hospital during the required period.

The Admissions clerical team may be responsible for consenting and registering patients at admission. Challenges may arise in operationalizing this key service when patients are admitted through various access points in the hospital. Under the consent and patient registration umbrella, the Admissions clerical team may be responsible for obtaining Consent to Treat, disseminating Patient Rights to inpatients, confirming external provider contact information, obtaining consent to notify an external provider of a patient's admission, notifying the family or personal representative of a patient's admission, and obtaining consent for a patient to be listed in the hospital directory. Exhibit 4.4 provides a sample workflow incorporating the various consent and registration functions.

Exhibit 4.4: Consent and Registration Workflow

Title: **Collecting and Documenting Patient Family Member/External Involved Provider Information – Emergency Center**
Creation Date: 7/23/19
Process Owner: EC FCC & Admissions
Last Updated: 2/10/20

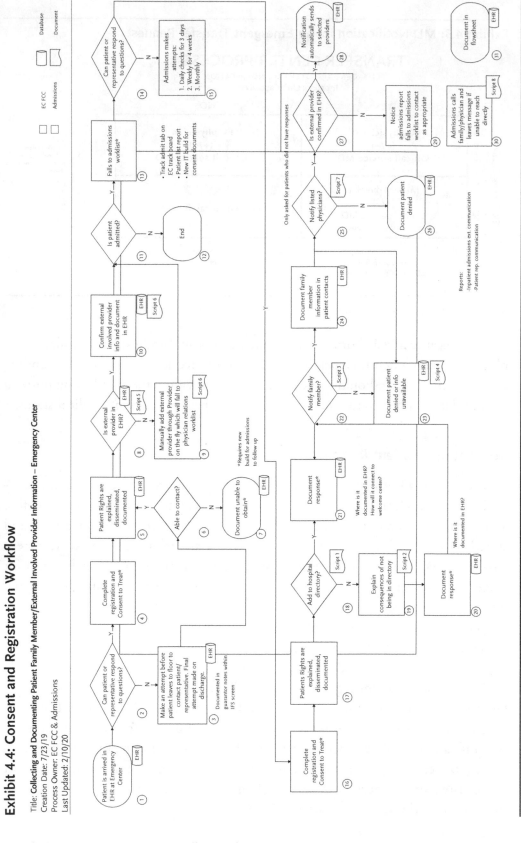

KEY UNITS OF WORK AND VOLUME STATISTICS TO MONITOR

Measuring and improving hospital department productivity has come under scrutiny as department leaders balance controlling cost with ensuring safety, quality, and staff morale (Ali, Salehnejad, and Mansur 2019). Key units of work is a methodology to compute the number of units of work done daily by each role in a department. Understanding key units of work will help department leaders measure and improve employee productivity. Productivity measures the relationship between the quantity of output and the quantity of input used to generate that output. An easy formula for measuring productivity is shown in exhibit 4.5.

Exhibit 4.5: Productivity Formula

$$Productivity = \frac{Output}{Input}$$

A volume statistic every Admissions Department should measure is total inpatient admissions, as displayed in exhibit 4.6. Department leaders should be aware of admisssion volumes, both total and segmented by specific access points shown in exhibit 4.6. Hospital volumes will affect the Admissions key units of work.

Exhibit 4.6: Inpatient Admissions Volume

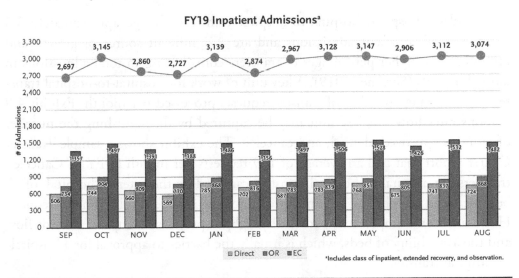

Note: EC = Emergency Center; OR = operating room.

Bed Assignment

Assigning inpatient beds to admitted patients is an important task that contributes to the strategic and operational flow of hospital patients. Bed assignments require more than the availability of a bed. Admitting the right patient to the right bed, at the right time, is a complex process that is further complicated when bed demands exceed availability. Long delays in bed assignments can result in emotional and physical stressors and a poor patient experience. Waste in the admission process and repetitious data collection that adds no value should be eliminated. If possible, manual processes should be replaced with real-time data collection integrated into the patient's EHR. The key unit of work for the Admissions clerical staff is bed assignments. Exhibit 4.7 illustrates the various ways this key unit of work can be measured.

Exhibit 4.7: Key Unit of Work: Bed Assignments

Key unit of work	Metric	Bed assignment productive hours per unit
Bed assignments	Average daily census	# of bed assignments/average daily census
Bed assignments	Patient days	# of bed assignments/# of patient days
Bed assignments	Patient and observation days	# of bed assignments/# of patient days + observation days

Hospital-to-Hospital Transfers

In a midsize hospital, hospital-to-hospital transfers average approximately 3.5 percent of all inpatient admissions and are a significant source of growth and revenue, with higher percentages of transfers contributing to total admissions in larger hospitals (Sommer 2019). A key unit of work for hospital-to-hospital transfers is the average number of transfer requests processed per month. Exhibit 4.8 demonstrates how this key unit may be captured by distinguishing the number of requests approved, denied, and canceled. The exhibit shows a sample Transfer Center report that had an average of 199 requests per month in FY19. Canceled transfers are hospital-to-hospital transfers canceled by the external hospital, often because of an inability to obtain approval for the transfer at the time of request. Hospitals should implement patient throughput projects to improve patient flow and the availability of beds, which is usually the barrier to approval for a hospital-to-hospital transfer.

Exhibit 4.8: Key Unit of Work: Transfer Requests per Month

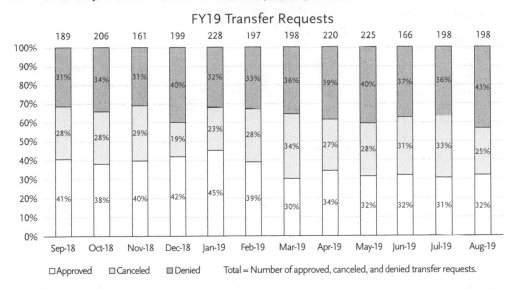

FY19 Transfer Requests

Category	Sep-18	Oct-18	Nov-18	Dec-18	Jan-19	Feb-19	Mar-19	Apr-19	May-19	Jun-19	Jul-19	Aug-19
Total	189	206	161	199	228	197	198	220	225	166	198	198
Denied	31%	34%	31%	40%	32%	33%	36%	39%	40%	37%	36%	43%
Canceled	28%	28%	29%	19%	23%	28%	34%	27%	28%	31%	33%	25%
Approved	41%	38%	40%	42%	45%	39%	30%	34%	32%	32%	31%	32%

☐ Approved ☐ Canceled ▦ Denied   Total = Number of approved, canceled, and denied transfer requests.

Consent and Patient Registration

The Admissions clerical team serves as an information resource and liaison between physician requests for admission or transfer; nursing departments; clinical coordinators; and any area requiring admission, including Surgery, the Emergency Center, Post-Acute Care Unit (PACU), clinics, diagnostics departments, and interfacility transfers. Exhibit 4.9 outlines the essential functions for all admitted patients regardless of access point. Admission types and access points

Exhibit 4.9: Consent and Patient Registration Key Functions

Key functions
Obtaining Consent to Treat
Disseminating Patient Rights
Obtaining consent to list in hospital directory
Confirming external provider
Updating external provider information
Collecting patient family member to notify of admission
Notifying family of patient's admission (via telephone)
Notifying external provider of patient's admission (via telephone)
Quality improvement process to monitor and correct functions 1–8

Exhibit 4.10: Key Unit of Work: Number of Patient Rights Administered Within 24 Hours of Admission

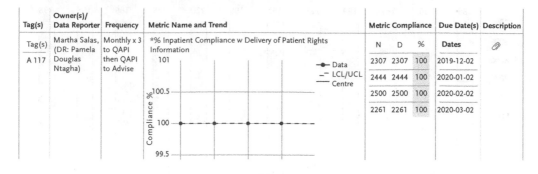

Tag(s)	Owner(s)/ Data Reporter	Frequency	Metric Name and Trend	Metric Compliance			Due Date(s)	Description
Tag(s) A 117	Martha Salas, (DR: Pamela Douglas Ntagha)	Monthly x 3 to QAPI then QAPI to Advise	*% Inpatient Compliance w Delivery of Patient Rights Information	N	D	%	Dates	
				2307	2307	100	2019-12-02	
				2444	2444	100	2020-01-02	
				2500	2500	100	2020-02-02	
				2261	2261	100	2020-03-02	

Note: LCL = lower control limit; QAPI = Quality Assurance Performance Improvement; UCL = upper control limit.

may include emergency admits from the Emergency Center; scheduled admits in Admissions; change in status from observation patients to inpatients; external transfers from the Transfer Center; and direct admits from clinics, Operating Room/PACU, Interventional Radiology, and Pediatrics.

Monitoring compliance with the delivery of Patient Rights information is a key unit of work for the Admissions team (exhibit 4.10). To comply with Centers for Medicare & Medicaid Services (CMS) requirements, Admissions should work with the IT team to develop real-time reports notifying Admissions of all admitted patients who have not received Patient Rights. Thereafter, the Admissions clerical team can develop a process to ensure delivery of Patient Rights information to all inpatients regardless of access point within 24 hours of admissions.

KEY METRICS TO MONITOR: PEOPLE, SERVICE, QUALITY/SAFETY, FINANCE

The Admissions Department plays a key role in analyzing and improving patient flow and its associated metrics. Monitoring key metrics of people, service, quality/safety, and finance will help the Admissions Department understand where problems exist and assess their causes and impact. Exhibit 4.11 indicates the People, Service, and Finance metrics to measure and report.

Bed Assignment

Bed assignment is determined by the patient's particular clinical service and the available beds shown on the EBMS for that nursing unit at time of admission.

Exhibit 4.11: Admissions Key Metrics

Type	Metric	Measurement
People	Workload satisfaction	Employee satisfaction with workload (by shift)[a]
People	Monthly retention rate	% of employees retained each month
People	Performance evaluation completion	% of evaluations completed on time
People	Recognition letter	# of recognition letters sent to department employees
People	Employee rounding	% of employees responding "Very Likely" to recommend employment at hospital[a]
Service	Customer rounding	% responding "Very Good" to overall impression of service[b]
Service	Customer phone service	% of audited calls that demonstrate telephone service skills
Service	Abandoned calls rate	Abandoned calls/total calls
Finance	Status of company center audits	Pass/Fail
Finance	Year-to-date variance: Operating margin	Actual-to-budget operating margin
Finance	Year-to-date variance: FTE	Actual-to-budget FTE

[a]From Hospital Employee Engagement or Satisfaction Survey.
[b]From Department Customer Satisfaction Survey.
Note: FTE = full-time equivalent.

Monitoring the history of bed occupancy by clinical service is the most common way to determine the number of beds to allocate for a particular clinical service. Exhibit 4.12 shows the key metrics for bed assignments.

Hospital-to-Hospital Transfers

The main goal of hospital-to-hospital transfers is to maintain the continuity of medical care. A good system of measurement is crucial to achieving this goal. Exhibit 4.13 indicates the metrics to measure and monitor for service and quality/safety.

Hospital-to-hospital transfers are regulated by CMS. There are strict guidelines regarding emergent EC-to-EC transfers. A key measure of safety and efficiency for emergent cases that must be monitored is called the Transfer Request to Disposition Time. Exhibit 4.14 shows an example of how to monitor this metric.

Exhibit 4.12: Admissions Key Metrics for Bed Assignments

Type	Metric	Measurement
Quality/safety	Advance directives	% of advance directive inquiries documented in medical record
Quality/safety	IM Letter	IM Letter compliance %
Quality/safety	Boarders	# of patients in overflow units, observation units, boarding areas, and hallways waiting to be admitted by day and hour
Quality/safety	Boarders ALOS	ALOS (hours) of patients in overflow units, observation units, boarding areas, and hallways waiting to be admitted by day and hour
Quality/safety	Admission percentage	The percentage of patients seen in the ED and then placed in an inpatient area of the hospital. This percentage includes the total number of admitted patients taken to an inpatient area, including those defined as observation patients by hospital processes. This is important for hospital administrators to know because ED patients who need inpatient services require a disproportionate amount of time and energy from emergency physicians and ED staff.
Quality/safety	Off-service patients	# and % of inpatients placed in inappropriate unit
Quality/safety	Admissions by hour	# of admissions by hour
Quality/safety	Admitted patients' arrival time	Time between admit order and time patient arrives to inpatient bed
Quality/safety	Admitted patients' satisfaction	Patient satisfaction/experience score related to waiting for admission

Note: ALOS = average length of stay; ED = Emergency Department; IM Letter = Important Message from Medicare.

Exhibit 4.13: Admissions Key Metrics for Hospital-to-Hospital Transfers

Type	Metric	Measurement
Service	# of transfers	Count of total number of hospital-to-hospital transfer requests initiated during the month
Service	Transfer disposition time	Time transfer request is made (transfer intake form initiated) until the time a final transfer decision is made to accept, deny, or cancel the transfer request

(continued)

Type	Metric	Measurement
Service	On-call notification of transfer request time	Time transfer request is made (transfer intake form initiated) until the time the on-call physician is notified of transfer request
Service	On-call physician response time	Time transfer request is made (transfer intake form initiated) until the time the on-call physician contacts the Transfer Center
Service	Medical appropriateness decision time	Time transfer request is made (transfer intake form initiated) until the time the medical appropriateness is determined
Quality/safety	% approved transfers	# transfers approved / # of transfer requests
Quality/safety	% denied transfers	# transfers denied / # of transfer requests
Quality/safety	% canceled transfers	# transfers canceled / # of transfer requests
Quality/safety	% new patient transfers	# new patients requesting transfer / # of transfer requests
Quality/safety	% existing patient transfers	# existing patients requesting transfer / # of transfer requests
Quality/safety	% transfers to EC	# transfers admitted via EC / # of transfers approved
Quality/safety	% transfers to inpatient units	# transfers admitted via inpatient Unit / # of transfers approved
Quality/safety	% transfers to ICU	# transfers admitted via ICU / # of transfers approved
Quality/safety	% transfers to Pediatrics	# transfers admitted via Pediatrics / # of transfers approved
Quality/safety	% transfers by service	# of transfers accepted by specific service / # of transfers approved
Quality/safety	Transfer type	# of transfers by type (i.e., routine/urgent/emergent) / # of transfers approved
Quality/safety	% of transfers requested while on diversion	# of transfers requested while hospital on diversion status/ # of transfer requests
Quality/safety	% of transfers denied while on diversion	# of transfers denied while hospital on diversion status/ # of transfer requests
Quality/safety	Transfer cancelation reasons	Count of reason for transfer cancelation (e.g., patient transferred to another hospital, patient discharged, patient expired)

Exhibit 4.14: EC-to-EC Emergent Transfer Disposition Time

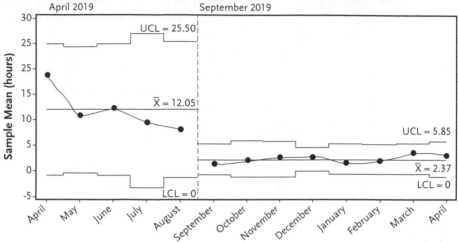

2019–2020 Disposition Time for Emergent EC Transfers

N = 25 N = 27 N = 25 N = 18 N = 23 N = 31 N = 22 N = 23 N = 52 N = 32 N = 34 N = 23 N = 19

Tests are performed with unequal sample sizes.
Results include rows where "floor type" = "EC" and status = "E."

Note: LCL = lower control limit; UCL = upper control limit.

Consent and Patient Registration

Key metrics identify strengths and weaknesses within processes, which gives teams an opportunity to correct course and drive improvements. To ensure compliance with the CMS Discharge Planning and Patient Rights Conditions of Participation, several key metrics should be measured and monitored (exhibit 4.15).

Exhibit 4.15: Admissions Key Metrics for Consent and Registration

Type	Metric	Measurement
Quality/safety	Consent to Treat compliance	% completion of Consent to Treat
Quality/safety	Patient Rights compliance	% completion of Patient Rights
Service	Admit notification to external provider compliance	% completion of admission notification to external provider
Service	Admit notification to patient family member/representative compliance	% completion of admit notification to patient family member/representative

KEY INFORMATICS ISSUES

Admissions should avoid documenting bed management processes manually on paper and via fax. Manual processes are cumbersome, inefficient, error prone, and redundant. The EBMS should be integrated with the EHR and Admission/Discharge/Transfer systems to maximize bed resources through real-time monitoring. Also, the Admissions team can travel to inpatient units as needed; therefore, the team must incorporate wireless technology (e.g., iPads, personal devices, computers-on-wheels) into operations.

The Admissions Department is key in patient surge planning, emergency and disaster planning, and hospital diversion implementation. Therefore, the department is often called to assist with hospital bed expansion. To accomplish this goal, real-time patient data and bed availability are required, and information must be shared securely and quickly with healthcare providers and the inpatient clinical team. Advancements in technology resulting in electronic bed boards and EBMSs have improved efficiencies of the care system and increased hospital capacity.

A robust bed management system is highly beneficial for improving bed turnover and patient flow (Tortorella et al. 2013). The hospital bed management system should be intuitive and provide alerts to the Admissions team. The system collects clinical data such as diagnosis, level of care, gender, isolation status, precautions, behavioral issues, and other patient characteristics needed for appropriate placement. Using these data, the bed management system recommends an "ideal bed" for each patient.

Health Insurance Portability and Accountability Act (HIPAA)–compliant electronic bed boards should provide easy access for the Admissions team to track where patients are in real time. The bed board should be color coded and display information in several different formats. The Admissions team will require access to data on the hospital, inpatient unit, and bed levels. The ability to analyze bed data in granular detail can lead to improved patient flow and hospital operations.

Dashboards of real-time data should be created to track key patient flow metrics. Senior leaders, clinicians, and managers should be able to easily access and analyze real-time bed availability information. Clinical and nonclinical Admissions staff should collaborate with the information management reporting team to develop needed reports. In addition to historical reports (e.g., census reports, discharge reports, compliance reports), this collaboration should develop admissions forecasting reports.

STAFFING MODELS

As bed planners, Admissions plays a key role in assigning patients to inpatient beds. With the Emergency Center being the primary access point for admissions in most hospitals, Admissions must have adequate staffing to handle the demands

Exhibit 4.16: Admissions Position Control: Budgeted Positions

FY20 Budgeted FTEs Admissions (204100)									
#	Position Number	Name	Title	Filled FTE	Vacant FTE	Status	Date Submitted to Taleo	Previous Incumbent	Total FTEs
1	000123456	Jane Doe	Patient Svcs Representative	1.00	0.00				
2			Patient Svcs Representative	1.00	0.00				
3			Patient Svcs Representative	1.00	0.00				
4			Patient Svcs Representative	0.00	1.00			Donald Duck	
5			Patient Svcs Representative	0.00	0.50				
6			Patient Svcs Representative	1.00	0.00				
7			Patient Svcs Representative	1.00	0.00				
8			Patient Svcs Representative	1.00	0.00				
9			Patient Svcs Representative	1.00	0.00				
10			Patient Svcs Representative	1.00	0.00				
11			Patient Svcs Representative	1.00	0.00				
12			Patient Svcs Representative	1.00	0.00				
13			Patient Svcs Representative	0.50	0.00				
14			Patient Svcs Representative	1.00	0.00				
15			Patient Svcs Representative	1.00	0.00				
16			Patient Svcs Representative	1.00	0.00				
17			Patient Svcs Representative	1.00	0.00				
Admissions Totals				14.50	1.50				16.00

Note: Shaded area indicates vacant positions. FTEs = full-time equivalents.

for bed assignments. Golmohammadi (2016) found the inability to move patients promptly to inpatient beds creates a bottleneck in the Emergency Center. Admissions Department leaders can ensure adequate department staffing by using a position control process (exhibit 4.16). Position control allows department leadership to maintain and monitor positions within their budget, monitor department-level staffing, and manage department labor cost authoritatively.

Bed Assignment

Most Admissions departments are staffed 24/7. In the following case study, the Admissions Department is not a 24-hour department, which illustrates there may be a time when the Admissions leadership team will need to consider expanding hours, services, or key functions.

Case Study: ABC General Hospital

ABC General Hospital is a 500-bed hospital located in a major US city. The Admissions Department was initially staffed seven days a week with hours between 7 a.m. and 11 p.m. Essential department functions were typical of most community hospital Admissions departments as illustrated in exhibit 4.17.

After-hour bed assignments and other key functions of the Admissions clerical team were fragmented and inconsistent, conducted by several different groups including the off-shift administrator, Emergency Center unit clerk, and inpatient nursing unit clerks. There was no designated contact person for bed

Exhibit 4.17: ABC General Hospital Admission Department Key Functions

Key functions	% of time
Bed Placement (multiple parties involved)	35%
Transfer Center (multiple parties involved)	25%
Customer Service	10%
Front Desk reception	10%
Pre-Admits/Admission	10%
Reports	8%
Performance Improvement project	1%
Other duties	1%

assignments after hours, leading to additional frustration and confusion when patients were being admitted from the Emergency Center, transferred from an external hospital, or needing an inpatient-to-inpatient transfer for a higher or lower level of care.

The Admissions clerical team possessed the expertise to place patients in the appropriate care setting. After hours, however, several roles not associated with Admissions shared this essential function. The process was piecemeal, inefficient, and ineffective, resulting in patients being placed in inappropriate beds, inpatient units, and levels of care. Using qualitative and quantitative data, a business case was made to expand Admissions to a 24-hour, seven-days-a-week department. A survey was conducted of a representative sample of community hospitals located in the region, top-tier hospitals across the United States, and *US News & World Report* Top Hospitals. Healthcare facilities surveyed all operated a 24/7 Admissions Department.

Bed assignments at ABC General Hospital consisted of patients being admitted to a bed for the first time (admission), along with patients changing rooms and inpatient units because of a need for a higher or lower level of care. Patient preference as a reason for transfer was very minimal. Although the majority of admissions and transfers occurred on the second shift (3 p.m.–11 p.m.), the third shift (11 p.m.–7 a.m.) had the greatest number of admissions and transfers, followed by the first shift (7 a.m.–3 p.m.). A data-driven justification was made that the Admissions clerical team's bed assignment expertise was of greater need for improving bed assignments on the third shift compared to the first shift; therefore, the third shift should be staffed with a representative from the Admissions clerical team. Upon determining the department was not adequately resourced after hours to respond to requests for bed assignments, a request was made for 2.5 full-time equivalents (FTEs) on Admissions clerical staff to run 24/7 operations. The request was approved. Appropriate bed placement on the second and third shifts after hours improved significantly after the plan was implemented.

For hospital-to-hospital transfers, ABC General Hospital cross-trained all members of the Admissions clerical team to be competent to perform bed assignment, hospital-to-hospital transfers, and consent and registration. One person was dedicated primarily to manage the hospital-to-hospital transfers on first and second shifts. With the department expanding to 24/7 operations, the new third-shift Admissions clerical team member will work bed assignments and hospital-to-hospital transfers.

A physician should serve as the Transfer Center medical director to oversee the clinical coordination. Admissions departments vary as to whether physicians will serve part-time or full-time in this role. ABC General Hospital has a hospitalist serving as the Transfer Center medical director part-time (20 percent of their time). The hospital staffs the Admissions Department with 2.0 registered nurse (RN) FTEs to provide clinical oversight. The Admissions Clinical Team is composed of RNs trained in critical care or emergency medicine to provide clinical oversight to bed assignments and hospital-to-hospital transfers.

For the consent and patient registration functions, the ABC General Hospital Admissions Department is now being asked to assume responsibility for front-door registration of all hospital-to-hospital transfers, and for satisfying the CMS requirements for external provider and family member notification of a patient's admission. An analysis was performed to determine the time required to complete these new duties and how many FTEs would be required.

The registration standard for registering a patient is seven minutes (excluding confirming and updating external provider information). Updating external provider information usually takes 15 to 20 minutes. The Admissions leadership team is projecting the routine registration functions (obtaining Consent to Treat, disseminating Patient Rights, and obtaining consent to list in hospital directory) will take three minutes per patient. Updating external provider information, collecting and notifying family member/external provider of admission, and related quality improvement (QI) processes add an additional 31 minutes if all factors are applicable as illustrated in exhibit 4.18.

Exhibit 4.19 displays the actual work time the Admissions clerical team will need for their new functions. This analysis does not include travel time to and from patients, training, and paid time off. From this analysis, 6.0 FTEs were requested.

Exhibit 4.18: Front-Door Registration Cycle Time

Phase	Cycle time (minutes)
Obtaining Consent to Treat	1
Disseminating Patient Rights	1
Obtaining consent to list in hospital directory	1
Confirming external provider	2
Updating external provider information	15
Collecting patient family member to notify of admission	2
Notifying family of patient's admission (via telephone)	3
Notifying external provider of patient's admission (via telephone)	3
Quality improvement process to monitor and correct above processes	3
Total	**31**

Exhibit 4.19: Front-Door Registration FTE Requirements

	Phase	Admissions			
		Cycle Time (Min)	Annual Volume	Annual Hours	FTEs Required
1	Obtaining Consent to Treat and Patient Rights	1			
2	Disseminating Patient Rights	1	35,776[a]	597	0.29
3	Obtaining Consent to List in Hospital Directory	1	35,776[a]	597	0.29
4	Confirming External Provider	2	35,776[a]	1,193	0.58
5	Updating External Provider Information	15	17,888[b]	4,472	2.15
6	Collecting Patient Family Member to Notify of Admission	2	8,944[c]	299	0.15
7	Notifying Family of Patient's Admission (via telephone)	3	8,944[c]	448	0.22
8	Notifying External Provider of Patient's Admission(via telephone)	3	8,944[c]	448	0.22
9	QI Process to Monitor and Correct Above Processes	3	35,776[d]	2,982	1.44
10	**Total**	**31**		**11,036**	**5.34**

(continued)

Exhibit 4.19: Front-Door Registration FTE Requirements *(continued)*

^aBased on FY19 total patients with call of inpatient, extended recovery, and observation.
^bAssumption: 50% of admitted patients will need external provider information updated.
^cAssumption: 25% of admitted patients will request a family member be notified of admission.
^dAssumption: 50% of admitted patients will request their external provider be notified of admission; half of these requests will need to be done via telephone.

FTEs Required	
FTEs Required	**5.34**
Nonproductive Hours	5.34 anticipated FTEs × 240 nonproductive hours annually = 1,281.60 nonproductive hours per 5.34 FTEs
FTEs Required for Nonproductive Time	1,281.60 nonproductive hours per 5.34 FTEs / 2,080 hours annually per FTEs = 0.62 FTEs to cover nonproductive hours for 5.34 FTEs
FTE Requirement with Nonproductive Hours	5.34 FTEs (to provide additional essential functions) + 0.62 FTEs (nonproductive hours) = 5.96 or 6 FTEs

For this analysis, six weeks of nonproductive time per FTE were utilized.
Note: FTE = full-time equivalent; QI = quality improvement.

PRODUCTIVITY MODELS, INCLUDING WORK-TO-STAFF RATIOS AND INDUSTRY PERFORMANCE TARGETS

Bed Assignment

To obtain optimal bed assignment productivity, all beds need to be assigned by a centralized authority. The Admissions clerical team can be trained to do bed assignment once rules and guidelines are developed. When problems arise, the Admissions clerical team can escalate to the Admissions clinical team for resolution. Potential problems include assigning patients to an off-service unit when the primary and secondary units are full, inadequate telemetry availability, and barriers to patient movement. Last, priorities for bed assignment should be developed that ensure the highest-acuity patients are assigned beds first.

The Admissions clerical staff's key unit of work is bed assignments. Once the optimal level of bed assignments per staff member is determined from historical volumes or external benchmarks (i.e., one Admissions clerical staff to X number of bed assignments per eight-hour shift), staffing will need to be adjusted to match the demand. Admissions Department leaders need to carefully monitor bed assignments and do not solely rely on hospital volumes when monitoring bed assignment productivity. This phenomenon was evident during the COVID-19 pandemic, when many hospitals experienced a decreased census (because elective

Exhibit 4.20: Admissions Clerical Staff Productivity: Bed Assignments

Month	Comparing ADC to PSR KUOW		
	ADC	KUOW	ADC:KUOW
Apr-19	633	6010	9.49
May-19	626	6075	9.70
Jun-19	624	5606	8.98
Jul-19	631	5844	9.26
Aug-19	631	5817	9.22
Sep-19	630	5624	8.93
Oct-19	653	9071	9.30
Nov-19	630	5495	8.72
Dec-19	606	5840	9.64
Jan-20	632	6000	9.49
Feb-20	619	5364	8.67
Mar-20	573	5260	9.18
Apr-20	386	3432	8.89

Note: ADC = average daily census; KUOW = key unit of work for PSRs (measured as number of completed bed assignments); PSR = patient service representative.

procedures were canceled) but increased bed assignments. The increase arose from patients being assigned a bed at admission, reassigned to a Patient Under Investigation (PUI) unit after a COVID-19 test was administered, and reassigned once again after COVID-19 test results were returned. One patient resulted in three patient moves. An example of this concept can be seen in exhibit 4.20, where hospital inpatient volumes went down in March and April, but the key units of work did not decrease proportionately with average daily census because of the frequent movement of patients from the Emergency Center to an inpatient unit to the PUI unit to their service unit or COVID-19 unit.

Hospital-to-Hospital Transfers

The productivity metric for hospital-to-hospital transfers is disposition time. Disposition time is defined as the time from the initial transfer request to the final decision to accept, deny, or cancel the transfer. A stretch goal for disposition of emergent transfers to the Emergency Center is one hour with a target of two hours. Exhibit 4.21 demonstrates a control chart of the disposition times for emergent Emergency Center transfers showing an average disposition time of 2.33 hours.

Exhibit 4.21: Disposition Time for Emergent EC Transfers

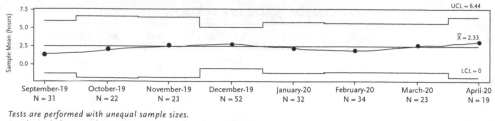

Tests are performed with unequal sample sizes.
Results include rows where status = "E" and floor type = "EC."

Note: E = emergent; EC = Emergency Center; LCL = lower control limit; UCL = upper control limit.

Consent and Patient Registration

Cycle-time measurements segmenting components of the consent and registration process may be used to measure productivity in this area. One cycle time used for productivity is called "initial time," measured from the time a patient is first checked into the hospital (regardless of access point) until the registration process is initiated. Another cycle time is "registration time," defined as the time from the initiation of the registration process until the conclusion.

STRATEGIES TO IMPROVE RECRUITMENT AND RETENTION

The training process for a new employee is lengthy and costly. Nevertheless, it is worth investing the time and energy needed to select the most qualified personnel on both the clinical and clerical sides of Admissions. A successful recruitment process begins with Admissions leadership being keenly aware of institutional leadership's vision and goals for the department. The process of finding the right personnel will focus on individuals who can help the department meet those goals. The ideal recruit for the clinical Admissions team is an experienced registered nurse, preferably with a critical care or emergency medicine background. This clinical experience will be beneficial when triaging and prioritizing patients to an inpatient setting. Recruitment for the clerical Admissions position will focus on a person with a customer service background and excellent communication skills. A willingness to learn and the ability to work well with others in a small group are also important traits.

Retention methods for both groups are similar. Maintaining competitive salaries and benefits will aid retention. Annual assessment of industry compensation packages and necessary adjustments should be part of the retention plan.

Depending on the size of the department, growth opportunities into management roles may be available, which can also improve retention. Having different levels within the clerical team from novice to master will provide the motivated employee with a goal for advancement. A positive work environment that provides employee appreciation events and promotes work–life balance is another important part of an effective retention plan. Educational opportunities that provide continuing education hours will be beneficial to the Admissions nurse. The budget should include funds both for the nurses' continuing education and cardiopulmonary resuscitation (CPR) training and for uniforms if the job requires scrub attire.

KEY REGULATORY ISSUES

CMS develops Conditions of Participation and Conditions for Coverage that healthcare organizations must meet to begin and continue participating in Medicare and Medicaid. The Conditions of Participation listed in exhibit 4.22 are relevant to the Admissions Department.

CMS requires all Medicare inpatients receive a written notice called the Important Message from Medicare (IM Letter) about the hospital discharge appeal rights. A second letter or notice is to be provided to the patient no more

Exhibit 4.22: CMS Conditions of Participation—CMS Tags

Tag	Condition of participation language
A-0117	§482.13(a)(1)—A hospital must inform each patient, or when appropriate, the patient's representative (as allowed under State law), of the patient's rights, in advance of furnishing or discontinuing patient care whenever possible.
A-0131	§482.13(b)(2)—The patient or his or her representative (as allowed under State law) has the right to make informed decisions regarding his or her care. The patient's rights include being informed of his or her health status, being involved in care planning and treatment, and being able to request or refuse treatment. This right must not be construed as a mechanism to demand the provision of treatment or services deemed medically unnecessary or inappropriate.
A-0133	§482.13(b)(4)—The patient has the right to have a family member or representative of his or her choice and his or her own physician notified promptly of his or her admission to the hospital.
A-0143	§482.13(c)(1)—The patient has the right to personal privacy.
A-0837	External Provider Communication.

than two days before discharge. The IM Letter cannot be altered from its original form, and the Office of Management and Budget control number must appear on the form. The department responsible for delivering the IM Letter is determined by the hospital and is usually Admissions, Registration, Case Management, Nursing, or Social Work. Delivery of the IM Letter must be documented. CMS requires 100 percent compliance with administering the first and second IM Letters.

The Joint Commission drives healthcare organizations to excel in providing safe, effective, high-quality care by surveying and accrediting more than 22,000 healthcare organizations in the United States. The Joint Commission Standards listed in exhibit 4.23 are relevant to the Admissions Department.

Exhibit 4.23: The Joint Commission Patient Flow Standards

Standard	Patient flow standards
LD.04.03.11	The hospital manages the flow of patients throughout the hospital.
LD.04.03.11 EP5	The hospital measures and sets goals for the components of the patient flow process, including the following: • The available supply of patient beds • The throughput of areas where patients receive care, treatment, and services (such as inpatient units, laboratory, operating rooms, telemetry, radiology, and the post-anesthesia care unit) • The safety of areas where patients receive care, treatment, and services • The efficiency of the nonclinical services that support patient care and treatment (such as Housekeeping and Transportation) • Access to support services (such as Case Management and Social Work)
LD.04.03.11 EP6	The hospital measures and sets goals for mitigating and managing the boarding of patients who come through the Emergency Center.
LD.04.03.11 EP7	The individuals who manage patient flow processes review measurement results to determine whether goals were achieved.
LD.04.03.11 EP8	Leaders take action to improve patient flow processes when goals are not achieved.
LD.04.03.11 EP9	When the hospital determines that it has a population at risk for boarding due to behavioral health emergencies, hospital leaders communicate with behavioral health care providers and/or authorities serving the community to foster coordination of care for this population.

KEY TERMS FOR ADMISSIONS

Admissions clerical team: Nonclinical, customer-facing staff, responsible for constantly monitoring hospital admissions, discharges, and patient movement within the hospital to ensure the right patient is assigned to the right bed at the right time. Also responsible for gathering personal information, insurance, and symptoms about the patient and communicating this information to the Admissions clinical team and medical staff.

Admissions clinical team: Registered nurses responsible for ensuring the effective use of beds throughout the hospital by finding open hospital beds and optimizing functional capacity by ensuring smooth patient flow. Provides clinical oversight to Admissions clerical team.

Bed assignment guidelines: A guide to bed assignment for patients based on clinical service. This bed assignment model, categorized by primary, secondary, and, as applicable, tertiary assignment, is reviewed and revised by a multidisciplinary group based on operational needs of the institution.

Bed management: Ensuring the right patient is placed in the right bed at the right time.

Electronic bed management system: A digital application that manages patient flow by providing real-time data on bed availability and status.

Electronic health records: A hospital's integrated system of applications that work together to support patient care processes by integrating data from multiple sources; capturing data at the point of care; supporting caregiver decision-making; enabling appropriate documentation of and reimbursement for the care provided; and facilitating the dissemination of that data with patients, referring providers, and other entities with a clinical, research, or business reason to access patient information.

Emergency Center capacity: A point in time when no external transfers or admissions to the Emergency Center would generally be accepted because of lack of beds, equipment, or personnel; capacity is dynamic and may be multifocal or unifocal.

Emergency medical condition: A condition in which a patient is in immediate danger of losing life, limb, or function. Further defined as a medical condition, manifesting itself by acute symptoms of sufficient severity (including severe pain) that the absence of immediate medical treatment could reasonably be expected to result in placing the health of the individual in serious jeopardy.

Hospital capacity: A point in time when no inpatient admissions or transfers to a hospital would generally be accepted because of lack of beds, equipment, or personnel; capacity is dynamic and may be multifocal or unifocal.

Hospital-to-hospital transfers: A transition of care occurring between two hospitals in which a patient is admitted to a hospital and subsequently transferred from the hospital where the patient was admitted to another hospital for additional treatment.

Inpatient-to-inpatient hospital transfer: A transfer occurring within the hospital from one service area to another or from one inpatient unit to another.

On-service placement: A correct patient assignment into an inpatient bed by the Admissions clerical and clinical team. The correct patient bed has been predetermined to be the most appropriate area to care for a specific patient's needs based on their diagnosis and acuity. Designated units are identified with key stakeholder involvement.

Patient services representative: A member of the Admissions clerical team.

Planned admission: A scheduled hospital inpatient acute care stay requiring specialized treatment arising from a clinical decision made by a physician.

Planned downtime: A period of time when normal access to the electronic health record is disrupted. This downtime is an anticipated outage that allows the departments to prepare for and communicate departmental procedures in advance. Examples may include system upgrades or maintenance.

Routine medical condition: A non-emergent, non-urgent condition.

Transfer Center: The point of access responsible for coordinating all aspects of requested transfers to a hospital.

Transfer Center medical director: A physician who serves as a medical resource to the Transfer Center for clinical decisions regarding acceptance. This person also works to encourage accurate and appropriate clinical hand-off communication between external and internal providers, may provide information to medical staff regarding hospital transfer–related issues, and provides guidance and oversight for Transfer Center staff.

Unplanned admission: An unscheduled in-hospital stay for an urgent or emergent condition requiring specialized treatment, arising from a clinical decision made by a physician.

Unplanned downtime: An unscheduled or unexpected interruption in the service of the electronic health record regardless of duration. This downtime occurs without prenotification. Impact is minimized by backup systems in place during these rare occurrences. Examples may include network or power outages.

Urgent medical condition: An urgent, non-emergent condition for which a transfer would seem to potentially benefit the patient.

REFERENCES

Ali, M., R. Salehnejad, and M. Mansur. 2019. "Hospital Productivity: The Role of Efficiency Drivers." *International Journal of Health Planning and Management* 34 (6): 806–23.

Golmohammadi, D. 2016. "Predicting Hospital Admissions to Reduce Emergency Department Boarding." *International Journal of Production Economics* 182: 535–44.

Herrigel, D. J., M. Carroll, C. Fanning, M. B. Steinberg, A. Parikh, and M. Usher. 2016. "Interhospital Transfer Handoff Practices Among US Tertiary Care Centers: A Descriptive Survey." *Journal of Hospital Medicine* 11 (6): 413–17.

Raeisi, A., M. A. Rarani, and F. Soltani. 2019. "Challenges of Patient Handover Process in Healthcare Services: A Systematic Review." *Journal of Education and Health Promotion* 8: 173.

Schäfer, F., M. Walther, and A. Hübner. 2017. "Patient-Bed Allocation in Large Hospitals." In *Health Care Systems Engineering: HCSE, Florence, Italy, May 2017* (Springer Proceedings in Mathematics & Statistics, vol. 210), edited by P. Cappanera, J. Li, A. Matta, E. Sahin, N. Vandaele, and F. Visintin. New York: Springer.

Schäfer, F., M. Walther, A. Hübner, and H. Kuhn. 2019. "Operational Patient-Bed Assignment Problem in Large Hospital Settings Including Overflow and Uncertainty Management." *Flexible Services and Manufacturing Journal* 31: 1012–41.

Sommer, D. 2019. "Solving Hospital to Hospital Transfers in Healthcare Today." *Innovator Health*. Published May 17. www.innovatorhealth.com/blog/solving-hospital-to-hospital-transfers-in-healthcare-today.

Tortorella, F., D. Ukanowicz, P. Douglas-Ntagha, R. Ray, and M. Triller. 2013. "Improving Bed Turnover with a Bed Management System." *Journal of Nursing Administration* 43 (1): 37–43.

CHAPTER 5

Case Management

Sue Wilson and Donna Ukanowicz

DEPARTMENT DESCRIPTION

Since the 1990s, Case Management departments have become invaluable hospital assets for helping patients navigate transitions between levels of care in the ever-so-confusing healthcare system, staying compliant with the Centers for Medicare & Medicaid Services (CMS) Conditions of Participation (CoPs), and ensuring appropriate payment with private payers. Case Management services in an acute care hospital focus on shifting the patient to the next appropriate level of care, to achieve high-quality care and positive outcomes while ensuring appropriate reimbursement for services provided. A solid case management program is essential to delivering full-continuum patient care while supporting the clinical, financial, and quality outcome metrics for the hospital.

The title *case manager* may be used by a variety of professionals, but in the hospital setting, a registered nurse or social worker most commonly fulfills this role. Hospitals are now actively seeking bachelor's-prepared nurses and master's-prepared social workers. These education levels align with the standards in nationally recognized hospital-level designations, such as the American Nurse Credentialing Center's Magnet Recognition Program. Additionally, certification as a case manager is becoming a preferred recruitment qualification. Although certification is not required by all organizations, it establishes a level of proficiency. Certification requirements usually include having one to two years of case management experience and passing a comprehensive exam of case management principles.

KEY DEPARTMENT SERVICES

Utilization review is one of the key services provided by Case Management. It encompasses determining bed status (i.e., outpatient status, inpatient admission), ensuring documentation supports the appropriateness of admission, reviewing continued stays, monitoring level of care (i.e., intensive or intermediate care, telemetry, medical-surgical bed), and obtaining final approval from the patient's insurance for all inpatient services provided. Utilization review case managers are stationed at access points to be the gatekeeper for the hospital and to ensure a patient's condition requires acute care. To optimize resources, bed status determination should be done before the admitting physician writes the initial bed status order. The utilization review case manager is expected to understand payer-related rules to provide payer-specific recommendations to the admitting physician, such as the Medicare two-midnight rule. (Medicare established the threshold criteria for admission to be based on documented hospital level of care that spans two or more midnights.) If these elements are met, the inpatient admission is deemed appropriate according to Medicare; however, other payers may make a different determination based on other guidelines.

Whereas admission review determines the appropriateness for inpatient admission, continued stay review determines the necessity of each day to ensure a lower level of care is not available. Admission and continued stay reviews may be conducted at different intervals, as designated in the hospital's Utilization Review Plan. This Utilization Review Plan outlines the specifics of how the hospital will evaluate the appropriate utilization of healthcare resources to include ongoing assessment of an inpatient stay. Several companies sell evidence-based guideline software for utilization review case managers to validate the appropriateness of an admission or continued hospital stay. These guidelines are intended to be utilized by non-physician reviewers and suggest that cases not meeting criteria be escalated to the next level for review. Hospitals often refer to a physician adviser for review of these cases and to intervene when clinical indications for admission or continued stay are not evident. Failure to have a robust program to review such cases can result in increased denials, prolonged length of stay, and misuse of limited healthcare resources.

More and more Case Management departments are taking the lead on addressing initial denials. An initial denial occurs when authorization for the hospital stay is not approved. The denial can be issued for a portion of the hospital stay or the entire admission. If hospital services are not approved for the patient, the utilization review case manager coordinates with the patient's payer and physician to facilitate the initial appeal for reconsideration. The advantage of having the utilization review case manager address the initial denial is their firsthand knowledge of what transpired during the admission and their access to the physician. Some hospitals have a designated Denial Management Department functioning separately from utilization review. A denial is easier to overturn as close to the date of discharge as possible, rather than appealing denied days or services at a later date, because of the ease of gathering additional documentation. Consider this fact when identifying how denials will be managed.

The other primary responsibility for a Case Management Department is discharge planning. Discharge planning involves ongoing patient-needs assessment to ensure a smooth and sustainable transition of care at time of discharge. This can be performed by either a nurse case manager or social worker. Which discipline performs the discharge planning function often depends on the clinical complexity of the discharge. Clinically complex discharges are often coordinated by the nurse case manager.

Discharge planning generally begins with the first patient contact, which can occur at the time of the patient's admission or beforehand. Hospitals with CMS accreditation are required to screen patients for potential discharge needs as close to admission as possible to prevent delays in discharge. This screening can be done in various ways. One technique is to have the bedside nurse complete the initial screen for discharge needs and identify those patients whose discharge plan requires further assessment. Patient screening tools can identify certain patient needs, such as post-acute care services that would require collaboration with case management for transition-of-care intervention. Many electronic health record (EHR) software programs have automated programs to help identify at-risk patients who may require additional screening or care coordination.

DEPARTMENT ORGANIZATIONAL STRUCTURES

The size and structure of the Case Management Department may be determined by the size of the hospital, scope of services to be provided, and available resources. The department's management is typically headed by a registered nurse regardless of the various types of licensed professionals in the department. A very large organization (i.e., 500+ beds) may have multiple levels of leadership to directly support Case Management staff. At minimum, most departments have a director who reports to a member on the executive team, usually the chief nursing officer, chief financial officer, or the chief medical officer. The director is responsible for the department's strategic planning and provides high-level oversight to ensure the department remains aligned with regulatory guidelines and stays ahead of any changes in the profession. The operations of the department may be delegated to its next level of leadership. This position would be responsible for implementing strategy, tracking performance-metric standards, leveraging technical solutions for issues, realigning focus as needed, and providing direct staff support.

In addition to the case management functions, there is always an administrative component that should be aligned to the most appropriate staff. Administrative duties include timekeeping, managing incoming calls and faxes, data entry of authorized days, and coordination of durable medical equipment. Having the right support for these duties allows the case managers and leaders to function at the highest level of their degrees. Nonclinical positions can decrease the burden of these tasks. See exhibit 5.1 for a sample case management organizational chart.

Various case management models can be used depending on the organization's needs. Each model has pros and cons that need to be weighed to determine what is best for that specific organization at that time. Factors that may affect what model to choose include size of the organization, scope of services provided, payer mix, and complexity of the patient population. Two of the most common models are the triad model and the dyad model.

Exhibit 5.1: Sample Organizational Chart

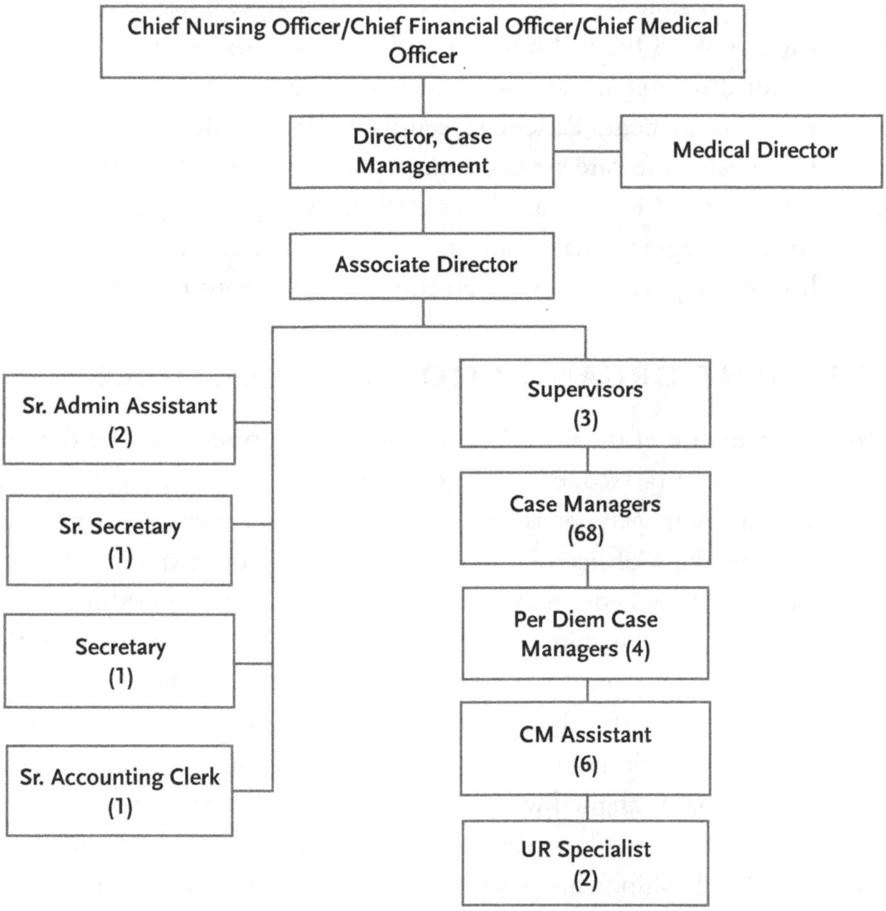

Note: CM = case manager; UR = utilization review.

A triad model has three distinct roles: utilization review, social work, and clinical case managers. Each discipline has a unique function. The utilization review nurse ensures appropriate bed status determination (i.e., the patient is in the right bed at the right time receiving the right services) and provides clinical information to payers to justify continued stay and payment. The social worker primarily focuses on the psychosocial needs of the patient along with other discharge planning activities. The clinical case manager nurse is responsible for coordinating care and assisting with the more clinically complex cases.

In the dyad model, the nurse case manager performs utilization review, whereas the social worker is the primary discharge planner.

Exhibit 5.2 lists the pros and cons of both models. Some of the discharge planning activities may be shared. Whichever model is used, close partnerships with the medical team must be developed to ensure the best quality of care is delivered.

Exhibit 5.2: Case Management Models

	Dyad model	Triad model
Pros	• One case manager interacts with team • Utilization review and discharge planning roles are interchangeable, which increases coverage • Reduces duplication of efforts, fragmentation, and redundancy	• Expertise in one focused area, either discharge planning, psychosocial needs, or utilization review • Fewer competing priorities • Availability to customers (e.g., patient, teams, insurance companies)
Cons	• Case manager needs to balance utilization review needs with discharge planning demands • May be less visible to the patient and team because of multiple tasks	• Several individuals interact with teams; may result in repetitive questions • Less ability to cross-cover other assignments because of specialization • Requires more staff

KEY CUSTOMERS AND THEIR PERFORMANCE EXPECTATIONS

Case Management affects almost every aspect of the patient experience in the hospital setting. Key customers include the patient, family/caregiver, physicians, nurses, ancillary staff, payers, and community providers (see exhibit 5.3). The primary customer will always be the patient, but the case manager needs to establish

Exhibit 5.3: Case Management Customers and Expectations

Customer	Expectations
Patient	• Advocate for the best care possible • Align discharge plan with patient's preference
Family/caregiver	• Ensure their loved one receives the best possible care
Physicians	• Interpret payer rules and understand regulations • Provide recommendations to facilitate a safe, sustainable transition of care at discharge
Nurse	• Understand clinically what the patient requires for a successful transition of care plan
Ancillary staff	• Anticipate the needs for consults • Possess the ability to provide patients the recommended services
Payers	• Anticipate the needs for consults • Provide clinical information to support the stay • Expedite discharge as soon as medically appropriate
Community providers	• Provide advance notice of discharge needs • Prevent premature discharges • Provide a sustainable discharge plan

solid relationships with the medical team to align the discharge plan with the anticipated needs of the patient. The case manager is expected to be the advocate for the patient and their family/caregiver. The case manager provides options and guidance to the patient and family/caregiver to assist them in developing their discharge plan.

The medical team expects the case manager to have in-depth clinical knowledge about the needs and care for the patient's condition while in the hospital and post-discharge. Given the complexity of the patient's insurance rules and CMS regulations, the medical team relies on the case manager to interpret payer rules and identify how patient needs can be met in an often financially and resource-constrained environment. Case managers frequently need to be creative to find alternatives when developing a successful discharge plan.

KEY PROCESS FLOWS

Utilization review and discharge planning are two key processes in case management. When performing utilization review, case managers are responsible for conducting daily clinical review to ensure the patient is receiving the right care, at the right time, in the right status. Before the patient is formally admitted, the utilization review case manager reviews the patient's medical record for documentation of medical necessity and provides a bed-status recommendation to the medical team. Screening for appropriate bed status before admission allows the case manager to identify those patients that lack the documented medical necessity to support being hospitalized, then provide opportunities for appropriate interventions to occur. The case manager can provide recommendations to the physician explaining the rationale for the determination. This explanation enables the physician to change the proposed status, modify the plan, or improve documentation to justify the requested status. Internal processes should be established to escalate cases when the physician and case manager disagree on either an initial bed-status determination or continued stay review. The utilization review case manager should review documentation daily to support initial bed-status determination, level of care, continued stay, and readiness for discharge.

The discharge-planning case manager works directly with the patient to develop a safe and sustainable discharge plan. Identifying issues that may affect discharge planning during the admission is crucial to prevent any barriers or delays when the patient is clinically ready for discharge. Most organizations use a screening tool at admission (exhibit 5.4) that the bedside nurse completes when the patient is admitted. The screening tool identifies key issues that may require more in-depth discussion between the case manager and patient. Regardless of the initial screening results, case managers need a process for a more in-depth review. For instance, case finding through chart review, discussion with the medical team, or in-person patient interviews may identify additional concerns. Because the patient's condition is ever evolving, the case manager needs to stay abreast of any clinical or social changes that may alter the discharge plan. It is important for the case manager to review the goals for care and potential care transitions, including alternate settings and levels of care, with the patient and family/caregivers. The timing and frequency of the reassessment needs to be revisited throughout the hospital stay and outlined in hospital policies.

Exhibit 5.4: Screening Tool

☐ Are you currently able to care for yourself at home?
☐ If no, do you have someone that provides assistance to you?
☐ Do you have any issues in obtaining prescription medications?
☐ Do you have any current medical equipment needs?
☐ Would you like to speak with a case manager regarding any discharge needs at this time?

If any answers are "yes," hospital staff places a consult for case management to conduct a more thorough assessment.

If organizations have separate case manager roles for discharge planning and utilization review, the two roles customarily act as partners. Each partner is responsible for identifying any delays with the transition of care. These issues should be escalated to case manager leadership for review and needed actions. The delays may be external or internal; although not all can be mitigated, understanding why the delays occur may explain length of stay outliers and identify opportunities for improvement.

KEY UNITS OF WORK AND VOLUME STATISTICS TO MONITOR

With the use of EHRs, capturing case management activities has become much easier. Exhibit 5.5 lists key utilization review and discharge planning metrics to consider. For utilization review, monitoring the number of cases reviewed can

Exhibit 5.5: Key Units of Work in Case Management

Utilization review	Frequency of monitoring	Target
Number of cases reviewed	Monthly	100%
Number of cases meeting medical necessity	Monthly	100%
Number of changes made to bed status (i.e., changed from inpatient to observation, observation to inpatient)	Monthly	< 5%
Compliance in delivering the Medicare Outpatient Observation Notice and Important Message from Medicare	Monthly	100%
Denials	Monthly	0%
Total number of admissions, observations, and extended recovery patients	Monthly	Ratio for case manager 1:30
Discharge planning	**Frequency of monitoring**	**Target**
% of inpatients with a case management admission assessment	Monthly	100%
Number of cases that required case management intervention	Monthly	N/A
Number of changes made to bed status (i.e., changed from inpatient to observation, observation to inpatient)	Monthly	< 5%
Total number of admissions, observations, and extended recovery patients	Monthly	Ratio for Case Manager 1:20

assist in evaluating productivity and staffing requirements. Other metrics, such as the denial rate, can help evaluate the appropriateness of physician documentation and the effectiveness of the clinical reviews provided to the payer. Evidence-based utilization review guidelines may aid in identifying cases that do not meet criteria for an acute care stay. Using these guidelines may reveal trends to investigate for possible quality and efficiency improvement.

Discharge planning metrics involve the number of initial case management assessments completed, number of cases requiring case management intervention, and total readmission rate. Initial case management assessments should be compared to the number of admissions for the specific period. The goal for case review, for instance, would be to complete and document a case management assessment for 100 percent of all new admissions within 24 hours of admission. The purpose is early identification of any coordination that needs to occur for a successful discharge (see exhibit 5.6 for sample discharge questions). Discharge planning coordination includes referrals and linkages to community resources and services when obtaining durable medical equipment or coordinating post-acute care services to promote positive outcomes for the patient and family/caregiver.

Exhibit 5.6: Discharge Planning Questions

- Who is the primary caregiver?
  - If someone other than yourself, please provide name and contact number
- Will there be a different caregiver after discharge?
  - If so, please provide name and contact number
- Current support system (check all that apply):
  - ☐ None   ☐ Family members   ☐ Children (and ages)   ☐ Other
  - ☐ Home care staff   ☐ Church or faith   ☐ Friends/Neighbors
- Where do you normally reside?
  - ☐ Home by self   ☐ Home with others   ☐ At a facility
  - ☐ Homeless   ☐ Other
- Current medical equipment at home:
  - ☐ Walker   ☐ Wheelchair   ☐ Oxygen
  - ☐ Bedside commode   ☐ Other
- Established services prior to admission:
  - ☐ Home health   ☐ Providers' services   ☐ Dialysis   ☐ Other
- Reason for admission:
- Do you anticipate having any issues in returning to your previous residence? (access to the home, transportation, change in status or financial situation)

(continued)

Exhibit 5.6: Discharge Planning Questions *(continued)*

- Anticipated needs such as durable medical equipment (specifically what item) or the need for placement
- Barriers to discharge:

  ☐ None   ☐ No support system   ☐ Insurance does not cover anticipated discharge needs

  ☐ Lacks insurance or limited   ☐ No transportation   ☐ No established outpatient insurance coverage   provider

  ☐ Other

- Does the patient have a relationship with a provider for ongoing care? If no, the following resources were provided:

- Have you been readmitted in the last 30 days to any hospital?

- If yes, was it a planned admission?

- If not a planned admission, what caused you to be readmitted to the hospital?

KEY METRICS TO MONITOR: PEOPLE, SERVICE, QUALITY/SAFETY, FINANCIAL

People are always the most valuable asset to any organization. Monitoring employee satisfaction and employee turnover can indicate the ongoing health of the department. Employee satisfaction surveys can be a valuable tool to identify areas that might need increased focus. The unique skill set of the case manager is not easy to recruit, and losing experienced staff can greatly hamper not only the department but also the whole organization.

Quantifying all the services Case Management provides is critical to justify staffing. Measures of such services include number of patients screened, number of cases that required post-discharge needs, appropriate bed status determination, and length of stay metrics. Such quantification aids in determining the effectiveness of the Case Management program. Case Management staffing for the Emergency Department (ED) is a very common practice and is often done 7 days a week and up to 24 hours per day. As service volumes for Case Management intervention in the ED increase or decrease, Case Management staffing may need to be adjusted accordingly.

The HCAHPS (Hospital Consumer Assessment of Healthcare Providers and Systems) measures quality of the hospital stay from the patient's perspective.

HCAHPS is a national data repository that can be used to compare organizations locally, regionally, and nationally (CMS 2020). All hospitals that participate in the Inpatient Prospective Payment System are required to report this data to HCAHPS. The results are made available to the public on the CMS Hospital Compare website (https://www.medicare.gov/hospitalcompare/search.html). Although the HCAHPS questions pertain to the entire hospital experience, several are specific to the discharge process.

Case management has a direct influence on the financial outcome of the organization. The utilization review case manager ensures appropriate payment for services rendered in the inpatient setting. This process includes determining and assigning the appropriate bed status at admission and facilitating appropriate levels of care throughout the inpatient stay. Failure to adhere to appropriate bed status or level of care determination can result in denials for services rendered. The discharge planning role has a direct impact on length of stay and readmissions. The Case Management team must ensure patients are transitioned appropriately by following the concept that the patient receives the right care, at the right place, at the right time. Premature discharges and delays in transitioning patients to the appropriate level of care can harm the financial outcomes of the organization. Discharging a patient too soon could place the patient at risk for readmission and incur penalties for the organization. Likewise, a prolonged hospital stay may exceed the anticipated length of stay, triggering insurance companies to examine documentation of medical necessity and ensure it supports the need for the excessive days. If they find the additional days to be not medically justified, they may issue a denial.

The utilization review function of Case Management also directly affects hospital reimbursement. How well an organization completes this task can be reflected in the denial rate. Providing payers with key clinical information in a timely manner to justify admissions and continued stays decreases the risk of denials. Case managers need to partner with the medical team to ensure sufficient documentation is evident in the medical record. They also need a strong clinical background to understand complex medical conditions and identify what needs to be included when documenting them to optimize authorization for services.

Since 2012, readmission rates have become a major focus for the healthcare industry. Not only does a readmission indicate the effectiveness of hospital discharge planning, it also may reduce reimbursement. CMS instituted the Hospital Readmissions Reduction Program in 2012 (CMS 2020). The intent of this program was to link payment to the quality of hospital care by using readmissions to indicate poor performance. Although this program is specific to Medicare and Medicaid beneficiaries, other insurances have followed suit.

A readmission related to the patient's previous admission may result in denial of payment for those services. In addition to their financial implications, readmissions may affect patient choice of healthcare providers. Because readmission rates are reported through multiple organizations and made available to the public, low readmission rates can be a marketing tool to attract new patients.

Abiding by CMS policies, hospitals are required to deliver the Medicare Outpatient Observation Notice (MOON) and the Important Message from Medicare (IMM) to Medicare beneficiaries. The regulations do not stipulate who must deliver these forms, but Case Management is often involved. Metrics to support the delivery of the MOON and IMM need to be tracked to ensure hospital regulatory compliance. Exhibit 5.7, the case management scorecard, displays this data point along with other metrics that may be monitored monthly. Reaching the target of 100 percent compliance with issuance of the MOON and IMM is often difficult to sustain and must be in line of sight for improvement opportunities by the operational leader of the department.

Exhibit 5.7: Case Management Scorecard

		Scorecard					
		Case Management					
		Under-performing	Threshold	Target	Stretch	MM/YYYY	YTD
People							
P1	Recognition or awards received	0		3			
P2	Year-to-date turnover: % of staff who (voluntarily/ involuntarily) left the organization during this fiscal year	>20%	11%–20%	1%–10%	<1%		
P3	First-year turnover: % of staff who (voluntarily/ involuntarily) left the organization less than 1 year from their date of hire	>14%	11%–14%	9%–10%	<9%		
Service							
S1	Ratio of discharge planning case managers to average daily census	>1:20	1:17–1:19	1:16	1:12		

(continued)

Scorecard					
Case Management					
	Under-performing	Threshold	Target	Stretch	MM/YYYY YTD

		Under-performing	Threshold	Target	Stretch	MM/YYYY	YTD
S2	% of initial case management assessments completed	<85%	86%–94%	95%	≥98%		
S3	Length of stay index	>1.5	1.4–1.2	1.1	1		
Quality							
Q1	Percent of unplanned readmissions	>20%	19%–18%	17%	15%		
Q2	Number of discharge planning–related issues after discharge	>5	4–3	2	1		
Q3	Percent of Medicare Notices delivered (IMMs and MOONs)	<85%	86%–89%	90%	95%		
Finance							
F1	Personnel expenses	>Budget		<Budget			
F2	Other operating expenses	>Budget		<Budget			
F3	Total operating expenses (ratio)	>1.5	1.4–1.2	1.1	1		
F4	Total dollar amount of services denied	<10%	9%–6%	5%	<3%		

Note: IMM = Important Message from Medicare; MOON = Medicare Outpatient Observation Notice.

KEY INFORMATICS ISSUES

The EHR has greatly increased the efficiency of Case Management. Most mature EHRs have a built-in Case Management module or a third-party system embedded into the EHR to support Case Management activities. The use of these programs standardizes Case Management documentation and can support regulatory requirements in regard to the discharge planning process. Unlike the historical paper-based medical records, the EHR allows multiple people to access the medical record at the same time regardless of location. This offers flexibility for the case manager to access patient information anywhere to perform Case Management duties.

From a utilization review standpoint, well-built EHRs can help package clinical information to be easily transmitted electronically to payers, which improves productivity and timeliness while reducing organizational costs. If a hospital stay is denied, case managers no longer need to file and maintain paper copies, because the correspondence is readily available in the EHR. Additionally, most EHRs have the capability to integrate evidence-based tools that assist the case manager when reviewing cases for medical necessity. Having these tools embedded in the EHR allows the case manager to easily send this information with the other clinical information.

Work-queue tools in the EHR allow the case manager to focus on cases requiring attention and perform daily tasks more efficiently. Work queues may be designed to identify subgroups such as short stays, observation patients, accounts where inpatient days are not reconciled, or outstanding changes with specific accounts. The ability to export data into reports allows quick analysis that would normally require extensive time to collect for case manager review. Compliance with key regulatory indicators, such as with the delivery of MOON and IMM notices, can be accomplished through EHR work queues and subsequent reports.

Adequate information technology (IT) support is essential to maximize the system of choice for the hospital's EHR. If possible, a dedicated IT resource for the Case Management Department is ideal for making workflows, reports, troubleshooting, and outcomes most efficient.

STAFFING MODELS

Case Management staffing assessment must be based on the needs of the organization. Case Management is primarily an 8 a.m. to 5 p.m. weekday role; however, extending case manager availability on weekends and after hours can be useful. For instance, having sufficient weekend staff can reduce the utilization review burden on Monday morning because new clinical reviews can be completed on the weekend and sent to the payer. Additionally, having a case manager available outside typical hours to aid bed status determination can prevent denials and decrease the potential appeal process workload in real time. A case manager for planning weekend discharge would be available to execute anticipated discharges and possibly to expedite unplanned discharges. Unplanned discharges that remain inpatient over the weekend would be considered avoidable days if coordination for discharge services caused the delay in discharge. The hospital should analyze the volume of admissions by hour and day of week to determine the amount of coverage needed. Most organizations have a period of extended coverage for this reason and may include the evening hours, up until midnight, seven days a week; however, the hospital's peak times for admissions and discharges will determine what would work best for the organization.

Daily assignment of Case Management staff can follow various models. Two of the most popular models are geographic and team-based assignments. Geographic staffing allows the case manager to be assigned to a group of beds or an entire specific unit or floor, whereas team-based staffing focuses on aligning with the hospital service. Both models have pros and cons. With the geographic model, the case manager partners closely with the unit's nursing staff. This partnership improves communication with the interdisciplinary team and increases access to updates that may affect the discharge plan. Another benefit is having all the patients assigned to the case manager on the same unit, which saves time and increases Case Management presence and availability so unit staff can immediately address issues or concerns. One of the disadvantages of the geographic model is the case manager may be required to work with multiple medical teams if specific hospital services span more than one unit. Additionally, Case Management assignments may not be fairly balanced, because each hospital service may have a different census and thus be less predictable than the team-based staffing model.

In the team-based model of staffing, the case manager is assigned to one or more hospital services, aligned with specific physicians rather than nursing staff. The benefits to this model are the case manager has more timely access to the physicians for obtaining the most current medical plan and informing the clinical team of any limitations pertaining to discharge planning. A major disadvantage to this model is that patients might be placed across several units, causing confusion for the nursing and ancillary support staff when identifying which case manager is assigned to that specific patient on the unit. Also, team-based models make it difficult for case managers to cover for one another. Case managers assigned to patients on multiple units need to prioritize their day and responses to services requests. When the units are geographically distant from one another, case managers must spend time navigating between units, which can result in extended delays and dissatisfaction to the patient and staff.

PRODUCTIVITY MODELS, INCLUDING WORK-TO-STAFF RATIOS AND INDUSTRY PERFORMANCE TARGETS

Several factors must be considered when determining the actual number of case managers required in a department. A review of the census history, payer mix, utilization review plan, and case management model will provide insightful information when planning the number of manager positions. Exhibit 5.8 provides two examples of proposed staffing for a Case Management Department: one where

Exhibit 5.8: Required Staffing for Two Case Management Models

Discharge planning and utilization review functions kept separate

Example facility	Patient complexity	Average daily census	Patient: Discharge planning case management ratio	Patient: Utilization review case management ratio	Estimated case manager FTEs needed
Oncology specialty hospital	High	450	1:16	1:32	42
Academic medical institution	High	450	1:20	1:32	37
Midsize general hospital	Moderate	300	1:24	1:32	22
Community hospital	Low	100	1:30	1:32	6.5

Discharge planning and utilization review functions combined

Example facility	Patient complexity	Average daily census	Patient: Case management ratio	Estimated case manager FTEs needed
Oncology specialty hospital	High	450	1:10	45
Academic medical institution	High	450	1:15	30
Midsize general hospital	Moderate	300	1:20	15
Community hospital	Low	100	1:24	4

Note: FTE = full-time equivalent.

utilization review and discharge planning are integrated and performed by the same case manager, and another where separate, dedicated case managers perform these functions. For models to support combined roles of utilization review and discharge planning, ratios would need to be lower to allow sufficient time to complete each task. The advantage of combining roles is the case manager will have a smaller patient-to-case-manager ratio and will be responsible for all aspects of the patient's plan. The challenge of having a combined role is there will always be competing priorities. Several payers now require a patient's clinical information to be provided within a short time window, which may force case managers to divide their attention between meeting the payer's timeline for clinical submission and facilitating a timely patient discharge. In organizations with separate discharge planning and utilization review components, ratios need to be determined on the expectation of each role. Factors influencing utilization review staff ratios are management of observation and extended recovery patients, payer mix, cadence established by the organization to conduct reviews, and who is responsible for denial management. In the discharge planning role, key metrics such as new case management assessments completed, and discharge arrangements made, can provide insight into the number of case managers required.

STRATEGIES TO IMPROVE RECRUITMENT AND RETENTION

A shortage of a quarter-million nurses is anticipated by 2025 (American Association of Colleges of Nursing 2019). Along with this predicted shortage, changes in legislation such as the Affordable Care Act will require organizations to depend on the case manager role to navigate the complexities of regulatory and payer guidelines. Considering the likely expansion of the case manager role, healthcare organizations will have greater cause to retain qualified case managers to meet new demands. A phenomenological study was done by Wilson (2014) to identify factors that influence case manager retention. The results revealed that manageable workloads were one of the highest satisfiers for retention. Staffing can vary by organization and case management model in use; therefore, making a generalized statement on caseloads would not be appropriate without considering these factors.

Department leadership was another key factor in Wilson's (2014) findings that led to dissatisfaction and turnover. Establishing a strong and supportive leadership team is the key to a successful Case Management Department. Having leaders that are available and approachable provides the necessary support to the team and fosters a sense of collaboration and shared responsibility. The leadership team is responsible for ensuring a structured orientation for new hires to provide a solid base of understanding of the case management role.

Other factors that influence case manager satisfaction are professional growth and work–life balance. Some organizations have developed case management titles that differentiate level of experience. Clinical ladders are one such technique that promotes professional growth, but they are more common with bedside nursing. A clinical ladder is used to recognize professional development and differentiate levels of nursing expertise (Coleman and Desai 2019). Recognizing the variation in case managers' proficiency while allowing for growth increases satisfaction and provides advancement opportunities. Experienced case managers are often paid similarly to those case managers with one to two years of experience, but case-load and complexity are often not equitable (Wilson 2014). Case managers with experience often get assigned the more clinically complex cases. Differentiating the case managers' experience levels allows their proficiency in the role to be recognized. Experienced case managers are necessary to provide the sound basis and understanding of Case Management practice in order to train and educate novice case managers on core competencies.

KEY REGULATORY ISSUES

Both CMS and The Joint Commission have regulatory standards for acute care hospitals. The goal of both organizations is to set an industry standard for quality care and patient safety. The CoPs for CMS include utilization review and discharge planning standards. Under the COPs, each hospital is required to establish a Utilization Review Plan that sets the tone and cadence for each of these functions.

In accordance with the COPs, the hospital must establish a Utilization Review Committee (URC). This committee must have at least two or more practitioners to conduct hospital utilization review functions, which include a review of medical necessity for admissions, extended stays, and professional services. The URC oversees the implementation of the utilization review plan and identifies opportunities to ensure the appropriate use of healthcare resources. The Case Management Department is an integral participant of the URC and often serves as the first line of review for such cases. The URC and Case Management must have a strong relationship because one directly affects the other. If the URC lacks authority, Case Management may not have sufficient support for interventions required to implement practice changes that align with regulatory requirements. Likewise, if there is a strong URC but the Case Management Department lacks the appropriate knowledge and understanding of how to implement the CoPs, gaps in utilization review will persist.

Another facet of CMS hospital CoPs is the importance of patient choice. As outlined in 42 CFR § 482.43(c), "Condition of Participation: Discharge Planning," patients must be informed of their right to choose post-hospital providers. Hospitals are required to provide the patient a list from which the patient may choose a provider. In 2019, CMS published an update to the discharge planning rule that requires hospitals not only to provide a list, but also to ensure the list includes measures of quality and resource use (CMS 2019). The Case Management Department needs a solid process to ensure adherence to this rule.

Accreditation is an evaluative process in which the hospital undergoes an examination of its policies, procedures, practices, and performance by an external organization to ensure that it is meeting predetermined criteria. The accreditation survey usually involves both on- and off-site surveys. In The Joint Commission standards, the chapter "Provision of Care, Treatment, and Services" is important to the Case Management Department. The team will review CMS standards (CFR § 482.30) against the hospital's utilization review plan. Under the "Provision of Care" chapter, the survey team will review discharge planning processes to ensure adherence to CMS requirements.

In addition to CMS CoPs, payer reimbursement and coverage play a major role in care coordination. Understanding the scope and limits of each patient's insurance coverage is important in understanding discharge options. The case manager needs to discuss options and limitations to coverage with the patient and family/caregiver to assist with making informed decisions for their post-hospital care. Coordination of benefits when a patient has more than one insurance and knowing which insurance is primary is critical when coordinating care. Patients and families need case managers to help them understand their financial obligations so they can make good decisions during a difficult time in their trajectory of care.

KEY TERMS FOR CASE MANAGEMENT

Admission review: An initial review of the medical documentation to support the need for hospital-level services. Although this is best done in real time, it can be performed retrospectively.

Bed status determination: Involves the review of medical documentation to support a specific bed status (e.g., inpatient or outpatient). Outpatient status includes observation and extended recovery statuses.

Continued stay review: Intermittent review of medical documentation that supports the ongoing need of hospital-level care.

Denial rate: Number of inpatient denials over the number of hospital inpatient discharges.

Discharge planning: An evaluation, assessment, and coordination of a patient's need for services post-discharge. This involves understanding the insurance coverage and limitations, the patient's medical and psychosocial needs, and their preferences and requests. The case manager needs to ensure requested services are appropriate.

Evidence-based case management tools: Tools that are based on scientific evidence and support a specific expected course of care. This includes the type of setting where a service should be rendered, projected length of stay, anticipated recovery milestones, and readiness for discharge. These tools often serve as a guide to aid the case manager in justifying the appropriateness of the service or status being requested. They are most commonly embedded in a software program but can be available in other forms.

Level of care: This level differentiates specific care that a patient may receive while in an inpatient setting. Each level of care has charges associated with the type of services provided and may affect reimbursement. Some of the more common levels of care are private, intermediate, intensive care, or rehabilitation.

Utilization review: A review process that determines the appropriateness of a hospital service. This determination of appropriateness is a requirement through the CMS Conditions of Participation. Most payers also require clinical information to support payment of clinical services.

REFERENCES

American Association of Colleges of Nursing. 2019. "Nursing Shortage." Updated April 1. www.aacnnursing.org/News-Information/Fact-Sheets/Nursing-Shortage.

Centers for Medicare & Medicaid Services (CMS). 2020. "Hospital Readmissions Reduction Program (HRRP)." Updated August 24. www.cms.gov/Medicare/Medicare-Fee-for-Service-Payment/AcuteInpatientPPS/Readmissions-Reduction-Program.

———. 2019. "CMS' Discharge Planning Rule Supports Interoperability and Patient Preferences." Published September 26. www.cms.gov/newsroom/press-releases/cms-discharge-planning-rule-supports-interoperability-and-patient-preferences.

Coleman, Y. A., and R. Desai. 2019. "The Effects of a Clinical Ladder Program on Professional Development and Job Satisfaction of Acute Care Nurses." *Clinical Journal of Nursing Care Practice* 3: 44–48.

Wilson, S. 2014. "Factors That Influence Retention of Nurse Case Managers." California Intercontinental University, DBA dissertation.

CHAPTER 6

Clinical Nutrition

Ann-Marie Hedberg and Jenny Koetting

DEPARTMENT DESCRIPTION

Clinical Nutrition Services provided in an accredited hospital are regulated by external accrediting bodies (discussed in the Key Regulatory Issues section of this chapter) and by the Centers for Medicare & Medicaid Services (CMS; www.cms. gov). A qualified dietitian registered by the Commission on Dietetic Registration (CDR; www.cdrnet.org) with the RD (Registered Dietitian) or RDN (Registered Dietitian Nutritionist) credential is recommended for acute care institutions. The CDR administers the RD or RDN credential once the candidate has completed all required degrees and clinical training hours and has passed a national examination. The RD provides science-based food and medical nutrition therapy to clients under the guidelines of the Code of Ethics for the Nutrition and Dietetic Profession and the Scope of Professional Practice (Academy of Nutrition and Dietetics 2018a; Academy Quality Management Committee 2018). Additional licensure or certification may be required by each state and can be found on the CDR website (Academy of Nutrition and Dietetics 2018b).

Adequate clinical RD and support personnel staffing is important to meet patients' clinical nutrition needs. Patient case-mix index and acuity level are factors in determining the department's required clinical nutrition staffing, as discussed in the Key Process Flows, Key Units of Work, and Productivity Models sections of this chapter.

A Mission and Vision Statement should be in place to describe the focus areas for the Clinical Nutrition Services Department or Section. Examples include the following:

- Mission Statement: Through our expertise, innovative practices, and commitment to quality, the Clinical Nutrition Services Team provides personalized nutrition care to promote health and healing for our patients.

- Vision: Through the excellence of our people and caring for others, we will lead the world in evidence-based nutrition care for our patients, caregivers, and staff.

Nutrition services are critical to patients to prevent the complications of malnutrition, which include delayed wound healing, fatigue, decrease in functional status, increased infection risk, greater length of stay, readmission, and death (Fingar et al. 2016; Funamizu et al. 2018; Hedberg 2018; Julius et al. 2017; Leiva-Badosa et al. 2017; Saghaleini et al. 2018; Tobert, Mott, and Nepple 2018; White et al. 2012).

KEY DEPARTMENT SERVICES

The clinical services that Clinical Nutrition staff provide include, but are not limited to, the following:

- Addressing all Patient Admission Screening referrals in a timely manner: The clinical staff admitting the patient (generally the nurse or nurse assistant) completes an admission screening tool to identify patients at nutrition risk. Other areas of potential risk are also identified including social and emotional, fall risk, skin breakdown, and so forth. The Patient Admission Screen prompts used to detect nutrition risk should include validated objective indicators to assess pre-admission weight loss and adequacy of intake.
- Identifying patients requiring nutrition services: A process should be established in collaboration with the Medical Staff, Nursing, other ancillary departments, and the patient or caregiver to refer patients meeting established risk criteria (e.g., inadequate intake, skin breakdown, weight loss, food/drug interaction). All inpatients should be eligible to receive a nutrition assessment by a qualified RD to assess nutrition requirements and adequacy of intake.
- Obtaining Documentation of Nutrition Assessment and a Nutrition Care Plan for each patient in the medical record: Policies should be in place that describe the process for referrals to an RD, the time frame for completing the consultation, and the services provided as a result of the nutritional assessment. The assessment may include a diet history, medical and surgical history, a nutrition-focused physical assessment for lean muscle and fat reserves/wasting, laboratory data, and plans for the individualized Nutrition Care Plan (see exhibit 6.1). The Nutrition Care Plan should be documented in the medical record for the medical care team and communicated with

Exhibit 6.1: Sample Nutritional Assessment and Nutrition Care Plan Template

Details	Includes relevant subjective and objective information related to nutritional status. Lists details such as diet history and appetite, social and cultural information, food allergies and preferences, weight history, medical history and condition, lab results, and physical findings.
Assessment	Determination of nutritional status using patient details. May include items such as estimated nutritional requirements, degree of nutritional impact of the medical condition, interpretation of lab results, and malnutrition diagnosis.
Recommendations	Recommended plan crafted from the assessment. May include interventions such as dietary counseling for the patient and caregiver, or recommendations for the provider such as enteral tube feeding or parenteral nutrition support.

the patient and caregiver. The RD should discuss with the medical team recommended interventions such as nutrition supplements, enteral tube feeding support, or, if indicated, parenteral nutrition support.

DEPARTMENT ORGANIZATIONAL STRUCTURES

Clinical Nutrition Services provided by RDs are generally part of the Food and Nutrition Services Department. Depending on the size of the institution and reporting structure of the organization, Clinical Nutrition may also report to these departments:

- Clinical Support Services, including other clinical services such as Social Work, Case Management, Respiratory Therapy, Spiritual Care, and Physical or Occupational Therapy
- Inpatient or Outpatient Division, alongside other ancillary clinical services in the inpatient or outpatient arenas
- Nursing Services: RDs may be assigned under nurse managers by specific units or clinical services
- Medical service lines: RDs may be assigned to medical service lines reporting to service line directors

Exhibit 6.2 is a structural representation of a model Clinical Nutrition Department at an academic medical institution or large healthcare facility. Smaller organizations will generally have fewer layers.

Exhibit 6.2: Sample Clinical Nutrition Organizational Structure

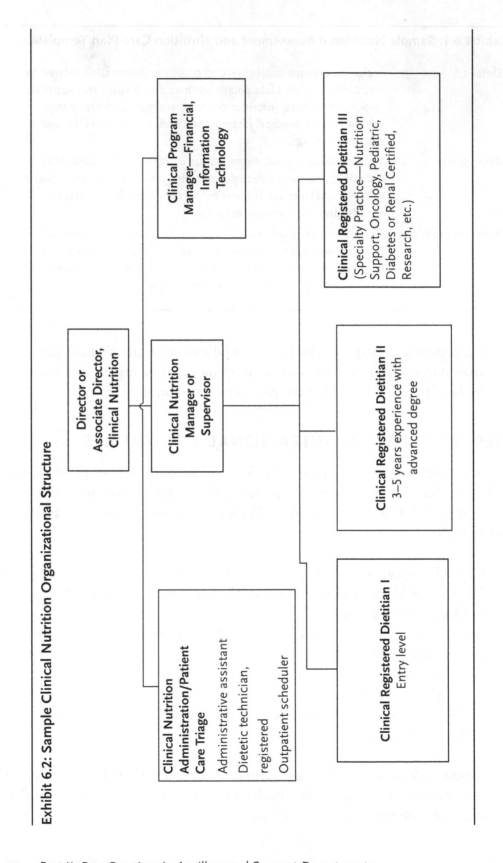

KEY CUSTOMERS AND THEIR PERFORMANCE EXPECTATIONS

Clinical Nutrition Services has numerous key internal and external stakeholders in the organization. The RD is uniquely qualified to perform comprehensive nutritional assessment, including a nutrition-focused physical assessment to identify nutrition risk factors that, if not addressed, can result in increased morbidity, length of stay, and risk of mortality. Therefore, medical teams must have documented, individualized Nutrition Care Plans for each patient from the RD.

Exhibits 6.3 and 6.4 list performance expectations for internal and external stakeholders, respectively, in relation to RDs' collaborative roles with these parties and their performance expectations.

KEY PROCESSES FLOWS

Interdisciplinary protocols with workflow processes indicating the role of the RD are important for delineating critical patient-care intervention time frames and expected patient-care outcomes. The Clinical Nutrition Department should seek input from key stakeholders and update the following procedures or workflows at least every two years or as appropriate, then distribute the final version to key stakeholders. Leaders should review processes annually to assess opportunities for improving efficiency.

- Admission Screening for Nutrition Risk
- Nutrition Assessment
- Documentation in the Electronic Health Record
- Food–Drug Interaction Education Process
- Patient Safety–Related Protocols
  - International Dysphagia Diet Standardization Initiative (https://iddsi.org/)
  - International Organization for Standardization (ISO) Enteral Feeding standard ISO 80369-3 (ENFit: http://stayconnected.org/enteral-enfit/) was adopted to prevent tubing misconnections. See The Joint Commission Sentinel Event 53, "Managing Risk During Transition to New ISO Tubing Connector Standards" (https://www.jointcommission.org/sea_issue_53/). Exhibit 6.5 shows an example ISO workflow for managing ENFit devices.
- Nutrition-Focused Physical Assessment and Malnutrition Diagnosis Recommendation (exhibits 6.6a and 6.6b)

Exhibit 6.3: Internal Stakeholders' Performance Expectations

Internal stakeholders	Collaborative role with stakeholder	Performance expectation from RD
Patient and family/caregivers	• Provide relevant nutrition history • Receive nutrition education	• Inclusion of diet history and nutrition-related inquiries in the development of Nutrition Care Plan to ensure optimal recovery
Physician	• Verification of final approval for the institution enteral formulary, Diet Manual, and Patient Education Materials related to area of practice • Documentation of agreement with Nutrition Care Plan and, if applicable, malnutrition diagnosis recommendation	• Recommendation of appropriate diet and nutrition support orders clearly documented in the Nutrition Care Plan • Confirmation of nutrition-related problems such as malnutrition on Patient Problem List
Nurse	• Admission screening for nutrition risk and referral to RD • Assessment of wounds and RD consultation • Referrals for nutrition education and malnutrition risk (e.g., inadequate intake, weight loss, loss of functional status)	• Assessing nutritional status of referred patients and development of individualized Nutrition Care Plan
Pharmacist	• Coordination of the Drug/Food Interaction education program with RD • Collaboration with RD for TPN indication, formulary, prescription, and monitoring processes • Approval of Enteral and Parenteral Formulary	• Delivery of drug/food interaction education • Development of recommendations for enteral formulary • Collaboration with pharmacist for TPN prescriptions

Social worker/case manager	• Implementation of a Social-Emotional Plan of Care that can include adequacy of intake and functional status evaluation • Conduct discharge planning rounds with RD • Organization of discharge process for patients on home enteral or parenteral nutrition support
Rehabilitation team: physical and occupational therapy	• Collaboration with RD to assess oral intake and hand-grip strength (dynamometry) during therapy sessions • Development of exercise prescription in coordination with Nutrition Care Plan to encourage lean muscle anabolism • Development of Nutrition Care Plan to support lean muscle anabolism
Respiratory therapist	• Coordination of Indirect Calorimetry testing for critical care patients team to ensure appropriate nutrition support prescription • Assessment of ventilator-dependent patients with RD for those on enteral and parenteral support to prevent overfeeding and associated metabolic complications • Recommendation for Indirect Calorimetry testing and follow-up integration of these results into Nutrition Assessment and Nutrition Care Plan • Adjustment of enteral and parenteral nutrition support recommendations to prevent overfeeding and associated metabolic complication for ventilator-dependent patients
Food Service director and managers	• Collaboration with RD regarding menus for patients and guests to ensure nourishing meals that patients tolerate and meet their specialized nutrition requirements • Review menu items and advise Food Service leadership regarding menus that meet specialized nutrition requirements

Note: RD = registered dietitian; TPN = total parenteral nutrition.

Exhibit 6.4: External Stakeholders' Performance Expectations

External stakeholders	Collaborative role with stakeholder	Performance expectation from RD
Professional organizations	• Provision of continuing education for the RD • Publication of diet manual that can be reviewed and approved by medical staff • Provision of patient education material	• Complete continuing education requirements to maintain registration • May choose to serve on professional organization boards or committees
Durable medical equipment companies	• Provision of discharge supplies for patients on home enteral and parenteral nutrition support	• Develop individualized recommendations for home enteral and parenteral support • Coordinate home enteral nutrition support prescription with equipment companies
Pharmaceutical companies	• Produce nutritional formulas and food products that meet advanced patient care nutrition-support requirements	• Review product options and recommend formulary products that meet the specialized nutritional needs of their patient population

Note: RD = registered dietitian.

KEY UNITS OF WORK AND VOLUME STATISTICS TO MONITOR

Analyzing benchmark data is important for demonstrating effectiveness of any clinical program. Justification for staffing should be based on objective benchmark data supported in the literature. Key units of work to demonstrate effectiveness of Clinical Nutrition staff are listed next, followed by an example template (exhibit 6.7) as a framework for monitoring key units of work.

1. Productivity: The Academy of Nutrition and Dietetics publishes staffing model data for Clinical Nutrition staffing (Phillips 2015). The parameters evaluated to demonstrate productivity in Clinical Nutrition patient care may include the following:
    • Number of patients seen
    • Number of patients seen per productive period

Exhibit 6.5: Patient Safety Example: ISO Standards for Enteral Feeding Connectors

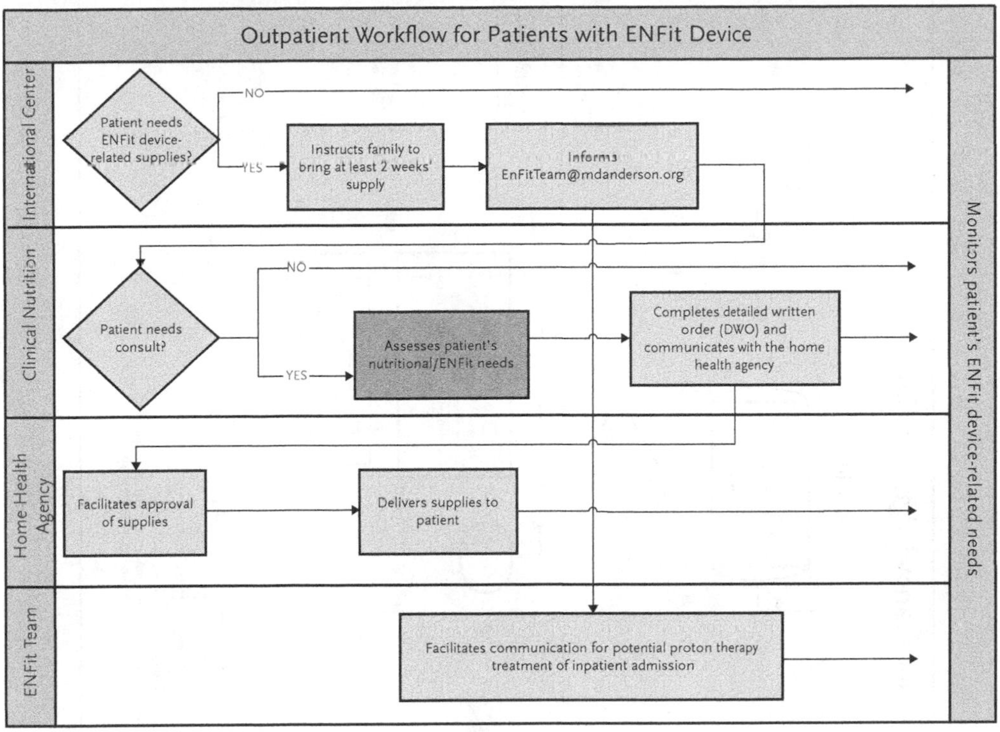

2. Fiscal Health: Budgetary management (as measured by comparing funds allocated monthly to actual) is important to ensure sustainability of the organization. Parameters may include the following:
   - Number of FTE staff
   - Personnel expense per period
   - Total operating expense per period
   - Total operating expense per patient seen per time period (exhibit 6.8)

KEY METRICS TO MONITOR: PEOPLE, SERVICE, QUALITY/SAFETY, FINANCIAL

Management of a Clinical Nutrition Program in a healthcare organization should include performance monitoring. Performance targets should conform to evidence-based industry professional standards. If professional standards are not available, then performance targets can be based on incremental improvement

Exhibit 6.6a: Malnutrition Diagnosis Recommendations to Providers for Acknowledgment: Flow by Role

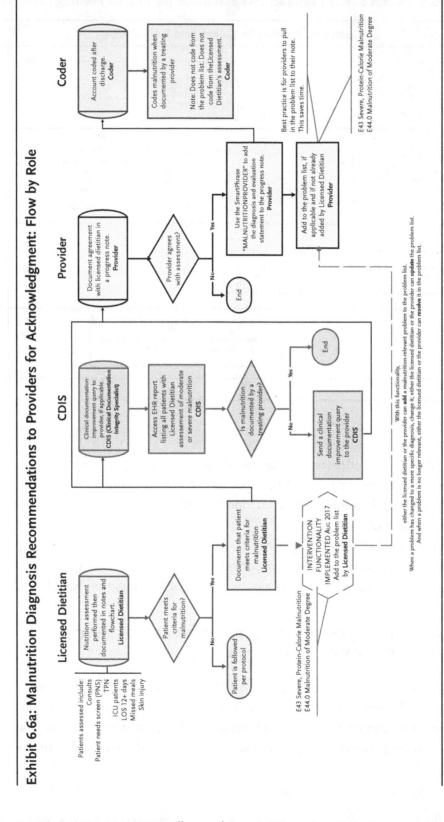

Exhibit 6.6b: Malnutrition Diagnosis Recommendations to Providers for Acknowledgment: Data by Role

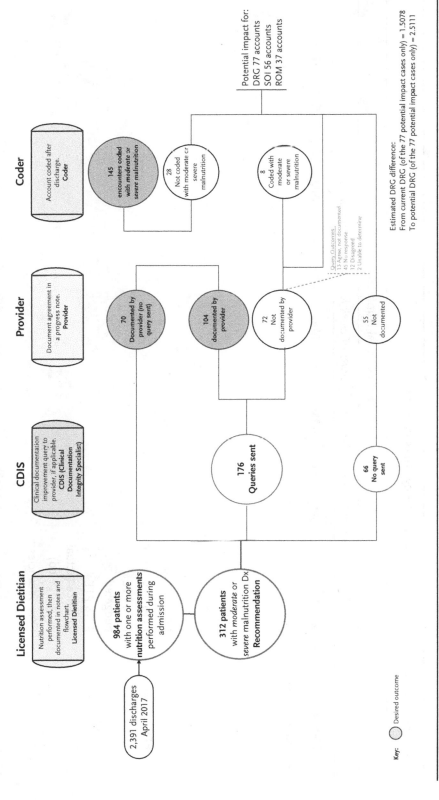

Note: DRG = diagnosis-related group; EHR = electronic health record; ICU = intensive care unit; LOS = length of stay; ROM = risk of mortality; SOI = severity of illness.

Exhibit 6.7: Template Framework to Monitor Key Units of Work

| | | | | | | | | Key Units of Work: Clinical Nutrition | | | | | |
| | | | | | | *Purpose: Monitor volume of key units of work for each department* | | | | | | | |
Measure	Month	Jan	Feb	Mar	Apr	May	Jun	Jul	Aug	Sep	Oct	Nov	Dec
1 **Patients Seen**	FY15												
	FY16												
	FY17												
	FY18												
	FY19												
	% Change (FY18–FY19)												
2 **FTE**	FY19 FTE actual												
	FY19 FTE budgeted												
	FY19 FTE variance (actual vs. budgeted)												
	FY19 vacancies												

3	**Personnel Expense**	FY19 personnel expense variance
4	**Overtime Expense**	FY19 actual YTD
5	**Total Operating Expense**	FY15
		FY16
		FY17
		FY18
		FY19
6	**Total Operating Expense/Patient Seen**	FY15
		FY16
		FY17
		FY18
		FY19

Note: FTE = full-time equivalent.

Exhibit 6.8: Clinical Nutrition—Total Operating Expense per Patient Seen

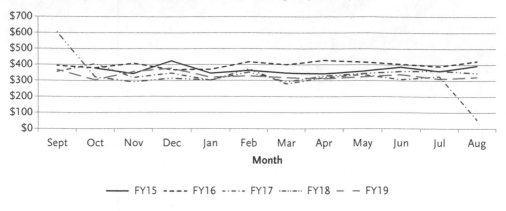

on historical performance. All aspects of a Clinical Nutrition Program should be monitored for performance. They will include people, service, quality, safety, and financial metrics.

- People: Qualified clinical staff are essential for providing evidence-based nutrition assessment and patient care. Effectiveness is best quantified using multiple measures, including patient and caregiver feedback on satisfaction surveys and social media to obtain more candid feedback. Recruitment, training, and retention of qualified staff are the responsibility of Clinical Nutrition leadership. Recruitment and training of clinical professional staff are time-consuming and expensive endeavors. Therefore, programs to improve job satisfaction and reduce unnecessary turnover of highly trained clinical staff are vital. Employee turnover rate and reasons for separation should be tracked and analyzed. Employee engagement surveys should be given at least every two years with action plans to address opportunities for improvement. People metrics include
  - feedback on surveys of employee engagement and culture of safety, and
  - first-year and total RD turnover rates.
- Service: Organizational procedures and workflow processes are critical for prioritizing provision of patient care services. Operational measures to evaluate service excellence may include the following:
  - Time to complete consultation orders
  - Percentage of appropriate referrals for patients at nutrition risk, as determined by evidence-based criteria
  - Number of patients at nutrition risk that have not been seen by an RD
  - Percentage of nutrition needs met by patients identified with wounds

- Quality/Safety: By measuring patient care outcomes and reporting results that demonstrate clinical effectiveness, Clinical Nutrition staff can more effectively guide quality improvement efforts. Clinical outcome studies quantifying the impact of nutrition care are time-consuming but imperative to justify resources. Early clinical nutrition intervention can affect patient outcome measures such as length of stay, incidence of nosocomial infection, and cost (Hedberg et al. 1999). In the oncology population, increased malnutrition contributes to higher rates of costly events such as falls, pressure injury, catheter-associated urinary tract infection, central-line-associated bloodstream infection, surgical site infection, prolonged length of stay, and 30-day readmission (Funamizu et al. 2018; Jackson et al. 2017; National Cancer Institute 2020; Planas et al. 2016; Zhu et al. 2018). The importance of nutrition intervention is demonstrated through Quality Improvement and Enhanced Recovery Programs by collecting patient outcome metrics (Winkler and Hedberg 2003). The Infection Prevention and Control Portal on the Joint Commission website is a reference for high-reliability processes (Joint Commission 2020). Guidelines for hand hygiene, tube-feeding hang time, parenteral nutrition processes, food storage, and safety on patient care units are some areas in which RDs should be involved. Quality/safety metrics include the following:
  - Number of safety incidents reported, if any
  - Percentage of patients that meet malnutrition diagnostic criteria
  - Percentage of patients diagnosed with pressure injury that are seen by an RD
  - Patient compliance with nutrition components of Enhanced Recovery Programs
  - Nutrition risk screening referrals and provider consults addressed per period
  - Malnutrition assessment/diagnosis recommendations per period
  - Percentage of unique patient admissions evaluated by an RD before discharge
  - Average length of stay until RD evaluation
  - Enhanced Recovery Program to ensure optimal patient outcomes
- Financial Performance: The RD can improve the bottom line by preventing malnutrition. Diagnosing patients with malnutrition using evidence-based criteria may affect case-mix index and more properly reflect patients' acuity status (Jackson et al. 2017; White et al. 2012). The RD is the expert trained to clinically assess patients and determine if they meet standardized criteria for malnutrition. The RD has the expertise to evaluate transition

of patients on enteral and parenteral formulas to less costly products if medically indicated, and to determine when patients can be weaned from these specialized feeding modalities. Discharge planning processes to ensure patients have necessary education and feeding supplies for home care are essential to prevent the expense of a prolonged stay (Hedberg 2018). Financial metrics include the following:

- Variance of actual expense from budget
- Variance of actual to budgeted full-time equivalents (FTEs)
- Patients seen per nutritionist FTE per working day
- Productivity measures, including the percentage of patients at nutrition risk seen within the expected period.

KEY INFORMATICS ISSUES

Building an electronic health record (EHR) with the functionality to allow data mining is recommended to ensure reporting of key informatics related to patient care provision. Data mining of key patient care metrics from the EHR should be identified proactively during the EHR build, if possible, to ensure reporting will meet organizational needs. Efficiencies to allow optimal time for direct patient care (face-to-face interventions with the RD) are possible through efficient EHR documentation of care if the RD is involved in developing the EHR documentation processes. The EHR build should focus on preventing duplication of processes. Workflow processes should be mapped, and informatics support team members should be trained to develop streamlined data-entry flowsheets and documentation templates. Policies and procedures for documentation requirements should include the time for entering notes from patient intervention and any required data, including face-to-face time, credentials, plan of care, and patient education. Key patient care metrics that should be included in documentation templates include dietary intake, weight history, nutrition-impact symptoms, and malnutrition diagnosis recommendations.

The EHR build should also allow for medication administration report or intake/output recording of enteral and parenteral nutrition support provided for patient billing, if applicable, and determination of nutrition support adequacy. Reports for patients on medications with food–drug interactions, extended length of stay without RD intervention, prolonged periods of inadequate intake (liquids only, NPO—"nothing through the mouth"), and nonhealing wounds are tools that improve triage of patients for early nutritional intervention. Training of patient care providers on data entry to ensure accurate reflection of nutrition support provided is important, and the RD should be involved in this training. If patients are discharged home on enteral or parenteral nutrition, the RD should work closely with Social Work or Case Management to build documentation processes that improve effectiveness of justification for home nutrition support (Hedberg 2018).

STAFFING MODELS

The Institute for Healthcare Improvement (IHI) defines value-based care in the IHI Triple Aim initiative, which includes optimization of the following (IHI 2020):

- Patient experience
- Population health
- Per-capita healthcare cost

Clinical Nutrition can produce data that demonstrates its impact on each of the IHI aims; therefore, appropriate staffing to provide timely nutrition interventions is justifiable.

An important step to determine appropriate Clinical Nutrition staffing would be to meet with internal stakeholders and determine the following parameters:

- Essential and desired services: Essential services are defined by accreditation bodies. Desired services may include classes, community events, and the like.
- Hours of operation: Accreditation entities require consistent inpatient clinical nutrition care provided to all patients. Therefore, weekend and holiday coverage are required. After-hours on-call may be required for providers to have an RD available to answer clinical inquiries regarding nutrition support orders, discharge education, and so forth.
- Patient acuity levels: RD involvement in patient care rounds for discharge planning and in the rehabilitation and critical care units is time-consuming but can provide valuable continuity of care. Patients in critical care units with increased metabolic needs because of wounds or organ failure, and those requiring enteral or parenteral nutrition support, require a higher level of care with more frequent follow-up by the RD.
- Outpatient services: Determination of non-billed or fee-for-service outpatient nutrition consultations that providers request, and whether these services will be billed, would be performed by the healthcare institution.
- Specialty services: Specialty nutrition services that increase patient and employee satisfaction may include patient classes, employee education events (e.g., nursing in-services on nutrition screening and referral), community services (e.g., presentations, health fairs, grocery store tours, home visits),

and participation at institutional meetings (e.g., Pharmacy and Therapeutics Committee, Nursing Practice Council, Ethics Committee).

- Increased scope of practice: The Academy of Nutrition and Dietetics published a "Revised 2017 Scope of Practice for the Registered Dietitian Nutritionist," which outlined the roles of dietetics practitioners (Academy Quality Management Committee 2018). Individual state licensure and regulations may permit advanced practice such as writing diet orders for patients (Academy of Nutrition and Dietetics 2019). This order-writing privilege would typically be subject to Medical Staff approval.
- Extenders or paraprofessionals as supportive staffing: A Clinical Nutrition Department typically requires support personnel such as nutrition and dietetic technicians, registered, or trained support personnel. These extenders assist with patient calls for RD intervention or outpatient consultation scheduling while triaging referrals from nursing staff and other clinical team members based on risk assessment, thereby allowing the RD more direct patient care time.

Justification for staffing is based on the number and type of patient care interventions or patients seen per productive period. In addition, outcome data such as incidence of malnutrition, wound care, rehabilitation effectiveness, weaning from expensive modalities (i.e., parenteral and enteral specialty products), and decrease in ventilator days are valuable metrics to demonstrate interventions' effectiveness. Enhanced Recovery Programs are often used to establish evidence-based care procedures and collect outcome data (Winkler and Hedberg 2003).

Acute care dietitian staffing needs differ considerably depending on organizational polices and patient population, and no single staffing model can be applied to all facilities. Estimates ranging from 30 to 75 admitted patients per RD have been reported (Marcason 2006). Low patient-to-RD-staff ratios will be required in facilities serving patient populations with high rates of malnutrition, which correlates with severity of illness and medical complexity. For instance, patients undergoing major surgery or with gastrointestinal disease, cancer, or pulmonary disease experience higher rates of malnutrition (Weiss et al. 2016). Patients aged 65 or older are at greater risk for malnutrition, as are those treated in critical care units (Osooli et al. 2019).

A baseline RD staff size can be projected by evaluating the preceding factors. Estimated baseline RD staff needs for sample facilities are listed in exhibit 6.9. However, because policies and job duties differ by facility, demand for nutritional services and RD productivity should be monitored to determine the actual average number of nutritional patient-care visits. RDs can generally complete seven to ten (median = 9) patient assessments and interventions per working day (Hand et al. 2015).

Exhibit 6.9: Clinical Nutrition Staffing Examples

Example Facility	A Patient:RD ratio	B Average daily census	C Estimated RD FTEs needed (B ÷ A)
Oncology specialty hospital, high patient complexity	30	450	15
Academic medical institution, high patient complexity	35	450	13
Midsize general hospital, moderate patient complexity	50	300	6
Community hospital, low patient complexity	70	65	1

Note: FTEs = full-time equivalents; RD = registered dietitian.

PRODUCTIVITY MODELS, INCLUDING WORK-TO-STAFF RATIOS AND INDUSTRY PERFORMANCE TARGETS

Personnel expense is significant in a clinical department such as Clinical Nutrition. Most Clinical Nutrition departments do not produce revenue and are considered expense departments. A clinical RD can see an average of six to ten patients per day depending on the acuity level and services provided. Productivity benchmarks can be obtained from the literature (Phillips 2015). The director of clinical nutrition should contact similar facilities and obtain comparative data regarding the types of services provided, census data, and productivity expectations.

Additionally, the director of clinical nutrition should monitor nutritionists' productivity, as shown in the two control charts in exhibits 6.10 and 6.11. Exhibit 6.10 includes all FTEs, including administrative staff, whereas exhibit 6.11 only includes the dietitians.

STRATEGIES TO IMPROVE RECRUITMENT AND RETENTION

Recruitment and training of new clinical personnel is a significant investment to ensure safe, reliable, evidence-based patient care. Continuity of care is critical to providing evidence-based clinical nutrition services while meeting all regulatory guidelines. An employment package that includes opportunities for professional growth, continuing education, and allowances for training days each year is attractive to the RD. Clinical dietitians increasingly need to attain an advanced degree to

Exhibit 6.10: Sample Patients Seen per Total Clinical Nutrition FTE (Including Administrative Staff) per Workday

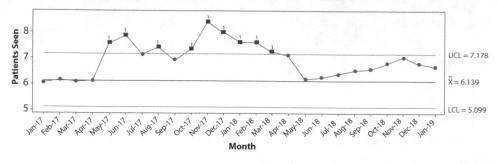

Note: FTE = full-time equivalent; LCL = lower control limit; UCL = upper control limit; X = central line. The 1s indicate a month when the metric exceeds the upper control limit.

Exhibit 6.11: Sample Patients Seen per RD FTE per Workday (8-Hour Productive Time)

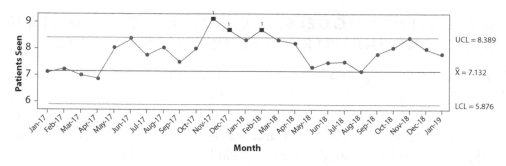

Note: FTE = full-time equivalent; RD = registered dietitian; LCL = lower control limit; UCL = upper control limit; X = central line. The 1s indicate a month when the metric exceeds the upper control limit.

compete in the marketplace. In addition, the CDR requires completion of ongoing continuing education. Many RDs have completed a research-based master's degree, and a rising number hold advanced practice certifications. The RD is an important part of the patient care team and interacts closely with providers (physician, physician assistant, nurse practitioner), nurses, pharmacists, social workers, physical and occupational therapists, and so forth. Allowance of direct patient-care time for rounding is one method that management can use to demonstrate the value it places on interdisciplinary collaboration. This reinforces to the RD that his or her role is important to total patient care, and this recognition of the RD value contributes to retention. Last, staff feedback regarding job satisfaction and discussion of recommendations in team settings helps foster team collaboration and sustainability, thereby reducing turnover of highly trained clinicians.

KEY REGULATORY ISSUES

Healthcare organizations that accept payment from Medicare and Medicaid must meet the CMS (CMS.gov) Conditions for Coverage and the Conditions of Participation (CoPs) (Academy of Nutrition and Dietetics 2014). CMS CoPs for Food and Dietetic Services include guidelines related to meeting the patient nutritional needs for specific processes such as

- appropriate staffing;
- Diet Manual;
- therapeutic menus;
- diet orders;
- nutritional assessment and dietary counseling;
- specialty feedings such as enteral and parenteral nutrition, or nutrition supplements; and
- Quality Assurance Performance Improvement and Infection Control programs.

Voluntary accreditation by one of the national vendors such as The Joint Commission (jointcommission.org), DNV GL Healthcare (dnvglhealthcare.com), the Center for Improvement in Healthcare Quality (cihq.org), or the Healthcare Facilities Accreditation Program (hfap.org) requires the healthcare facility to maintain standards of performance as a high-reliability organization, as defined by the Agency for Healthcare Research and Quality (2019). For clinical nutrition services, these requirements include:

- Culture of safety with employee training to identify safe patient-care processes for proper patient identification; handwashing; use of personal protective equipment to protect patients and staff when indicated; assurance of correct prescriptions for oral diets and parenteral, enteral, and tube feedings; allergies; and food–drug interaction education
- RD competency training program for new employees and annual training program to verify competencies for performance within scope of practice
- Quality improvement program to include impact of nutrition support on patient outcomes such as nosocomial infection, wound healing and pressure sore incidence, malnutrition diagnoses, and the like
- Accurate and timely documentation of patient care provided
- Approval by medical staff of Diet Manual on an annual basis and Formulary for Enteral Products as needed
- Policies and Procedures regarding appropriate staffing for consistent level of patient care, identification of patients at nutrition risk, process for

patient referrals to the RD by nursing and medical providers, nutrition assessment and follow-up of patients at nutrition risk, food–drug interaction identification and patient education, and documentation of patient care in the medical record

- RD involvement in evaluation of patient nutrition-education materials, adequacy of patient menus, ethnic or cultural food options, special feeding schedules, nutritional supplements, and altered-texture modified diets

The RD is a valuable member of the patient care team. Patient safety includes ensuring adequate nutrient intake during acute and chronic disease states to prevent complications of treatment. Optimal nutrition support during all stages of recovery prevents complications of malnutrition that can extend length of hospital stay, which influences patient experience and cost of care. By improving patient outcomes and patient care experience, the Clinical Nutrition Department plays a significant role in the healthcare institution.

KEY TERMS FOR CLINICAL NUTRITION

Evidence-based practice: Clinical practice based on strategies incorporating scientific research, quality improvement data, clinical expertise, consensus statements, and knowledge/recommendations of experts in the field (Academy of Nutrition and Dietetics 2018a).

High-reliability organization: Complex organizations such as healthcare entities that may experience potentially catastrophic failures (e.g., death, wrong-site surgery, hospital-acquired infection or malnutrition) (Agency for Healthcare Research and Quality 2019).

Malnutrition: Nutrition imbalance affecting patient outcome, arising from inadequate nutrient intake, increased needs, or altered nutrient use because of disease processes (White et al. 2012).

Medical nutrition therapy: Evidence-based, cost-effective nutrition care plan based on nutrition assessment by an RD, and coordination of the care plan with the interdisciplinary medical team (Academy Quality Management Committee 2018).

Nutrition assessment: Incorporates a complete evaluation of a patient's nutritional status with a review of medical history, patient interview and diet history, malnutrition assessment including nutrition-focused physical assessment, laboratory and medication history, and so forth, to develop a comprehensive individualized nutrition care plan (Academy Quality Management Committee 2018; White et al. 2012).

Nutrition care plan: Recommended education and nutritional interventions based on a comprehensive nutritional assessment by an RD.

Parenteral nutrition: Intravenous administration of nutrition for patients who cannot eat or absorb enough food through tube-feeding formula or by mouth (American Society for Parenteral and Enteral Nutrition 2020).

Registered Dietitian (RD): A nutrition expert who has met qualifications to earn the RD credential, including completing a bachelor's degree or higher and coursework requirements approved by the Accreditation Council for Education in Nutrition and Dietetics (ACEND), completing an ACEND-accredited supervised practice program, passing a national examination, and completing continuing professional education requirements to maintain registration. RDs may choose to use the optional title Registered Dietitian Nutritionist (RDN), which highlights that "all registered dietitians are nutritionists but not all nutritionists are registered dietitians" (Academy of Nutrition and Dietetics 2020a, 2020b).

REFERENCES

Academy of Nutrition and Dietetics. 2020a. "Every Registered Dietitian Is a Nutritionist, but Not Every Nutritionist Is a Registered Dietitian." Accessed August 24. www.eatrightpro.org/about-us/what-is-an-rdn-and-dtr/what-is-a-registered-dietitian-nutritionist/every-registered-dietitian-is-a-nutritionist-but-not-every-nutritionist-is-a-registered-dietitian.

———. 2020b. "What Is a Registered Dietitian Nutritionist." Accessed August 24. www.eatrightpro.org/about-us/what-is-an-rdn-and-dtr/what-is-a-registered-dietitian-nutritionist.

———. 2019. "Therapeutic Diet Orders in Hospitals and Long-Term Care Facilities." Updated September. www.eatrightpro.org/advocacy/licensure/therapeutic-diet-orders.

———. 2018a. "Code of Ethics for the Nutrition and Dietetics Profession." Commission on Dietetic Registration. Accessed December 4. www.eatrightpro.org/practice/code-of-ethics/what-is-the-code-of-ethics.

———. 2018b. "State Licensure." Commission on Dietetic Registration. Accessed December 6. www.cdrnet.org/state-licensure.

———. 2014. "Centers for Medicare and Medicaid Services." Accessed January 2. www.eatrightpro.org/practice/quality-management/national-quality-accreditation-and-regulations/centers-for-medicare-and-medicaid-services.

Academy Quality Management Committee. 2018. "Academy of Nutrition and Dietetics: Revised 2017 Scope of Practice for the Registered Dietitian Nutritionist." *Journal of the Academy of Nutrition and Dietetics* 118 (1): 141–65.

Agency for Healthcare Research and Quality. 2019. "Patient Safety Primer: High Reliability." Updated September 7. https://psnet.ahrq.gov/primers/primer/31/high-reliability.

American Society for Parenteral and Enteral Nutrition. 2020. "What Is Parenteral Nutrition." Accessed August 24. www.nutritioncare.org/about_clinical_nutrition/what_is_parenteral_nutrition/.

Fingar, K. R., A. J. Weiss, M. L. Barrett, A. Elixhauser, C. A. Steiner, P. Guenter, and M. H. Brown. 2016. "All-Cause Readmissions Following Hospital Stays for Patients with Malnutrition, 2013." *Healthcare Cost and Utilization Project (HCUP) Statistical Briefs.* Published December. https://hcup-us.ahrq.gov/reports/statbriefs/sb218-Malnutrition-Readmissions-2013.jsp.

Funamizu, N., Y. Makabayashi, T. Iida, and K. Kurihara. 2018. "Geriatric Nutritional Risk Index Predicts Surgical Site Infection After Pancreaticoduodenectomy." *Molecular and Clinical Oncology* 9: 274–28.

Hand, R. K., B. Jordan, S. DeHoog, J. Pavlinac, J. K. Abram, and J. S. Parrott. 2015. "Inpatient Staffing Needs for Registered Dietitian Nutritionists in 21st Century Acute Care Facilities." *Journal of the Academy of Nutrition and Dietetics* 115 (6): 985–1000.

Hedberg, A. M. 2018. "Improved Discharge Planning for Patients on Home Enteral Nutrition: Role of the RDN 'Case Manager.'" *Future Dimensions in Clinical Practice Newsletter*, Academy of Nutrition and Dietetics, Clinical Nutrition Management Practice Group. Winter, 1–6.

Hedberg, A. M., D. R. Lairson, L. A. Aday, J. Chow, R. Suki, S. Houston, and J. A. Wolf. 1999. "Economic Implications of an Early Postoperative Enteral Feeding Protocol." *Journal of the American Dietary Association* 99 (7): 802–7.

Institute for Healthcare Improvement (IHI). 2020. "Quality, Cost, and Value." Accessed August 25. www.ihi.org/Topics/QualityCostValue/Pages/default.aspx.

Jackson, S. S., S. Leekha, L. S. Magder, L. Pineles, D. J. Anderson, W. E. Trick, K. F. Woeltje, K. S. Kaye, K. Stafford, K. Thom, T. J. Lowe, and A. D. Harris. 2017. "The Effect of Adding Comorbidities to Current Centers for Disease Control and Prevention Central-Line-Associated Bloodstream Infection Risk-Adjustment Methodology." *Infection Control and Hospital Epidemiology* 38 (9): 1019–24.

Joint Commission. 2020. "Infection Prevention and Control." Accessed August 25. www.jointcommission.org/hai.aspx.

Julius, M., D. Kresevic, M. Turcoliveri, L. Cialdella-Kam, and C. J. Burant. 2017. "Malnutrition as a Fall Risk Factor." *Federal Practitioner* 34 (2): 27–30.

Leiva-Badosa, E., M. Badia Tahull, N. Virgili Casas, and G. Elguezabal Sangrador. 2017. "Hospital Malnutrition Screening at Admission: Malnutrition Increases Mortality and Length of Stay." *Nutricion Hospitalaria* 34 (4): 907–13.

Marcason, W. 2006. "What Is ADA's Staffing Ratio for Clinical Dietitians?" *Journal of the Academy of Nutrition and Dietetics* 106 (11): 1916.

National Cancer Institute. 2020. "Nutrition in Cancer Care (PDQ®)—Health Professional Version." Accessed August 24. www.cancer.gov/about-cancer/treatment/side-effects/appetite-loss/nutrition-hp-pdq.

Osooli, F., S. Abbas, S. Farsaei, and P. Adibi. 2019. "Identifying Critically Ill Patients at Risk of Malnutrition and Underfeeding: A Prospective Study at an Academic Hospital." *Advanced Pharmaceutical Bulletin* 9 (2): 314–20.

Phillips, W. 2015. "Clinical Nutrition Staffing Benchmarks for Acute Care Hospitals." *Journal of the Academy of Nutrition and Dietetics* 115 (7): 1054–56.

Planas, M., J. Alvarez-Hernandez, M. Leon-Sanz, S. Celaya-Perez, K. Araujo, A. Garcia de Lorenzo, and PREDyCES researchers. 2016. "Prevalence of Hospital Malnutrition in Cancer Patients: A Sub-analysis of the PREDyCES® Study." *Supportive Care in Cancer* 24 (1): 429–35.

Saghaleini, S., K. Shadvar, K. Dehghan, and S. Sanaie. 2018. "Pressure Ulcer and Nutrition." *Indian Journal of Critical Care Medicine* 22 (4): 283.

Tobert, C. M., S. L. Mott, and K. G. Nepple. 2018. "Malnutrition Diagnosis During Adult Inpatient Hospitalizations: Analysis of a Multi-institutional Collaborative Database of Academic Medical Centers." *Journal of the Academy of Nutrition and Dietetics* 118 (1): 125–31.

Weiss, A. J., K. R. Fingar, M. L. Barrett, A. Elixhauser, C. A. Steiner, P. Guenter, and M. H. Brown. 2016. "Characteristics of Hospital Stays Involving Malnutrition, 2013." In *Healthcare Cost and Utilization Project (HCUP) Statistical Briefs*. Published September. www.hcup-us.ahrq.gov/reports/statbriefs/sb210-Malnutrition-Hospital-Stays-2013.jsp.

White, J. V., P. Guenter, G. Jensen, A. Malone, M. Schofield, Group Academy Malnutrition Work, A.S.P.E.N. Malnutrition Task Force, and A.S.P.E.N. Board of Directors. 2012. "Consensus Statement: Academy of Nutrition and Dietetics and American Society for Parenteral and Enteral Nutrition: Characteristics Recommended for the Identification and Documentation of Adult Malnutrition (Undernutrition)." *Journal of Parenteral and Enteral Nutrition* 36 (3): 275–83.

Winkler, M. F., and A. M. Hedberg. 2003. "Quality and Performance Improvement." In *Contemporary Nutrition Support Practice: A Clinical Guide*, edited by L. E. Matatese and M. M. Gottschlich, 616–24. Philadelphia, PA: Saunders.

Zhu, C., B. Wang, Y. Goa, and X. Ma. 2018. "Prevalence and Relationship of Malnutrition and Distress in Patients with Cancer Using Questionnaires." *BMC* Cancer. Published December 19. https://bmccancer.biomedcentral.com/articles/10.1186/s12885-018-5176-x.

CHAPTER 7

Environmental Services

Robert Ray

DEPARTMENT DESCRIPTION

The Environmental Services (EVS) Department of a healthcare organization is responsible for the upkeep of its physical space, much the same as the EVS in other industries. However, as with the other ancillary and support departments in a healthcare organization, EVS is also responsible for controlling infection and complying with regulations while providing excellent customer service. Additionally, in academic medical centers, EVS's scope of services includes cleaning research and educational spaces, so understanding the sensitivity of lab cleaning, along with timing, frequency, and materials (i.e., the chemicals used for cleaning) is vital to this success.

This chapter will describe the EVS Department's organizational structures, roles, and services. Healthcare facilities operate 24 hours a day, 7 days a week; therefore, having the appropriate staff size and the correct talent mix on a particular shift is important. The structure of EVS will include an executive-level staff member, several layers of operational management, and frontline supervisors and staff. To get the proper skills and staffing levels for thorough cleaning, organizations have three options: insource the services, outsource them, or combine the two approaches. All three have advantages and disadvantages; an organization must choose the option or combination that will work best for its situation. The Department Organizational Structure section will discuss these options.

KEY DEPARTMENT SERVICES

The customary services EVS provides are well defined. Routine tasks include collecting and removing trash, sweeping and mopping floors, cleaning and disinfecting restrooms, and dusting horizontal surfaces. The healthcare EVS team offers several services that distinguish them from other industries' EVS teams, such as collecting and disposing of regulated medical waste (e.g., biohazard waste) and following proper disinfecting protocols to prevent the spread of infections and contaminants. Internal to the healthcare organization, the Infection Control and Occupational Health and Safety departments are integral in reviewing and approving the EVS processes for biohazard waste and preventing infection. Another factor unique to EVS in a healthcare organization is the numerous regulatory agency standards EVS must comply with. These will be discussed in the Key Regulatory Issues section.

Infection Control departments in healthcare organizations partner with EVS to verify standards are in place to prevent the spread of pathogens and ensure the safety of those cleaning and occupying the space. For example, EVS and Infection Control will confirm the proper chemical mixture is being applied to surfaces for disinfection and that its contact or dwell time is sufficient for decontamination. Dwell time is defined as the time a surface is required to be wet with the chemical to provide adequate disinfection. The manufacturer for each chemical specifies this dwell time.

The Infection Control Department will also team with EVS to ensure the proper personal protective equipment (PPE) is used while cleaning designated isolation rooms. Two forms of isolation exist in a healthcare organization: isolation and reverse isolation. In isolation, the worker wears PPE because the patient has a pathogen that can infect the worker (e.g., tuberculosis). With reverse isolation, PPE protects the patient who occupies the room from germs carried by those who enter (e.g., a patient undergoing cancer treatment who has a compromised immune system).

The biohazard waste stream contains large quantities of bodily matter. EVS in healthcare organizations is responsible for collecting this waste stream. In many organizations, EVS also manages oversight for the shipping requirements of this stream. This industry is highly regulated, and standardized methods for collecting, monitoring, and tracking waste streams in a facility, during transport, and at point of disposal are mandatory. The Occupational Health and Safety Department will provide handling guidance to EVS.

DEPARTMENT ORGANIZATIONAL STRUCTURES

EVS organizational structures are relatively standard, with a few exceptions depending on the size of the organization. Exhibit 7.1 shows a sample organizational structure for the Environmental Services Department.

EVS will typically report to a vice president of support services. A larger organization may have an associate or assistant vice president to whom the director of

Exhibit 7.1: Sample Environmental Services Team Organizational Chart

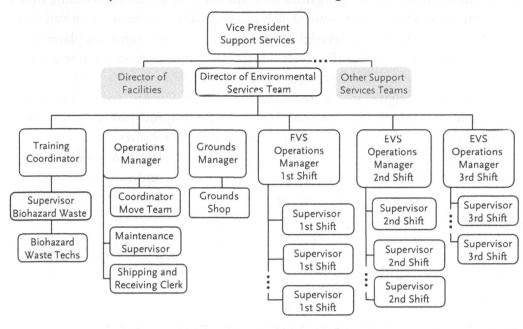

Note: Dashed lines for organizational size scalability purposes.

EVS would report. The vice president's role includes leading the strategic planning efforts to develop a three- to five-year plan. By contrast, the director focuses on the operational plans for the next 3 to 18 months. A director will have some day-to-day interaction with EVS team members, but most such activity is the operations manager's responsibility.

The operations manager focuses on what is coming up in the next 2 to 12 weeks and ensures the team has adequate training for their duties and the proper equipment in their work area. Depending on the organization's size and complexity, there will be three to four supervisors reporting to the operations manager. Managers may divide the work of the supervisory team into areas of responsibility. The operating room environment requires focus around the expensive medical equipment to avoid damaging it, including specialized cleaning knowledge and attention to detail. The successful operations manager will confirm that supervisors responsible for such areas can provide expected and consistent outcomes.

Supervisors oversee the tactical hour-to-hour, day-to-day workload of the frontline staff, adjust staffing to ensure all areas are covered, approve vacation, evaluate staff frequently and provide feedback, and ensure training requirements are being completed. Supervisors are essential in hiring and educating staff, controlling about 10 to 15 full-time equivalents (FTEs).

The supervisor position is critical because it is an entry-level role onto the management track. In many organizations, the supervisor is an outstanding front-line employee who has demonstrated leadership skills or the self-motivation to get the job done with little oversight; supervisors also have been team players who worked well with other frontline staff. This success leads to promotion to a supervisory position, where they are required to oversee and comment on the work of their former colleagues and provide evaluative feedback as needed. Leadership must stay focused on the supervisor's area of control and provide appropriate training to ensure proper leadership practices are being followed.

Another key position in the EVS Department is training coordinator. Today's EVS teams typically have a diverse demographic makeup and varied backgrounds. The industry has also moved from paper, face-to-face training to online training. This combination may lead to misunderstandings of cleaning standards and styles. A training coordinator can prevent such misunderstandings by developing and implementing a standard training program that will help guide, train, and develop staff from all backgrounds and experience levels.

KEY CUSTOMERS AND THEIR PERFORMANCE EXPECTATIONS

Customers for the EVS team will be anyone who enters the healthcare organization, including staff, visitors, patients, or other people doing business there. The challenging aspect of measuring performance expectations for the EVS team is that every customer has a different vision of "clean." For example, individuals have different views on tidiness, what is considered unkempt, and how frequently an area must be swept to be clean. Such variations make it nearly impossible to satisfy all customer expectations all the time.

One solution is to develop a service-level agreement (SLA) to set the performance expectations with the customer and the EVS team. This document allows the groups to negotiate an outcome that satisfies the cleanliness expectations and operational parameters of the customer within the budget and staffing allowances of the EVS team. Several standards of cleanliness exist; for example, the Association of Physical Plant Administrators (APPA) developed the following scale and descriptions of cleanliness (APPA 1998, p. 266):

1. Orderly Spotlessness
2. Ordinary Tidiness
3. Casual Inattention
4. Moderate Dinginess
5. Unkempt Neglect

During the SLA negotiations, these levels of cleanliness with APPA's more detailed descriptions can help to ground the discussion. The allocation of budget and FTE resources will drive the achievement of these standards. The more money and FTEs the EVS team has to work with, the closer to Level 1 the organization can reach.

KEY PROCESS FLOWS

Key process flows for an EVS team are critical to successful operations. Defining key processes allows the operations manager and supervisors to provide the framework required to train new frontline personnel consistently for the desired outcome. This training approach is important because the annual turnover rate for the frontline EVS team can be as high as 100 percent (Swanberg, Nichols, and Perry-Jenkins 2016). One standard process flow the EVS team can use is referred to as Work Instructions, which define a systematic process for completing a task.

Given the diverse backgrounds of the frontline EVS team, the Work Instructions provide a baseline for performance expectations. For example, a Work Instruction for a patient room may start with instructions on wiping down all high surfaces (which would include any surface above shoulder height that may collect dust), followed by removing the trash, cleaning the items in a patient restroom, and sweeping floors, closing with mopping floors. It can come with pictorial images showing in what direction to mop the floors so the EVS worker ends up at the patient door. Instructions will include the type and quantities of chemicals used in the cleaning process. Work Instructions should be provided for each type of space cleaned in a healthcare environment.

Another standard workflow process is removing waste from facilities. Established routes exist to provide a systematic process for the frontline staff member to travel within the hospital while collecting the waste stream. The frontline EVS staff member will travel a route to each space with a cart, deposit all gathered trash, and transport it from the building to a dumpster or trash compactor. Defining routes through the building completes the workflow. Each route includes the frequency at which it needs to be completed. For example, operating rooms will require multiple trash removal visits over an eight-hour shift.

Another workflow to document is the collection of the biohazard waste stream. This workflow will be highly specific because of the regulatory requirements associated with collecting and transporting such waste. The management defines biohazard collection routes for the frontline staff to follow. As with the normal waste stream, the biohazard route also includes collection frequency; however, proper frontline staff instructions and education are all the more crucial to successful outcomes. The instructions will include proper sealing of biohazard bags, their proper packaging in transportable cardboard containers, and correct labeling. Such documentation is included on a waste manifest sheet before it is hauled away for proper disposal. The packaging, handling, and transportation requirements can vary slightly from state to state. Some organizations have the capability of processing the biohazard waste stream on their campus; although this chapter will not detail that process, know that the option does exist.

A key consideration in planning of routes on Work Instructions relates to transportation travel time. Environmental Services and other ancillary and support functions use service elevators to access different floors. When planning routes, the manager must build in the wait time associated with these frequently used modes of transportation, understanding that they are not always in the most convenient locations for route activities to be most efficient.

KEY UNITS OF WORK AND VOLUME STATISTICS TO MONITOR

Among the key units of work that Environmental Services monitors, the most commonly used is gross square footage. In the most basic sense, gross square footage is defined from exterior wall to exterior wall, accounting for the entire floor area.

However, assigning work activities based purely on a square-foot metric is not always the most productive method. Time/motion studies can be completed in lieu of assigning work based on a certain square footage. For example, the EVS staffer walks to an area, disposes of the waste in a chute, and proceeds to the next space; or they collect the waste in a cart and move to the next space. A time/motion study for this work activity would allow the manager to understand during certain times of the day how long it takes the staff member to traverse their route. Study outcomes can lead to the modification of the route, the time allotted, its frequency, and if required, a reallocation of staff to accommodate the true need.

Certain spaces, such as operating rooms (ORs) and conference spaces, need to be particularly well cleaned and available for the next use. For ORs, EVS staffing is allotted depending on need and skill of the workforce, not square footage. Routine cleaning is done between cases; all trash is removed, and all floors swept and mopped with proper disinfection. After cases are done for the day, the operating suite receives a terminal clean—a higher-level, more intense cleaning. EVS staffing for such cleaning will be whatever is needed to get the rooms completed for the next business day. Conference areas are another example where consulting their daily use schedule is a better way to plan for cleaning this space, versus using a square-foot metric.

KEY METRICS TO MONITOR: PEOPLE, SERVICE, QUALITY/SAFETY, FINANCIAL

A well-run EVS department sets and monitors key metrics to ensure products and services are being delivered with the proper outcomes. Some organizations base these metrics on their organization's goals. For example, if an organization is interested in maintaining a high score on the HCAHPS (Hospital Consumer Assessment of Healthcare Providers and Systems) patient satisfaction survey, providing a clean environment for the patient and visitor as measured by HCAHPS is the priority metric. Another method for defining key metrics for the EVS team is to track them more formally using the Balanced Scorecard developed by Robert Kaplan and David Norton (Kaplan and Norton 1992).

People

Required annual training for institutional safety and other topics mandated by regulations is an important metric. Confirming each team member is up to date provides consistently successful outcomes. Training and retraining associated with work instructions likewise improves product quality.

Service

The key service metric (and the main driver for the customer) is the satisfaction scores from either the HCAHPS survey result or other internally generated surveys. Survey scores represent an effective way to monitor performance from the customer's perspective. The HCAHPS survey is administered to all discharged patients and includes a specific question about the cleanliness of their room. Such feedback directly reports the outcomes of the EVS team's work.

Another form of customer feedback is through internal surveys to healthcare organization staff. Surveys should include non-patient-care areas along with patient areas, to determine how effective the cleaning program is across the institution from the staff viewpoint.

A further critical service metric is the time to deliver products or services. One important timing metric in the healthcare industry is room turnaround time. After a patient is discharged, the EVS team should be accountable for cleaning the room within a defined time; the typical benchmark is 60 minutes. Monitoring the process and performance to meet this benchmark is critical for making adjustments to the process or staffing.

Quality/Safety

The SLA can provide metrics for tracking quality and safety, but achieving successful outcomes requires considerable training. If SLA outcomes are not being met, staff (including management) may need retraining.

Financial

The two main financial metrics for EVS are the expenses of personnel and material as part of operating budgets. The personnel expense consumes approximately 70 percent of the operating budget (International Facility Management Association [IFMA] and American Society for Healthcare Engineering [ASHE] 2010). Performance on EVS budget metrics can be considered if actual expenses come within a 2 percent variance from budget.

PRODUCTIVITY MODELS, INCLUDING WORK-TO-STAFF RATIOS AND INDUSTRY PERFORMANCE TARGETS

To justify staffing levels, an organization must have executive leadership support for the work-to-staffing-ratio benchmark. Without leaders' understanding and acceptance of the benchmark, staffing levels will be questioned. Often there are nuances in operations that cause the calculated staffing levels to be higher or lower than the benchmark standards. However, the EVS leaders should use their benchmarks as a catalyst for discussion if the actual staffing levels differ.

For example, benchmarking by IFMA for EVS is by gross square foot, and the median amount of floor area cleaned by one FTE is 37,000 square feet for office space (IFMA 2017). Being a median, this target depends on the type of space being cleaned. Benchmarks like these allow organizations to plan staffing needs, validate their distribution of the workforce, and set budgets. Another benchmark is the average cost for janitorial services per gross square foot, which was $4.41 at the 50th percentile for healthcare organizations (IFMA and ASHE 2010). These benchmarks should be compared with the same metrics in similar institutions to identify any opportunities for improvement.

STAFFING MODELS

In healthcare organizations, the EVS team does more than just empty trash and sweep floors; they are responsible for preventing the spread of pathogens in a setting operating 365 days a year. EVS leaders must provide an accurate staffing model to fit this demand. The physical work this team performs requires a certain level of staffing and equipment to perform tasks at the level of quality expected and needed in a healthcare setting. For example, a staffing ratio of 12 to 15 frontline staff to one supervisor provides enough supervision to maintain productivity throughout the shift. Additionally, a ratio of three to five supervisors for each manager works well in many larger organizations. This ratio ensures proper oversight to accomplish the operational objectives defined by management and policy. Finally, the director of EVS in larger organizations will have three to five managers reporting to them. This structure provides the opportunity to accomplish the work tasks and address any shortfalls in productivity or performance targets. The EVS team may be called away from scheduled tasks to address emergencies; the leadership team must consider these unexpected situations and have sufficient backup plans and equipment. Staffing models vary greatly depending on the demand of the workload, the organization's capacity to manage it, and the institution's financial situation. There is not a right or wrong answer to insourcing (i.e., employing staff) or outsourcing (through a vendor contract) as long as the decision provides the desired outcome.

As with any organization, work demand shifts each day, requiring the staffing model to accommodate those swings. This flexibility can be addressed several ways, starting with an overarching plan of whether the organization insources, outsources, or does both for its EVS work. The question of whether to insource or outsource EVS is determined by each individual healthcare organization given its circumstances at the time. This section will discuss the advantages and disadvantages of both approaches.

Insourcing simply means all EVS staff, including leadership, are employees of the organization, and no contracts are involved in the working agreement. In the strict sense of an insource product, the advantages are complete control over personnel decisions and the strategies used in providing environmental products and services. There are no hidden costs associated with the total financial picture. If the organization decides to increase or decrease staffing, the impact of those decisions is limited to the organization. Insourced employees who consistently work in the same area and do a good job for the occupants tend to become part of the culture in that area, especially for inpatient care areas.

Some of the disadvantages of insourcing are the constant recruitment demands of employee turnover, the costs associated with retraining a new employee, and the inconsistent outcomes new employees present. Additionally, in some organizations, staffing levels are difficult to increase amid sudden demand because of budgetary constraints. Insourcing also requires the management to have the right skill set to develop policies and procedures for cleaning activities.

Outsourcing strategies offer the flexibility of working with a vendor to provide all EVS staffing. In these contract structures, the organization sets a level of expected service and quality, and the vendor must provide the necessary staffing to achieve that goal. The vendor makes all staffing decisions; however, if there are issues with a staff member, the organization can request a replacement. The organization does not have to carry any of the labor costs and overhead associated with the outsource contract on its books, and neither gets involved in the hiring process nor provides regulatory training. Finally, the chosen vendor will possess expertise in managing EVS; therefore, its knowledge and resources can be a tremendous advantage.

Outsourcing EVS can prevent the organization from knowing the true costs associated with the products and services offered. If the vendor can provide the level of services and products outlined in the contract, the organization will not have input into the number of staff members that the vendor is providing. The vendor is running its business in a fashion that is profitable for it. For example, outsourcing strategies can include working staff less than full-time to avoid overtime pay, which can mean a variety of staff members over a normal eight-hour shift. Consistency of service can be problematic in this scenario.

Many large healthcare organizations and academic medical centers follow staffing models that combine insourcing and outsourcing. For instance, they may outsource management while insourcing frontline staff, or vice versa. Larger organizations also may have multiple building-use types categorized as "business occupancy," "ambulatory occupancy," and "healthcare occupancy," as defined by the National Fire Prevention Association (NFPA) Life Safety Code 101 (NFPA 2012). The organization may split its EVS duties among these buildings, completely outsourcing one type and insourcing another. For example, EVS staff for business and ambulatory occupancy buildings are sometimes outsourced because of the vendor's expertise in these building types, whereas EVS for healthcare occupancy buildings is insourced to leverage the organization's internal expertise with healthcare building regulations.

STRATEGIES TO IMPROVE RECRUITMENT AND RETENTION

Undoubtedly one of the most important aspects of a successful EVS department is the ability to recruit and retain good staff. As noted, turnover can be as high as 100 percent (Swanberg et al. 2016). The work is physically demanding; having a well-disinfected space requires rigorous cleaning that complies with multiple regulatory agency requirements.

The workforce applying for EVS tends to be younger adults who come from diverse backgrounds with minimal education beyond high school. Organizations typically only require a high school diploma or equivalent, yet some only require an education up to eighth grade. The positions at these levels would be considered entry level, and the pay is usually much less than that of other positions in the healthcare organization. EVS staff members who are the primary income earners for their families will typically need to work two or more jobs to meet their personal financial needs. Recruitment for these positions is challenging, and many organizations are often competing for the same labor pool. Recruitment strategies can consist of higher pay than competitors, a better comprehensive benefit package, flexibility in scheduling and shifts, and (in larger organizations) a variety of job tasks along with advancement and continuing education opportunities.

Healthcare institutions can use several strategies to reduce EVS turnover. One basic strategy is a simple "Thank you" or "We appreciate your hard work," starting from the president down to the EVS supervisor. Another way to limit turnover is a robust onboarding program. One organization found that if new frontline EVS staff stayed for one year, then the staff would likely stay five years. Understanding the reason turnover was occurring in the first year helped it develop its new employee onboarding program. Onboarding included a schedule for 365 days of touch points to engage the new employee so they felt rooted into the culture and its organizational goals. These touch points consisted of routine 1:1 meetings with the supervisors, skip-level meetings with the managers, training, tours, and introductions to key organizational employees they will interact with during their daily work. Feedback was provided to management on the new employees' progress and engagement from this onboarding process.

Other offerings to reduce turnover include offering advanced training and developing new skill sets the employee did not possess before hire. Examples include learning how to operate a computer, improving their English language skills, and becoming certified as a nurse assistant and transferring from EVS to nursing. Another retention strategy is to offer new hires opportunities to become an EVS technician and career-track advancement opportunities to supervisor or manager.

KEY REGULATORY ISSUES

Healthcare organization EVS teams are required to understand and comply with the regulations of the authorities that have jurisdiction over the organization. The Centers for Medicare & Medicaid Services (CMS) is one of the leading regulatory groups for hospitals that certify compliance with operating standards, which is required to receive reimbursement for patients covered under these programs. CMS provides deemed status to organizations such as The Joint Commission, which performs inspections of healthcare organizations and their key processes to ensure compliance with the CMS Conditions of Participation. If compliant, the healthcare organization is authorized for reimbursement for services to Medicare and Medicaid patients. For many organizations, this reimbursement is a significant revenue stream and their institutions would not be viable without it. EVS must comply with the codes and standards adopted by CMS. These requirements include, but are not limited to, explaining fire safety procedures, knowing the proper procedures for using cleaning chemicals, effectively disinfecting an area, and keeping personnel files current. A surveyor can ask leadership and staff about these standards and many more areas of focus during an inspection. EVS teams must comply with The Joint Commission chapters, including Environment of Care, Life Safety, and Human Resources; however, if the EVS team is found to be significantly out of compliance with these chapters, EVS and the organization can get documented as noncompliant in the Leadership chapter.

Environment of Care Chapter

To meet the standards of the Environment of Care chapter, the EVS team should focus on the cleanliness of the environment. When the surveyor asks, the EVS employee should be able to explain what chemicals are being used and the proper dwell time for them to effectively do their job, then demonstrate their process for cleaning an area. The frontline staff should be able to answer questions from memory or refer from Work Instructions.

Life Safety Chapter

For the Life Safety chapter, the surveyor will want to determine if the frontline staff understands the importance of preventing hallway obstructions. For example, corridors cannot be blocked with an unattended cart; carts cannot block stairwell doors and other access paths of egress; and housekeeping carts cannot block key access points on a patient unit. Equipment cannot prevent access to the medical gas shutoff valves, electrical panels, or fire life-safety devices such as pull stations. The frontline staff will also be asked to demonstrate their knowledge of several common acronyms, such as RACE; they will be allowed to use pocket cards as reminders. During a fire, RACE (**R**escue, **A**larm, **C**onfine, **E**xtinguish or **E**vacuate) is a reminder of action steps the employee must take to keep people safe.

Human Resource Chapter

The EVS team also must be compliant with the Human Resource chapter. This chapter will require the frontline staff member to complete all annual mandatory training the institution requires for their job and to comply with the organization's policies. In addition, the surveyor will randomly pull human resources files to review compliance with annual performance evaluations.

In addition to The Joint Commission and CMS, most healthcare organizations must be compliant with several other regulatory agencies such as their state department of health and department of environmental quality. Another name for these groups is Authorities Having Jurisdiction (AHJs). As defined by the NFPA, the AHJ is "an organization, office, or individual responsible for enforcing the requirements of a code or standard, or for approving equipment, materials, an installation, or a procedure" (NFPA 2018). Other examples of AHJs include the state fire marshal, the owner's insurance agent, and the state elevator inspector. As the local AHJs, these organizations will set the standards required in healthcare by the state. Services provided by EVS are vital to successful inspections by these agencies.

KEY TERMS FOR ENVIRONMENTAL SERVICES

Authorities Having Jurisdiction: Agencies that define regulatory standards and inspect for compliance within the healthcare system. These agencies can be at the city, state, or national levels.

Dwell time: The time a surface is required to be wet with chemical to provide adequate disinfection. Typically the chemical manufacturer defines this time period.

Insourcing: Use of in-house labor and resources to accomplish the operational needs of the healthcare facility.

Isolation: A room status for which a healthcare worker wears appropriate personal protective equipment to prevent being infected by a patient.

Outsourcing: Use of external resources to accomplish the operational needs of the healthcare facility.

Personal protective equipment: Equipment used in a healthcare environment to protect staff members and patients from transmitting pathogens. This equipment will consist of gloves, gowns, and hair protection with goggles and face shields.

Reverse isolation: A room status for which a healthcare worker wears appropriate personal protective equipment to protect a susceptible patient from becoming ill through exposure to the worker's germs (e.g., a patient undergoing cancer treatment who has a compromised immune system).

Routes: Pathways designated in the healthcare setting along which EVS teams will travel to collect the trash and other waste streams.

Service-level agreement: An arrangement between the customer and the EVS team that sets performance expectations. The groups negotiate an outcome that is satisfactory for the cleanliness expectations and operational parameters of the customer within the budget and staffing allowances of the EVS Department.

REFERENCES

Association of Physical Plant Administrators (APPA). 1998. *Custodial Staffing Guidelines for Educational Facilities*, 4th ed. Alexandria, VA: APPA.

International Facility Management Association (IFMA). 2017. *Operations and Maintenance Benchmarks: International Facility Management Association (IFMA)*. Houston, TX: IFMA.

International Facility Management Association (IFMA) and American Society for Healthcare Engineering (ASHE). 2010. *Operations and Maintenance Benchmarks for Health Care Facilities Report*. Houston, TX: IFMA.

Kaplan, R. S., and D. P. Norton. 1992. "The Balanced Scorecard—Measures That Drive Performance." *Harvard Business Review*, January–February, 21.

National Fire Protection Association (NFPA). 2018. "Health Care Facilities Code NFPA 99." Quincy, MA: NFPA.

———. 2012. "NFPA 101 Life Safety Code 2012 Edition." Quincy, MA: NFPA.

Swanberg, J. E., H. M. Nichols, and M. Perry-Jenkins. 2016. "Working on the Frontlines in U.S. Hospitals: Scheduling Challenges and Turnover Intent Among Housekeepers and Dietary Service Workers." *Journal of Hospital Administration* 5 (4): 76–86.

CHAPTER 8

Facilities

Robert Ray

DEPARTMENT DESCRIPTION

In today's healthcare industry, there is no single standard Facilities Department. Few organizations have the same Facilities setup, methods of doing business, or metrics. Reasons for this variation include organization size and type, uniqueness of systems in the facilities, skill set of the local workforce, and financial resources allocated to the Facilities Department. Generally speaking, Facilities is responsible for maintaining the many buildings and systems in the organization's property portfolio 365 days a year. Additionally, these departments must adhere to regulatory requirements, including the Centers for Medicare & Medicaid Services (CMS) Conditions of Participation. The Joint Commission or other agencies with deemed status to inspect healthcare facilities enforce and verify regulatory compliance through routine inspections. Facilities Department staff therefore require a comprehensive set of skills and knowledge to comply with regulatory requirements while providing a safe work environment and reliable utilities in a dynamic and challenging setting.

Although this chapter will focus on the primary duty of system maintenance generally accepted as part of the typical Facilities Department, in some institutions the department may include one or more of the following support and ancillary services:

- Facilities Team
- Security
- Certified Police Department
- Electronic Surveillance
- Clinical Engineering

- Landscaping and Grounds
- Project Management
- Capital Project Planning
- Parking Operations
- Environmental Services
- Laundry
- Dining Services

KEY DEPARTMENT SERVICES

Facilities departments provide a core set of services regardless of institution size, be it a hospital with a few medical office buildings or a full-service academic medical center with multiple inpatient and outpatient buildings offering patient care, research, and education. In addition to the core infrastructure of the mechanical, electrical, and plumbing systems, Facilities also oversees operation of the following specialty systems:

- Medical gas system
- Pneumatic tube system
- Refrigeration system
- Vertical conveying system
- Water features
- Fire alarm system
- Fire suppression system
- Lock system
- Regulatory compliance
- Energy plant operations

These systems include scheduled, unscheduled, predictive, and preventive maintenance actions that will be described later in the chapter.

DEPARTMENT ORGANIZATIONAL STRUCTURES

Facilities departments will be led by a vice president who manages multiple teams. Exhibit 8.1 shows a sample Facilities Department organizational chart.

Reporting to the vice president are the directors for Facilities and Environmental Services (sometimes called Housekeeping), along with other directors responsible for support departments listed in exhibit 8.1. Larger organizations often have assistant director positions as well. Managers will have assistant managers or supervisors who oversee the frontline staff.

Exhibit 8.1: Sample Facilities Team Organizational Chart

```
                          ┌─────────────────────┐
                          │   Vice President     │
                          │  Support Services    │
                          └─────────────────────┘
                      ┌─────────────┴──────────────┐
        ┌──────────────────────────┐      ┌──────────────┐
        │ Director of Environmental │      │ Director of  │
        │  Services (Housekeeping)  │      │  Facilities  │
        └──────────────────────────┘      └──────────────┘
```

Financial/ Compliance Manager	Power Plant Manager	Electric Shop Manager	HVAC/Plumbing Shop Manager	Customer Services Manager
Material Management Manager	Power Plant Assistant Manager	Assistant Manager	Assistant Manager HVAC/Controls	Assistant Manager Scheduled Work
	Plant Maintenance Supervisor	Skilled Trades Supervisor	HVAC Shop	Key Shop
	District Energy Operators	Journeyman Electricians	Controls Shop	Sign Shop
		Lamp Technicians	Assistant Manager Plumbing/Night	
		Assistant Manager Preventive Maintenance Programs	Plumbing Shop	
		Preventive Maintenance Programs	Night/Weekend Team	

KEY CUSTOMERS AND THEIR PERFORMANCE EXPECTATIONS

The Facilities Department serves the entire campus and everyone who visits the campus; patients, family members, administrators, staff, and faculty and students in an academic medical center are their customers. The healthcare physical environment is a dynamic setting operating 365 days a year. Continuous operation greatly stresses the physical plant and leads to a rapid failure of equipment (more so than with office buildings), which customers may perceive as inconsistent performance in systems serving their areas.

Time needed to complete work orders is monitored to assess whether the Facilities Department is meeting performance expectations. Assessment can be based on hours, days, weeks, or months. For example, regarding filter changes on an air-handling unit, Facilities Department managers will set up preventive work orders on a frequency of once every three months. They will examine the completed work to assess whether it was done within an acceptable time frame and by the due date. Another example is completion time on work order tickets for standard tasks. If replacing a light bulb takes an employee one hour to complete, the manager can examine the time employees entered on their tickets to ensure the work is being done in a timely manner. The response time to high-priority work order tickets is also monitored. Most organizations have time requirements for such tickets, like a Facilities staff member reporting within ten minutes to fix a water leak. The manager can examine these tickets in the work order system to ensure response times are being met.

Regardless of organization size, the Facilities Department will use a software system referred to hereafter in this chapter as the Computer Maintenance Management System (CMMS). The CMMS acts as a data management hub for the department's key process flows. It contains information on all departmental system assets maintained in the organization. Facilities staff will use the CMMS to schedule and track all work done through work orders. Exhibit 8.2 shows an example of a typical work order to test the emergency generators on a weekly basis. Most organizations will have at least four key work processes, within which there can be a variety of subcategories unique to the organization's needs:

- Unscheduled or Demand Work
- Scheduled Work
- Preventive Maintenance
- Predictive Maintenance

Unscheduled or Demand Work

Unscheduled work orders are requests that interrupt service delivery to customers and must be completed immediately. Examples include an overflowing toilet, a pipe leaking water, or a malfunctioning medical gas system or electrical circuit. These work orders cannot be predicted, so when the call is received, the most effective and efficient team will be pulled off their current assignment and dispatched to resolve the issue.

Scheduled Work

Scheduled work orders are those requests that are not considered an emergency and do not have to be completed immediately; for example, a request to hang a picture or paint a wall. Being able to schedule these tasks helps management improve productivity and stretch scarce resources.

Exhibit 8.2: Example of an Open Work Order for a Weekly Preventive Maintenance Task

Work Order					
WO Type:	Preventive Maintenance	**Location ID:**		**Request #:**	
Subtype:	Weekly PM	**Facility:**		**Reference #:**	
WO Placed On:		**Building:**	MRI	**Status:**	Created By PM Schedule
Primary Ph:		**Floor:**		**Requested:**	12/9/2018 12:00 AM
Requestor:	PM Scheduler	**Department:**	Facilities	**Est. Start:**	
Requestor Ph:		**Priority:**	TJC1 – Priority 1 TJC	**Est. End:**	12/9/2018 12:00 AM
Repair Center:	Facilities	**Completed:**		**Est. Hours:**	
Acct No:		**Project:**	–	**Est. Costs:**	0.00
#:	MRI-GEN-#01 – Emergency Generator			**Modified By:**	
Risk Level:	1	**Supervisor:**		**Time:**	12/9/2018 10:38 PM
Sub-location:	Outside, West (Diesel)			**Total Hours:**	
Model:	1A2B3C	**Serial:**	100200	**Mfr:**	
Action Requested:	Emergency Generators (diesel)				
Comments:					
Svc. Interruption:	Provides emergency power to MRI.				
Task:	Emergency Generators (diesel)	**Task Due Date:**		00:00	
Failure Code:		**Task Status:**			
Failure Sub-Code:		**Completion Date:**			
Authorized By:		**Finished Date:**			
Contractor:		**WO #:**		123456	
Trade:	PM Shop	**PM Interval:**		1 Week	
Schedule	*(EO-239394: LSS-6202 - Emergency Generators (diesel))*				

Technician	Trade	Start		Comment	
John Smith	PM Shop	12/9/2018 10:37 PM			
Emergency Generators (diesel)	Labor	Materials	Other	Contractor	Total Charges
Total	0.00	0.00	0.00	0.00	0.00

Note: TJC = The Joint Commission.

Preventive Maintenance

Preventive maintenance (PM) is performed to eliminate unplanned outages and extend the useful life of an asset. PM work is scheduled and tracked through the CMMS system. The schedule can be generated from a frequency of needed work, such as quarterly filter changes on air-handling units. Frequency of PM will be driven by industry best practices, manufacturer's recommendations, or regulatory and code-required intervals. These frequencies, coupled with the scope of work required to complete the PM task, can lead to more efficient and productive use of staff's time while extending the uptime and useful life of the equipment.

Predictive Maintenance

Predictive maintenance is a form of preventative maintenance in which staff monitor assets in place and schedule work depending on their findings. In addition to the CMMS system, most Facilities departments will use a Building Automation System (BAS) as part of their predictive maintenance process. Exhibit 8.3 illustrates an example of a system's graphics page, illustrating the key components of an air-handling unit that serves operating rooms and its operating characteristics. The Facilities team reviews critical parameters such as positions of valves and dampers, relative humidity, and air temperatures at supply discharge and outside the facility. These parameters are critical to regulatory compliance and help minimize utility costs. By monitoring them daily, Facilities staff can better predict when a system component is beginning to show signs of wear.

This system can be used to identify equipment that is not performing optimally, which helps the Facilities staff predict when maintenance will be needed and prevent catastrophic failure.

Other common examples of predictive maintenance include thermal imaging and vibration analysis. Thermal imaging is used to analyze roofs and electrical panels. Breakers in the electrical panel can be scanned with thermal cameras to show loose electrical connections from the surrounding breakers. Rather than tightening all the connections as is typical, Facilities staff can address only the connections that are loose. Roofs can be scanned for temperature variations that indicate insulation breakdown.

Vibration analysis can be used on moving or rotating machinery to determine an excessive amount of vibration in the operation of the equipment. This excess is a signal that some part of the equipment is not working properly (e.g., loose mechanical belts, bearings going bad), which can lead to catastrophic failure if not addressed. The predictive approach to maintenance has proven to be more cost-effective than the preventive (Reliable Plant 2018).

Exhibit 8.3: Example Building Automation System Graphic for an Air-Handling Unit Serving an Operating Room

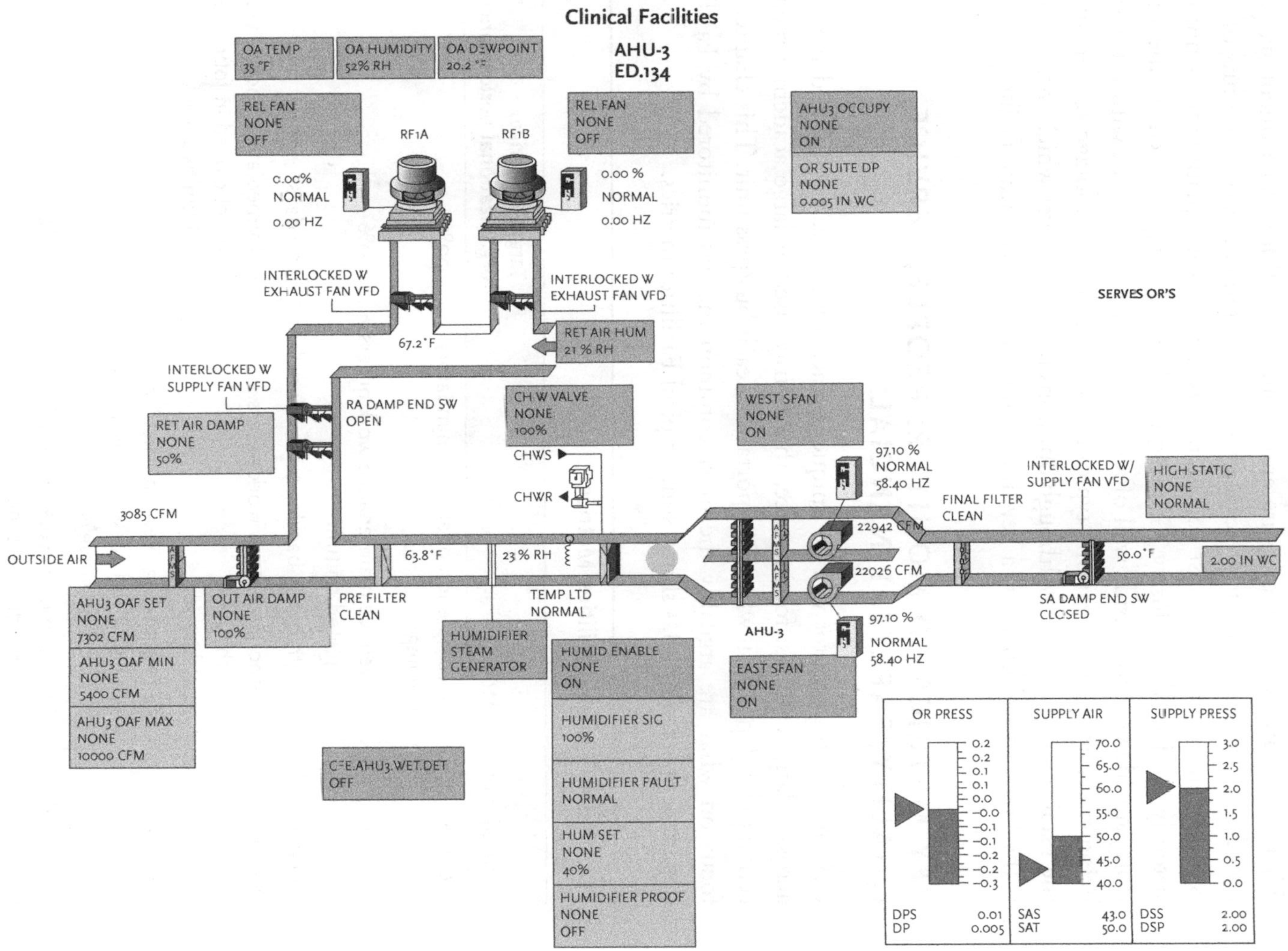

SERVES OR'S

Clinical Facilities

AHU-3
ED.134

OUTSIDE AIR

KEY UNITS OF WORK AND VOLUME STATISTICS TO MONITOR

There are many ways to measure and monitor Facilities Department work. As noted, no two departments are exactly alike and standardization of units of work is a challenge. Even the most commonly used unit, the square foot, is not consistently used in the industry. Gross square footage is represented by measuring from outside wall to outside wall of a space and includes all area within the space being measured. Organizations typically use gross square footage to benchmark the Facilities Department. Although opinions may differ over which measurement is the best, square footage is a key unit to monitor in healthcare facilities.

KEY METRICS TO MONITOR: PEOPLE, SERVICE, QUALITY/SAFETY, FINANCIAL

Key metrics to monitor will be unique to each healthcare facility and may vary across a large campus; for instance, the metrics used at large academic medical centers will depend on what is important to each business unit. This chapter will focus on what are arguably the most common metrics monitored by Facilities departments. Exhibit 8.4 shows some typical Facilities metrics.

Exhibit 8.4: Typical Facilities Metrics

Type of metric	Metric	Target/historical organizational performance
People	% completion of annual mandatory training	100%
Service	Preventive maintenance work orders completed on time	100%
Service	Length of the backlogged work orders	< 30 days
Service	Response time to work orders • Scheduled • Demand	• Immediate response with ticket closed in four hours • Within two weeks
Service	% responding "very satisfied" or "satisfied" on customer work order satisfaction surveys	> 95%
Financial	Time spent on work order tickets to total productive time	> 80%
Financial	Actual expense	Budget
Financial	Overtime charged to work orders	Budget

People

The key people metric is the Percentage Completion of Annual Mandatory Training, which typically consists of annual safety, conflict of interest, and other departmental-level training, such as preventive or predictive maintenance training associated with key equipment and systems for regulatory compliance. Regulatory compliance training for maintenance activity centers on understanding the importance of schedules, proper recordkeeping of the results, and understanding what to do in case of a problematic or missed test. In addition to the annual institutional mandatory training, the craft and trade disciplines require annual training to maintain their licenses and certifications. For example, in most states a licensed journeyman electrician will require an annual update of NFPA 70, the National Electric Code, to maintain their license. In addition, most healthcare organizations have the following complex systems and equipment that require specialized training:

- Ultra-low freezers
- Pneumatic tube system
- Building automation system
- Medical gas system
- Fire alarm system

Along with these people metrics, the performance-evaluation cycle includes annual employee evaluations along with routine performance discussions with the employee throughout the year. Facilities Department leaders should engage with each staff member on performance, attitude, and general well-being while understanding the person's professional and personal aspirations. The annual evaluation is required, but routine discussions are further components of being a good leader and taking an interest in staff.

Service

Key service metrics come from two sources: work orders and customer feedback surveys. Work order service metrics can be a combination of those orders that keep the systems functional and those that directly relate to customer expectations. A key metric for scheduled maintenance is Work Orders Completed on Time. Equipment deemed critical to hospital life safety systems is considered priority equipment. An example of a priority work order in a healthcare organization is the work performed on the emergency generator system. For priority work orders, a date to complete the work will be included for scheduling purposes, but a range of time associated with completion is also permitted. For example, if a work order is completed quarterly, a ten-day acceptable time interval to complete the work is given (Joint Commission 2020). Exhibit 8.5 shows the grace periods in the Acceptable intervals column for the Facilities group to be successful with on-time completion given the numerous unforeseen circumstances that arise in healthcare organizations.

A healthcare facility will benefit from how preventive and predictive work orders ensure systems function as designed. However, customers will not notice this work, as much of it happens behind the scenes, unlike work order tracking where the customer is directly involved. For example, a water leak, a light fixture not working, and a hot or cold area within the customer's space are certainly going to have the attention of the customer. Therefore, Facilities leadership must track Time for Completion, Length of the Backlogged Work Orders, and Time to Respond to the Work Orders. Organizational goals and expectations determine which service metrics Facilities departments choose to track.

Another service metric that measures the success of the work order process is the Percentage Responding "Very Satisfied" or "Satisfied" on Customer Work Order Satisfaction Surveys, usually obtained via a customer survey. Facilities departments should solicit customer feedback on several dimensions, such as whether the work was completed in a timely manner, whether the craftsperson who completed the task was professional and respectful, and whether there was

Exhibit 8.5: Inspection Time Frames and Acceptable Internals

Time frame	Equivalent descriptions for time frame			Requirement	Acceptable intervals after requirement
Every 36 months	Every 3 years			36 months from the last event	45 days
Every 12 months	Annually	Once a year	Every year	1 year from the last event	30 days
Every 6 months				6 months from the last event	20 days
Every quarter	Quarterly			Every 3 months	10 days
Every month	Monthly	30-day intervals		12 times a year	Once per calendar month
Every week				Once per calendar week	Once per calendar week

Source: Adapted from Joint Commission (2020).

effective communication about the work from the craftsperson to the customer. Feedback can help Facilities Department leaders determine if customers' expectations are being met and identify opportunities to improve service.

Quality/Safety

A key quality metric is Percentage Satisfactory on Routine Inspections of the physical environment, which determines whether all items in the environment are functional and in good condition. If not, reviews are required of what tasks are routinely being completed and at what frequency. Facilities leaders then need to make the necessary adjustments to ensure improved outcomes during the next inspection.

Another metric for quality is monitoring and tracking Equipment Downtime, which can determine quality of the process for maintaining physical plant. Each piece of equipment monitored will have a different standard level of downtime, but tracking these data points over time will reveal whether the equipment maintenance program is effective.

Financial

The key financial metrics for Facilities include comparison of Actual Expense Versus Budget on a month-to-month or year-to-date basis, as well as year over year for a historical comparison of operating and utilities budgets (which includes electric, water, and gas). Labor expenses will typically account for about 75 percent of the total operating budget. The operating budget and the utility budget should be separated to accurately analyze the components of each. Facilities leaders need to understand the major reasons for budget variances. In a healthcare facility, those differences can depend on the volume of patients in the organization. If the organization is experiencing a prolonged high census, some routine maintenance expenses may be higher than anticipated when the budgets were created. Understanding this relationship between patient census levels and maintenance costs is particularly important when there are discrepancies between budget and actual expenses.

The Facilities Department is also responsible for monitoring Expenses for Capital. Typically in a small to medium-size organization the Facilities Department will have oversight of the capital-project budget. In larger organizations a Capital Planning Department will oversee those activities, coupled with a multidisciplinary capital planning committee. No matter the size of the organization, the Facilities Department will generate and manage a budget for capital equipment that supports its specific needs.

Having supervisory staff track more detailed financial metrics is important for needed course corrections in processes or staff habits. Because labor is such a significant percentage of the operating budget, management needs to understand how the time is being spent. Staff time spent on a work order corresponds to a direct monetary outlay, so if work time on a ticket exceeds the allowable time, adjustments are needed. Monitoring the amount of Time Charged to Work Orders is important to understanding financial performance. Tracking and monitoring staff's productivity levels is another important financial metric that should be performed at a supervisory level.

Each organization must address what key metrics are important to the success of the Facilities Department and the whole organization. Once identified, roles and responsibilities can be assigned and processes put in place to begin monitoring these key metrics.

STAFFING MODELS

Standardized staffing models are difficult to define for healthcare organizations. Facilities leadership must consider several factors when determining staff count, including the uniqueness of the organizational structures, the physical environment, the sophistication of the clinical work being performed, the technical complexity of building systems, and the operational expectations of the organization. Therefore, when modeling the staff required, Facilities leadership must review staffing needs from a system-specialization perspective, a general maintenance-needs perspective, and a special knowledge-based requirement.

Unless an organization has gone through a major new building campaign, the typical campus will have multiple generations of buildings, with many different systems and maintenance staff spanning several generations. Healthcare organizations have many specialized systems that require a special skill set to be kept running properly. Some of the skill required can only be provided by external organizations (e.g., a well-designed and well-executed contract with an elevator maintenance firm to ensure reliability).

One specialized system with a unique skill set the organization can choose to outsource or insource is the ultra-low freezers that are standard and critical pieces of equipment, especially in academic medical centers. Training on these freezers is typically provided by the manufacturer and can cost thousands of dollars to provide. Although this investment is large, the cost of losing the products in these freezers can easily range in the hundreds of thousands of dollars.

Another example of such specialized equipment is the pneumatic tube system, used to deliver small packages around the facility, such as lab samples and pharmaceuticals. Depending on the size of the organization, these systems can have miles of tubing and multiple pieces of electromechanical equipment, all controlled by a sophisticated software system. Staffing requirements for these specialized systems depends on the size of the organization, the tolerance for system or equipment failure, and how much the organization is willing to invest to achieve its desired outcomes.

General-maintenance staffing models consist of the more typical positions found in a Facilities Department, such as electricians, plumbers, HVAC workers, carpenters, and general technicians. These positions are typically the easiest for which to find benchmark data; however, the level of executive leadership buy-in for the staffing ratio benchmarks determines the success of the staffing model. As with any benchmarking data, accuracy of the data must be scrutinized to gauge if the organization has enough staff for the work to be completed.

Staffing plans for the Facilities Department also must address the specialized knowledge throughout the department to account for the workload and the complex environment. Specialized knowledge areas focus on regulatory knowledge, such as infection control as related to Facilities work.

Most hospitals undergo a routine survey process to assess compliance with the CMS Conditions of Participation. Most healthcare facilities in the United States have contracts with The Joint Commission, which typically has a triennial inspection process (Pelletier 2017, 33). The Facilities staffing plan must include frontline staff that understands Joint Commission testing, inspecting, and reporting requirements. Supervisors, managers, and other leadership in the Facilities Department should have knowledge of Joint Commission regulatory requirements. The data collected by the frontline staff during the routine testing and inspecting of equipment must be stored and available for summary presentation to the Joint Commission surveyor. Number of staff required would be based on facility size and how the roles and responsibilities of these inspections are distributed. During the triennial survey, the inspector will expect to hear from the staff involved in the testing, not just the management team in charge of the program.

The staffing plan for the Facilities Department should include staff who know the local and state departments of healthcare codes, and the codes and standards that govern building systems such as the National Fire Protection Codes—in particular National Fire Protection Association (NFPA) 101, Life Safety Code, and NFPA 99, Health Care Facilities Code, among many others in the NFPA group of codes (see https://www.nfpa.org). One or more team members will be responsible for all issues concerning the state agency that governs air quality. With larger healthcare organizations and academic medical centers, permit requirements must be tracked, documented, and reported. Ancillary departments described in the Key Regulatory Issues section also affect Facilities staffing metrics.

With the increased prevalence and focus on hospital-acquired infections, the Facilities staffing plan must also include staff knowledgeable in preventing potential infections from the work they perform. Major construction projects, remodeling work, and routine maintenance work can produce air quality issues that are not conducive to healing. Even routine maintenance work can cause a poor environment that is not conducive to healing. Therefore, Facilities must have a program with sufficient controls and documented training for these infection-control potentials. This program requires the staffing plan to include individuals to oversee and manage this effort.

Finally, although many industries were early adopters of the Lean Six Sigma process, healthcare was not one of them. In recent years, however, more healthcare organizations have begun to adopt Lean Six Sigma practices to reduce waste and improve process variations. As this transformation takes place at an organizational level, the Facilities staffing plan should include individuals with Lean Six Sigma knowledge.

PRODUCTIVITY MODELS, INCLUDING WORK-TO-STAFF RATIOS AND INDUSTRY PERFORMANCE TARGETS

The International Facility Management Association (IFMA) and the American Society for Health Care Engineering (ASHE) have staff ratio benchmarking that uses gross square foot per unit calculations for total FTEs required (IFMA and ASHE 2010). For example, if the benchmark mandates one electrician for every 213,000 gross square feet of space, and the organization is 1 million square feet, the ratio implies the need for five electricians (IFMA and ASHE 2010). These benchmarks are available to members of these organizations. Staffing ratios should be reviewed and understood among Facilities leadership as general guidelines, but they also must account for the uniqueness of organizational structures and physical environments. A director of the Facilities Department may use a recognized industry standard to justify required staffing levels. If executive leadership has not accepted the benchmark, the staffing justification will not be successful. The director must ensure the benchmark is accurate and applicable for the campus and the building use groups, such as research, education, and healthcare.

Facilities leadership should have a system to monitor staff productivity. For example, productivity is reported from the work order system comparing Time Spent on Work Order Tickets to Total Productive Time. Typically this metric is monitored weekly or monthly. Each organization must define productive time for a craftsperson. Lunchtime and breaks are typically not included, but some organizations may include travel time to the repair location or administrative time spent on the work order system as productive time.

STRATEGIES TO IMPROVE RECRUITMENT AND RETENTION

Recruits traditionally have sought opportunities in the Facilities Department because of the steady and reliable work, good pay, exceptional benefit packages, and favorable work conditions. Given the current climate of aging employees, however, and limited interest among younger generations in entering the crafts and trades, healthcare system leaders must find new strategies to recruit and retain staff to maintain hospital systems. The complexity and uniqueness of the systems being maintained in a healthcare system demand a specially trained workforce. The challenge in most organizations is the operational blending of much older systems with those using the latest technology; this hybrid requires a knowledgeable workforce who can maintain the spectrum of systems.

One strategy to promote staff satisfaction and retention is to ensure they have the necessary tools to do their jobs, like a comprehensive set of diagrams for the systems that the Facilities team is responsible for maintaining. These diagrams, in electronic and hard copy format, allow new staff members to learn the systems without having to rely on veteran staff, and enable staff of disparate technical competencies to succeed. New staff will feel they have the ability to contribute early on in their career.

Providing pathways for growth and advancement for all levels of staff in the Facilities Department is another retention tactic. Historically, much of the workforce for the crafts and trades at healthcare facilities gained experience through the military or heavily unionized industries. These two avenues have a clear path of progression and subsequent pay increases. For example, an electrician entering the Facilities Department would clearly see a path of progression as an electrician I, II, and III in the organizational structure along with supervisory and managerial roles. Being able to see paths for advancement can promote longer job tenure, even if promotions are not guaranteed.

KEY REGULATORY ISSUES

CMS provides deemed status for organizations to inspect hospitals on their behalf, including the following:

- The Joint Commission
- Det Norske Veritas Healthcare, Inc.
- Healthcare Facilities Accreditations Program

Each has its own survey process but must ultimately comply with the CMS Conditions of Participation. The Joint Commission has been the premier player in this industry for more than 50 years, and will be the focus for this section (Pelletier 2017).

The Joint Commission has an annual publication, the *Comprehensive Accreditation Manual for Hospitals* (*CAMH*; Joint Commission 2020), outlining the inspection requirements that align with the Conditions of Participation published by CMS. The two chapters in *CAMH* most pertinent to the Facilities Department are the Environment of Care (EOC) and Life Safety (LS) chapters. The EOC chapter covers all aspects of the physical space, including air pressure relationships in the healthcare areas and utility-infrastructure testing requirements. Many of the standards in the *CAMH* require the Facilities Department to keep records of testing frequency and compliance rates. Much of these data are collected and stored in the BAS or CMMS. Test failures must be documented and corrected, and a retest of the standard must be done with the successful test documented.

The LS chapter in the *CAMH* outlines the requirements for systems that provide life safety features in the hospital area. These LS systems include the fire alarm system, the fire sprinkler system, and the life safety plans that document paths of egress from the building. Each of these systems has requirements for testing and documenting the results.

The EOC and LS chapters represent the majority of the work that is pertinent to the Facilities Department; however, other chapters in the *CAMH* are the primary responsibilities of other departments that involve Facilities. The Facilities budget should include the appropriate expense necessary to meet compliance of standards in the following ancillary and support departments.

- Emergency
- Radiology
- Nuclear Medicine
- Dining Services
- Infection Control
- Pharmacy
- Perioperative
- Laboratory

In addition to Joint Commission regulatory requirements, the Facilities Department is required to help departments meet their regulatory obligations that fall outside the CMS Conditions of Participation. For example, Facilities will be expected to show proper HVAC system performance for academic medical centers with vivarium labs where animals are housed that are inspected by representatives of the American Association for Accreditation of Laboratory Animal Care. The local health department will typically have routine or on-demand inspections for the kitchen and other food areas that require Facilities assistance to comply with standards. The city or state Department of Environmental Quality will inspect the diesel storage and generator exhaust volume. Facilities leadership must understand the volume of work and resources required for successful inspection, testing, and documentation for the various regulatory agencies, because underestimating the need can mean dire consequences for the organization.

KEY TERMS FOR FACILITIES

Building Automation System (BAS): A software solution that controls the asset operations in the field by using input parameters from monitoring key equipment activities, with the purpose of maximizing efficient operation of utility systems.

Computer Maintenance Management System (CMMS): A software solution for tracking and reporting on-campus physical assets and processing work requests generated by customers of the Facilities, Security, Environmental Services, and Clinical Engineering departments.

Predictive maintenance: A form of preventive maintenance in which staff monitors the assets in place and schedules work according to the data. Besides monitoring key components in the BAS, two common predictive maintenance tasks are thermal imaging and vibration analysis.

Preventive maintenance: Work performed to eliminate unplanned outages and extend the useful life of an asset. This work is scheduled and tracked through the CMMS system. Schedules are set as per manufacturer's recommendation or an alternate method created by the Facilities Department.

Scheduled maintenance: Work orders that are not considered an emergency and do not have to be completed immediately.

Unscheduled maintenance: Also known as demand tickets, these orders need to be completed immediately because of some concern or issue with either a customer or the utility system.

Work order: The method of tracking work requested and completed on a physical asset in a facility as well as work requested by a customer. The work order is created and stored with the CMMS system.

REFERENCES

International Facility Management Association (IFMA) and American Society for Healthcare Engineering (ASHE). 2010. *Operations and Maintenance Benchmarks for Health Care Facilities Report*. Houston, TX: IFMA.

Joint Commission. 2020. *Comprehensive Accreditation Manual.* Oakbrook Terrace, IL: Joint Commission Resources.

Pelletier, M. 2017. *Accreditation Guide for Hospitals.* Oakbrook Terrace, IL: Joint Commission Resources.

Reliable Plant. 2018. "Predictive Maintenance Explained." Accessed August 30, 2020. www.reliableplant.com/Read/12495/preventive-predictive-maintenance.

CHAPTER 9

Food and Nutrition Services

Leisa Bryant

DEPARTMENT DESCRIPTION

This chapter will address essential and practical information for managing the inpatient meal service (sometimes called room service) and retail dining operations (sometimes called dining services) of the Food and Nutrition Services (FNS) Department. The FNS Department in healthcare organizations establishes evidence-based and best-practice guidelines for the Clinical Nutrition, Patient, and Retail Dining services. (Clinical Nutrition, which is staffed by registered dietitians, provides individualized nutrition assessments, medical nutrition therapy, nutrition support, and education, and is addressed in a separate chapter.) In alignment with the organization, the FNS Department must establish a mission and vision that clearly defines why the department exists and what it wants to achieve. A simple example of a mission for the department's operational area is to exceed the dining expectations of patients and customers by providing high-quality, nutritious food and services in a safe and efficient environment. Similarly, a simple vision statement is to become the leader in healthcare foodservice by perpetuating a culture of healthy eating and exceptional service.

To support its mission and vision, a best practice for FNS is to develop and have in writing its scope of services, which describes the activities and expected services of the department. The model and scope of FNS vary among institutions and depend on factors such as the mission, vision, goals, and size of the institution and the population it serves. Some FNS departments are self-operated, some outsource either management or all functions to foodservice contract companies, and some operate as a hybrid of contracted and self-operated areas. A 2016 Healthcare Survey in *Foodservice Director Magazine* showed that 76 percent of the institutions surveyed were self-operated, 20 percent were contract managed, and 4 percent were hybrids (FSD Staff 2016).

Like the healthcare industry, FNS is heavily regulated and must follow federal, state, and local laws and licensing or regulatory requirements. The Conditions of Participation (CoPs) in Centers for Medicare & Medicaid Services (CMS) Requirement A-0168 dictate that the hospital's food and dietetic services must be organized, directed, and staffed in a manner that ensures patients' nutritional needs are met in accordance with practitioners' orders and acceptable standards of practice. For services that are not addressed by CMS or other regulatory bodies or where more definitive professional standards do not exist, the department must collaborate with subject matter experts and professional organizations (e.g., Academy of Nutrition and Dietetics, Association for Healthcare Professionals, Association of Nutrition & Foodservice Professionals) to adopt standards that meet safety requirements and industry best practices. CMS Interpretive Guideline 482.28 requires that, at minimum, the department have policies and procedures that address the following areas:

- The availability of a Diet Manual and therapeutic diets
- Frequency of meals served
- A system for ordering diets and meal deliveries
- Accommodations for non-routine nutrition services
- Integration of the hospital-wide Quality Assurance Performance Improvement (QAPI) and Infection Control (IC) programs
- Personal hygiene
- Kitchen sanitation
- Emergency Preparedness

KEY DEPARTMENT SERVICES

FNS plays an integral role in providing safe, high-quality care and service, and promoting health and healing, to patients, guests, and customers. Menus for patient and retail operations must be planned in accordance with well-defined policies and meet Food and Drug Administration food labeling laws and the nutritional standards and diets of the patient and customer population it serves. Menus should include therapeutic and modified diets that are defined in the institutionally approved Diet Manual and meet the United States Department of Agriculture's Recommended Dietary Allowances. Defined diets include but are not limited to Regular, Consistent Carbohydrate/Calorie Controlled, Heart Healthy, Modified Texture (e.g., for dysphagia), and short-term test diets such as Clear Liquids.

Patient care foodservice includes patient meal services, guest meal services, celebratory meal services, and—becoming more mainstream—post-discharge meal delivery to combat food insecurity. Over the years, many foodservice departments have transitioned from the traditional inpatient dining-service delivery to a room service model or some other enhanced version of service to improve the patients' nutrition and dining experience. The on-demand room service model allows patients to order high-quality restaurant-style meals that meet both their preferences and the goals of the prescribed diet. The meals are prepared fresh and delivered to the patient's room within a specified time of about 45 to 60 minutes. Research has shown that hospitals with a room service program have seen higher patient satisfaction scores with meals, improved nutrient intake, and lower food waste and meal cost (McCray et al. 2018). The room service model is not for every facility and patient population. FNS must ensure that whatever service a facility uses aligns with the institution's goals and priorities and meets the patient's nutritional needs.

Healthcare foodservice retail operations encompass all revenue-generating cafés, catering, convenience stores, coffee bars, food courts, vending, and office coffee services. The goals of retail dining should be to set the highest standards in the industry for exceptional dining experiences and to optimize revenue growth through innovative dining services and initiatives. These goals should be defined in writing and communicated to the FNS leadership team and staff to ensure a common understanding, so the success of retail dining can be evaluated using financial, sales, and customer satisfaction metrics. Identified as one of the revenue contributors to the institution, many retail food operations have reimagined and renovated their retail spaces to be on trend with consumer expectations for flavors, quality, health, ambience, and value while seeking revenue growth and expansion. Retail concepts such as healthy grab-and-go, made to order, rotating local restaurants, franchises, and licensee concepts for recognized brands are now common staples of the healthcare retail portfolio. Healthcare retail dining continues to innovate to drive revenue while responding to customer demand and changes in the environment. For example, when the COVID-19 pandemic disrupted the foodservice industry, healthcare retail operations responded with initiatives such as grocery to go, family meals to go, order and pickup, order for delivery, mobile ordering via apps, and self-checkout services.

DEPARTMENT ORGANIZATIONAL STRUCTURE

FNS departments are dynamic in operating structure and business models, as guided by the hospital's mission, values, internal policies, and regulatory guidelines. Their dynamic status can sometimes lead to operational complexities and variance in the department's structure, oversight, and scope. Whichever business model it uses, the department must be adequately staffed by qualified employees to provide safe, quality nutrition care and dining services to patients, guests, and customers. To lead and manage FNS programs, the department is required to have a full-time employee who is qualified by experience or training to serve as its director. The hospital's governing body and staff must grant or delegate the director all needed authority and responsibility to manage FNS's daily operations. The director should report to a senior member of the hospital administration who can advocate for the needs and requirements of the department. Depending on the healthcare organization's size, the department may be part of a division such as Clinical Support Services, Ancillary Support Services, Facilities, or Patient Experience. The department must have policies that define the reporting relationships to IC, Environmental Health and Safety (EH&S), QAPI, Clinical Nutrition (if it is not a part of the FNS Department), and other hospital committees that affect patient and customer safety, care, and services.

In addition to the director, and depending on the department's size and scope of services, FNS may need additional layers of department leaders and managers, such as associate directors for both the inpatient and retail areas, and an executive chef to oversee production, sanitation, and recipe development. Midlevel and frontline managers and supervisors also may be needed to support back of house (kitchen), front of house (serving area), patient-facing service, call center or diet office, purchasing and receiving, sanitation, and production. The department may also have a business support team that oversees the budget; cash handling; accounts payable, receivable, and transfers; and all departmental transactions and finances. Finally, the department must hire adequate administrative staff. Exhibit 9.1 provides an example of an FNS department in an academic medical center.

KEY CUSTOMERS AND THEIR PERFORMANCE INDICATORS

The FNS Department has numerous internal and external customers and stakeholders, such as staff, visitors, patients, vendors, and community partners who do business with the organization. The department's operational priority should be to develop and sustain high reliability and a customer-centric, value-driven culture of service that is efficient and innovative. Some customers are patients, guests, and fellow employees and medical staff. Expectations and performance indicators of key customers are illustrated in exhibit 9.2 and are guided by regulatory requirements; contractual obligations; service-level agreements; and the organization's culture, mission, and values.

Exhibit 9.1: Organizational Chart for an Example FNS Department in an Academic Medical Center

Director (1) — Sr AA (1)

Program Manager (1) [3 FTE]
- Admin Coord (1)
- Sr Sec (1)

Associate Director Retail (1) [20.6 FTE]

Retail Director Catering (1)
- Catering Manager (1)
- Supervisor (1)
- Sr Catering Asst (2)
- Catering Asst (8)
- PerDiem (0.96)
- Cook I (1)
- Cook III (1)
- Sr Admin Clerk (1)

Food Service Director (1)
- Health & Wellness Mgr (1)
- Mgr Food Ops (1)
  - Cashier (1)
  - FSW (1)
- Asst Mgr (1)
  - Sr FSW (4)
  - FSW (7)
  - Cashier (1)
- Asst Mgr (1)
  - Sr Cashier (4)
  - FSW (9)
  - Cook II (1)
- Asst Mgr (1)
  - Sr Cashier (2)
  - Cashiers (13)
- Supervisor (1)

Food Service Director (1)
- Mgr Food Operations (1)
  - Cook I (4)
  - Cook II (5)
  - Cook III (1)
  - Sr FSW (3)
  - Sr Cashier (4)
  - Cashier (4)
- Sous Chef (1)
  - Cook I (3)
  - Cook II (2)
  - Cook III (1)
- Asst Manager (1)
  - Sr FSW (3)
  - FSW (5)
  - Sr Cashiers (3)
  - Cashiers (4)

Manager Retail Ops (1)
- Cook I (2)
- Cook II (1)
- Cook III (2)
- Sr FSW (8)
- FSW (9)
- Sr Cashier (2)
- Cashiers (7)
- Supv (2)

Sr Executive Chef (1)
- Mgr Food Operations (1)
  - Sous Chef (1)
  - Cook I (5)
  - Cook II (7)
  - Cook III (4)
  - Sr FSW (2)
  - FSW (1)
- Sous Chef (1)
  - Cook I (7)
  - Cook II (1)
- Chef Manager (1)
- Asst Manager (1)
  - Stores Clerk (3.5)
  - Sr Stone Clerk (1)
- Mgr Food Operations (1)
  - Cook I (2)
  - Cook II (1)
  - Cook III (1)
- Asst Manager (1)
- A2I FSM (1)
- Sr Instr Tech (1)
- Instr Tech (1)

Associate Director Room Service (1) [24.3 FTE]

Executive Chef (1)
- Sous Chef (4)
  - Cook I (8)
  - Cook II (12)
  - Cook III (4)
  - Sr FSW (2)
  - FSW (1)
  - Exp (13)
- Supervisor FS (1)
  - Cook I (3)
  - Cook II (2)
  - FSW (3)
- Storekeeper (1)
- Stores Clerk (1)

Manager RS (1)
- Asst Mgr RS call center (1)
- Sr RS Asst (3)
  - RS Asst (8.25)
- RS Captain (1)
- Sr RS Asst (3)
  - RS Asst (12.25)
- Database Coordinator (1)
- Info Sys Tech (1)

Manager RS (1)
- Asst Manager (1)
  - Transport (1)
  - Wait Staff (21)
  - RS Captain (1)
  - Transport (9)
  - Wait Staff (72)
  - RS Captain (1)
  - Transport (6)
  - Wait Staff (16)
- Asst Manager (1)
  - Transport (6)
  - Wait Staff (18)
  - RS Captain (1)
  - Transport (5)
  - Wait Staff (18)
  - RS Captain (1)
  - Transport (4)
  - Wait Staff (18)

Associate Director Clinical Nutrition (1) [44 FTE]
- Sr C lnical RD Funded by HAL/PTC (7.6)
- Clinical Nutrition Mgr (1)
  - Sr Clin RD (18.5)
  - Clin RD (14.5)
  - Clin Nutr Spc (6)
- Clinical Nutrition Triage Team
  - Clinical RD (2)
  - Diet Tech (1)
- Clinical Program Mgr (1)

Finance Manager (1) [1 FTE]
- Accounting Spc (1)

Note: AA = administrative assistant; FSW = food service worker; FTE = full-time equivalent; RD = registered dietitian; RS = room service.

Exhibit 9.2: Key Customers, Expectations, and Performance Indicators

Key customers	Expectations	Performance indicators
• Patients • Patients' guests • Patients' caregivers • Café customers • Catering customers • Vending customers • Office coffee customers	Provide nourishing and high-quality meals to optimize nutritional outcomes	Satisfaction with: • Quality of meals • Courtesy of staff • Temperature of food • Accuracy of meals • Timeliness of delivery • Value of meals • Variety of meal selections
• Physicians • Advance practice providers • Nursing • Ancillary support staff	Provide services as outlined in institutional or interdepartmental policies and regulatory requirements	• Timeliness in the delivery of meals and service requests
• Environmental Health Services • Facilities	Provide services as outlined in the service-level agreement	• Highest level of cleaning, sanitation, and pest management • Percentage score on kitchen sanitation audit inspection • Timeliness in reporting infrastructure and operational maintenance incidents
• Departmental staff	Satisfaction with the work culture, environment, and leadership	• Overall satisfaction on the employee opinion survey • Overall satisfaction on the employee safety survey
• Vendor partners	• Timely payment of invoices • Timely escalation and resolution of concerns • Communication and collaboration to ensure expectations are managed	• Quarterly business and quality review meetings • Quarterly contract obligations review

KEY PROCESS FLOWS

Patient, customer, and staff safety comprise the number one priority for FNS departments. The department's success is grounded in safe food practices through procurement, storage, and preparation to service. Food safety, prevention of allergy interactions, diet order compliance, personal hygiene, and sanitation procedures are critical to ensuring safe and quality patient and customer care. The

Exhibit 9.3: Process Flow for an Inpatient Room Service Tray Delivery

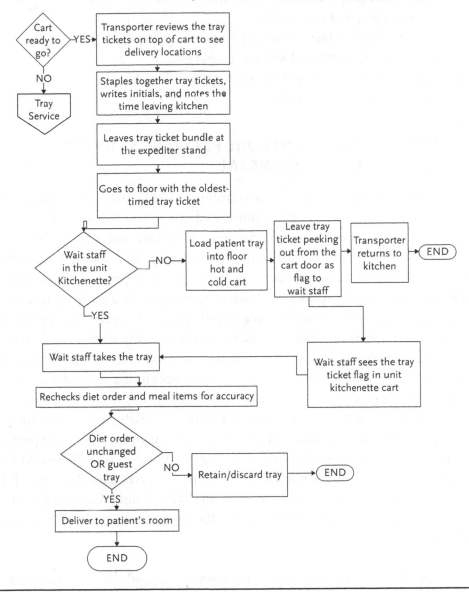

department must have and maintain standard operating procedures to ensure safety and regulatory compliance with applicable laws and licenses. Depicting process flows in a flowchart is one way the FNS Department can standardize operating procedures. A flowchart is a pictorial representation of the sequential steps in a process. Exhibit 9.3 shows an example of a process flow for delivering meal trays to inpatients. Key process flows include, but are not limited to, the following:

- Food allergy management for dietary orders
- Cleaning surfaces, walls, equipment, utensils, small wares, and floors

- Disposing of trash, grease, and kitchen waste
- Directing meal preparation, delivery, and services
- Labeling, dating, and storing food
- Conducting kitchen inspection and pest management
- Providing staff training and knowledge assessment
- Managing cash handling and financial oversight
- Complying with food recalls

KEY METRICS TO MONITOR: PEOPLE, SERVICE, QUALITY/SAFETY, FINANCIAL

A successful FNS Department has a continuous QAPI program in place. This process should be dynamic, well planned, and systematic to monitor and assess the safety, quality, value, and appropriateness of the care and services the department provides. Continuous quality improvement enables managers to achieve benchmark levels of performance. Benchmarking is a proactive tool used to identify comparative strengths and weaknesses and provide a pathway to enhancing the experience of patients, customers, and staff while optimizing operational efficiencies. Benchmarking can be done internally to compare historical and current performance levels, industry-wide relative to foodservice industry standards and best practices, competitively against similar operations with like scope and size, or functionally where internal functions are compared with those of the best regardless of the industry. Key performance indicators (KPIs) are used to measure quality of care and service delivered to patients and customers. KPIs support and influence food service strategic goals, objectives, and decisions. KPIs should focus on who the department serves, what it serves, how it serves, and the value of that service or product. In general, the department's KPIs should focus on its people, service, quality/safety, and finances. Exhibit 9.4 shows an example FNS scorecard template.

- **People:** Customer and staff experience matters. Engaged staff and customers will be aligned and loyal, and will become advocates for the business and brand.
- **Service:** Excellent service is key to improving customers' experience. Measuring the impact of the level and standard of service provided is essential.
- **Quality and Safety:** Quality and safety are top priorities for the department. Quality and safety metrics help the department measure or quantify processes, outcomes, and patient and customer perceptions of meals.
- **Financial:** FNS is a business. Well-managed finances lead to a healthy and successful department.

Exhibit 9.4: Example of a Food and Nutrition Services Scorecard Template

	Performance indicators	Data source	Target	Qtr. 1	Qtr. 2	Qtr. 3	Qtr. 4
People	Number of recognition awards given to employees	Human Resources	>50				
	Employee year-to-date turnover	Human Resources	<10%				
	Employee satisfaction with the workplace	Survey	>80%				
Service	Patient satisfaction with the courtesy of staff	Survey	>90%				
	Patient satisfaction with food temperatures	Survey	>90%				
	Customer satisfaction with cafeteria services	Survey	>80%				
Quality and Safety	Patient Safety: Right diet, right patient	Audit	100%				
	Employee Safety: Workplace accidents resulting in injury	Audit	0				
	Patient satisfaction with the quality of food	Survey	>90%				
	Kitchen sanitation and cleanliness	Audit	>95%				
Finance	Number of inpatient meals served	Operating Statement					
	Total revenue	Operating Statement					
	Productive hours/meals served	Operating Statement					
	Personnel expense	Operating Statement					

KEY INFORMATICS ISSUES

The intersection of technology, nutrition, and information has given rise to innovations, workflow optimization, high reliability, and customer and patient satisfaction in the FNS industry. FNS leaders must remain relentless to achieve operational excellence and invest in technology to manage and meet customer and patient demand. Despite the rapid growth in technological advancement and many challenges to get approval to invest in technology for the department, FNS leaders must continue their best efforts to remain knowledgeable and advocate for the benefits of technology in their operations. Exhibit 9.5 shows three key areas where technology has improved operations and safe patient care.

Exhibit 9.5: Key Food and Nutrition Services Technologies

Key technology	Functions
Menu Management Software System: Allows foodservice professionals to develop or modify recipes, provide nutritional and allergen data on food ingredients, help to calculate cost and price of menus, and address compliance with food labeling requirements	• Electronic diet order and allergy transmission—increase reliability for timely and accurately transmitting diet orders to the diet office and tray line • Accurate nutrient analysis and recipe management—satisfies CMS and other regulatory agencies such as TJC and DNV • Right diet, right foods—flags food with allergens and diet compliance • Supports inventory and procurement contracts • Staff optimization with reduction in manual work • Tracks patient meal orders and deliveries
Point of Sale System: An integrated software and hardware solution for the retailer operation to manage sales	• Processes all types of payments including self-checkout • Tracks inventory • Manages the department's accounting needs and calculate sales tax • Tracks employee work hours, vacation time, and absences • Manages loyalty programs • Tracks sales history and sales mix • Calculates pricing and discounts • Improved customer satisfaction with easy access and mobile ordering
Electronic Temperature Monitoring Systems: Food temperature monitoring and logging are essential for food safety and are regulatory requirements	• Protect patients and customers from foodborne illnesses • Automate manual food and equipment temperature logging • Reliable food and equipment temperature monitoring 24/7/365 • Immediate notification of food safety hazards • Timely corrective actions that can mitigate food waste because of spoilage • Monitor critical limits with an electronic alert at any time • Optimize work process and temperature documentation

Note: CMS = Centers for Medicare & Medicaid Services; DNV = Det Norske Veritas; TJC = The Joint Commission.

PRODUCTIVITY MODELS, INCLUDING WORK-TO-STAFF RATIOS AND INDUSTRY PERFORMANCE TARGETS

Labor costs in healthcare foodservice continue to increase year over year. The shift to pay a "living wage" rather than the minimum wage and competition for skilled and qualified staff have increased not only wages but also the cost of fringe benefits. The FNS Department is labor intensive, and labor expense accounts for approximately 50 percent or more of the operating budget. Managing productivity is one of the key metrics for evaluating and improving performance and efficiency and controlling labor cost. Productivity is the amount of output gained from a given amount of input (BC Cook Articulation Committee 2015). Inpatient meal service productivity is the number of meal equivalents (meal volume), and retail productivity is the number of transactions or revenue for each labor hour worked, as shown in exhibit 9.6.

The department must have metrics and processes in place to continually manage labor cost by mitigating nonproductive time (Gregoire and Theis 2015). Proactively managing what drives labor cost and accurately forecasting labor need are essential to the department's staffing model and work schedule. Too much labor at the wrong time of day will result in waste; too little will result in poor service and dissatisfied customers. In addition to benchmarking to set productivity targets, the department must hardwire the process to have accurate job descriptions, good onboarding and orientation programs, ongoing employee trainings, and engaged supervision with bidirectional feedback about job performance. Some institutions have also implemented zero-overtime policies, which have been shown to improve employee productivity and the department's bottom line. Exhibits 9.7 and 9.8 provide examples of FNS productivity monitoring.

Exhibit 9.6: Key Productivity Metrics

Retail Operations	Inpatient Meal Services
• Revenue (sales) per FTE • Average retail transactions per FTE	• Meals per labor hour • Meals per FTE • Trays per minute

Note: FTE = full-time equivalent.

Exhibit 9.7: Example of Room Service Productivity Monitoring

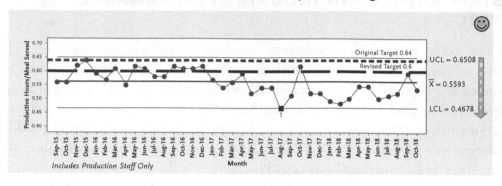

Note: LCL = lower control limit; UCL = upper control limit; X = central line.

Exhibit 9.8: Example of Dining Service Productivity Monitoring

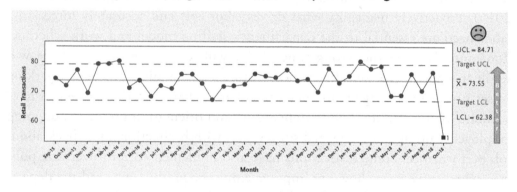

Note: LCL = lower control limit; UCL = upper control limit; X = central line.

STRATEGIES TO IMPROVE RECRUITMENT AND RETENTION

Foodservice workers contribute to the healthcare institution's mission to provide safe and quality care. The work is physically demanding, with long hours seven days a week, and requires strict attention to details. Qualified staffing is one of the top challenges of foodservice operators (Association for Healthcare Foodservice 2020). A 2017 Retention Report conducted by the Work Institute concluded that 75 percent of the causes of employee turnover are preventable (Bolden-

Barrett 2017). Thus, foodservice leaders must intentionally strategize to maximize employee recruitment, retention, and development.

Hiring and Onboarding Process

The Center for Hospitality Research at Cornell University reported the cost of staff training as just about 25 percent of the total expense of replacing an employee, and the cost of staff turnover as high as $5,864 per employee (Jaffee 2016). FNS leaders therefore must collaborate with Human Resources to develop recruitment, hiring, and development strategies that focus on hiring the right candidate who is coachable and a good cultural fit. Exhibit 9.9 provides an example of a comprehensive and collaborative recruitment process. The department must deliberately invest in staff training and development, starting with its onboarding process. The training should be hardwired into the departmental culture and can be done during staff huddles, or via communication using platforms such as visual boards (e.g., bulletin boards, whiteboards, e-blackboards), newsletters, emails, and meetings. Managers should be intentional with employee encounters by establishing regular manager and employee touchpoints throughout the probationary period to ensure expectations and needs are being met.

Competitive Compensation

Wages are a determining factor for job satisfaction and influence an employee's decision to join or leave an organization. Research has shown that wage is one of the most important categories contributing to job satisfaction in the service industry (Miller 2016). FNS leaders therefore must advocate for competitive employee wages and benefits. Competitive compensation will minimize turnover, given that employees will transfer to a competitor for as little as an additional $0.25 per hour. To retain staff, advocate for additional benefits such as night and weekend differentials, tuition assistance, and free or discounted meals.

Employee Engagement

Create a culture of caring where employees are aligned, recognized, and motivated to serve patients, customers, and each other. Department leaders should start by building trust and fostering a growth mindset that enables each employee to learn and stretch their potential beyond their current role. This process will help employees find value in their work and be aligned with the mission.

Exhibit 9.9: Example of a Food and Nutrition Services Recruiting Process

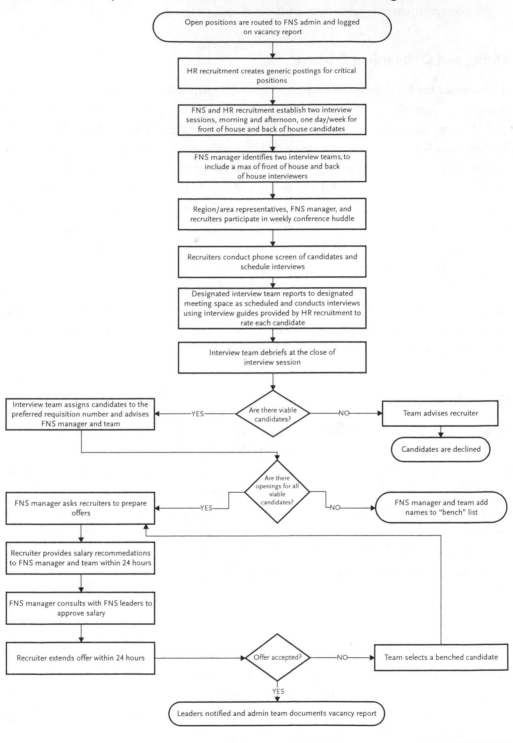

KEY REGULATORY ISSUES

FNS is heavily regulated by federal, state, and local ordinances. As mentioned, CMS is a federal regulatory agency of the US Department of Health and Human Services, which administers the Medicare program. CMS monitors hospitals' compliance with CoPs and Conditions for Coverage (Academy of Nutrition and Dietetics 2020). CMS surveys healthcare institutions for compliance using its *State Operations Manual*. Healthcare institutions must be 100 percent compliant with the minimum requirements for safety 100 percent of the time. CMS provides deemed status to other organizations, such as The Joint Commission and Det Norske Veritas, to perform regulatory inspections for safety and quality. Additionally, the pressure for high performance was heightened with the federally mandated Hospital Consumer Assessment of Healthcare Providers and Systems, which standardized patients' hospital ratings. The CMS Food and Dietetics CoPs requirements are also fully integrated into many other CoPs such as IC, QAPI, EH&S, and Emergency Management, to name a few. FNS directors must complete a crosswalk of all the CMS CoPs with TJC or DNV standards to ensure compliance and a deeper understanding of the required standards.

Disasters and emergencies come in all forms and sizes, small to large, and on the local, state, or national level. The FNS Department must have plans and processes in place to readily provide meal service to patients, staff, and stakeholders during disasters. State and local requirements may vary, but it is always best practice to have a minimum of four days of food and potable water on hand. Water needs should be estimated at one gallon per person per day, and food at three meals and a substantial snack. Regulations and food trends, along with diversity among patients, customers, and employees with varying expectations, have added a level of complexity to the delivery of emergency meals. The department must have emergency feeding and business continuity plans in place to provide nourishing meals and snacks in a safe environment.

FNS must also have a robust sanitation program that is integrated into the institution's QAPI program. In many organizations, FNS reports its safety and quality improvement initiatives and performance metrics through the IC or Safety committees. Exhibit 9.10 provides some examples of performance metrics for kitchen safety, cleaning, and sanitation. The sanitation program must meet federal, state, and local regulatory guidelines and ordinances for safety, proper cleaning, sanitation, and infection procedures to prevent foodborne illnesses. Kitchen cleanliness is crucial to ensure a pathogen- and pest-free environment that meets regulatory standards. The FNS Department must also have routine unannounced inspections by a registered sanitarian from the county, city, or state.

Exhibit 9.10: Sample Metrics for Kitchen Safety, Cleaning, and Sanitation

Metrics and goals	Metric selection rationale	Responsible party	Method of data collection	Benchmark source
Achieve 100% compliance with hand hygiene and isolation procedures during patient delivery	Regulatory and food safety	Room service manager	Weekly	Internal
Achieve >95% compliance with food safety standards during receiving, storage, preparation, and service of food	Regulatory and food safety	Registered sanitarian	Monthly	Internal
Achieve 100% compliance with dock audits, and designated kitchen area audits relating to Infection Control	Regulatory and food safety	Executive chef and infection control liaison	Daily	Internal

KEY TERMS FOR FOOD AND NUTRITION SERVICES

Balanced scorecard: A strategic performance management tool managers use to track execution of activities within their control and monitor performance arising from these actions.

Benchmark: The practice of comparing business processes and performance metrics to industry standards and best practices from other companies.

Business continuity: The process of creating systems of prevention and recovery to deal with potential emergencies and threats to a business.

Emergency plan: The organization and management of resources and responsibilities for dealing with all aspects of emergencies.

Metric: A measure of quantitative assessment commonly used for comparing and tracking performance or production.

Outsource: When one company hires another to be responsible for a planned or existing activity that is or could be done internally.

Self-operated: Describes foodservice operations that are "in house"—that is, managed by the healthcare facility's own staff.

Service-level agreement: An arrangement between an internal customer and the FNS team that sets performance expectations for work to be done by both parties. The two groups negotiate and agree on satisfactory measurable outcomes for the services to be monitored and reported.

REFERENCES

Academy of Nutrition and Dietetics. 2020. "Centers for Medicare and Medicaid Services." Accessed September 2. www.eatrightpro.org/practice/quality-management/national-quality-accreditation-and-regulations/centers-for-medicare-and-medicaid-services.

Association for Healthcare Foodservice. 2020. "Publications and Newsletters." Accessed September 2. www.healthcarefoodservice.org/resources/publications.

BC Cook Articulation Committee. 2015. "Managing Labor Costs." In *Introduction to Food Production and Service,* edited by B. Egan. University Park, PA: Pennsylvania State University Open Resource Publishing.

Bolden-Barrett, V. 2017. "Study: Turnover Costs Employers $15,000 per Worker." *HR Dive.* Published August 11. www.hrdive.com/news/study-turnover-costs-employers-15000-per-worker/449142/.

FSD Staff. 2016. "2016 Healthcare Census: Hospitals Raise Their Game." Published May 16. www.foodservicedirector.com/operations/2016-healthcare-census-hospitals-raise-their-game.

Gregoire, M. B., and M. L. Theis. 2015. "Practice Paper of the Academy of Nutrition and Dietetics: Principles of Productivity in Food and Nutrition Services: Applications in the 21st Century Health Care Reform Era." *Journal of the Academy of Nutrition and Dietetics* 115 (7): 1141–47.

Jaffee, A. I. 2016. "The Real Cost of Restaurant Staff Turnover: $146,000/Annually." *The Rail.* Accessed September 2, 2020. www.therail.media/stories/2016/3/17/hidden-costs-restaurant-staff-turnover.

McCray, S., K. Maunder, R. Krikowa, and K. MacKenzie-Shalders. 2018. "Room Service Improves Nutritional Intake and Increases Patient Satisfaction While Decreasing Food Waste and Cost." *Journal of the Academy of Nutrition and Dietetics* 118 (2): 284–93.

Miller, S. 2016. "Better Pay and Benefits Loom Large in Job Satisfaction." Society for Human Resources Management. Published April 26. www.shrm.org/resourcesandtools/hr-topics/compensation/pages/pay-benefits-satisfaction.aspx.

CHAPTER 10

Health Information Management

Elit Gonzalez

DEPARTMENT DESCRIPTION

The Health Information Management (HIM) Department is responsible for managing and protecting patient health information. The American Health Information Management Association (AHIMA) describes it as "the practice of acquiring, analyzing, and protecting digital and traditional medical information vital to providing quality patient care" (AHIMA 2020). HIM staff review, process, maintain, store, and release electronic and paper health records. Protecting and preserving the integrity of patient health records is crucial to the quality and continuum of patient care. HIM roles and responsibilities have changed significantly in the past 30 years. HIM was formerly known as the "the Medical Records department," staff were called librarians, and finding a patient file entailed searching index cards in cabinets, similar to a library book catalog. Today, "the HIM field is comprised of business, science and information technology" (AHIMA 2020).

HIM positions range from frontline staff to leadership roles. HIM associates must work with various electronic systems and have basic knowledge of medical terminology and of anatomy and physiology. Preferred HIM credentials are the Registered Health Information Technician (RHIT) or Registered Health Information Administrator (RHIA) certifications. Project managers, data analysts, project analysts, and medical record audit staff require a bachelor's degree and preferred RHIA credential. Clinical documentation specialists require a bachelor's degree in HIM or RN, and a preferred RHIT, RHIA, or coding certification such as Certified Coding Specialist (CCS). In most organizations an HIM associate director requires a bachelor's degree or higher and a preferred RHIA credential, and an HIM director requires a master's degree or higher and an RHIA preferred. Along with credentials, experience in HIM functions is a plus.

KEY DEPARTMENT SERVICES

A larger, more comprehensive HIM Department may include the following teams and services:

- Document Imaging: Retrieves, preps, scans, indexes, and performs quality assurance checks on paper and electronically imported inpatient, outpatient, and external patient medical record documents for uploading into the electronic health record (EHR). Some Document Imaging teams use Workstations on Wheels to process paper documents on inpatient and outpatient units instead of in the HIM Department.
- Deficiency Tracking: Ensures patient medical records are complete, including but not limited to the presence and authentication of discharge summaries, history and physicals (H&Ps), progress notes, consultations, physician orders, emergency provider notes, and open encounters (outpatient encounters); and assigns deficiencies for missing documentation.
- Medical Record Audit: Performs structured audits of possible missing elements in the content of patient healthcare documentation as required by various regulatory agencies and hospital policies. Audits include, but are not limited to, death note, autopsy consents, release of remains, universal protocol, anesthesia consent, surgical consent, procedure consent, consent to diagnose and treat, research consent, blood consent, chemotherapy consent, moderate sedation consent, required elements of H&Ps, and discharge summary. Audit findings are entered in a database and reported to quality officers, the Medical Records Committee, The Joint Commission, other stakeholders and committees, and any other requesting regulatory agencies.
- Clinical Documentation Improvement (CDI): Reviews clinical documentation and provides feedback to physicians that improves documentation (Shearwater Health 2020). In simpler terms: Medical Coding 101 says, "You can only code what you can document." CDI 101 says, "Let's fill in the gaps of what's documented so we can code better." Documentation queries are sent for additional information that may promote coding success. Based on clinical indicators in the record and clarity of documentation, queries may affect the diagnosis-related group and case mix index, severity of illness, or risk of mortality for the hospitalization.
- Data Integrity: Comprises data analysts who perform a variety of job functions, including but not limited to making EHR chart corrections and

merging duplicate patient medical-record numbers (MRNs); assisting EHR users (providers, clinical support, internal, and external) in navigating the EHR and instructing them how to make their own corrections; working with EHR information technology (IT) teams to troubleshoot various issues; handling special projects or requests that require abstracting and presenting data; and managing or maintaining downtime and daily paper patient-care forms.

- Release of Information (ROI): Releases patient health information critical to the quality and continuity of care provided to the patient. ROI also plays an important role in providing the information needed for billing, reporting, research, legal proceedings, and other requests for patient health information.

- Coding: According to the American Academy of Professional Coders (2020), coding provides the transformation of healthcare diagnosis, procedures, medical services, and equipment into universal alphanumeric medical codes. The diagnoses and procedure codes are taken from medical record documentation, such as transcription of physician's notes, laboratory and radiologic results, and so forth. Coding is still present in some HIM environments; however, a more recent trend is for coding to fall under the umbrella of the chief financial officer (CFO) for the revenue cycle instead of HIM.

DEPARTMENT ORGANIZATIONAL STRUCTURES

A HIM Department's organizational structure will depend on the size of the healthcare facility and whether it is using an EHR. A smaller facility may be able to function with one director or manager and two to five staff to perform HIM job functions depending on the services and volumes it provides. In a larger facility (e.g., 500+ beds), the HIM Department may have a director, associate director, three or four managers, and a support staff of 60 or more full-time equivalents (FTEs), possibly more for even larger facilities. (See exhibit 10.1 for an example of an HIM organizational chart that includes Coding.) However, Coding often reports to the CFO for the revenue cycle. Because of the various services HIM provides in most hospitals, the HIM director may report to one of the following executives and departments: the chief operating officer, Inpatient Medical Practice; the CFO, Finance; the chief nursing officer, Nursing; or the chief information officer, Information Technology.

Exhibit 10.1: Sample Organizational Chart with Coding in HIM

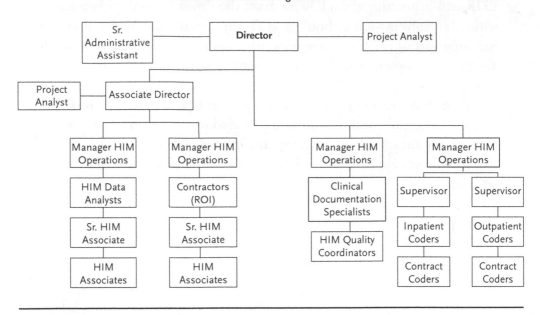

Note: HIM = Health Information Management; ROI = release of information.

KEY CUSTOMERS AND THEIR PERFORMANCE EXPECTATIONS

HIM's key customers are patients, their families, caregivers, providers, ancillary staff, legal, and compliance. Customers expect a timely, accurate, and complete patient care record to be available in the EHR. Patients request the release of their patient information for the continuum of care, patient care benefits, payment, and legal proceedings, and they expect the requests to be fulfilled in a timely fashion. Providers, caregivers, multidisciplinary teams, and researchers expect patient information to be available in the EHR to treat the patient accurately and efficiently. See exhibit 10.2 for an example of customers and the services HIM provides.

Exhibit 10.2: Examples of HIM Customers and Services Provided

Customer	HIM services provided
Patient	• Release of information • Assistance with EHR portal (access/opt out) • Assist with amendments to patient records per patient request

(continued)

Customer	HIM services provided
Patient's family	• Release of information
Provider	• Timely processing of paper or electronic records, including timely uploading of external documents for new patient referrals for provider to review • Assist with completing chart, including but not limited to tracking chart deficiencies, CDI queries, and audit results for improved documentation • Help troubleshoot EHR
Ancillary staff	• Timely processing of MRN merges • Timely processing of paper or electronic records • Help troubleshoot EHR
Legal/compliance	• Assist with amendments to patient records per legal or patient's request
Regulatory agencies	• Provide patient health records as requested for review
External facilities	• Prep or import and process electronic and paper medical records in a timely manner for immediate viewing in the EHR

Note: CDI = clinical documentation improvement; EHR = electronic health record; HIM = health information management; MRN = medical record number.

KEY PROCESS FLOWS

HIM departments are multidimensional, with numerous key process flows for their top services. See exhibit 10.3 for HIM Department areas and process flow descriptions.

KEY UNITS OF WORK AND VOLUME STATISTICS TO MONITOR

Key units of work (KUoW) are used to track and monitor key HIM services. KUoW help track trends over time, such as changes in volumes of work compared with FTEs per unit of work over months and years. This information should be very transparent and communicated monthly to leadership and at least quarterly to all HIM staff. An example of some KUoW used in HIM are number of medical record audits, document images processed, CDI reviews, release of information requests processed, duplicate MRNs merged, and chart corrections processed. Exhibit 10.4 is an example of KUoW for number of document images processed for a period of five years (the numbers are sample data). Please note the number of document image FTEs is set at 20; realistically, however, this number would fluctuate with new hires, retirements, resignations, terminations, and the like.

Exhibit 10.3: HIM Department Areas and Process Flow Descriptions

Area	Process flow description
Document Imaging	Retrieves paper and electronically imported patient records; preps, scans, indexes, and performs quality assurance; and stores patient records.
Deficiency Tracking	Performs a retrospective analysis and reviews patient records for missing or unauthenticated documentation using EHR work queues; marks records as deficient/delinquent; tracks and completes deficiencies; and sends notifications of delinquency.
Medical Record Audit	Performs concurrent and retrospective analysis and custom audits, reviews patient documentation, documents and reports missing documentation or missing required elements.
Clinical Documentation Improvement	Reviews patient records and queries physicians to provide accurate and complete documentation, to improve documentation and report query rates.
Data Integrity	Performs chart corrections, merges duplicate patient medical record numbers, and troubleshoots other EHR issues. Manages patient care forms.
Release of Information	Receives information release requests from various requestors, and fulfills requests by mailing, emailing, exporting to online patient portals, or faxing requested documents.

Exhibit 10.4 allows leadership to easily trend data discrepancies using charts and graphs. An example of such trending is exhibit 10.5, which shows the number of processed document images decreased in March and April 2016. The exhibit indicates that the significant decrease was attributed to the implementation of an EHR and post-EHR event.

Exhibit 10.6 shows a steady trend of documents imaged per imaging FTE per working day for 12 months that consistently fall between the upper and lower control limits. Holiday and summer months show a slight decrease, which is expected based on previous years.

KEY METRICS TO MONITOR: PEOPLE, SERVICE, QUALITY/SAFETY, FINANCIAL

Basing scorecards on a fiscal year defines and helps track HIM's key metrics for People, Service, Quality/Safety, and Financial. Exhibit 10.7 is an example of key metrics for the HIM Department. The People category helps track employee

Exhibit 10.4: Sample Health and Information Management Key Units of Work

	HIM KUoW												
Purpose: Monitor volume of key units of work for each department													
Measure	**Sept**	**Oct**	**Nov**	**Dec**	**Jan**	**Feb**	**Mar**	**Apr**	**May**	**Jun**	**Jul**	**Aug**	**Sept**
FY15	12,72,605	12,72,605	10,88,191	12,25,708	12,23,714	11,92,019	12,72,404	12,57,426	11,9,094	12,57,426	13,47,509	12,14,958	12,14,958
FY16	14,22,880	13,86,836	12,62,540	13,14,819	12,05,343	12,95,220	3,83,307	1,95,982	11,22,651	13,75,796	15,26,113	12,84,328	12,84,328
FY17	7,20,324	6,70,090	9,28,701	9,93,438	8,52,459	7,84,181	8,82,554	7,47,774	7,59,069	7,80,682	7,28,157	6,19,678	6,19,678
FY18	5,41,836	7,08,004	5,86,394	7,06,004	7,20,339	8,05,057	7,86,997	7,18,576	7,96,506	8,12,826	8,23,797	8,54,958	8,54,958
FY19	7,99,449	9,54,378	8,41,856	7,81,385	9,48,214	9,23,844	8,89,340	9,72,580	8,90,961	8,52,926	8,92,353	9,50,905	9,50,905
% Change in volume (FY18 to FY19)	148%	135%	144%	111%	132%	115%	113%	135%	112%	105%	108%	111%	111%
Number of Document Images Processed													
FY19 # of DocImgFTEs	20	20	20	20	20	20	20	20	20	20	20	20	20
FY19 # of working days	19	23	22	19	21	20	21	22	22	20	22	22	22
FY19 Docs Imaged per FTE per day	2,104	2,075	1,913	2,056	2,258	2,310	2,117	2,210	2,025	2,132	2,028	2,161	2,161
FY19 Control Line (mean)	2,130	2,130	2,130	2,130	2,130	2,130	2,130	2,130	2,130	2,130	2,130	2,130	2,130
FY19 Upper Control Line	2,509	2,509	2,509	2,509	2,509	2,509	2,509	2,509	2,509	2,509	2,509	2,509	2,509
FY19 Lower Control Line	1,752	1,752	1,752	1,752	1,752	1,752	1,752	1,752	1,752	1,752	1,752	1,752	1,752

Note: FTE = full-time equivalent.

Exhibit 10.5: Sample Data Derived from 5 Years of Key Units of Work Trends

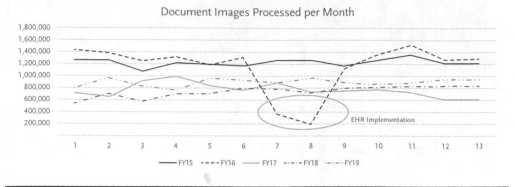

Document Images Processed per Month

Exhibit 10.6: Sample Monthly Control Chart

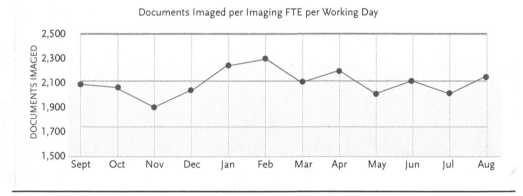

Documents Imaged per Imaging FTE per Working Day

recognition, promotions, turnover, and training with regard to their health, safety, or personal development. The Service category focuses on customer service and turnaround times. The Quality/Safety category measures the quality of key services provided by HIM; some quality measures reflect internal processes and others external. Last, the Financial category tracks personnel and operating expenses to ensure HIM is on track with budgeted expenses. Tracking these types of metrics monthly aids a department in planning, trending, reporting, and adjusting as needed to keep itself running optimally and efficiently.

KEY INFORMATICS ISSUES

HIM departments are fortunate to have an expansive understanding not only of HIM, but also of most clinical, inpatient, and ancillary areas and their workflow processes. New technology, healthcare innovation, and the introduction

Exhibit 10.7: Scorecard—People, Service, Quality/Safety, and Financial

Scorecard
HEALTH INFORMATION MANAGEMENT

	Metric	Under-performing	Threshold	Target	Stretch	Sept	Oct	Nov
PEOPLE								
P1	**Employee Recognition Letters:** # of recognition letters given	0		≥1				
P2	**Year-to-Date Turnover:** % of staff who (voluntarily + nonvoluntarily) left the institution during the fiscal year	≥4	3%–4%	1%–2%	≤-%			
P3	**First-Year Turnover Rate:** % of staff who (voluntarily + nonvoluntarily) left the institution less than 1 year from the date of hire				≤1%			
P4	**Employee Development:** # of employees attending an in-person employee development course (online or in person)	<2	2–3	4	>4			
SERVICE								
S1	**Timely processing of merges:** Average time elapsed from receipt of request to completion	≥3 days	2 days	1 day	<1 day			
S2	**Timely processing of ROI requests:** Time elapsed from receipt of request to availability	>10 days	6–10 days	5 days	<5 days			
S3	**% of all document imaging processed within 24 hours:** Time elapsed from scan to availability	<50%	50%–69%	70%–79%	>80%			
QUALITY								
Q1	**Medical Record Delinquency Rate:** % of delinquent medical records	>50%	50%–16%	15%–2%	<1%			

(continued)

Exhibit 10.7: Scorecard—People, Service, Quality/Safety, and Financial (continued)

Scorecard
HEALTH INFORMATION MANAGEMENT

	Metric	Under-performing	Threshold	Target	Stretch	Sept	Oct	Nov
Q2	**CDI % of admissions reviewed by CDI specialists within 48 hours:** # of reviews including initial DRG within 48 hours of the admission order / # of admissions	<60%	60%–69%	70%–79%	≥80%			
Q3	**CDI Provider Query Response Rate:** Total # of provider responses / total # of queries sent	<70%	70%–79%	80%–89%	≥90%			
Q4	**Patient Safety and High Reliability:** Number of HIM patient mismatches identified and corrected before published to EHR	>200	100–200	<100	0			
Q5	**Vendor Dashboard:** Completed monthly vendor tracking	<5		5				
Q6	**Audits and Regulatory Requirements:** % compliance with contingent worker's HR files	*Performance ranges under development*						
FINANCE								
F1	**KUoW Team Productivity:** # of KUoW metrics achieving productivity goals	<3		3				
F2	**Personnel Expense Variance YTD**	>Budget		≤Budget				
F3	**Other Operating Expense Variance YTD**	>Budget		≤Budget				
F4	**Total Operating Expense Variance YTD:** Personnel Expense + Other Operating Expense (Department Financial Goal)	>Budget		≤Budget				
F5	**Operating Income/Loss Variance YTD:** % Variance Actual to Budget	−5% to +5%	−5% to +5%	−4% to +4%	−3% to +3%			

Note: CDI = Clinical Documentation Improvement; DRG = diagnosis-related group; KUoW = key unit of work; ROI = release of information.

and implementation of very robust EHRs provide new opportunities for HIM. New roles, job functions, and teams need to be developed to meet these innovative needs in healthcare support. For example, once a healthcare institution has selected an EHR vendor, HIM must ensure its representation at the table when the planning phase of the EHR project commences.

For instance, the HIM team needs to ensure the EHR not only meets user and patient care needs, but also complies with HIM workflow processes. The EHR needs to have a good system for tracking deficient charts and must be able to integrate with a good document management system for scanning, importing, and storing patient healthcare images. Coding and auditing need to be robust, and CDI and ROI modules both must meet HIM needs. HIM will have many decisions to make: for example, who in HIM will be involved in software development, training, and implementation? Who will ensure that users understand how everything works, such as new workflows? Additionally, EHRs must undergo significant testing before adoption to guarantee the product meets HIM user needs. One key step before implementing an EHR is to clean up the current master patient index as much as possible before transferring this information to the new EHR so past problems are not repeated in the new electronic index. Also, with the implementation of an EHR, the department in charge of a certain function may no longer be the department responsible for this same function in the new EHR. Job functions will be reevaluated before implementing an EHR, so departments must be prepared to take on new roles and maybe even lose current roles to another department. For example, merging MRNs, which before EHR implementation had been the responsibility of Patient Access/Registration eMPI IT support, could get reassigned to HIM afterward. "HIM professionals are the experts at preserving data integrity, whether it's staying on top of duplicates and overlays in EHRs, managing the master patient index, or acting as strong stewards of data by monitoring core clinical systems" (Butler 2018).

Part of the EHR implementation process is to train superusers and provide them with the expertise they need to train others in their specific EHR module. HIM leadership must ensure that HIM employees selected as superusers are technologically proficient, knowledgeable, and skilled trainers. HIM superusers are responsible for training and providing support to other HIM staff on their respective EHR modules before, during, and after EHR launch. Therefore, skilled superusers must be chosen to ensure the necessary training for HIM staff and a successful EHR implementation.

When new EHRs are launched, there will be a steep learning curve when the system goes live that will last for months. A best practice is to establish an HIM Data Integrity team that includes data analysts who can serve as the initial point of contact for EHR corrections. End users from all healthcare disciplines will need assistance in correcting EHR errors after launch. The HIM Data Integrity team should have the same troubleshooting tools as IT staff assigned to work on the EHR to assist customers. For example, the HIM Data Integrity team needs a support environment application to troubleshoot end user issues and various chart correction tools to fix the issues. A knowledgeable and skilled HIM Data Integrity team can be at the forefront, assisting in troubleshooting key informatics issues and providing valuable input to resolve issues.

The EHR is a valuable tool for patient care, especially with the added value of Health Information Exchange (HIE). HIE is the electronic health information exchange that allows doctors, nurses, pharmacists, other healthcare providers, and patients to appropriately access and securely share a patient's vital medical information electronically (Health IT 2020). However, the EHR can also result in physician burnout and residents and fellows documenting around the clock. For example, before the EHR, physicians and residents could dictate their notes by speaking into a phone from anywhere (office, car, home). A transcriptionist would type the notes and make any corrections, and the notes would appear in the patient's chart. Today, most EHRs have voice recognition software, where providers dictate into the EHR system; but if there are errors in the dictation, the provider has to make the corrections, which can be time consuming.

Many users think that after the EHR is launched, most of the "paper" issues will be fixed. Indeed, some of the issues formerly encountered with paper records will be eliminated or decline with the implementation of EHR. For example, patient records used to be collected in file folders that were filled with paper and separated by document-type identification tabs. These folders were filed on HIM Department shelves using systems such as terminal digit order, straight filing, or middle digit, depending on the facility. Some facilities even used patient Social Security numbers to file patient paper charts (today a HIPAA violation). These files could become large enough to be broken into volumes and often were stored off-site because HIM departments lacked the storage space. Adopting EHR has helped HIM departments significantly reduce spending on paper, file folders, storage (both internal and external), and other supplies needed for the filing process.

However, EHRs will never eliminate human-created issues such as duplicate MRNs and accidentally documenting in the wrong patient's chart. HIM professionals are well prepared to resolve this new set of issues because of the profession's knowledge and training in health information technology. In the case of duplicate MRNs, algorithms exist that can help identify potential duplicates, but this process still requires a human to review and correct the case. The prevalence of duplicate records in most hospitals has been generally estimated between 5 percent to 10 percent of all stored records (Harris and Houser 2018). EHRs can provide duplicate MRN reports using algorithms and user reporting that can help HIM track and trend the source of the issues creating such duplicates. HIM can then provide extensive training to those areas and reduce the duplicate rate to less than 1 percent. The formula used to determine the potential duplicate rate is the following:

$$\frac{\text{Total \# of duplicate patient records} \times 100}{\text{Total \# of patient records in database}} = \text{MRN Duplicate Rate}$$

STAFFING MODELS

Staffing models will vary by size of facility and services provided. Some factors to consider for a smaller facility (<100 beds) that may drive staff size and services provided include the following. Are patient health records paper based, hybrid (paper and electronic), or electronic? Is the HIM Department located on-site, off-site, or both? Will coding and CDI report to HIM or the revenue cycle? A typical smaller hospital may be able to staff with one director or manager and two to five FTEs. If the hospital has paper medical records, three to five FTEs may be needed depending on the volume of paper that needs processing. If the hospital has a hybrid or fully functional EHR, then two to three FTEs should suffice. The functions of a typical smaller HIM department include processing and maintaining the patient health record, release of information services, deficiency tracking, and coding.

A larger hospital (>500 beds) typically needs to provide more services with additional staff. Such hospitals most likely will have fully functional EHRs, which eliminates the need to process paper charts. The services of a typical larger hospital include processing and maintaining the EHR, Deficiency Tracking, Medical Record Audits, CDI, ROI, Data Integrity, and Coding if not under the revenue cycle. Please see exhibit 10.8 for an example of plausible staffing in some areas for a hospital with more than 500 beds.

PRODUCTIVITY MODELS, INCLUDING WORK-TO-STAFF RATIOS AND INDUSTRY PERFORMANCE TARGETS

Productivity models for most HIM areas are calculated from an eight-hour day with seven hours of productive time. One hour is subtracted to allow for breaks and other unproductive time. Calculations for productivity expected for a typical month can vary by institution and volume of work. Typical productivity targets based on volume of work are listed in exhibit 10.8. The areas referenced in the exhibit are calculated from historical and current experience from data that has been extracted from productivity reports and compared with several comparable local and national hospitals.

Exhibit 10.8: Sample Staffing Model for a Hospital with 500+ Beds

Team	Volume	Productivity target (based on 7 productive hours/day)	Number of FTEs
Document Imaging	800,000 images (M) 36,350 images (D)	230–260	20
Deficiency Tracking	8,000 deficiencies (M) 365 deficiencies (D)	14–15	4
Medical Record Audit	660+ audits (M) 30–40 audits (D)	2–3 Varies by audit type	4
Clinical Documentation Improvement	4,200 reviews (M) 190–200 reviews (D)	2–3	10
Data Integrity	440 MRN merges (M) 20 MRN merges (D) 250 chart corrections (M) 10–11 chart corrections (D) 300 interface error checks (M) 14 interface error checks (D)	3–4	2
Release of Information	5,000 ROI (M) 230 ROI (D)	4–5	8

Note: D = daily; M = per month; MRN = medical record number; ROI = release of information.

STRATEGIES TO IMPROVE RECRUITMENT AND RETENTION

When hiring an HIM employee, the interviewer needs to ask the appropriate questions for the particular position. With the multiple titles in HIM areas, the interviewer must confirm that the candidate has the suitable degree and credentials:

- An HIM associate whose functions include processing, retrieving, tracking, and maintaining documents associated with managing health information should have three years of HIM experience; the RHIT certification is preferred but not required.
- A senior HIM associate, who assists with the coordination and oversight of HIM associates, should have an associate's degree and three years of HIM or healthcare experience. An RHIT or RHIA certification is preferred but can be substituted with five or more years of experience in HIM that includes leading teams.

- A CDI specialist, whose primary responsibility is to promote appropriate clinical documentation in the patient's medical record, should have a bachelor's degree in HIM or nursing; either a CCS, RHIT, or RHIA certification; five years of clinical coding or nursing experience; and, preferably, a Certified Clinical Documentation and Improvement credential.
- A medical record quality coordinator (also known as a medical record auditor), responsible for collecting, analyzing, and reporting data quality, should have three years of HIM experience, a bachelor's degree in HIM or nursing, and one of the following preferred credentials: RHIT, RHIA, Certified Professional in Healthcare Quality, or Certified Professional Medical Auditor.
- An HIM project analyst, who leads projects to support improvement of operational and financial performance in HIM functional areas, should have at least five years of HIM experience and a bachelor's degree in HIM or healthcare administration.
- An HIM operations manager should have at least four years of HIM experience with at least three years of supervisory experience; a bachelor's degree in healthcare, business, or a related field; and an RHIT or RHIA preferred credential.
- An HIM associate director should have at least five years of management experience, a bachelor's degree in HIM or healthcare, and an RHIT or RHIA credential, with a master's degree in HIM, healthcare administration, or health informatics preferred.
- An HIM Director should have three to five years of HIM and management experience and a master's degree, plus an RHIA or other healthcare or informatics credential.

The HIM Director should regularly evaluate competition in the local market for HIM candidates. The director needs to ensure that the hospital remains competitive in pay and employee benefits with annual cost of living increases. The leadership team must be knowledgeable and passionate about HIM to improve employee morale and turnover rates. Employee morale plays a major factor in employee retention. A toxic working environment can cause good and even long-term reputable employees to quit. "According to many sources, a bad boss is the number one reason people quit their jobs" (Heathfield 2019). To boost retention, HIM leaders should offer growth opportunities (e.g., professional development courses) and empower employees to solve issues in their areas of expertise to use their skills to the fullest. Given that many HIM staff work behind the scenes in the healthcare setting, where their contributions may not be acknowledged by members of the care team, providing robust employee recognition is a must. To keep employees engaged, HIM leadership should be sure to celebrate department successes.

KEY REGULATORY ISSUES

Various federal, state, and internal bodies guide HIM practices. The external accrediting agencies, such as The Joint Commission, the Centers for Medicare & Medicaid Services (CMS), and the US Food and Drug Administration (FDA), each have standards used to survey or audit healthcare institutions. The Joint Commission surveys hospitals every three years, and one of its primary foci is information management, where HIM is highly involved. Information must be timely and accurate, with all required documentation and elements therein present, and provider delinquency rates low (Joint Commission 2020). CMS can survey a hospital at any time. For example, if a complaint incident has been reported to the CMS, it may conduct a thorough investigation immediately. Some examples of CMS Conditions of Participation that pertain to HIM are that medical record service organization and staffing, form and retention of records, and content of record (including all medical record entries) must be legible, complete, dated, timed, and authenticated, in addition to the actual content of the medical record (Customs Mobile Regulations 2020). The FDA also conducts frequent audits of patient health information. Most facilities have an Institutional Review Board, and it is routine for the FDA to frequently audit the Research Department on their clinical trials. According to the FDA, they conduct clinical investigator inspections to determine if the investigators are conducting clinical studies in compliance with applicable statutory and regulatory requirements. Researchers who conduct FDA-regulated clinical investigations are required to permit FDA inspectors to access, copy, and verify any records or reports made by clinical investigators regarding the disposition of the investigational product and participants' case histories, among other records. Additionally, HIM adheres to the Health Insurance Portability and Accountability Act (HIPAA) relating to privacy and patients' rights to access medical records (FDA 2010).

HIPAA stipulates important regulatory standards for privacy. HIM employees are required to take a HIPAA patient privacy and security course once a year to remind them of the importance of protecting health information. HIM staff are privy to all patient health information; therefore, staff of all levels must know the importance of keeping patient information confidential at all times. In some cases, accessing a patient's record with no business need, or breaching a patient's record, could result in fines, termination, and even imprisonment. The Privacy Rule requires HIPAA-covered entities to provide patients access to their patient health information (PHI), including the patient's right to review or obtain a copy of it (Health Information Privacy Division 2020). The HIM Department plays a vital role in providing patients' PHI. Requests for medical records come through the department by phone, fax, electronic health portals, or in person. HIM release of information personnel must stay abreast of all regulatory requirements when releasing PHI.

The main internal hospital committee whose adherence to regulatory and institutional policies HIM supports is the medical staff's Medical Record Committee (MRC). Ideally, the MRC is a multidisciplinary team that includes a physician or clinical representative from each clinical and inpatient area. Other beneficial members should come from Nursing, Information Technology, Legal, Compliance, Internal Communications, and other ancillary departments and clinical support services. The MRC enforces Medical Staff Rules and Bylaws and other rules and regulations.

KEY TERMS FOR HEALTH INFORMATION MANAGEMENT

Certified Coding Specialist: One of many coding credentials.

Electronic health record: An electronic version of the patient's medical history obtained over time; these have replaced paper medical records.

Health information management: The practice of managing and maintaining the integrity and completeness of patient health records, paper and electronic, to ensure quality patient care.

Health information technology: Electronic systems used to store, share, and analyze health information.

Health Insurance Portability and Accountability Act: Passed by Congress in 1996, it requires the protection and confidential handling of protected health information.

Hybrid record: A combination of an electronic and paper health record.

Registered Health Information Administrator: Earned after obtaining a bachelor's degree in health information administration (HIA) and passing a national HIA certification exam.

Registered Health Information Technician: Earned after obtaining an associate's degree in HIT and passing a national HIT certification exam.

Support environment: An exact copy of the EHR's production environment, commonly used by IT and HIM staff to initially troubleshoot issues when assisting EHR users such as physicians and nursing.

Workstations on Wheels: A cart with a laptop and portable scanner that HIM uses to prep and scan paper medical records outside of the HIM Department (i.e., on inpatient units).

REFERENCES

American Academy of Professional Coders. 2020. "What Is Medical Coding?" Accessed September 3. www.aapc.com/medical-coding/medical-coding.aspx.

American Health Information Management Association (AHIMA). 2020. "What Is Health Information?" Accessed September 3. www.ahima.org/careers/healthinfo.

Butler, M. 2018. "Ensuring Data Integrity During Health Information Exchange." *Journal of AHIMA* 89 (10): 14–17.

Customs Mobile Regulations. 2020. "Condition of Participation: Medical Record Services. Standard: Content of Record." CFR § 482.24. Accessed September 3. www.customsmobile.com/regulations/expand/title42_chapterIV_part482_subpartC_section482.24#title42_chapterIV_part482_subpartC_section482.24.

Harris, S., and S. H. Houser. 2018. "Double Trouble—Using Health Informatics to Tackle Duplicate Medical Record Issues." *Journal of AHIMA* 89 (8): 20–23.

Health Information Privacy Division. 2020. "Individuals' Rights Under HIPAA to Access Their Information 45 CFR § 164.524." Accessed September 3. www.hhs.gov/hipaa/for-professionals/privacy/guidance/access/index.html.

Health IT. 2020. "What Is HIE?" Accessed September 3. www.healthit.gov/topic/health-it-and-health-information-exchange-basics/what-hie.

Heathfield, S. M. 2019. "Top 10 Reasons Why Employees Quit Their Jobs: A Checklist for the Retention of Your Talented Employees." Balance Careers. Published December 9. www.thebalancecareers.com/top-reasons-why-employees-quit-their-job-1918985.

Joint Commission. 2020. "Facts About The Joint Commission." Accessed September 3. www.jointcommission.org/about-us/facts-about-the-joint-commission/.

Shearwater Health. 2020. "The Importance of CDI for Healthcare Providers." Accessed September 3. https://swhealth.com/providers/the-importance-of-cdi-for-healthcare-providers/.

US Food and Drug Administration (FDA). 2010. "Information Sheet Guidance for IRBs, Clinical Investigators, and Sponsors: FDA Inspections of Clinical Investigators." Published June. www.fda.gov/media/75185/download.

CHAPTER 11

Language Assistance

César Palacio

DEPARTMENT DESCRIPTION

The primary focus of the Language Assistance Department (LAD) is to provide meaningful healthcare access to Limited English Proficient (LEP) patients by delivering language services that facilitate clear and accurate communication between healthcare providers and their patients, so they can make informed decisions. These services not only make communication among speakers of different languages possible; in the United States, they are also a federal mandate under the requirements of the Civil Rights Act of 1964, as ratified and amplified in Section 1557 of the Affordable Care Act of 2010.

Language Assistance departments typically deliver services for spoken languages and deaf patients needing sign language assistance or auxiliary aids to help them communicate. In certain healthcare institutions, LAD may also be responsible for supporting visually impaired patients and even providing housing communication aids, such as communication boards for patients whose native language is English but who are unable to communicate verbally for various reasons.

Most of the LAD's language services fall into two basic categories, interpretation and translation. Although many people use these terms interchangeably, they refer to two different aspects of this area of service. *Interpretation* is the rendering of communication verbally, whereas *translation* refers to the conversion of written text from one language into another.

In healthcare, the majority of the services the LAD provides involve interpretation, because most of the interactions between healthcare providers and their patients occur in person and are verbal in nature. In addition to these responsibilities, and depending on the organizational structure of the hospital, the LAD may also be accountable for testing the language skills of bilingual employees for medical interpretation, maintaining records on these employees, consulting other hospital departments in matters related to languages, and other tasks.

The academic and language-skills requirements for medical interpreters in position descriptions vary greatly among institutions. Although federal law requires medical interpreters to be qualified, meaning that they must have demonstrated proficiency in English and at least one other spoken language, the law does not specify training or certification requirements. The most widely accepted minimum requirements for entry-level medical interpreters include a language-skills assessment and at least 40 hours of training in medical interpretation. Depending on the organization, interpreters could be required to have a college degree, one or more years of verifiable experience in the field, and even national certification as a medical interpreter.

KEY DEPARTMENT SERVICES

The most fundamental services the LAD provides are interpretation and translation, which should aim to provide LEP individuals with meaningful access to healthcare services. Interpretation must be offered for spoken and sign languages, whereas translation is required for the most common languages of the populations served by the facility.

Depending on the size and resources of the entity, interpretation can be delivered in one or more modalities. The three available methods of interpretation are in-person (sometimes referred to as on-site), video, and telephonic (exhibit 11.1). Although a large healthcare facility with ample resources should offer a mix of all three types, smaller operations may only need to use a combination of two, or even one. Other considerations for the provision of interpretation might be the location of the facility and availability of interpreters in the area.

Interpretation may occur during any phase of a patient visit, including registration, appointments, imaging, tests, treatments, surgery, counseling, patient

---

Exhibit 11.1: Interpretation: Methods of Delivery

- **In-person interpretation:** Interpretation provided live on site. Used for both spoken and signed languages.
- **Telephonic interpretation:** A type of remote interpretation where the three parties (patient, provider, and interpreter) participate in an interpreted conversation that takes place over phone lines.
- **Video remote interpretation:** Another type of remote interpretation where the participants connect to each other over the internet and are able to see and hear each other while an interpreter assists with language.

---

education, discharge instructions, and many other clinical and nonclinical interactions related to the patient's condition and treatment. The interpretation may extend beyond these examples, to include phone calls to and from the patients that may be generated for diverse reasons. Note that interpretation services should also cover LEP family members as long as they are involved in caring for the patient.

The translation side of language services should focus on the translation of vital written materials into the language of each frequently encountered LEP group eligible to be served or likely to be served. The classification of documents as vital or nonvital depends on the importance of the program, information, or service involved, along with the consequence to the LEP person if the information is not provided accurately or in a timely way. In both interpretation and translation, the services may be provided by contract personnel, provided that they comply with the requirements of the law. Smaller healthcare facilities may be able to provide language services without hiring employees, whereas larger hospitals may have a mix of offerings that will include hired and contract language professionals. Depending on the scope of responsibility placed on the LAD at each institution, the department may have other equally important services to provide, such as auxiliary aids for the deaf, communication devices or methods for the blind, and communication boards for patients with verbal communication challenges.

DEPARTMENT ORGANIZATIONAL STRUCTURES

The size and complexity of language service departments vary according to the patient population of the facility, its geographical location, and even the specialties and services provided. These operations may range from one on-site interpreter for only one language to a hundred or more interpreters working in several languages over different shifts throughout the day, plus translators, dispatchers, and support staff. In the former case, the interpreter may report directly to an administrator in charge of a larger department in the institution; in the latter case, the LAD may have a director, supervisor, and shift leaders over the interpreters.

The organizational structure of the LAD may also be organized around types of languages, volume of work, or shifts. It is not uncommon to see LAD personnel reporting to different areas or divisions, such as Clinical Support Services, Nursing, Clinical Operations, Social Work, and the like. However, the LAD should be under the supervision of a group that has a similar or common mission, one that understands that interpreters are an important part of the patient care team and that their mission is to assist patients in their journey through the healthcare system. Exhibit 11.2 shows a sample organizational chart for a large LAD that includes translation and interpretation sections along with an internal call center.

Exhibit 11.2: Sample Organizational Chart

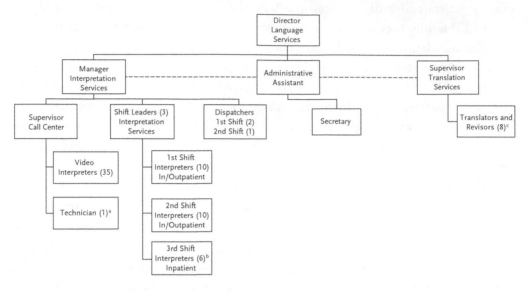

Language Services Department with 500+ Inpatient Beds and Multiple Outpatient Services

Notes: (a) Technician provides support and repair for video remote interpretation tablets. (b) Third-shift interpreters are contacted via pagers; no dispatchers are needed on third shift. (c) Revisors are translators who revise translated documents for grammatical and technical issues before document translation is finalized.

KEY CUSTOMERS AND THEIR PERFORMANCE EXPECTATIONS

The customers of the LAD require interpretation, translation, or both. The vast majority are patients and healthcare providers in outpatient and inpatient areas. A smaller number come from other institutional departments that may need translation services to reach patient or employee audiences for various reasons. A few potential customers may be departments providing ancillary services. These departments, such as the Food and Nutrition Department, Police or Security Services, Human Resources, and Legal Services, may require assistance with translation or interpretation for their own purposes, not necessarily to interact with patients. In some cases, the LAD will also count family members of their patients among their customers. If any family members are involved in the patient's care and do not speak English, the healthcare organization must assist them in communicating with the care team, even if the patient speaks English.

In all these cases, the crucial expectations from the internal LAD customers are to receive quality language services in a timely manner. Other expectations include professionalism, good customer service, prompt response to requests, and adherence to deadlines in the case of document translation.

Depending on the volume of the operation, providing timely interpretation every time can be challenging, especially if resources may be limited. Other important factors in providing timely interpretation are the inherent delays within the requesting units or areas, and coordinating the simultaneous meeting of patient, interpreter, and provider.

Communication is of paramount importance to manage the customer's expectations. Meeting with the appropriate service area or unit stakeholders to provide them with guidelines for language services, apprise them of departmental limitations, and learn about their language services needs is very important for strengthening relationships with internal customers and creating awareness of LAD's services and procedures.

KEY PROCESS FLOWS

Although the process flows in the LAD are relatively simple, they can be handled in different manners. The main processes in the LAD are

- request and provision of interpretation services and
- request and provision of translation services.

A basic flow for the interpretation process is shown in exhibit 11.3.

This process can include many variations, depending on the resources available, the dispatch system selected for this purpose, and the complexity of the operation. The process can be manual, electronic, or a hybrid of both. Requests may be placed by phone, email, web page, or other electronic means. The key information needed for an interpretation request includes patient name, room number, medical record number, and requestor. The information needed to reach the requestor to provide the service may be gathered manually during the interaction with the requestor, or may be entered directly by them. The assignment of interpreters may also be handled manually, or automatically by a computer application with several

Exhibit 11.3: Basic Interpretation Flow

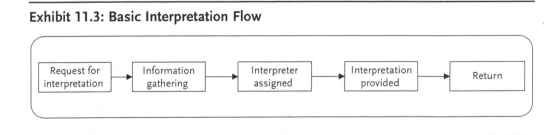

methods for assigning requests, such as rotation, preferred or assigned units, sectors, inpatient versus outpatient, and others. In a rotation method, interpreters would be rotated in order of availability as requests come in for all areas of the organization. Interpreters could be assigned to specific sectors or units of the institution, where they would work directly with the unit staff to provide service only to patients in their area of responsibility as appointments occur. Assignment also could be split between inpatient and outpatient areas, in which interpreters assigned to one of these sides would not cross into the other, and provide service only to the patients and staff within those areas.

Besides in-person interpretation, the requests can also be handled via video or telephone. The interpretation itself can also be handled in one of the four basic types of interpreting, consecutive being the most widely used method in medical interpretation. Exhibit 11.4 provides an explanation of the four types. Once the interpretation is completed, the interpreter returns to an available status. As with the other parts of the process, the return can also be logged manually or electronically.

Translating documents follows a similar workflow as interpretation. The linear, uncomplicated process, as seen in exhibit 11.5, can be handled in other ways, depending on the specific needs of the organization.

Exhibit 11.4: Types of Interpretation

- **Simultaneous interpreting:** Also known as conference interpretation, involves the processes of instantaneously listening to, comprehending, interpreting, and rendering the speaker's statements into another language.
- **Consecutive interpreting:** Commonly used in meetings with few participants. The interpreter listens to a set number of utterances from the speaker and then gives their rendition in the target second language.
- **Whispered interpreting:** This method of interpreting, also known as *chuchotage*, is used in meetings with few participants. The interpreter, who is positioned right next to the listener, simply whispers to the listener precisely what the speaker is saying.
- **Sight translation:** The oral rendition of text written in one language into another language, usually done in the moment.

Exhibit 11.5: Basic Translation Flow

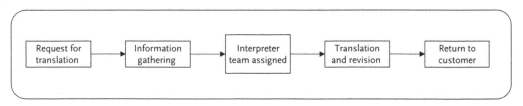

| Request for translation | → | Information gathering | → | Interpreter team assigned | → | Translation and revision | → | Return to customer |

Documents for translation can be sent in their original form, via email, or uploaded to a specific website or cloud server, among other methods. Requestors can enter their information directly regarding the requirements for the translation. Once LAD knows the scope of the project, it assigns a translation/revision team to the project, depending on language, topic, availability, and other requirements, such as whether formatting is needed. Regardless of whether the translation can be handled in house or has to be outsourced, the length of the text should be known, to estimate cost and the amount of time the project will take.

Depending on the type of document, the translation could be handled manually by one translator, who would then pass it to another translator, who revises the original translation for accuracy and other factors, depending on the client's needs. The text also could be processed through different computer-assisted methods to obtain a machine-generated translation that would have to be revised or post-edited by a human translator or reviewer. Any formatting needed should be requested at the beginning of the project, so the new text is dropped in the desired format, then adjusted to the customer's requirements within the allotted time. Once the final translation is completed, the new document in the target language is sent back to the customer for their approval. If any corrections are needed, the document has to be sent back to the appropriate area for rework. One other process to consider is invoicing. The decision to set up an LAD as revenue generating depends on institutional preferences and accounting practices, and will drive the need for invoicing with the appropriate process flow.

KEY UNITS OF WORK AND VOLUME STATISTICS TO MONITOR

The data gathered while providing language services are very useful to the department and the institution. LAD data reveal the resources needed to provide language services and can be used to justify the need for more resources, track staff productivity, allocate resources, and determine if any issues may be developing in certain areas of the department.

LAD should keep track of the number of assignments, length of time per assignment, labor expenses, and number of full-time equivalent positions. The data should be gathered by type of service (in person, telephone, video, or translation) to look at growth, trends, and needs by type of service. The director should also monitor services by language and combine type of service and language to determine more specifically how the department uses needed resources. Comparing the data from one year to the next can reveal changes in numbers and trends that can explain or justify growth. To report trends to division leadership, a summary of the data, along with comparisons to previous years, can be presented monthly.

KEY METRICS TO MONITOR: PEOPLE, SERVICE, QUALITY/SAFETY, FINANCIAL

Monitoring these four areas keeps leadership informed of changes and allows the necessary modifications to more adequately control operations and stay within institutional parameters. People metrics provide valuable information regarding the need for recruitment, whether or not retention issues are present, and keeps track of staff recognition. Service metrics help monitor productivity and enable appropriate action should an issue surface. Quality metrics include response time and can show improvement in this area as operations are modified, and can also be used to monitor any safety issues. Financial metrics are related to expenses for personnel, contracted services, and department supplies. These data are helpful in adhering to budget. Personnel expenses are normally the largest LAD expense, but depending on the volume and management of the operation, contract services could be the largest. Exhibit 11.6 shows a sample scorecard used to track key monthly metrics the LAD can monitor. The specific metrics for target, stretch, threshold, and underperformance should be developed according to the metrics observed at each organization.

STAFFING MODELS

Adequately staffing a Language Services operation involves several factors, including hours of operation, patient volumes, languages needed, and the types of cases encountered in each practice.

Note that most of the work LAPs perform takes place during regular office hours, Monday through Friday during the daytime. An activity plot for most hospitals providing both outpatient and inpatient care would show a well-defined bell curve with a sharp increase in both areas in the demand for language services shortly after opening, and a sharp decrease at the end of the business day in the outpatient areas.

The need for interpreters shifts from outpatient clinics during the day to the Emergency Department and inpatient units at night. Some institutions may prefer to assign interpreters to specific units, whereas others may find rotating their interpreters among all services more efficient. A rotating operation keeps all interpreters exposed to many different specialties, making it easier for any interpreter to provide service in any area. Assigning interpreters to specific areas specializes them in a particular field, making them more difficult to replace, and even creating dependency on the interpreters by both staff and patients, who may prefer to work with the interpreter assigned to the unit. This dependency may create challenging situations when the assigned interpreter is on leave or otherwise unavailable.

Exhibit 11.6: Language Assistance Department Scorecard

		Scorecard LANGUAGE ASSISTANCE DEPARTMENT					
Metric	Under-performing	Threshold	Target	Stretch	Sept 2019	Oct 2019	Nov 2019
PEOPLE							
P1 **Recognition Letters:** # of recognition letters given (mail or other)	0		≥1				
P2 **Vacancies:** Total # of vacancies							
P3 **Year-to-Date Turnover:** % of staff who (voluntarily+involuntarily) left the institution since 9/1/19							
SERVICE							
S1 **Service Complaints:** # of service complaints received	>10	8–10	4–7	<4			
S2 **Dispatch Time:** Decrease the average time from receipt of request for in-person interpretation to time when interpreter is dispatched to assignment from 9.47 minutes to <9.25 minutes	≥9.47 min	9.46–9.25 min	9.24–9.03 min	<9.03 min			

(continued)

Exhibit 11.6: Language Assistance Department Scorecard (continued)

| | | Scorecard | | | | | |
| | | LANGUAGE ASSISTANCE DEPARTMENT | | | | | |
Metric	Under-performing	Threshold	Target	Stretch	Sept 2019	Oct 2019	Nov 2019
S3 **Productivity:** # of KUoW metrics achieving productivity goals (refer to KUoW report)	<1		1				
Quality							
Q1 **Interpreter Interaction Time:** Average number of minutes of interpretation per interpreter and interaction	<10 min	10–13 min	14–16 min	>16 min			
Audits and Regulatory							
Q2 **Requirements:** % compliance with HR files	*Performance ranges under development*						
FINANCE							
F1 **Personnel Expense**	>Budget		≤Budget				
F2 **Other Operating Expense**	>Budget		≤Budget				
Total Operating Expense:							
F3 Personnel Expense + Other Operating Expense (Award Department Financial Goal)	>Budget		≤Budget				
F4 **Operating Income/Loss:** % Variance Actual to Budget							

Note: KUoW = key unit of work.

Another way of staffing is to follow a daily list of appointments and procedures. In this method, any delay in the appointment flow creates a delay in the interpretation flow, which increases as the day goes by, stacking up in different areas, and may prevent interpreters from servicing some of their patients, because they have to wait for already scheduled ones.

In institutions with a very diverse patient population, Language Assistance departments cannot have staff interpreters employed for every language needed. Such patient populations make it necessary to schedule appointments well ahead of time to request contract interpreters for other languages. In cases when there are walk-ins for languages not offered on staff and no live interpreter is available, the service can be provided over the phone, or via video, because these services are available on demand.

To demonstrate how to calculate the number of staff interpreters needed, exhibit 11.7 shows the assumptions and calculations used to determine the number of interpreter FTEs needed in a specific situation.

Exhibit 11.7: Language Assistance Staffing Model

Calculate the number of full-time equivalent positions needed to work an interpretation assignment.

1. Exclude Nonproductive Time
   - Exclude paid hours that are considered nonproductive such as paid time off, sick leave, jury duty, or Family Medical Leave
   - This is likely to be around 90% of total paid hours
   - Total = 4 hours per week per FTE is lost to nonproductive time
2. Exclude Time Spent on Non-Direct Patient Care Activities
   - 30 minutes per day for organizational tasks or 2.5 hours/week
   - 1 hour/month with committee work
   - 1 hour/month for continuing education
   - Total = 1 hour/week in non-direct patient care, leaving 88% of their productive hours for direct patient care
3. Direct Patient Care Demand: Interpretation Assignment
   A. Each intervention takes an average of 42 minutes (understanding some patients take more time and some take less time)

Example: Interpreter Model Assumptions:
   - 87.5% nonproductive time per interpreter: 154 worked hours per month
   - Deduct another 10% from productive hours to account for non-direct patient care time: $154 - 17 = 137$
   - Estimate that each intervention will take 42 minutes (0.7 hours)

(continued)

Exhibit 11.7: Language Assistance Staffing Model *(continued)*

A.	Total number of appointments needing interpretation per month	7,150
B.	Interpretation hours needed per month (0.7 × A)	5,005
C.	Available interpretation hours per interpreter per month	137
D.	Interpreter FTE needed (B / C)	36.53

As a general rule, an interpreter can see 6–10 patients per day.

PRODUCTIVITY MODELS, INCLUDING WORK-TO-STAFF RATIOS AND INDUSTRY PERFORMANCE TARGETS

Measuring productivity and work-to-staff ratios in language services varies across institutions. Factors that affect productivity include type of institution, its volume and bed size, schedules and hours of operation, and methods of service delivery.

Delivery method (in person, telephone, video) makes a big difference in staff productivity. Some of the monthly metrics suggested to keep track of productivity include the number of assignments per employee and the total time they spend on those assignments. The data can yield productivity information, such as average minutes per call, hours spent interpreting per month, average number of hours interpreted per day, and average number of assignments per day.

These data, as well as the data collected from vendors of telephonic, video, and contract in-person interpretation, can be converted to interpretation units as a common unit of work. One suggestion is to convert the number of minutes interpreted in each modality to interpretation units equivalent to 15 minutes of interpretation per unit. This calculation can be modified to different numbers of minutes of interpretation per unit, depending on preference. Exhibit 11.8 shows a sample control chart with interpretation units per month tracked over a period of more than four years.

Exhibit 11.8: Total Staff Interpretation Units per Month

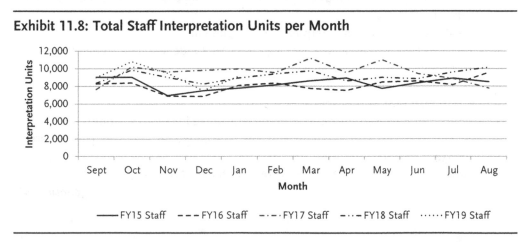

Benchmarks for language services are not readily available in the industry, so language services directors are advised to create relationships with directors at other institutions similar in size and working under similar circumstances, to compare performance standards.

In general, though, in-person interpreters can handle between 6 and 12 assignments per eight-hour shift. This workload may vary, depending on the nature of the interpretation work. An interpreter working at a community clinic taking care of more common medical appointments could face up to 30 assignments per day, whereas another at an oncology specialty hospital may only have an average of six assignments daily. An average of ten assignments per day per interpreter is a good starting point for in-person interpretation. Once productivity data is tracked for some time, and certain averages are known, work-to-staff ratios can be calculated for the specific situation, and benchmarks can be set for the operation, which can help determine work activity and decide the number of labor hours needed to cover the demand for language services.

STRATEGIES TO IMPROVE RECRUITMENT AND RETENTION

Depending on the level of experience required for each institution, different strategies can be applied to recruit good candidates for interpreter and translator positions. In certain situations there may be a need to recruit candidates as they graduate from a training institution. Creating relationships with local institutions that provide medical interpreter/translator training can prove useful to recruit graduates. Being able to do a presentation to students prior to graduation introduces the institution to potential candidates who might not have thought about certain organizations otherwise.

Other institutions may need to hire staff with experience in medical interpretation. Directors should build relationships with members and leaders of language assistance trade associations and volunteer to make educational presentations. Working with trade associations at the local, state, and national level can open a dialogue about the institution, the requirements for candidates, and what the institution can offer employees.

To promote retention, the director should provide staff with clear expectations of work, a complete understanding of their job functions, and a comprehensive orientation to the department and position. This approach should include an introduction to departmental staff, training on how work is expected to be conducted, and exposure to the work environment prior to new staff interpreting on their own. Having new interpreters shadow more experienced ones helps them learn the processes and understand the workplace culture.

Creating opportunities for advancement within the department is also good for employee retention. Having a tiered structure, where the interpreter or translator can advance in title and compensation, can help retain staff. Hiring for supervisory positions from within is also highly recommended, as this provides another opportunity for advancement.

Another factor that improves retention is providing professional development opportunities. Having a budget to assist with certification, conferences, and other development will help employees focus on doing their best in the department. Other important factors to strengthen retention are recognizing the valuable work of interpreters, asking for their input on improvement, and following up on their suggestions with regular staff updates.

KEY REGULATORY ISSUES

According to federal regulations, healthcare organizations receiving federal funds must provide LEP individuals with meaningful access to their services (US Department of Health and Human Services [HHS] 2016a). This regulation must be met by providing effective language assistance free of charge to the patient. The federal mandate is true for all healthcare providers receiving federal funds, regardless of their size, from large hospitals to individual practitioners. The regulations account for differences in size and available resources and allow for different methods of interpretation delivery. For example, an individual practitioner with only a few LEP patients may provide interpretation through a vendor of telephonic interpretation. This interpretation would only cost a few dollars per patient, and the service would be provided by calling an 800 number that would give the practitioner access to a wide range of languages on demand. On the other hand, large healthcare organizations are expected to provide a mix of interpretation services (i.e., face to face, contract video, and telephonic) to handle a much larger demand and diversity of language services.

Proper training of interpreters is also stipulated by law that requires interpreters to be qualified for medical interpretation and specifies what constitutes qualification. According to Section 1557 of the Affordable Care Act, a qualified medical interpreter for an individual with limited English proficiency is an interpreter who via a remote interpreting service or an on-site appearance

A. adheres to generally accepted interpreter ethics principles, including client confidentiality;

B. has demonstrated proficiency in speaking and understanding both spoken English and at least one other spoken language; and

C. is able to interpret effectively, accurately, and impartially, both receptively and expressly, to and from such language(s) and English, using any necessary specialized vocabulary, terminology and phraseology (HHS 2016b).

Medical interpreter certification is not mandated by law whether they work in person, over the phone, or via video. The law prohibits minor children (under the age of 18) from interpreting, except for short-term emergency situations where an interpreter is not available (HHS 2016a). Using family or friends as interpreters is also prohibited, unless the patient specifically requests it (HHS 2016a). Should the patient request this, the hospital should determine if the person designated to interpret to/for the patient is capable of interpreting. The healthcare organization should still provide an interpreter to monitor the ad hoc interpreter, and the hospital-appointed interpreter should intervene if the designated interpreter does not provide adequate interpretation (accurate, impartial, and transparent). Other healthcare staff should refrain from interpreting, unless they are qualified to do so, because interpreting is an official job duty (HHS 2016b).

Regarding video interpretation, current regulations require certain standards. Video must be of high quality. The video interpretation must be done in real-time, full-motion video over a high-speed, wide-bandwidth video connection delivering high-quality images. The transmission of voices must be clear and audible, and users of the technology must be adequately trained to operate the equipment (HHS 2016c). Exhibit 11.9 provides a timeline showing the laws and regulations affecting language services for healthcare organizations.

Exhibit 11.9: Laws and Regulations Governing Language Services in Healthcare

- Title VI of the Civil Rights Act of 1964 prohibits discrimination of persons based on their race, color, or national origin by entities receiving federal funds.
- Since 1964, the Department of Justice has issued regulatory requirements that have been interpreted to prohibit denial of equal access to programs or services because of an individual's limited proficiency in English.
- On August 11, 2000, President Bill Clinton issued Executive Order 13166, "Improving Access to Services by Persons with Limited English Proficiency" (LEP).
- The same day, the Civil Rights Division of the US Department of Justice issued an initial Guidance document titled "Enforcement of Title VI of the Civil Rights Act of 1964—National Origin Discrimination Against Persons with Limited English Proficiency," in which it advised recipients of federal funding they were required to take reasonable steps to ensure meaningful access by LEP persons.
- On March 23, 2010, President Barack Obama signed the Affordable Care Act (ACA).
- On May 18, 2016, the US Department of Health and Human Services, Office for Civil Rights issued the implementing regulation for Section 1557 of the ACA, indicating covered entities must take reasonable steps to provide meaningful access, free of charge and in a timely manner.
- The Joint Commission has adopted several of the regulations related to language services included in the preceding documents and has converted them into standards for its customers to follow.

KEY TERMS FOR LANGUAGE ASSISTANCE

Interpretation: The facilitation of spoken or signed language communication between users of different languages.

Limited English Proficient: A term used in the United States for a person who is not fluent in the English language, often because it is not their native language.

Sight translation: The oral rendition of a written text.

Translation: The process of converting the written word from one language to another in a way that is culturally and linguistically appropriate so it can be understood by its intended audience.

REFERENCES

US Department of Health and Human Services. 2016a. "Nondiscrimination in Health Programs and Activities; Final Rule." 81 Fed. Reg. 31470. May 18 (45 CFR Part 92).

————. 2016b. "Nondiscrimination in Health Programs and Activities; Final Rule." 81 Fed. Reg. 31468. May 18 (45 CFR Part 92).

————. 2016c. "Nondiscrimination in Health Programs and Activities; Final Rule." 81 Fed. Reg. 31470–31471. May 18 (45 CFR Part 92).

CHAPTER 12

Pathology and Laboratory Medicine*

Joyceann Musel-Winn

DEPARTMENT DESCRIPTION

Clinical laboratories perform scientific tests on specimens (blood, tissue, body fluids) taken from patients to assist clinicians in assessing or evaluating their health status. Clinicians use these results to diagnose, treat, monitor, and prevent disease. As required by the Clinical Laboratory Improvement Amendments (CLIA), clinicians interpret laboratory results as normal or abnormal, according to ranges statistically determined when the tests are validated (Centers for Medicare & Medicaid Services [CMS] 2019a). Although the patient may present with clinical symptoms indicating a specific diagnosis, often the diagnosis is confirmed only after the clinician receives the laboratory results. Clinicians then may use additional testing to better define the diagnosis and monitor the treatment. Should the patient's clinical condition not meet the expected outcome of treatment, the clinician may modify treatment depending on different test results.

Patients in different environments vary in the frequency of tests their clinicians request and complexity of testing. According to Ngo, Gandhi, and Miller (2017), 98 percent of hospitalized patients receive laboratory testing, whereas emergency room and outpatients are tested less often (56 percent and 29 percent, respectively). It has been almost a decade since Hallworth (2011) claimed that 70 percent of all diagnostic data in patients' medical records were laboratory test results. Although Hiltunen (2017) disagrees with this claim, he states that the true value of the patients' testing results is the added value that helps the

---

*In healthcare settings, the Clinical Laboratory Department is often referred to as the Laboratory (Lab) or Pathology (Path). For ease of convention, *laboratory* is used here.

clinician better meet the patients' diagnostic needs. Testing may be performed at the patient's bedside, in an on-site laboratory, and/or at a larger off-site laboratory facility, depending on the tests. The clinical laboratory's testing menu available at each institution is based on the clinicians' testing needs, the criticality of patients, and number of patient visits per institution, but it is the value of those tests to the patients to ensure appropriate treatment and diagnosis that must be recognized (Hiltunen 2017).

KEY DEPARTMENT SERVICES

Laboratories vary greatly in size, as do their testing platforms and menus. Smaller laboratories in clinics or doctor's offices, especially in rural areas, offer pocket-size tests, whereas commercial laboratories, and very large laboratories featured in academic centers, use automated robotic lines to handle the large volume of specimens. Testing complexity may also vary according to the size of the labora-tory. The general sizes of laboratories are as follows:

- **Small Laboratories and Patient-Side Testing:** Point-of-care testing is often performed on small, simple devices designated as "waived" by the US Food and Drug Administration (FDA) and therefore usable by individuals under a physicians' oversight. These tests may measure blood sugar, A1C, strep throat, influenza, urine chemistry, pregnancy, and other simple conditions and values that provide quick results for diagnosis or treatment. Small laboratories may also use "nonwaived" tests, which are more complex and require a higher level of education. Most point-of-care devices are designed as screens and often confirmed in a more complex laboratory, especially if abnormal or unexpected results are produced.
- **Midsize Laboratories:** Community hospital settings or larger clinics often have midsize laboratories. The testing is performed on more complex and validated analyzers. These routine panels and tests are broader and screen for multiple health conditions. Diagnostic and screening tests done at midsize laboratories include complete blood counts (CBCs), chemistry panels (including CMS-designated panels such as basic metabolic panels and comprehensive metabolic panels), urinalysis with microscopic evaluations, and routine coagulation. These tests provide standardized information to assess the patients' health:
  - Hematology: CBCs indicate whether the patient has one of many abnormal conditions such as an infection, anemia, abnormal blood cells, or decreased thrombocytes, all of which require medical intervention for the best outcomes.

- Chemistry: Routine chemistry panel results permit the clinician to evaluate the patient's basic bodily functions and the activity of the bones, heart, kidney, liver, lungs, and pancreas, in addition to providing information related to general abnormal conditions such as inflammation.
- Body Fluids: Urinalysis assesses kidney and bladder function, and microscopic evaluation allows more information on the functionality of those organs.
- Coagulation Studies: Coagulation testing evaluates both bleeding and clotting function and will typically be ordered to monitor anticlotting medications used to prevent strokes.
- Transfusion Service: If maternity, surgery, or oncology services/ treatments are provided on-site, it is expected that the laboratory also provide a transfusion service. This service provides blood and blood products to patients should they need it as a consequence of their diagnosis, surgery, or chemotherapy treatment or as a result of an emergency incident or trauma.
- Microbiology Testing: Many midsize laboratories provide minimal microbiology, such as gram stains, blood cultures, and other simple cultures, that requires the laboratory to identify and grow the pathogens on nutrient-rich growth media. More modern laboratories will include analyzers to help identify organisms more rapidly using polymerase chain reaction (PCR) techniques, instead.
- Highly Specialized Testing: Molecular, next-generation sequencing (NGS), flow cytometry, cytogenetic testing, human leukocyte antigen (HLA) testing, and other highly complex analyses are generally referred out to contract laboratories that have the specialized equipment and pathologists or specialists.
- **Pathology Laboratories:** In midsize hospitals and ambulatory surgical facilities, specialized labs ensure the patient's tissues or tumors are secured and properly identified.
  - Surgical Pathology: If procurement of tissues through biopsies or surgical procedures is expected at the site, the laboratory must preserve the integrity of the specimen for later testing and interpretation. Some surgical units require interoperative interpretations performed on patient tissues referred to as *frozen sections*. Some midsize laboratories process the specimens on-site, whereas others transport them to a larger or more complex laboratory to interpret the results.
  - Immunohistochemistry Assays: Common specialized stains and chemical assays are performed on the patient specimens to help identify abnormal

cells present in the tissues and assist the pathologist in providing a diagnostic interpretation. Complex assays, when needed, are typically sent to a reference laboratory or academic center.

- **Academic or Large Laboratories:** These include both the routine testing just described plus an expanded menu of tests. The testing platforms (analyzers and machines) are more complex and often have robotics to handle higher patient-sample volumes. The analyzers include middleware (computer) solutions that allow for multifaceted algorithms to interpret the intricate results, which provides higher-quality results to the providers and meets the needs of the patient population (Mayo Clinic College of Medicine and Science 2020; Quest Diagnostics 2020; Skobelev et al. 2011). These academic laboratories provide the following services:

  - Training Programs: Laboratories in academic centers often include training programs for pathologists, clinical laboratory scientists (CLSs; also known as medical technologists, MTs), molecular diagnostics, cytogenetics, histology, cytology programs, and other laboratory-related specialties.

  - Routine Testing: The robotic analyzers perform pre-analytic processes to prepare the patient specimens, including centrifugation, separation of blood fractions, relabeling, aliquoting, and tracking of patient specimens. The patient samples are fed to the analyzer on a conveyor track and tested on complex analyzers.

  - Hematology Reviews: The CBC results are evaluated by laser beams and algorithms. If the results meet certain algorithmic criteria, the results are auto-verified and released automatically through a laboratory software computer system to a hospital-wide electronic health record (EHR) for a clinician's review. If the results do not meet the auto-verification and release criteria, a blood slide is made, a digital scan is produced, and a CLS/pathologist reviews, interprets, and reports the findings.

  - Chemistry: The robotic chemistry lines, designed with sophisticated algorithms, can establish whether the sample needs additional testing, the integrity of the results has been compromised and the sample needs to be redrawn, the sample should be retested to confirm abnormal results, or the sample passes the criteria for auto-verification and release.

  - Fluid Analysis: Urinalysis testing with microscopic analysis is typically automated and provides information that may route to specialized tests or microbiology testing. Body fluids are also processed in this manner.

  - Coagulation Studies: Coagulation results in larger hospital settings may occasionally route to specialized tests such as mixing or factor assay studies, but most testing and studies are performed to monitor anticoagulation medication to prevent strokes.

- Transfusion Services: Large medical-center laboratories are designed to support complex surgeries, premature births, chemotherapy patients, and emergency/trauma patients, and must include a robust transfusion service. This service collaborates with clinicians and the nursing service to administer units of blood, platelets, or plasma to meet patients' needs. Although many administrative processes are still manual, automation provides more technical assistance in affording the safest blood product. Specialized products such as irradiated blood and recombinant factor products are often found in these large centers. Whereas commercial laboratories may provide blood screening tests, hospitals or clinics administer the blood products, because patients require monitoring during transfusions.

- Microbiology: Large laboratories employ sophisticated analyzers such as mass spectrometry; multiplex PCRs for infection detection; pH-sensitive blood culture analyzers; and rapid yet accurate viral testing. These laboratories are also equipped with biohazard safety equipment such as biosafety laminar flow hoods and other precautions to protect the staff as they identify fastidious and unique infectious organisms. The microbiology laboratories collaborate with state and local public health agencies and the Centers for Disease Control and Prevention in the surveillance of infectious diseases during epidemics and pandemics.

- Highly Specialized Testing: Academic center laboratories are designed to assist with complicated patient cases by using highly complex testing to better define the diagnosis. Some large laboratories perform both somatic and germ-line molecular/genetic tests that are used to determine if a genetic mutation or deletion is causing a patient's health condition. This field has exploded as identification of genetic markers has provided clinicians with diagnostic and prognostic information to ease some patients' disease states. Although many disease states cannot currently be resolved, the genetic information is valuable to researchers studying medical interventions targeted at these more difficult diagnoses. For instance, NGS molecular testing has been revolutionizing oncology treatments with great promise by identifying the most effective patient treatment more rapidly and basing a prognosis of success on genetic mutations, a technique referred to as *personalized medicine*. In addition, flow cytometry, cytogenetic, and HLA test results are used to determine the genetic makeup of cells typically seen in leukemia and lymphoma patients' blood specimens. These areas are highly complex and require both specialized CLSs/

MTs and special board-certified pathologists to interpret and provide a diagnosis and prognosis.

— Surgical Pathology: This service is very active in academic and large healthcare centers. Pathologists work with surgeons to better define the extent of tissue removal or reconstruction necessary to ensure the best outcomes for patients. Frozen tissue sections from the operating room (OR) are reviewed and interpreted by pathologists while a patient is still in the OR suite. The patient's tissue removed is either frozen, preserved in formalin, or both, then transported to the histology/ pathology laboratory for sectioning, dehydrating, slide staining, and the pathologist's interpretation. At the pathologist's discretion, additional definitive immunohistochemistry testing, fluorescence in-situ hybridization, or molecular testing may be performed to definitively assign a patient diagnosis. The pathologists' interpretations are transmitted and available in the EHR for clinician and patient viewing.

— Research and Development: Academic centers and large laboratories perform research studies to advance the field of medicine, including the science of laboratory testing. Many researchers use the laboratories for their clinical trials and studies, and receive test results as evidence of outcomes. In addition, these large laboratories collaborate with vendors to act as beta or alpha sites to validate new testing platforms and test reagents to provide more rapid or accurate patient testing.

DEPARTMENT ORGANIZATIONAL STRUCTURES

CMS, the FDA, and other regulatory agencies have extensive organizational standards that need to be met to ensure that testing is appropriately supervised and performed by competent personnel, and that all processes are standardized to produce quality results, including the following requirements:

- **Director:** In CMS/CLIA-certified laboratories, a board-certified MD or PhD is required to direct laboratory testing. This individual is either designated a medical director or laboratory director depending on their credentials. According to the CMS/CLIA, only a board-certified physician is permitted to bill clinical testing interpretations that are used to treat patients, but private payors do not have this restriction. The departments' laboratory testing varies in methodologies and complexities, resulting in specialized laboratories requiring specialized skills and knowledge. Generally, the laboratories that study patients' body tissues are designated as Pathology

Exhibit 12.1: Sample Organizational Chart, Pathology and Laboratory Medicine Department

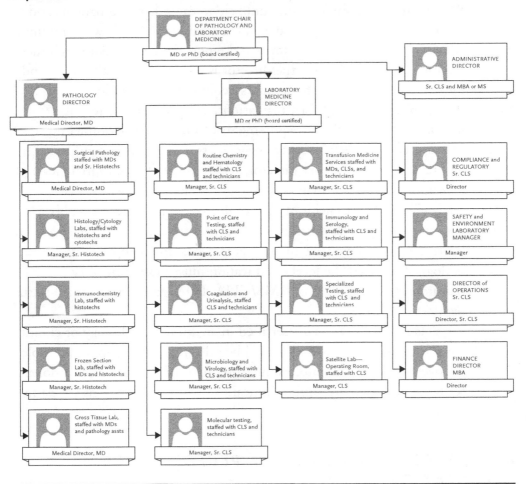

Note: CLS = clinical laboratory scientist.

or Anatomical Pathology, whereas laboratories processing bloods and fluids for testing are designated as Clinical Pathology. Each of these areas requires a board-certified laboratory director reporting to the chair of the Department of Pathology and Laboratory Medicine, as shown in exhibit 12.1.

- **Testing Personnel:** When CLIA is assessing the complexity level of testing, they rely on such factors as the required independent judgment; difficulty of examination or preparation; methodology testing; difficulty of interpretation or calculations; calibration and quality control procedures; training required to perform testing; and any other factor that CMS believes will affect the testing results. As testing complexity levels increase, so do the educational requirements of the individuals performing tests and reporting results (CMS 2013). The following are categories derived from CLIA:

- Waived Testing: Simple testing unlikely to cause harm to patients and not error prone are designated as waived, and individuals with minimum education are allowed to perform and report the testing. Although these requirements are minimal, the director is responsible for all testing and must ensure all FDA manufacturers' requirements are followed.
- Complex Testing: Per CLIA regulations, as complexity of testing increases, the educational requirements of the testing personnel must increase as well. The surveying agencies assess the testing complexity and require the laboratory director to determine the appropriate level of education required to maintain quality testing and patient safety.
- CLS/MTs with a bachelor of science degree are required for highly complex testing, whereas individuals processing and preparing specimens for testing may only need an associate's degree in an appropriate biological science. The level of education must meet regulatory requirements (e.g., those of CMS/CLIA, FDA, and other deemed-status regulatory agencies).
- Physicians and PhDs board certified in anatomical pathology or clinical pathology, or other CMS-approved board certifications, are responsible for overseeing the laboratories, interpreting some of the more complex testing, and providing clinical indications and interpretations of testing results.

KEY CUSTOMERS AND THEIR PERFORMANCE EXPECTATIONS

Patients and healthcare providers expect that testing results used to prevent, diagnose, and treat disease will be of the highest quality and deserving of their trust. Their satisfaction also depends on the timeliness of testing, with more urgent/stat testing meeting clinical-need time frames, as appropriate. Other key customers and their expectations include the following:

- Emergency Department: This department must evaluate the patients' conditions as quickly as possible, and therefore requests rapid routine testing available in 60 to 90 minutes, with blood gases within 20 minutes. Transfusion services must be available 24/7 to provide blood units as necessary, especially in healthcare settings that are designated as certified trauma emergency rooms.

- Surgery Department: The OR requires point-of-care testing or rapid complex testing with minimal waiting for results. Frozen sections are often requested intraoperatively. The transfusion service is expected to provide blood components as needed should a patient begin to bleed unexpectedly.
- Maternity Unit: Stat testing is expected should the clinicians need the results for reevaluating the mothers' or babies' health.
- All hospital inpatient units: Clinicians, providers, and patients expect that routine testing on samples taken in early morning be available to the clinicians later that morning, to permit the clinician to discuss the results with the patients while rounding.
- Ambulatory patients: Patients and clinicians have time expectations depending on the complexity of the processes involved in the testing. Routine testing is expected to be rapid or at least completed within 24 hours. Some tissue samples may take four days to diagnose, whereas molecular and microbiology testing may take from a week to two months to complete depending on the test.
- Nursing staff: Although the clinicians are in charge of the patients, nurses continuously monitor patients as part of their daily care. Laboratory results provide them assessment tools to determine if patients' health status is clinically stable, improving, or declining.

KEY PROCESS FLOWS

Laboratories consider the scientific testing process to comprise three phases: pre-analytical, analytical, and postanalytical. The Clinical and Laboratory Standards Institute (CLSI), a volunteer-driven not-for-profit organization, provides the quality control and testing standardization procedures for laboratories in each phase required for scientific quality results.

1. Pre-analytical: Patient samples are collected from the patients in various ways. Some specimens, such as urine, are collected by the patient themselves, whereas others are drawn from the patient through phlebotomy and IV lines. In addition, some specimens are surgically removed or collected in clinics and operating rooms. The procurement, identification, stabilization, handling, transportation, and receipt of the specimen affect the integrity of specimens, and therefore the laboratory results are only as good as the samples submitted (CMS 2013).
2. Analytical: This phase is the testing component controlled by the laboratory upon receipt and documented for regulatory agencies. Monitoring of this

phase includes not only the testing process but also the analyzer validation, information system, algorithms, environment, competency of the personnel, equipment maintenance, reagents, and any other variables that may affect test results.

3. Postanalytical: This phase is described as the reporting phase. The results must reach the clinicians in a timely way, with reference ranges, and must be available for physicians and patients through medical records. Critical (life-threatening) results are required to be called to the clinician to ensure the patients' safety. All results released to the patients' charts or EHR must allow for assay comparisons and provide reference ranges (as per the College of American Pathologists; https://www.cap.org/).

Exhibit 12.2 depicts the three phases of testing.

Exhibit 12.2: Three Phases of Testing

Pre-analytical Phase	Analytical Phase	Post-analytical Phase
Collection of patient specimen for testing	Submitted for scientific testing in the laboratory	Results available to clinicians and patients
↓	↓	↓
Specimen/sample collected by phlebotomist (blood), surgically collected (biopsy), or self-collected (urine, sputum, etc.)	Calibrated analyzers release validated results for interpretation to Laboratory Informatics System (LIS)	Physicians/nurses receive results through EHR
↓	↓	↓
Specimens transported to laboratories at required temperatures for testing	Algorithms are applied to analytical results	Patient diagnosed, treated, or monitored based on received results
↓	↓	↓
Pre-analytical variables, such as labeling and temperatures, validated and documented	Verified results and interpretations released to EHR	Patient medical records (electronically stored)

KEY UNITS OF WORK AND VOLUME STATISTICS TO MONITOR

The multitude of metrics that laboratories use to monitor efficiencies and effectiveness include but are not limited to the number and type of specimens, different time frames, origin of specimens per service and location of patients, case count, and worked relative value units (wRVUs). Each laboratory section monitors the testing results filed into the EHR and staff productivity metrics. Laboratory sections may have different levels of complexity and regulatory standards that need to be accounted for in productivity metrics.

Budget metrics are related to testing volumes, capital, and expenses including labor, services, and consumables expended to produce test results. Once the results are produced, a charge is generated and submitted to government insurance plans such as Medicare and Medicaid, private insurance companies, or patient self-pay. The net revenue generated from the testing minus the expenses equals the profit or margin of the laboratory. When preparing a budget, laboratory managers base revenue on the number of expected tests for the coming year. Full-time equivalents (FTEs) are also based on testing volumes in each laboratory and would be adjusted up or down depending on quantity of tests requested in a time frame. To establish the charge for a test, a time study is performed detailing the amount of CLS time devoted to producing one result. If automation is included, the test total is taken into account to arrive at the hands-on time it takes to produce one result; these are the labor costs. Performing single tests, especially manually, often adds more labor per test than automated testing done with higher volumes. The labor ratio is used to estimate how many tests can be performed per hour. This productivity metric would need to be adjusted for the expected or required turnaround times for test results. (Turnaround time is defined as the time from when a specimen is received in the laboratory to when the result is available in the EHR. Critical tests from the Emergency Department, such as a CBC, result are expected to take no longer than 30–60 minutes.) Staffing models must meet this expectation, taking into account volume of patient specimens per day.

Additional metrics to be considered are the metrics related to the pathologists. CLIA laboratories receive multiple specimen types for testing and interpretations. Biopsies, and tissue samples received from the OR, are sent to the Pathology Department for processing. Anatomical pathologists are trained to examine tissues for signs of disease or malformations by reviewing cell morphology and molecular testing. Clinical pathologists are responsible for the blood and fluid patient samples processed in Laboratory Medicine lab sections including additional molecular testing. Typically, clinical pathologists also oversee the Transfusion Medicine Service. Both anatomical and clinical pathologists are evaluated for productivity using relative value units (RVUs), patient cases reviewed and interpreted, or slides reviewed per unit of time. The clinicians await the pathologist's interpretation or diagnosis to proceed with treatment; therefore, patient cases are expedited to ensure timeliness. Because clinical pathologists' main responsibilities include the regulatory oversight of automated laboratories, reviewing difficult hematology cases, and managing transfusion services, their productivity metrics depend heavily on the laboratories' performance and compliance with regulatory requirements.

KEY METRICS TO MONITOR: PEOPLE, SERVICE, QUALITY/SAFETY, FINANCIAL

Clinical Laboratories produce numerous metrics that are monitored to improve operations, ensure patient and employee safety, and satisfy clinicians. Regulatory agencies such as CMS, CAP, and The Joint Commission (TJC) require key metrics on laboratory performance, identified errors with corrective action, and monitoring of all required personnel requirements including competencies and education. CMS has granted deemed status to several agencies to survey laboratories for compliance every two years; CMS resurveys 10 percent of those laboratories. The College of American Pathologists (CAP) is the most commonly used agency to meet the CMS/CLIA survey requirement. Other agencies that survey the hospital of an institution will require documentation from its laboratories for standards that interface between nursing and the laboratory. When the deemed-status regulatory agency visits the laboratory, they meet with the staff and administration, then review the environment, proficiencies, procedures, quality monitors, and flow processes for all testing performed in the laboratory. The regulatory surveyors meet with the laboratory medical director, who is responsible for any citations the surveyors find that need remediation. Surveyors submit their findings to CMS in response to the Federal Regulations (CMS 2013).

Exhibit 12.3 summarizes the key metrics used to monitor clinical laboratories' performance.

Exhibit 12.3: Summary of Key Clinical Laboratory Metrics

Issue	Metric	Variable 1	Variable 2	Requirement/ measurement
Staffing	Competency/ proficiency	Procedures/ analyzer	Frequency/ outcomes	Regulatory requirements
	Education	Level of education	Level of patient testing	CLIA and FDA regulatory requirements
	Productivity	Time testing	Results produced	Efficiency/safety

(continued)

Issue	Metric	Variable 1	Variable 2	Requirement/measurement
Service	Patient satisfaction	Waiting time	Patients' scores	Press Ganey
	Provider satisfaction	Testing times	Providers' scores	Press Ganey/provider survey
	Key customers	Testing access	Satisfaction survey (biannual)	Regulatory requirement
Quality	Proficiency testing for each assay	Proficiency sample result	Validated result	CLIA and FDA required
	Pre-analytical errors (e.g., mislabeled, collected incorrectly)	Number of specimens	Frequency over time	Regulatory requirement; also requires remediation plans
Safety	Use of personal protective equipment	Compliance in using personal protective equipment	Exposures/incident frequency over time	OSHA, TJC, and CLIA regulatory requirements
	Safe patient care	Number of critical patient values	Turnaround times from result availability to clinician notification	CAP and TJC standards
Finance	Expenses	Number of test results finalized	Cost of labor and consumables per test	Budgets/sustainability
	Margins percent	Revenues received for testing/lab	Cost of all expenses per/lab area	Budgets/sustainability
	Staffing	Number of staff/lab	Number of tests performed	Budgets/sustainability
	Faculty	Percentage of clinical efforts designated per faculty	Number of wRVU/Cases (timely)	Budgets/sustainability
	Revenue	CPT code	Reimbursement adjusted per payors	Budgets/sustainability

Note: CAP = College of American Pathologists; CLIA = Clinical Laboratory Improvement Amendment; CPT = Current Procedural Terminology; FDA = US Food and Drug Administration; OSHA = Occupational Safety and Health Administration; TJC = The Joint Commission; wRVU = worked relative value unit.

KEY INFORMATICS ISSUES

Laboratories produce volumes of patient and regulatory data daily, and thus depend on robust computer systems and electronic software to manage it all while providing test results to physicians and patients (Lukić 2017). Many healthcare institutions have adopted an EHR system that includes the Laboratory Informatics System (LIS) to eliminate multiple interfaces between departments. According to Petrides et al. (2017) and Yusof and Arifin (2016), any new LIS should be evaluated by multiple levels of laboratory staff, including the pathologists, for a successful implementation. Yusof and Arifin (2016) recommend that clinicians and laboratory staff can reduce the number of errors by working together in an effective evaluation framework. A survey to evaluate LIS systems across the United States was administered by Mathews and Marc (2017). Their research revealed low ratings on a System Usability Scale for common tasks performed on multiple LISs. Petrides et al. (2017) state that a new LIS changes work processes, algorithms, middleware rule builders, and functionality in order to produce quality, scientific patient test results. Alternatively, Islam, Poly, and Li (2018, 88) suggest that the "integration of the LIS with other systems is always a challenge" due to the complexity of multiple other hospital informatic systems that must interface with the LIS. They suggest that the ideal LIS would need to serve a "multitude of clinical and lab workflows," some complex and compounding. Exhibit 12.4 identifies some of the multifaceted informatics issues that support the need for pathologists' subject matter expertise in selecting a LIS.

Exhibit 12.4: Key Informatics Issues for Laboratory Informatics Systems

Attributes or services	Key points for deciding which LIS meets laboratory needs
Specialized modules	Requirements of highly complex areas (e.g., transfusion services, HLA lab, molecular labs) must be met
Pathology services	Software must provide the pathologist the ability to review test results, images, health state of patient, and diagnostic history to interpret the surgical specimen and provide digital imaging with algorithms
Laboratory services	Multifunctional modules to assist with multiple workflows, ability to interface with middleware solutions, multiple instrument interfaces, point-of-care testing, off-site laboratories, and outreach must be made available. Interface with other clinical informatic systems and the hospital EHR

(continued)

Attributes or services	Key points for deciding which LIS meets laboratory needs
Outside interfaces	Software needs to interface with public health reporting, reference laboratories, research sources, and tumor registries Laboratories providing reference testing for other organizations must have LIS that is able to interface with clients, provide financial reports, and track all specimens
Flexibility	Software must allow for implementation of new technologies and methodologies through interfaces and integrating the testing results seamlessly
Cost	Deciding to change LIS is costly and must be assessed with upgrade of current system
Features	Must allow for order entry, tracking of specimens, and concise and rapid reporting. Should a new LIS be planned, care must be taken to ensure maintenance/functionality of the old software/system while providing new features with the new system
Responsiveness	LIS vendor must be highly committed and respond quickly to issues that may arise
Revenue	Ability to capture subcomponents of testing panels to insure appropriate billing
Regulatory standards	Ability to capture all metrics required of agencies to meet standards
Middleware solutions	Ability to support algorithms that provide safe and scientific results for the patients

Note: EHR = electronic health record; HLA = human leukocyte antigen; LIS = Laboratory Informatics System.

STAFFING MODELS

Clinical laboratory staffing depends on the complexity and volume of testing performed to ensure accuracy and quality. CLIA requires CLSs and MTs in laboratories that perform moderate- and high-complexity testing. These individuals graduate from college with a bachelor's degree in allied health or science that includes a minor in mathematics. To qualify for a board certification in Laboratory Science, they must also intern for a year in a clinical laboratory and then pass the board examination. The board of certification most recognized is the American Society for Clinical Pathology (ASCP), which provides certification in all clinical laboratory specialties, including cytology, molecular, microbiology, blood bank, histology, and general medical technology. In states that require board certification, the ASCP is the organization of choice, but some states provide their own state boards. To improve patient care, the ASCP collaborates with many organizations to provide education and training in the field to pathologists, residents, students, and medical laboratory professionals to ensure competent lab workers who meet the CLIA requirements.

The staffing models used in laboratories are required to meet CLIA supervisory requirements. There must be a supervising individual in the laboratory, either a CLS or a pathologist. The supervisor must have the required years of laboratory experience related to the testing being performed in that laboratory. Although non-degreed individuals may perform the pre-analytical phase, only the CLS can perform the analytical or testing phase at moderate and higher complexities. Even the waived and nonwaived lower-complexity point-of-care testing must be overseen by CLS staff.

A pathologist or their designee commissions a new laboratory when there is a service need. When designing the laboratory, time studies are performed and non-personnel expenses are totaled to establish charges for the test(s) that will be performed in that laboratory. Management will expect a certain test volume to justify the new laboratory. Using both the labor time established in the time study and the projected test volume, the laboratory director can calculate how many CLSs and non-degreed individuals are needed to staff the laboratory and what the expected turnaround times for testing will be. The staffing model will gain efficiencies as testing processes becomes standardized and routine or when manual processes are replaced with automation. The staffing model must also allow time to perform proficiencies (regulatory specimens required to maintain CLIA certification) and complete regulatory documentation that will be reviewed on biannual surveys and yearly audits by CMS or a recognized deemed status regulatory agency. Exhibit 12.5 depicts the categories of staff that most laboratories use.

Exhibit 12.5: Categories of Laboratory Staff

Staffing	Service need	Credentials required
Laboratory/medical director	Smaller laboratories may only require one laboratory/medical director; larger laboratories require multiple directors to assure compliance with standards required by certifying agencies.	Medical directors require board certification in anatomical pathology and clinical pathology depending on their oversight.
Testing personnel (day labs)	Laboratories open for office hours hire according to testing volumes and test complexity for one shift. Vacation, sick time, and personal time must be addressed to ensure testing can be performed as required by clinic or office.	CLIA has waived all testing that is considered low risk to cause harm and is low error prone but is overseen by the physician on-site. All complex testing must be performed by higher-educated individuals under a physician's oversight.

(continued)

Staffing	Service need	Credentials required
Testing personnel (24/7 labs)	Laboratories open 24/7 must determine the labor required to staff the laboratory in accordance with the projected volume of testing. Staffing ratios must include 21 shifts (4.2 FTEs without allowance of PTO, emergency time, or sick time). For every five staff members, an additional FTE is required to cover benefit time.	CLSs and MTs require a bachelor's degree in medical technology or biological science. Many organizations require ASCP board certification or equivalent. California, Florida, New York, and Washington State require that CLSs and MTs obtain a professional license.
Testing personnel (cytology and histology)	Laboratories performing fine needle aspirates and cytology require cytotechnologists, who are highly regulated by CLIA. Histology laboratories require personnel that have documentation of competency in tissue processing.	Cytotechnologists require a board certification with a bachelor's degree in science; histology techs do not require a bachelor's degree.
Pathologists	Clinical testing, including clinical interpretations, requires medical doctors to finalize patient results to get reimbursed by CMS.	CLIA and CAP require board certification in the specialty area to approve them to be the laboratory director.
PhDs (alternative)	Clinical testing interpretations can be provided by PhDs but cannot be billed per CMS; they can be billed to private insurers.	The PhD holder must be board certified both to perform clinical interpretations and to be the laboratory director in a clinical laboratory.

Source: Adapted from CMS (2013).
Note: ASCP = American Society for Clinical Pathology; CAP = College of American Pathologists; CLIA = Clinical Laboratory Improvement Amendment; CLS = clinical laboratory scientist; FTE = full-time equivalent; MT = medical technologist; PTO = paid time off.

PRODUCTIVITY MODELS, INCLUDING WORK-TO-STAFF RATIOS AND INDUSTRY PERFORMANCE TARGETS

Labor Ratio: Test per FTE

The Department of Pathology and Laboratory Medicine comprises many sections devoted to testing, ranging from highly automated testing analytics to tests that require one test, one tech. To establish the ratio of testing to each FTE in each area, laboratory managers must perform a time study that accounts for the number of tests that can be performed in one workday. Accordingly, techs working in more automated sections will be expected to produce more tests in their workday: automated analyzers will perform some of the required steps in the testing procedures, which allows the techs to perform quality control reviews, evaluate calibrations, and troubleshoot any issues related to the produced testing results. In other labs, the technical staff may have more labor-intensive specimen processing or procedures that require more tech time to produce the test results. The number of test results would be lower per FTE. All test results are expected to meet all quality criteria before they are released in the software; algorithms may be designed to capture any lapse in quality or accuracy before the test result is released to the clinician.

Revenue Ratio: Revenue per FTE

Each lab or section will establish the revenue generated per FTE (or net revenue per FTE) by reconciling the number of FTEs completing the testing in the section. This ratio typically includes non-testing (support) staff and testing personnel.

Cases Versus wRVUs

Productivity metrics for pathologists need to be carefully assessed, with consideration given to the nuances of the pathology field. In academic medical centers, pathologists' work time is divided into four elements: clinical effort (work on cases), research time (work on research projects), administrative (support for institutional initiatives or committees), and education (teaching). Anatomical pathologists' productivity is quantified by the number of patient cases they finalize in a certain period by using wRVUs. Unfortunately, this strategy has its flaws because some cases are highly complex with multiple tissue samples to be reviewed before the pathologist makes a diagnosis, whereas other pathology specialties may have fewer tissue samples per case. Academic institutions with their highly specialized pathology departments can be underappreciated for their productivity because they often review highly complex cases referred for their expertise. Certain areas of anatomical pathology are rich with wRVUs because many immunohistochemistry or flow-cytometry tests are required per case, which incurs several wRVUs that may require less work effort, resulting in productivity inequalities among the subspecialties. See exhibit 12.6 for productivity metrics.

Clinical pathologists are also assigned clinical effort, research, administrative, and education responsibilities. Instead of single cases, they are responsible for hundreds or thousands of tests from many patients and cases, and these tests are charged daily in different laboratories. The wRVUs captured are the interpretations assigned

Exhibit 12.6: Pathologist Productivity Metrics

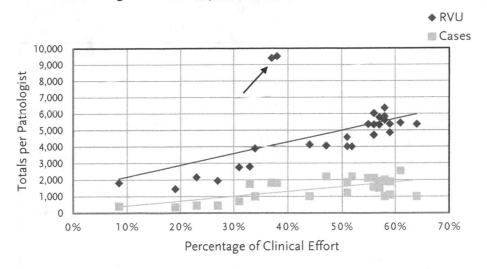

Note: Totals per Pathologist = total cases and wRVUs generated from different subspecialties per pathologist.

Note the large increase in the RVUs generated by two pathologists (indicated by the arrow) because their cases require multiple confirmatory tests, such as immunohistochemistry tests or flow-cytometry studies, which generate multiple wRVUs per case.

to a small percentage of these blood or body fluid tests, but the clinical pathologists' main responsibility lies in ensuring both laboratory regulatory compliance and safe, quality testing for patients. Their productivity metrics incorporate the laboratory proficiency program and the regulatory compliance surveyed annually. Some clinical pathologists are also responsible for transfusion medicine service cases, including transfusion reactions and patient consultations related to blood products, both of which generate wRVUs. In addition, clinical pathologists are responsible for blood conservation programs to ensure safe levels of blood supply in the institution. The number of transfusions in the institution and the timeliness of responses from transfusion services to clinicians is monitored to determine if additional clinical pathologists are needed to oversee transfusion services in accord with regulatory guidelines. Exhibit 12.7 charts metrics for clinical pathology productivity.

STRATEGIES TO IMPROVE RECRUITMENT AND RETENTION

Many larger laboratories and academic centers have addressed the diminishing number of CLSs/MTs in the market by supporting schools for health science professionals or hiring college graduates who majored in science and providing

Exhibit 12.7: Graph of Clinical Pathology Productivity

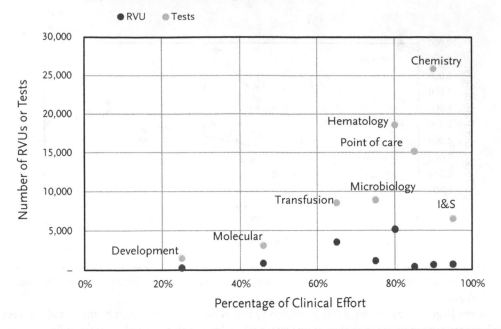

Note: I&S = Immunology and Serology; RVUs = relative value units. Clinical Pathologists' worked RVUs (wRVUs) may vary considerably among different laboratory specialties and may not directly correlate with the large testing volumes that they are responsible for overseeing. Some laboratory tests provide few if any wRVUs to the clinical pathologists.

them a year-long internship opportunity to meet CLIA requirements, along with monetary incentives to become certified by a regulatory agency such as ASCP.

Using career ladders to recognize the increasing skill levels of testing personnel has been effective in retaining technologists and developing them to progress to management levels. These programs provide expanded educational opportunities, additional pay for additional skills, leadership development, and mentoring.

Faculty retention programs include leadership development classes and programs to integrate CLSs/MTs into administrative initiatives and projects. In addition, institutions can offer recognition incentive programs and research opportunities through funding and collaborations with other institutions. Programs are intended to develop and mentor the clinicians but also retain them.

KEY REGULATORY ISSUES

All laboratory tests performed on humans in the United States must meet the regulatory requirements of the CLIA under CMS authorization if the test result will be used to treat or diagnose the patient. Therefore, CMS excludes basic research testing from the CLIA requirements because the results are not used to care for patients.

CMS certifies approximately 260,000 US laboratory entities, of which 69 percent are certified as waived laboratories (CMS 2020). To ensure compliance with quality and safety standards, CLIA or other deemed-status regulatory agencies survey the clinical laboratories every two to three years. CAP, TJC, COLA Inc., and the American Association for Laboratory Accreditation are the most common agencies laboratories use to maintain CLIA certification status. In addition, laboratories are required to meet their state's regulations, some of which require additional standards beyond the CLIA requirements. Larger laboratories are required to maintain multiple regulatory certifications because they incorporate specialty laboratories and must follow special FDA requirements. The FDA oversees medical devices such as testing platforms and blood bank activities, and surveys the blood banks often.

With the rapid expansion of methodologies in the clinical laboratory field, especially in genetic testing, the regulatory agencies overseeing regulations and reimbursements are falling behind the science. An example is molecular testing and its advances in the last five years. Although CMS and CLIA address issues related to routine testing, the new regulations addressing developing fields such as molecular diagnostics have not met the many complexities resulting from genetic testing (e.g., germline findings in a liquid biopsy sample). A second issue is patient privacy regarding genetic testing. Clinical trials targeting genetic testing on infants are being used for prognoses and researched for selective characteristics. Although genetic mutations can be identified and some clinical conditions mitigated, the massive amount of predictive data now available when performing these genetic panels raises concern about the baby's rights to privacy (see the National Institutes of Health, ClinicalTrials.gov).

A compounding regulatory issue is that laboratories have been challenged by decreasing reimbursement for testing as the cost of complex testing has risen to maintain quality standards. Although laboratory testing constitutes only 4 percent of the CMS annual budget, Congress continues to cut the reimbursement for laboratory services each year through the Protecting Access to Medicare Act of 2014 (PAMA) regulations, making it difficult to cover the cost of quality testing. Insurance companies typically follow CMS guidelines and will also pay less for testing (CMS 2019b).

For years, laboratory-developed tests (LDTs) have been designed by laboratories and surveyed by the regulatory agencies; now CMS/CLIA has adopted the charge of surveying laboratories for the clinical validity of LDTs. The agency has been expanded to survey more laboratories throughout the country, which has increased the volume of regulatory documentation and number of laboratory surveys. Any deviation from FDA-approved testing requirements delegates the tests as an LDT and requires a full validation per CLIA [CMS 2019a; see 42 CFR 1253(b)(2)]. The laboratories are responsible for maintaining regulatory documentation and validations for multiple agencies, which increases the cost of testing for the patients and increases the expense of healthcare as the population demands more quality tests with faster and higher-complexity results to help clinicians properly diagnose and treat patients.

KEY TERMS FOR PATHOLOGY AND LABORATORY MEDICINE

Centers for Medicare & Medicaid Services: Part of the US Department of Health and Human Services, CMS is responsible for federal healthcare programs, including incentive programs for electronic health records such as meaningful use. Oversees CLIA regulations.

Clinical and Laboratory Standards Institute: Provides quality control for and standardization of laboratory procedures in all laboratory disciplines. The standards are developed by scientific leadership worldwide and are considered the source of truth for clinical scientific human testing.

Clinical Laboratory Improvement Amendments: These 1988 amendments contain the federal regulatory standards required of all clinical laboratories performing human testing used to treat patients. (Basic research and clinical trials are exempt, unless required.)

COLA: Premier clinical laboratory accreditation, consultation, and education organization that has deemed status with CMS.

College of American Pathologists: An accreditation organization that comprises 18,000 board-certified pathologists. It holds deemed status with CMS to accredit laboratories, meeting many states' certification requirements, in lieu of a CMS inspection.

Electronic health record: A digital version of a patient's medical record or chart that makes information available immediately and securely to healthcare workers and patients.

Human leukocyte antigen: The system that produces proteins present on the surface of almost all human cells that factor in organ-transplant compatibility outcomes.

Microbiology: The study of organisms too individually small to see with the naked eye. Although these organisms are ubiquitous, some are beneficial to humans whereas others can produce infections in humans who are exposed to them.

Molecular diagnostic testing: Techniques used to identify genetic biological markers in the genome of patient samples that indicate mutations (changes) in genes, which may influence the development of a specific disease or disorder, such as cancer or cystic fibrosis.

Patient sample: A human specimen submitted for testing or assessment (e.g., blood, urine, and other bodily fluids, and tissues).

Polymerase chain reaction: A chemical reaction intended to amplify millions of copies of a specific DNA segment, also referred to as "molecular photocopying."

Specimen ID: Samples uniquely identified with patient information typically barcoded with unique patient numbers and accession numbers.

REFERENCES

Centers for Medicare & Medicaid Services (CMS). 2020. "Division of Clinical Laboratory Improvement and Quality Enrollment Data." Published March. www.cms.gov/Regulations-and-Guidance/Legislation/CLIA/Downloads/statupda.pdf.

———. 2019a. "Clinical Laboratory Improvement Amendments." Published January 18. www.cms.gov/Regulations-and-Guidance/Legislation/CLIA/index.html.

———. 2019b. "PAMA Regulations." Published January 22. www.cms.gov/Medicare/Medicare-Fee-for-Service-Payment/ClinicalLabFeeSched/PAMA-Regulations.html.

———. 2013. "CLIA Regulations and Federal Register Documents." Published August 6. www.cms.gov/Regulations-and-Guidance/Legislation/CLIA/CLIA_Regulations_and_Federal_Register_Documents.html.

Hallworth, M. J. 2011. "The '70% Claim': What Is the Evidence Base?" *Annals of Clinical Biochemistry* 48 (Pt 6): 487–88.

Hiltunen, M. J. 2017. "Dispelling the 70% Claim with Laboratory's True Value." *Medical Lab Management.* Published October. www.medlabmag.com/article/1406.

Islam, M. M., T. N. Poly, and Y.-C. J. Li. 2018. "Recent Advancement of Clinical Information Systems: Opportunities and Challenges." *Yearbook of Medical Informatics* 27 (1): 83–90.

Lukić, V. 2017. "Laboratory Information System—Where Are We Today?" *Journal of Medical Biochemistry* 36 (3): 220–24.

Mathews, A., and D. Marc. 2017. "Usability Evaluation of Laboratory Information Systems." *Journal of Pathology Informatics.* Published October 3. www.ncbi.nlm.nih.gov/pmc/articles/PMC5653961/.

Mayo Clinic College of Medicine and Science. 2020. "Medical Laboratory Scientist." Accessed October 6. https://college.mayo.edu/academics/explore-health-care-careers/careers-a-z/medical-laboratory-scientist/.

Ngo, A., P. Gandhi, and W. G. Miller. 2017. "Frequency That Laboratory Tests Influence Medical Decisions." *Journal of Applied Laboratory Medicine* 1 (4): 410–14.

Petrides, A. K., M. J. Tanasijevic, E. M. Goonan, A. B. Landman, M. Kantartjis, D. W. Bates, and S. E. F. Melanson. 2017. "Top Ten Challenges When Interfacing a Laboratory Information System to an Electronic Health Record: Experience at a Large Academic Medical Center." *International Journal of Medical Informatics* 106: 9–16.

Quest Diagnostics. 2020. "What to Know About Fasting Before Your Lab Test." Accessed October 6. www.questdiagnostics.com/home/patients/preparing-for-test/fasting.

Skobelev, D. O., T. M. Zaytseva, A. D. Kozlov, V. L. Perepelitsa, and A. S. Makarova. 2011. "Laboratory Information Management Systems in the Work of the Analytic Laboratory." *Measurement Techniques* 53 (10): 1182–89.

Yusof, M. M., and A. Arifin. 2016. "Towards an Evaluation Framework for Laboratory Information Systems." *Journal of Infection and Public Health* 9 (6): 766–73.

Patient Advocacy

Elizabeth Comcowich Garcia, Chris Hernandez,
Michele Walker, Judy Overton, and Randal S. Weber

DEPARTMENT DESCRIPTION

The Patient Advocacy program exists to provide patients in the healthcare system an opportunity to voice complaints, grievances, or requests, and to seek prompt resolution of their concerns. In most organizations, the ability to express concerns is a fundamental patient right that is typically embedded in an institutional patient bill of rights. Although each organization may customize its Patient Advocacy program to meet the specific needs of its patient population, policies are also in place at the state and federal levels to ensure patient-centered care and protect patients' rights (Centers for Medicare & Medicaid Services [CMS] 2020).

The purpose of a Patient Advocacy program is to help patients, families, visitors, and staff identify and remove perceived obstacles and barriers to patient care. A patient advocate serves as a liaison between the patient and their healthcare team to mediate and resolve complaints and grievances in a timely, reasonable, and consistent manner. Advocates also process specific requests and help connect patients to all resources and services available to assist in the healthcare journey. To serve their patients effectively, advocates should possess a thorough knowledge of their healthcare organization's patient care philosophy, organizational structure, and policies. Fundamental to this role is the advocate's ability to leverage strong professional relationships with key individuals in the organization (Jansson et al. 2016).

Successful Patient Advocacy programs train their staff to interact with patients in a highly professional, empathetic, diplomatic, and objective manner, especially on sensitive and complex issues. In an ideal patient-centered care culture, Patient Advocacy programs partner with patients and their families to create an environment of comfort and trust as a safe harbor to share their concerns. Piper and Tallman (2015) encourage a collaboration in which interventions are made, and resolutions accomplished, with the active participation of the patient and their family, which aligns with the four components of a family-centered culture: dignity and respect, information sharing, participation, and collaboration (Piper 2011). When patients are empowered to voice their opinions or concerns, advocates are able to identify trends and facilitate change and improvement.

Many professions have a set of core tenets, or fundamental values, that shape their departmental goals. In Patient Advocacy departments, these values are often rooted in the belief that all patients have the right to safe care, to have concerns acknowledged, to receive a response, and to see timely action on their behalf. This belief arises from the "Value = Outcomes / Cost" model, shown in exhibit 13.1, which Porter (2014) developed to encourage a major change in healthcare that centers on improved value for consumers. Since this concept debuted, healthcare institutions have created their own models that meet their organizations' needs. One approach to consider is the Value Equation (exhibit 13.2). Developed by members of a comprehensive cancer center, the Value Equation places an emphasis on the experiences of all key stakeholders—patients, caregivers, and providers. This team approach allows patients and their loved ones to receive key information from providers that allows them to make informed care decisions. In turn, patients and caregivers offer feedback to their providers and the institution, which could help improve its processes and programs.

Exhibit 13.1: Principles of Value-Based Healthcare Delivery

$$Value = \frac{\text{Health outcomes that matter to patients}}{\text{Cost of delivering the outcome}}$$

Source: Adapted from Porter (2014).

Exhibit 13.2: Healthcare Value Equation That Includes Experience

Note: Experience includes patients, caregivers, providers, and employees.

KEY DEPARTMENT SERVICES

In most organizations, leadership delegates to the Department of Patient Advocacy the primary responsibility for reviewing and resolving grievances. Grievances are presented to an organization in several ways, many of which involve Patient Advocacy. Patients may share their displeasure with a staff member for referral to a hospital representative, usually a patient advocate, who should investigate the issue and follow up with the patient. Patients may also directly contact the Patient Advocacy office to file their complaint, and may notify the state or federal agencies that oversee the facility. Patients have the further option of sharing experiences through systemwide surveys they receive after discharge. Once the institution is aware of an issue, the Patient Advocacy Department must take consistent and timely steps to acknowledge, investigate, and document the grievance and respond to the patient. Some of the patients' complaints can be directly linked to patient safety, poor professional behavior, risk management concerns, or inadequate operational processes. Ideally, the organization should compile the information on a unified platform to capture all patient incidents across a wide spectrum. Such an approach will better equip organizational leaders to respond quickly and address underlying "institutional blind spots," which facilitates a better patient outcome and experience.

DEPARTMENT ORGANIZATIONAL STRUCTURES

Patient Advocacy involves myriad responsibilities that are required to meet the operational needs of a patient-centered program. Because healthcare organizations place strong emphasis on exceptional customer service, their need for frontline communication experts extends well beyond the standard patient advocate position. Advocates' ultimate role is to serve as liaisons between patients and their family members with the institution's administration, healthcare providers, and staff, depending on the involved parties. In performing this role, patient advocates must surround themselves with a knowledgeable and capable support staff, because of the heavy reliance on the following administrative actions: documenting complaints and grievances, recording data and trends; creating reports; responding to regulatory audits and reviews; and providing customer service in person or via phone or email. Establishing an administrative infrastructure facilitates compliance with state and federal requirements and allows the advocates to focus primarily on meeting the needs of a distressed or dissatisfied patient population.

Patient advocate positions should be multi-tiered and offer opportunities for professional growth and development to allow team members to be promoted to senior patient advocate or team lead. Absent opportunities to advance, advocates may succumb to burnout or other stress-induced conditions. Department leaders should periodically survey their employees to assess employee satisfaction, both to establish credibility with employees and to address their needs (Studer 2008). (Fatigue and burnout will be further addressed in the Strategies to Improve Recruitment and Retention section.)

Another layer of the Patient Advocacy organization is leadership, which should include supervisors, managers, an executive-level leader, or a medical director for patient advocacy. The medical director often has received responsibility for the effective operation of the institution's grievance process, which is then delegated to the director of Patient Advocacy. The responsibilities include oversight of the institution's patient grievance process, review and resolution of patient grievances, and distribution of data regarding patient complaints and grievances to the institution's Quality Assessment and Performance Improvement Council. The medical director also serves as the lead investigator for medical quality issues and collaborates with other physician leaders throughout the organization. A vital role for the medical director, or their delegate, is initiating and leading family conferences with the patient's medical team. Often a family conference is the most effective way to address grievances, especially those pertaining to quality of care. Organizational models will vary with the size and scope of the department. However, filling key components of the organizational structure with administrative and support staff, patient advocates, and department leadership will help frame the core of a fully functioning Patient Advocacy team. Exhibit 13.3 shows a sample Patient Advocacy organizational chart.

Exhibit 13.3: Sample Patient Advocacy Organizational Chart

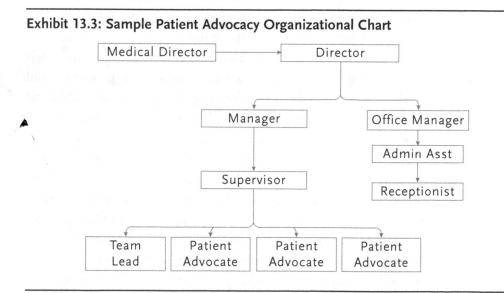

KEY CUSTOMERS AND THEIR PERFORMANCE EXPECTATIONS

A Department of Patient Advocacy has a wellspring of key customers, or stakeholders, who rely on its employees to administer important services in providing patient-centered care while adhering to regulatory requirements. Stakeholders include patients and their representatives, the institution's governing body, clinicians and their support staff, and Risk Management.

Patients or their representatives are the department's priority customers. Patient advocates are responsible to ensure that patient complaints and grievances are investigated, addressed, and resolved in a prompt, reasonable, and consistent manner. They are the frontline faces of an organization for patients and their representatives during this process. According to the CMS Conditions of Participation, a Patient Advocacy Department also has the responsibility to track and trend complaints and to assist the institution, where possible and appropriate, in taking steps to improve systems, safety, efficiency, and overall quality of patient care and service (GovRegs 2020b). As a result, each complaint and grievance contributes to improvement for all patients. Hospitals must establish a process for prompt resolution of patient grievances and to inform each patient whom to contact to file a grievance.

The institution's governing body typically is also a customer of the Patient Advocacy Department. The CMS Conditions of Participation state that the governing body is responsible for the operation of the grievance process, unless it delegates the responsibility in writing to a grievance committee. The grievance committee is most frequently chartered under, and led by, the Patient Advocacy medical director or executive leadership. Committee members are obligated to regularly report data and trends regarding complaints and grievances to the governing body (GovRegs 2020a). Such monitoring and reporting ensures that these trends are analyzed robustly so they can be used in a process improvement strategy to enhance safety, quality, and patient experience.

Every healthcare organization should establish policies to document, investigate, and resolve complaints and grievances, and patient advocates are the guardians of this process. Key elements of the policy should include an interview with the patient or patient representative, a review of the patient's medical record, interviews with staff members who may have knowledge of the grievance, and potential measures for resolving the grievance (Emergency Care Research Institute [ECRI] 2016). Physicians, advanced practice providers, and staff are also often customers of Patient Advocacy departments. Advocates must support and assist not only patients but also employees who facilitate grievance resolution. All employees of an institution must refer any grievance to the Patient Advocacy Department in order to follow the institution's established grievance policies. Throughout the process, the Patient Advocacy staff must establish and maintain professional, productive, and responsive relationships with providers and staff to facilitate open communication. Involving an advocate as soon as possible in a grievance situation will help to achieve timely resolution (GovRegs 2020b).

Another important role for advocates is to counsel and assist providers in disclosing medical errors to patients or their representatives. The evidence is strong that having a policy of disclosing medical errors reduces litigation, strengthens patient–provider relationships, and eases provider burnout (American College of Obstetricians and Gynecologists 2016). These can be difficult conversations for providers, but advocates can provide support and presence for the patients and providers involved in the disclosures. Finally, Risk Management is a close collaborator of Patient Advocacy. Risk Management professionals often manage medical errors or occurrences that are associated with a complaint or grievance, and they must follow the grievance resolution process.

KEY PROCESS FLOWS

Exhibit 13.4 summarizes the key steps in addressing patient complaints and grievances required under the CMS Conditions of Participation. Particular attention is given to the types of grievances and the responsibilities of the patient advocate in documenting, assigning, and resolving the issues that emanate from verbal or written complaints, including patient surveys.

Exhibit 13.4: Process for Addressing Patient Complaints

Process for addressing patient complaints and grievances

Pursuant to the Centers for Medicare & Medicaid Services (CMS) Guidelines

1. Any Staff Member who receives a verbal **Complaint** from a Patient or Patient Representative must:
   a. Obtain all relevant information related to the Complaint.
   b. Take all actions necessary to resolve the Complaint at the time of communication by Staff Present.
   c. **Report such Complaint and actions to Patient Advocacy if the Complaint is not resolved at the time of the Complaint by Staff Present and requires additional time for investigation, action, or referral to other staff for resolution.**

2. Any Staff Member who receives a **Grievance** from a Patient or Patient Representative must:
   a. Obtain all relevant information related to the Grievance.
   b. **Immediately forward the Grievance to Patient Advocacy.**

(continued)

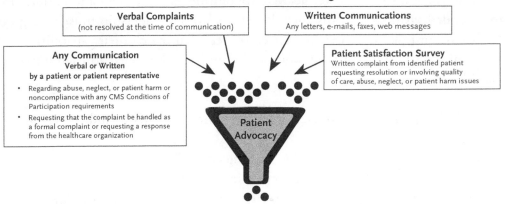

Grievances include the following:

Verbal Complaints	Written Communications
(not resolved at the time of communication)	Any letters, e-mails, faxes, web messages

Any Communication
Verbal or Written
by a patient or patient representative
- Regarding abuse, neglect, or patient harm or noncompliance with any CMS Conditions of Participation requirements
- Requesting that the complaint be handled as a formal complaint or requesting a response from the healthcare organization

Patient Satisfaction Survey
Written complaint from identified patient requesting resolution or involving quality of care, abuse, neglect, or patient harm issues

Patient Advocacy

Patient Advocacy Responsibilities

- Document receipt, assignment, and resolution of all Grievances and maintain the Grievance Log in accordance with the healthcare organization's Complaints and Grievances Policy.
- Send Resolution Letters, and if necessary, Acknowledgment Letters and/or Progress Letters.
  - **Resolution Letter**—A written communication sent upon resolution of the Grievance.
  - **Acknowledgment Letter**—A written communication regarding a Grievance that is not resolved within seven (7) business days.
  - **Progress Letter**—A written communication regarding a Grievance that is not resolved within thirty (30) business days.

All Medicare beneficiary billing complaints related to, for example, rights and limitations on allowable charges to beneficiaries for deductibles, coinsurance, and/or copayments as provided for in 42 CFR Part 489 are Grievances.

The healthcare organization's Billing Department is responsible for Medicare beneficiary billing complaints. The above documentation and resolution process will be utilized by the Billing Department to address Medicare beneficiary billing Grievances.

KEY UNITS OF WORK AND VOLUME STATISTICS TO MONITOR

Productivity metrics are difficult to measure in Patient Advocacy because of the heterogeneity of the complaints and grievances. Resolving a given grievance may require a three-minute phone call or several family conferences and the engagement of multiple providers. Often the patient advocate is addressing a complicated issue such as providing compensation to a patient for expenses as a result of service issues, such as travel-delayed appointments or housing and parking for an extended visit. In each instance, Patient Advocacy leadership must take great care to assign tasks and cases to their employees that match their capabilities and position descriptions. Units of work and volume apportioned to each advocate should consider

- patient/representative contacts such as phone calls, emails, and in-person meetings;
- number of grievance cases being investigated;
- frequency of family conferences coordinated; and
- number of required acknowledgment and resolution communications.

Leadership also should consider how much time is needed for each unit of work; this can vary with grievance complexity and severity. Departments may choose to generate more accurate data by doing studies over time.

Some Patient Advocacy departments assign levels to complaints and grievances as they are received to help measure productivity and more evenly distribute work among staff. Current literature provides no benchmarks for assigning levels of complexity to grievances; however, most institutions have developed internal criteria. Because many Patient Advocacy departments designate an on-call advocate to cover after-hours situations, the staffing model must account for the time commitment to perform on-call duty and daily hours worked. Although tracking this data monthly can be helpful, patient advocacy staff must always be ready to pivot assignments, because rarely is the grievance resolution process a straight line.

KEY METRICS TO MONITOR: PEOPLE, SERVICE, QUALITY/SAFETY, FINANCIAL

Patient Advocacy departments do not create a revenue stream. In addition to standard cost oversight, including personnel and expenses, Patient Advocacy departments monitor several key metrics, many of which are clearly outlined by regulatory agencies (D'Amico et al. 2020). Service metrics include ensuring 100 percent of all grievances, no matter the source, are addressed and have a written resolution sent to the patient or representative who lodged the grievance. Patient advocates must track all key units of work, such as the types of complaints and grievances received, and the average time in days taken to acknowledge and resolve them. Current CMS guidance is that most grievances be resolved within an average of seven days. However, CMS's greatest concern is that any complaint or grievance should be acknowledged in writing within seven days, and that the patient or patient representative be kept up to date on the investigation and resolution process. Any CMS survey will focus on whether the institution is following its complaint and grievance policy. This policy should define the targeted average timeline for acknowledgment and resolution, and should specify whether the timeline includes weekends (GovRegs 2020b). Patient Advocacy departments also monitor and account for compensation provided to patients and families for customer service reasons. Analyzing monetary expenses can help influence changes to the institution's processes that improve patient experience. Department leaders may also consider tracking the quality and process improvement that arises from complaint and grievance trends. These improvements can help measure the value that Patient Advocacy departmental contributions add to the institutional mission. Regulatory agencies require that these key metrics regularly be reported to the governing body and the quality assurance and process improvement committee. Exhibit 13.5 lists suggested key metrics to report.

Individual advocates may have benchmarks to measure performance success; for example, the percentage of patient complaints and grievances successfully resolved to the patient's satisfaction. Most patient advocacy data is documented and compiled into a complaint and grievance database. A quick review of this registry could indicate whether or not an advocate is meeting this particular standard. Another way to benchmark an advocate's performance would be to include a question about Patient Advocacy services on a patient satisfaction survey. The question could read, "If you required the services of a patient advocate, was your issue resolved to your satisfaction?" A further benchmark could be centered on an advocate's communication and organizational proficiency by tracking acknowledgment and response deadlines. The state and regulatory agencies that govern

---

Exhibit 13.5: Suggested Key Metrics to Report to the Governing Body

1. Trending quarterly number of complaints, topic of complaint, and the department or service from which the complaint originated.[a]
2. Trending quarterly number of grievances, topic of grievances, and the department or service from which the grievance originated.
3. Days to acknowledge, in writing, grievances to the patient or patient representative.
4. Days to resolve and communication resolution to patient or patient representative.
5. Detailed report of any grievance that caused harm to the patient or for which the institution paid out compensation.
6. Measurable improvements made to processes as per previously trending complaints or grievances.

---

[a]Complaints are resolved at the time they are communicated, so there is no time frame to report for acknowledgment or resolution.

Patient Advocacy programs have exacting timelines and standards that advocates must meet when resolving patient complaints and grievances. Ensuring these timelines and standards are met is an essential element of success for any Patient Advocacy program. One last benchmark to consider could be to measure the advocate's ability to meet quarterly reporting deadlines. Patient advocates are required to prepare and present information to executive leadership for quality improvement. Although this is a key indicator of success, notifying leadership of factors that increase patient dissatisfaction is also a crucial element in creating and maintaining a safe, patient-centered environment.

KEY INFORMATICS ISSUES

Addressing patients' grievances expeditiously is not only the right thing to do, but is also a federal and state mandate (Piper and Tallman 2015). Healthcare informatics is therefore becoming a key element at organizations nationwide in addressing operational issues and improving patient satisfaction. In the past, healthcare organizations focused primarily on the patient's medical condition versus the non-medical experience that resulted in patient displeasure or dissatisfaction. Today, medical informatics is changing that conventional way of thinking by collecting, analyzing, and responding to data generated during a poor patient experience. In a recent study funded by the Agency for Healthcare Research and Quality, Haldar et al. (2019) reported that medical informatics was found to "support patients at all stages of their experience by increasing awareness of [undesirable events], encouraging intervention and resolution, detecting and managing invisible harms [such as emotional trauma], and reducing barriers and sharing report updates."

Healthcare institutions worldwide are finding that a unified reporting and documentation system that tracks patient complaints and grievances, safety incidents, risk management, and (most recently) breaches of professionalism is vital to producing actionable data and trends or providing efficient regulatory and legal reporting as needed. Individuals across the organization enter incidents into the system, and staff from each department can review them to ascertain if their department has a role to play in resolving them. For example, some grievances involve both safety and risk management. Logging such grievances in a data system with universal department access is a much more organized way to manage work. Such a system increases efficiency by reducing duplication of effort or missed opportunities, which improves collaboration across departments and mitigates miscommunication. Several companies have developed these specialized unified reporting systems; however, some institutions choose to develop their own (Mack et al. 2017).

STAFFING MODELS

Patient Advocacy departments can choose from several staffing models, depending on an institution's structure, the ratio of complaints and grievances to institutional activity (e.g., census or visits), and the expectations of Patient Advocacy employees. In many institutions, local leadership manages complaints and grievances up to and including resolution, which is then documented centrally in their systems. This model is often used for organizations with multiple small unit or clinic locations. Leadership often conducts the consultations remotely with the advocates across all locations.

Any evidence-based research in the literature to quantify specific staffing ratios for patient advocates is grounded in models for other healthcare specialties. Two models that can be applied are similar to the traditional nursing Total Patient Care Delivery Model, introduced in the 1930s, in which one patient advocate is responsible for a group of patients in the inpatient or outpatient setting (Tiedeman and Lookinland 2004). For instance, patient advocates can be assigned to the location in which the patient is receiving care. Such assignments work well in the inpatient hospital setting where patients are assigned to a bed in a unit. When a patient or patient representative lodges a grievance, the advocate assigned to that unit is responsible for shepherding the grievance through the process. On occasion, the advocate may need to escalate complex cases that require multiple family conferences or consultations to their supervisor or manager.

Consideration should be given to the type of healthcare setting when developing a staffing model. In an inpatient setting, most complaints and grievances are handled and resolved by staff on hand because of the availability of rounding medical teams. Because the highest percentage of patient issues center on communication, the rates of inpatient complaints and grievances is often lower in the hospital setting, where communication with medical staff is more readily available for patients and families. One patient advocate therefore should be able to handle a 200-bed service line. On the other hand, a 600-bed hospital facility that solely provides inpatient medical care would need three patient advocates on staff.

In contrast to inpatient advocacy programs, those in the ambulatory setting receive a greater volume of complaints and grievances. Facilities that provide outpatient services often have many more dissatisfied patients, possibly because of the nature of clinical operations. Issues in these settings can include communication, wait time, scheduling, and billing. Patient Advocacy programs that work in these settings often use caseload to help determine the appropriate staffing ratios. A typical program may determine that 15 cases per week, or 60 cases per month, would be a reasonable target to achieve as they work toward building the right-size staffing model. Some hospitals deliver both inpatient and outpatient medical services. In this setting, more staffing coverage would be required in the ambulatory setting for the aforementioned reasons.

Another model often used is assigning patient advocates by service line. For example, a single advocate would handle all gynecology patient grievances, allowing the advocate to develop strong relationships with the providers and staff working in that service. At times, the balance of work can be skewed in this model—some services are larger than others, and some types of patients tend to lodge more complaints—so workloads should be closely monitored. One remedy is to assign one advocate to multiple smaller service lines, while another advocate covers one large service. Finally, patient advocates can be assigned to cases as the department receives them to more evenly distribute work among staff. Although this staffing model provides a fair workload assignment, the department manager will want to expeditiously assign and address every case.

PRODUCTIVITY MODELS, INCLUDING WORK-TO-STAFF RATIOS AND INDUSTRY PERFORMANCE TARGETS

Unlike many other quality and productivity statistics, healthcare institutions do not share their data about patient complaints and grievances outside their organizations. Because the public is not privy to this information, and the role and involvement of patient advocates vary between institutions, no standard productivity models or staff ratios exist. Future technology may help analyze the severity of grievances and assist in developing standardized staffing ratios and productivity models. The most accurate productivity metrics now available are (1) the number of complaints and grievances, (2) the average time in days before acknowledgment and resolution of grievances, and (3) the responsiveness of the Patient Advocacy Department to staff requests for assistance. Institutions can also use the ratio of complaints and grievances to the institutional activity to develop a productivity model and establish staffing ratios.

STRATEGIES TO IMPROVE RECRUITMENT AND RETENTION

As in many professions, hiring the right person at the right time is crucial. But particularly because of the sensitive nature of the complaints and grievances that Patient Advocacy fields daily, recruitment and retention efforts must reflect an organization's commitment to hire only those who are most qualified to take this role.

Organizations will want to design interviews to readily identify candidates with the best likelihood of success. One way to achieve this is by implementing

Exhibit 13.6: Questions to Elicit Behavior History

1. Describe a relationship with a patient that had a significant effect on you.
2. Tell me about a time you had to make an important decision but lacked critical information.
3. Tell me about a time you had to create a team.
4. Tell me about a time you had to educate a patient and family in some aspect of medicine.

Source: Adapted from Easdown et al. (2005).

panel interviews with behavioral-based questions (exhibit 13.6). Many Human Resources departments have behavioral-based templates available, or can help develop a question set for particular positions. This method, which industrial psychologist Tom Janz, PhD, developed in the 1980s, suggests that past behavior predicts future behavior (Easdown et al. 2005). Its use provokes situational thought and places the candidate in scenarios with various potential outcomes.

Literature suggests that organizations use a Patient Advocacy staffing skills scale to identify candidates who could thrive in this role (Jansson et al. 2016). Many of these staffing skills scales are developed from replies to behavioral interview questions, and then ratings are assigned to the job candidates using their real-life examples (Bariso 2018). The most successful patient advocates have the ability to communicate effectively at all levels of an organization, are subject-matter experts in relationship building, and are seen as champions for patients and families. They are able to sense the needs of their stakeholders, both patients and fellow employees (Piper and Tallman 2015). Additional skills to consider are resiliency, tact, diplomacy, being a good listener, and having an overarching sense of caring and compassion. An individual's ability to use critical thinking skills is a must-have quality for any applicant who hopes to work in this profession. In addition, successful patient advocates are natural problem solvers, and when they face difficult situations, they often have to consider an array of variables and factors to find the best possible solution. Finding applicants with some or most of these professional qualities is not always easy, but organizations should expend the energy to recruit and coach these talented and valuable individuals.

Once a Patient Advocacy team has been formed, department leaders should pivot to retention efforts to keep the best patient advocates on staff. One way to accomplish this retention is by creating an environment where high-energy staff members feel valued and appreciated (Studer 2003). All frontline customer service roles, particularly in healthcare, carry a risk of fatigue or burnout, especially when the nature of the department is complaint resolution (Takvorian et al. 2020). To mitigate staff dissatisfaction, department leaders should create a work schedule that is considered favorable to the employees. The department should have key benchmarks or goals in place that the staff should accomplish within a certain period. Advocates should also be given latitude and flexibility to manage their daily schedules.

A typical workday for a patient advocate is atypical and includes many variables that make it difficult to follow a standard or routine schedule. Some Patient Advocacy programs have been able to provide flexible work schedules with opportunities to conduct administrative or telephonic work from home. Placing trust and confidence in staff members by giving them the autonomy to manage their daily routines helps create a productive and welcoming work environment that may inspire retention and loyalty.

KEY REGULATORY ISSUES

Although the presence of a Patient Advocacy program can provide comfort, reassurance, and confidentiality to a patient's experience, federal, state, and organizational requirements are in place for healthcare facilities to meet Conditions of Participation and achieve accreditation. The primary regulatory agency that governs patient rights is CMS, which provides guidelines that protect the patient's right to file a complaint or grievance if the person is not satisfied with any aspect of their care. More specifically, as stated in US Code of Federal Regulations §482.13 (GovRegs 2020b), healthcare organizations must "establish a process for prompt resolution of patient grievances and must inform each patient whom to contact to file a grievance. The hospital's governing body must approve and be responsible for the effective operation of the grievance process and must review and resolve grievances, unless it delegates the responsibility in writing to a grievance committee." As mentioned, the governing body in many hospitals delegates authority to a grievance committee to ensure oversight, review, and resolution of all grievances. Because the grievance process is a regulatory procedure, Patient Advocacy is usually designated as the mechanism for handling all patient complaints and grievances. In accord with federal regulatory and accreditation guidelines, the Emergency Care Research Institute (ECRI) maintains that patient advocates must follow an established process to document all grievances in a database, maintain a Grievance Log, and send written correspondence as required (resolution letters, and, if necessary, acknowledgment or progress letters) (ECRI 2016). Exhibit 13.7 shows three sample letters to use for grievance response, updating, and resolution.

Exhibit 13.7: Sample Letters

[Acknowledgment Letter]

[Date of Letter]

[Patient / Patient Representative Name]
[Address 1]
[Address 2]
[City, State, ZIP]

Dear [Patient / Patient Representative Name]:

Thank you for the opportunity to respond to your concerns regarding your recent care at [hospital name]. These issues are being addressed and you will receive a written response upon completion of this review process or within thirty (30) business days. Please accept our apologies for not meeting your expectations.

We appreciate you choosing [hospital name] and providing feedback regarding your experiences. We are always striving to achieve the excellence that our patients expect and deserve. If you have any questions, please contact Patient Advocacy at [phone number].

Sincerely,

[Name]
[Position]

[Progress Letter]

[Date of Letter]

[Patient / Patient Representative Name]
[Address 1]
[Address 2]
[City, State, ZIP]

Dear [Patient / Patient Representative Name]:

We would like to take this opportunity to inform you of our progress toward resolving your concerns. The review process is ongoing at this time.

We appreciate your patience and understanding as we work to improve the quality of patient care at [hospital name]. Please be assured that you will receive a written response upon completion of the review process. If you have any questions, please contact Patient Advocacy at [phone number].

Sincerely,

[Name]
[Position]

[Resolution Letter]

[Date of Letter]

[Patient / Patient Representative Name]
[Address 1]
[Address 2]
[City, State, ZIP]

Dear [Patient / Patient Representative Name]:

Thank you for the opportunity to respond to your concerns regarding *[description of grievance]*. We would like to express our apology for any dissatisfaction you have experienced with the services provided by [hospital name].

On *[date of resolution]*, our review and resolution process was completed. The following steps were taken to address your concerns: *[steps taken to investigate, results of investigation, and actions taken to resolve grievance]*.

[Hospital name] is committed to an ongoing performance improvement process. It is feedback such as yours that allows us the opportunity to ensure that appropriate improvements are made throughout our organization. We appreciate you choosing [hospital name]. We hope that in the future we meet your expectations and ours for outstanding patient care and services. If you have any questions, please contact Patient Advocacy at [phone number].

Sincerely,

[Name]
[Position]

Patient Advocacy programs must meet specific standards. The most efficient way to ensure these standards are consistently being met is to outline them in the Complaint and Grievance Policy. The elements in the policy should follow the CMS Conditions of Participation for complaints and grievances. Some of the most important parts of the policy are

- definitions that differentiate a complaint from a grievance and the specific process and documentation for addressing each;
- designated responsibility for all employees to report grievances to the department responsible for resolving them;
- the procedure for submitting a verbal or written grievance by a patient or patient representative;
- the process, communication, and documentation for acknowledgment, investigation, and resolution;
- target timeline for acknowledgment and resolution including specifics regarding if the timeline includes or does not include weekends; and
- a mechanism for timely referral of patient concerns regarding quality of care or premature discharge to appropriate agencies (GovRegs 2008).

One of the most important elements in any grievance policy is a process for immediately addressing any complaint or grievance that may contribute to endangering the patient, such as abuse or neglect. Institutions need to specifically define the sort of grievance that meets the threshold for abuse or neglect, and to design an immediate process for removing patients from a situation that may potentially harm them, either physically or emotionally. This may include such provisions as staff being put on administrative leave during investigation, reassignment of staff, reporting to government agencies for safety and welfare, or providing 1:1 supervision for the patient during investigation and resolution.

The CMS Conditions of Participation standards are very similar to The Joint Commission standards. Reviewing and citing the Conditions of Participation, in addition to adhering to Joint Commission standards and state regulations, will meet all the necessary requirements in a policy and will allow for successful accreditation surveys. Deeming status is granted by CMS, which then empowers The Joint Commission to perform its regularly scheduled accreditation visit. CMS generally surveys after a pattern of grievances is registered with it or when it receives an egregious grievance involving harm to a patient. There can be serious implications for healthcare organizations if standards are not achieved and the hospital receives substandard scores. Because patient rights standards are a cornerstone of CMS and accrediting bodies such as The Joint Commission, the existence of a strong Patient Advocacy program is instrumental to the success of healthcare organizations.

KEY TERMS FOR PATIENT ADVOCACY

Advocacy skills: Specific attributes or skills that patient advocates exhibit in their interactions with patients and their family members. The most successful patient advocates have the ability to communicate effectively at all levels of an organization, are subject-matter experts in relationship building, and are seen as champions for the patients and families. They are able to sense the needs of their stakeholders, both patients and fellow employees.

Conditions of Participation: Rules of the Centers for Medicare & Medicaid Services (CMS) that a healthcare institution must follow to participate in the Medicare program.

Ethical leadership: The action taken by an institution's healthcare leaders to address complaints and grievances from patients and their family members in order to learn from indiscretions and mistakes and to improve patient care.

Patient Advocacy: A healthcare department whose members serve as patient representatives that support patients or family members with their healthcare issues.

Patient- and family-centered care: A healthcare model that involves the participation of the patient and family members, who serve as partners with the clinical care team in the healthcare journey.

Patient complaints: Patient issues that a member of a healthcare team can resolve at the time of complaint. CMS considers complaints to be minor issues that do not involve clinical care and do not require an investigation or peer review.

Patient grievances: According to CMS guidelines, these are formal complaints, delivered verbally or in writing, by the patient or family. Grievances are those issues that cannot quickly be resolved and involve in-depth concerns regarding such matters as patient care, confidentiality, or unethical behavior.

REFERENCES

American College of Obstetricians and Gynecologists. 2016. "Disclosure and Discussion of Adverse Events." Committee Opinion No. 681. *Obstetrics and Gynecology* 128: 257–61.

Bariso, J. 2018. *EQ Applied: The Real World Guide to Emotional Intelligence.* Germany: Borough Hall.

Centers for Medicare & Medicaid Services (CMS). 2020. "Revisions to Interpretative Guidelines for Medicare and Medicaid Services Hospital Conditions of Participations." Published May 19. www.cms.gov/Regulations-and-Guidance/Legislation/CFCsAndCoPs.

D'Amico, T. A., L. A. M. Bandini, A. Balch, A. B. Benson III, S. B. Edge, L. Fitzgerald, R. J. Green, W.-J. Koh, M. Kolodziej, S. Kumar, N. J. Meropol, J. L. Mohler, D. Pfister, R. S. Walters, and R. W. Carlson. 2020. "Quality Measurement in Cancer Care: A Review and Endorsement of High-Impact Measures and Concepts." *NCCN Policy Report* 18 (3): 250–59.

Easdown, L. J., P. Castro, E. Shinkle, L. Small, and J. Algren. 2005. "The Behavioral Interview, a Method to Evaluate ACGME Competencies in Resident Selection: A Pilot Project." *Journal of Education in Perioperative Medicine.* Accessed October 6, 2020. https://cdn.ymaws.com/www.seahq.org/resource/resmgr/JEPM/VII/VII_1_Easdown.pdf.

Emergency Care Research Institute (ECRI). 2016. "Managing Patient Complaints and Grievances." Published August 17. www.ecri.org/components/HRC/Pages/PtSup1.aspx.

GovRegs. 2020a. "US Code of Federal Regulations: §482.12—Condition of Participation: Governing Body." Accessed October 6. www.govregs.com/regulations/expand/title42_chapterIV_part482_subpartB_section482.13#title42_chapterIV_part482_subpartB_section482.12.

———. 2020b. "US Code of Federal Regulations: §482.13—Condition of Participation: Patient's Rights." Accessed October 6. www.govregs.com/regulations/expand/title42_chapterIV_part482_subpartB_section482.13#title42_chapterIV_part482_subpartB_section482.13.

———. 2008. "Revisions to Interpretive Guidelines for Centers for Medicare & Medicaid Services Hospital Conditions of Participation 42 CFR §§482.12, 482.13, 482.27 and 482.28." Published October 17. http://wayback.archive-it.org/2744/20111204095603/http://www.cms.gov/transmittals/downloads/R37SOMA.pdf.

Haldar, S., S. R. Mishra, A. H. Pollack, and W. Pratt. 2019. "Informatics Opportunities to Involve Patients in Hospital Safety: A Conceptual Model." *Journal of the American Medical Informatics Association* 27 (2): 202–11.

Jansson, B., A. Nyamathi, G. Hidemann, C. R. Rogers, K. Brown-Saltzman, and C. Kaplan. 2016. "Predicting Levels of Policy Advocacy Engagement Among Acute-Care Health Professionals." *Policy, Politics and Nursing Practice* 17 (1): 43–55.

Mack, J., J. Jacobson, D. Frank, A. Cronin, K. Horvath, V. Allen, J. Wind, and D. Schrag. 2017. "Evaluation of Patient and Family Outpatient Complaints as a Strategy to Prioritize Efforts to Improve Cancer Care Delivery." *Joint Commission Journal on Quality and Patient Safety* 43: 498–507.

Piper, L. 2011. "The Ethical Leadership Challenge: Creating a Culture of Patient and Family Centered Care in the Hospital Setting." *Health Care Manager* 30 (2): 128–29.

Piper, L., and E. Tallman. 2015. "The Ethical Leadership Challenge for Effective Resolution of Patient and Family Complaints and Grievances." *Health Care Manager* 34 (1): 62–68.

Porter, M. E. 2014. "Value-Based Health Care Delivery." Published January 15. www.hbs.edu/faculty/Publication%20Files/3_13615129-eeec-4987-bf1a-1261ff86ae69.pdf.

Studer, Q. 2008. *Results That Last*. Hoboken, NJ: Wiley.

———. 2003. *Hardwiring Excellence*. Gulf Breeze, FL: Fire Starter Publishing.

Takvorian, S., E. Balogh, S. Nass, V. Valentin, L. Hoffman-Hogg, R. A. Oyer, R. Carlson, N. Meropol, L. Kennedy Sheldon, and L. N. Shulman. 2020. "Developing and Sustaining an Effective and Resilient Oncology Careforce: Opportunities for Action." *Journal of the National Cancer Institute* 112 (7): dj2239.

Tiedeman, M. E., and S. Lookinland. 2004. "Traditional Models of Care Delivery: What Have We Learned?" *Nursing Administration* 34 (6): 291–97.

CHAPTER 14

Patient Transportation

Jermaine McMillan

DEPARTMENT DESCRIPTION

A healthcare facility's Patient Transportation Department is responsible for the safe and timely transport of patients and biological specimens 24 hours a day. Timeliness is a challenging but critical component in patient transportation that requires significant monitoring and tracking. Effective monitoring and tracking ensures that delays or workflow impediments can be identified and addressed promptly for optimal hospital operations. Transportation departments in large institutions rely on technology for successful monitoring; they use real-time performance dashboards, trend reports, and patient survey data. Such technology is necessary to form a complete picture of how well Patient Transportation is serving its patients.

Safety merits a little more explanation in the context of transporting patients: it means properly ensuring that patients are carefully assisted on and off transportation equipment in a manner that prevents injuries. Transportation equipment includes mobile beds, stretchers, and wheelchairs. Safety also means eliminating infection or contamination risks; transportation equipment must be sanitized before and after each patient has contacted any of its surfaces.

KEY DEPARTMENT SERVICES

Patient Transportation focuses exclusively on picking up patients and specimens, then delivering them to requested hospital destinations. However, customers require a series of additional services:

- Status notification of delays affecting drop time
- Additional staff for large or complex transport needs
- Data reporting and analysis for chronic impediments to efficiency

Other key features of optimal transportation services are bidirectional communication and advanced preparation to connect patients to the care and treatment needed. Clinical teams must anticipate patient admission and discharge as well as transfer requirements and time frames. A coordinated effort in clinical units will produce more accurate and timely transport information, which dispatchers can use to assign transporters. Through a team of dispatchers working in concert with transport personnel, Patient Transportation can promptly respond to any transport request around the clock. To provide such service in a large organization, Patient Transportation may employ more than 130 transporters. Teams of transporters must work in shifts, under supervision, to ensure protocols are followed and operations are performed seamlessly.

DEPARTMENT ORGANIZATIONAL STRUCTURES

A Transportation Department's organizational structure will depend on the size of the transport operation and the healthcare facility. The department should be led by a director who has solid knowledge of hospital operations and the logistical demands of patient transportation.

The most common challenges that Patient Transportation faces are stakeholders who do not understand or follow protocols, environmental challenges (e.g., inadequate egress, malfunctioning elevators, broken equipment), and insufficient staff. Inadequate onboarding or training may lead to downstream dissatisfaction from patients, process stakeholders, or Patient Transportation staff. Many Patient Transportation issues can be addressed through effective leadership and interdepartmental collaboration. The focus of such collaboration should be optimizing transportation workflows, continuously improving them by using data-driven benchmarks and achievable efficiency targets.

In addition to a director and managers, a Transportation Services Department operating 24 hours in a large organization requires tiered levels of leadership. A typical organizational structure includes

- a director, who develops and drives departmental strategy and vision;
- managers, who develop and execute plans to facilitate the strategy and vision;
- supervisors who monitor, track, and ensure performance and compliance with processes that facilitate operational plans and liaise with other departments;
- team leads, who respond to workflow barriers and process failures; and
- transporters, who execute transportation duties.

The director must establish and communicate a clear vision with milestones. The vision must be communicated to managers and supervisors, who will be responsible for helping to develop plans to bring the department vision to fruition. The director also must ensure that all levels of staff understand how its roles and functions affect the success of the department and the whole organization. More important, directors and managers must stress the importance of quality in the execution of duties at all levels of staff.

KEY CUSTOMERS AND THEIR PERFORMANCE EXPECTATIONS

Patient Transportation is considered a patient-touching clinical support service. As such, patient transportation provides services to a unique mix of customers who connect at different points along the continuum of care. Key customers include the following:

- Patients
- Family members
- Clinicians (nurses, physicians, care coordinators)
- Organizational leaders
- Other process stakeholders (e.g., admission and discharge locations)

Each customer has a specific performance expectation that influences their experience or value proposition. Organizational team members expect prompt services that will enable them to provide their patients timely and safe treatment. They expect responsiveness and data-driven solutions to new or chronic process challenges that may occur. Patients and their families expect an experience commensurate with the time and expense associated with the care they receive. They expect a consistent and high level of customer service and sensitivity relating to the condition that led them to seek treatment or evaluation.

KEY PROCESS FLOWS

Process flow and workflow monitoring is critical to maintaining seamless around-the-clock operations. For Patient Transportation, clear process flows enable transporters to know what needs to be done at each step in the transport process and how long it should take, along with the roles of other stakeholders.

Most electronic health record (EHR) systems have a patient transportation module that allows various periods to be monitored. Each Patient

Transportation Department will select which periods to monitor from among the following samples:

1. **Pending to Assign** is the time between when the request is entered into the system and when it is assigned to a transporter.
2. **Assign to Acknowledged** is the time between its assignment to the transporter and acknowledged receipt by the transporter.
3. **Acknowledged to In-progress** is the time between when the transporter acknowledges the request and when they put it in progress after arriving at the pickup location.
4. **Assigned to In-progress** is the time between assigned (dispatcher assigns request to transporter) and in-progress (transporter is moving toward pickup location).
5. **In-progress to Complete** is the time between in-progress (transporter leaving pickup location) and completed (transporter arrives at final destination).
6. **Assign to Complete** is the time between assigned to transporter and completed.
7. **Pending to Complete** is the time between pending (when the request is entered into the system searching for an available transporter) and completed.

Patient Transportation leadership can then monitor the actual time taken compared with targets, as shown in exhibit 14.1, where the last row indicates the average times over or under the targets for each time segment.

Having a clear understanding of roles enables transporters to communicate more effectively and respond more accurately in real time to obstacles or problems. By extension, monitoring these processes enables supervisors to conduct root-cause analysis of chronic process failures and collaborate with managers to develop sustainable solutions.

Exhibit 14.1: Patient Transportation Sample Workforce Performance

Quarter 1	Pending to assign	Assign to acknowledged	Acknowledged to in-progress	In-progress to complete	Pending to complete
Average time (minutes)	13	2	9	21	48
Target	9	3	16	20	45
Variance + = over target − = under target	+4	−1	−7	+1	+3

KEY UNITS OF WORK AND VOLUME STATISTICS TO MONITOR

Key units of work (KUoW) are effective for evaluating productivity and efficiency in achieving performance targets. KUoW include utilization by equipment type and the volume of patients and specimens transported within a targeted time frame. These measures will enable an organization to monitor performance and correct course when targets are not met.

KEY METRICS TO MONITOR: PEOPLE, SERVICE, QUALITY/SAFETY, FINANCIAL

Monitoring metrics establishes a basis against which to measure success and progress and for informing strategic decisions. Exhibit 14.2 shows a sample scorecard for Patient Transportation.

People

To ensure that Patient Transportation is sufficiently staffed to meet the patient volume demand, managers should monitor total and first-year turnover. Transportation staff must receive specific training when onboarding and when protocols are created or revised. Training for transporters generally includes patient safety, infection control, equipment operation and maintenance, customer service, and communication tools for use during transport. The training records of transporters should be monitored to ensure compliance and a knowledgeable workforce.

Service and Quality/Safety

Regular communication with key customers provides patient transportation leaders with important, subjective customer satisfaction feedback regarding service. The volume of transports completed in a given amount of time should be monitored to evaluate productivity and efficiency. Timeliness and safety are key quality metrics. At each step in the transportation process, elapsed time is tracked and compared with target times. Patient Transportation also monitors the ease of use and cleanliness of the equipment used during transport.

Safety includes sanitizing transport equipment and safe handling of patients on and off transportation equipment. Infection control protocols should comply with the Centers for Medicare & Medicaid Services (CMS) regarding the method and frequency of sanitizing transport equipment. The frequency for sanitizing equipment is an important safety metric that must be documented and tracked to minimize risks to patient safety.

Exhibit 14.2: Sample Scorecard for Patient Transportation

			Scorecard PATIENT TRANSPORTATION			
	Metric		Performance	Sept 2019	Oct 2019	Nov 2019
PEOPLE						
P1	**Recognition:** # of recognition given (mail or other)		0	≥ 1		
P2	Vacancies: Total # of FTE vacancies		*No performance ranges established*			
P3	**Year-to-Date Turnover:** % of staff who (voluntarily + involuntarily) left the institution since 9/1/19		*Performance ranges under development*			
P4	**Facility Award:** % of employees hired on or before May 31, 2020 to complete Advanced Directive Training		90%	90%	>90%	
P5	**Facility Award:** % of employees hired on or before May 31, 2020, to complete Advanced Directive Assessment		90%	90%	>90%	
SERVICE						
S1	**Productivity:** # of KUoW metrics achieving productivity goals		<2	2		
QUALITY						
Q1	**Dispatch Response Time (Average of Pending to Assign):** Time elapsed from "Pending" to "Assign"		>13 min	<11 min	<9 min	<7 min
Q2	**Average Escort Response Time (Average of Assign to Acknowledge):** Time elapsed from "Assignment" to "Acknowledgment"		>5 min	<5 min	<3 min	<2 min

Q3	**Escort Hold Time/Patient Readiness:** Time from when transporter places request on hold until patient ready for transport	≥17.18 min	17.07–17.17 min	16.96–17.06 min	≤16.95 min
Q4	**Escort Arrival Time (Average of Acknowledge to In-progress):** Time elapsed from escorting acknowledging to arrival to pick-up location	>13 min	<12 min	<11 min	< 1 min
Q5	**Escort Transport Time (Average of In-progress to Complete):** Time elapsed from status of "In progress" to status of "Complete"	>25 min	<24 min	<23 min	<22 min
Q6	**Escort Transport Time (Average of Acknowledge to Complete):** Time elapsed from status of "Acknowledged" to status of "Complete"	>24 min	22.5–24 min	20.1–22.4 min	≤20 min
Q6	**Transport Completion Time (Average of Pending to Complete):** Decrease the transport completion time (time elapsed between "pending" and "completion") from 36.5 minutes to 33.1–36 minutes	≥36.5 min	36.1–36.4 min	33.1–36 min	<33.1 min
Q7	**Transports Exceeding 30 Minutes:** % of total transports exceeding 30 minutes	>26 %	<26 %	<25 %	<15 %

FINANCE

F1	**Personnel Expense**	>Budget		≤Budget	
F2	**Other Operating Expense**	>Budget		≤Budget	
F3	**Total Operating Expense:** Personnel Expense + Other Operating Expense (Facility Award Department Financial Goal)	>Budget		≤Budget	
F4	**Operating Income/Loss:** % Variance Actual to Budget		*Performance ranges under development*		

Note: FTE = full-time equivalent; KUoW = key units of work.

Financial

Large organizations usually base budgets on the previous year's performance. For Patient Transportation, the largest expenditures are typically personnel and equipment. Throughout the fiscal year, the department needs to closely monitor actual expense versus budget. Overtime also should be closely tracked to cover for vacant positions and unexpected volumes. Patient Transportation leaders should inventory their wheelchairs and stretchers to identify any needs and budget for these costs.

KEY INFORMATICS ISSUES

Documentation and data management are critical. Organizations need effective tools and technologies to facilitate continuous data capture, management, reporting, and analysis. In an ideal setting, a robust EHR integrates clinical care and Patient Transportation processes by linking transport activity for each patient throughout their treatment.

No matter how sophisticated the EHR, the system is only as effective as the accuracy of the data entered. Other considerations include how the data is organized and the level of difficulty in extracting reports to gain performance insights. Noncompliance with or nonexistent standardized data entry protocols also present challenges to data analytics and leadership when attempting to evaluate performance. The remedy is to establish clear and standardized processes for data capture, educate users on the importance of compliance, and strictly monitor adherence to standard operating procedures.

STAFFING MODELS

Crafting a Patient Transportation Department staffing model is necessary to properly hire for current demands and for anticipating requirements for future growth. An organization should base its staffing model not only on patient volume but also on other key inputs, such as normal business hours, peak times and seasons, and down times. Hospital size, and travel time between pickup and drop-off locations, must also be factored into staffing models, because they affect response time between transport requests. Given these considerations, staffing models are central to ensuring that adequate personnel are scheduled at the appropriate times to meet routine operational needs. Department leaders also should have a business continuity plan for emergencies that includes a staffing plan. When there is an expanded or new hospital service line, the staffing plan will have to be adjusted.

PRODUCTIVITY MODELS, INCLUDING WORK-TO-STAFF RATIOS AND INDUSTRY PERFORMANCE TARGETS

Productivity is based on how many transports are completed by a transporter per hour over an eight-hour shift. Productivity can vary between two to three transports per hour, but depends on the physical size of the organization as well as patient and specimen volumes. Exhibit 14.3 shows a sample individual-productivity feedback report that supervisors can review with transporters to identify opportunities and any barriers to performance.

STRATEGIES TO IMPROVE RECRUITMENT AND RETENTION

Transporters escort patients to appointments and assist in discharging them after treatment, and move time-sensitive medications and specimens as needed. To ensure consistent quality and efficiency, the right staff must be selected during the recruitment process. Behavioral-based interview questions help identify if the candidate is a good fit. The essential skills and capabilities include the following:

- Extensive customer service experience
- Calm temperament during confrontational situations
- Problem-solving skills
- Comfort with being around biological materials
- Comfort with being around patients with various types/stages of illness
- Ability to take direction and to work autonomously
- Ability to meet the physical demands of the job (moving patients for an entire shift)

Once suitable candidates have been identified, they should be offered compensation that is commensurate with the market wage and complexity of the work required. A structured onboarding and training program is needed to educate new staff on the organization, job expectations, vision and goals of the department, and the importance of their role in the continuum of patient care. Cardiopulmonary resuscitation and oxygen tank safety training also should be included. Staff should be trained to respond appropriately to emergencies, even if these skills are not frequently applied. Identifying candidates during the interview process who have the necessary skills and capabilities is vital for avoiding a high first-year turnover rate, which can be costly given the considerable investment in training.

Exhibit 14.3: Sample Workforce Performance Feedback Report

Date	Productivity Avg transports per day		Productivity Avg transports per hour		Acknowledge to in-progress		In-progress to complete		Acknowledge to complete	
	Your Performance	Target	Your Performance	Target	Your Performance	Target	Your Performance	Target	Your Performance	Target

Great care must be taken to recruit the right staff, because making the wrong hires can have lasting and harmful consequences. For example, a transporter with poor customer service skills can add stress to patients with delicate conditions, which may aggravate their symptoms, or a new hire with poor interpersonal skills may fuel a negative culture or work environment. Both employees harm retention and affirm the need for a diligent recruitment process.

KEY REGULATORY ISSUES

CMS guidelines direct patient transportation protocols that govern the following:

- Condition of transportation equipment
- Sanitizing transportation equipment
- Storage conditions of transportation equipment
- Vendor performance regarding maintenance of transportation equipment
- Documented trainings to ensure compliance with federal and organizational requirements

Although compliance with CMS guidelines regarding the aforementioned areas is required, it is also critical to patient safety. Faulty or unsanitary equipment can create impediments to transporting a patient or infection control issues, both of which are detrimental to patient care.

KEY TERMS FOR PATIENT TRANSPORTATION

Performance dashboard: A performance management system that communicates strategic objectives and enables businesspeople to measure, monitor, and manage the key activities and processes needed to achieve their goals.

Process stakeholders: Each process requires staff to execute specific tasks in a standardized fashion to achieve sustainable efficiency and performance. Each staff member in a process is a stakeholder, and process changes may affect how they execute their tasks.

Sanitization: Cleaning wheelchairs and stretchers (e.g., sterilizing with delicate task wipes and bleach or other approved chemicals) is essential to minimizing the spread of germs and infection.

CHAPTER 15

Pharmacy

Lauren Goldberg, Megan McGugan, and Ryan K. Roux

DEPARTMENT DESCRIPTION

Hospital Pharmacy departments are directly involved in procuring, delivering, and managing medications as they serve the needs of patients throughout their duration of care. Through a collaborative approach alongside providers, healthcare institutions offer the necessary infrastructure to develop strong interdisciplinary teams and ensure safe medication practices under Pharmacy's support. Pharmacy may be involved in transitions of care, drug therapy management, optimizing patient adherence and outcomes, and cost-savings initiatives, all of which are critical to the health and maintenance of hospital operations and the provision of best practices.

There are more than 125 pharmacy schools in the United States. Since 2006, individuals training to be practicing pharmacists must obtain a Doctor of Pharmacy (PharmD) degree and pass two different exams: the pharmacy board exam called the North American Pharmacist Licensure Examination (NAPLEX), and the state law exam called the Multistate Pharmacy Jurisprudence Examination (MPJE) for the state where the individual is seeking licensure. Additionally, pharmacists may elect to pursue one to two years of postgraduate residency training to further hone their skills, making them more competitive in the hospital job market. As with medical residencies, pharmacy residencies vary in specifications, such as general pharmacy practice, cardiology, critical care, drug information, infectious diseases, and oncology. Residency applicants now exceed available positions, making pharmacy residency matching very competitive (Learn How to Become 2020a).

Becoming a pharmacy technician requires a high school diploma or equivalent, with the option of completing a formal pharmacy-technician training program that lasts from six months to one year. Whether the formal training program is completed or not, the individual must pass the Pharmacy Technician Certification Board (PTCB) or the Exam for the Certification of Pharmacy Technicians (ExCPT). Depending on the state or hospital, technicians may be required to have a certification to gain employment. Technicians are intimately involved in distributing and delivering medication orders, patient assistance programs, training and education functions, and auditing for regulatory compliance. As opportunities for the pharmacy technician continue to grow in the marketplace, additional training and competencies may be required (Learn How to Become 2020b).

KEY DEPARTMENT SERVICES

The scope of pharmacy services delivered within each hospital is influenced by factors such as the size of the institution and the practice model. Because of the wide variety of responsibilities Pharmacy has accrued throughout the years, many services are working synergistically to provide patient care needs while maintaining patient safety. A commonality between all Pharmacy departments is their involvement in coordinating drug procurement, secure inventory control practices, medication order review, and medication distribution, which may occur through both inpatient and outpatient service lines.

For admitted patients, the inpatient pharmacy oversees timely preparation and delivery of medications. Intravenous admixtures, individual oral doses, and potentially investigational agents are some examples of preparations that inpatient pharmacies provide. Depending on the geographic location of patient care areas from the main pharmacy, and the volume of preparations required, the inpatient pharmacy may have satellite pharmacies spaced throughout the hospital to aid in medication delivery. In some cases, certain functions may be distributed throughout the region, such as central fill and mail order for prescriptions, central bulk compounding for products frequently used among several commonly owned pharmacies, or patient-assistance-program activities (Schneider, Pedersen, and Scheckelhoff 2018).

Outpatient and retail pharmacies provide discharge or maintenance medications the institution's providers have prescribed. Typically, these medications are oral and require less special handling and preparation than IV admixtures. As done at a neighborhood retail or chain pharmacy, these prescriptions are processed through a patient's insurance; once they are approved, a pharmacy technician will fulfill the order, then have the medication verified by a pharmacist. Some health systems sublet space to a third-party commercial retail or specialty pharmacy operation, whereas others provide their own infrastructure. A benefit of having outpatient pharmacy services within the hospital is the close connection with the healthcare team, which can aid in the patient's transitions throughout the healthcare facility (Schneider, Pederson, and Scheckelhoff 2019).

Specialty pharmacy services are closely related to the retail model of billing and fulfilling an order, but must perform additional clinical and accreditation-required functions. Because of the complex nature of certain conditions, extensive storage or handling requirements, and the high cost of the medications, specialty pharmacies must also monitor adherence and clinical outcomes of therapeutic regimens prescribed.

Many health systems categorize pharmacist roles in different ways. Operational pharmacists are typically tasked with order review and verification to ensure appropriateness of therapy in relation to the patient's other treatments, disease conditions, lab values, drug–food interactions, patient-specific pharmacokinetics, and patient physical characteristics (weight, absorption, body surface area). In-process checks and final-product preparation verification are important to ensure medication quality and safety, and are often the last steps before delivery. Some health systems have dedicated pharmacists with specific medication safety responsibilities to evaluate processes, develop standard operating procedures, review adverse events, and identify further interventions to ensure medication safety.

With additional postgraduate residency training, pharmacists can be further integrated into the healthcare team by providing clinical services such as tailored therapy based on pharmacokinetic monitoring and dosing, metabolic support, and patient education. Some states have developed collaborative practice agreements that allow postgraduate-trained pharmacists to work under physicians as recognized healthcare providers. These pharmacists frequently manage drug therapy following a diagnosis; ensure patient education is complete before discharge; and assist with transitions of care between hospital, ambulatory care settings, and home.

Regardless of whether the Pharmacy Department is focused on the inpatient or outpatient setting, drug procurement, formulary management, and secure inventory control practices are critical components of medication delivery. Ensuring that a hospital has access to medications requires relationships with manufacturers and wholesalers. A working knowledge of the relationships between group purchasing organizations, wholesalers, distributors, and contracting is vital. The Pharmacy Department is also responsible for troubleshooting any potential drug shortages or drug procurement issues that may arise from expected or unexpected situations. Effective Pharmacy leadership is needed to balance financial restraints, inventory management logistics, and security with clinical care to ensure the right medications are available to patients in a timely manner.

Although the key Pharmacy Department services just mentioned are commonly seen regardless of the size of the institution, larger hospitals may support pharmacies with the capacity to disseminate drug information resources and conduct research.

DEPARTMENT ORGANIZATIONAL STRUCTURE

All pharmacies, including those within a hospital setting, must designate a pharmacist-in-charge who has the responsibility to establish an effective governance structure that can ensure compliance with all legal and regulatory entities. The size and structure of a Pharmacy Department will vary with the size of the organization and its possible status as part of a larger health system. The larger the entity, the more layered the department. The increase in size may yield the development of unique roles for pharmacists and pharmacy technicians. Exhibits 15.1 and 15.2 display sample organizational charts for two different-sized institutions.

Smaller institutions may have only two or three pharmacy staff members, with the director of pharmacy as the only pharmacist. However, larger teaching hospitals may have hundreds of pharmacy staff members. All pharmacies, including those within a hospital setting, must designate a pharmacist-in-charge who has the responsibility to establish an effective governance structure that can ensure compliance with all legal and regulatory entities. Depending on the size and scope of the institutions, Pharmacy Department employees may have multiple responsi-

Exhibit 15.1: Sample Leadership Structure in a Smaller Institution

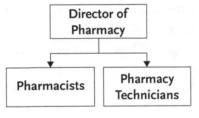

Exhibit 15.2: Sample Leadership Structure in a Larger Institution

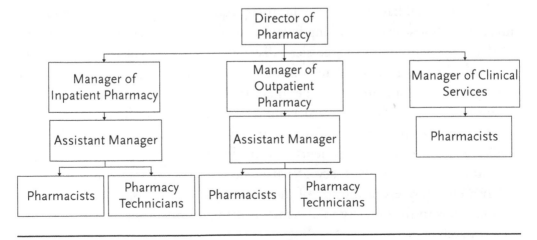

bilities to guarantee key functions are covered. Exhibits 15.1 and 15.2 depict the organizational structure of standalone institutions, but many hospitals are a part of a health system where a systemwide reporting structure oversees individual organizations. No matter the size of the hospital or health system, Pharmacy leadership should create a sound organizational and governance structure that supports the mission and vision of the institution. To do this, however, communication and collaboration with other departments to determine hospital needs is paramount.

KEY CUSTOMERS AND THEIR PERFORMANCE EXPECTATIONS

The patient is the central priority for providing and maintaining exceptional care; however, the Pharmacy Department also serves a broad range of other customers. Those providing direct patient care (nurses, physicians, advanced practice providers) and the patient's family members have consistent service expectations from Pharmacy, driven by the five rights of medication administration: right patient, right medication, right dose, right route, and right time. To achieve these performance expectations, many layers of the Pharmacy Department may be involved to ensure all customers benefit. Automated dispensing cabinets have allowed for decentralized work while reducing technician workload. However, if the number and types of equipment on the units are poorly implemented or designed, availability of timely medications may be hindered by too many individuals accessing the cabinets at the same time, thereby negating the anticipated efficiency and frustrating a large portion of the healthcare workforce.

Pharmacy collaborates with customers routinely through multidisciplinary committees to provide the infrastructure needed to support daily operations. Service begins with formulary management to determine which medications may be available for patients within the institution. For example, the Pharmacy & Therapeutics Committee (P&T) consists of pharmacists, physicians, advance practice providers, nurses, supply chain experts, finance, and patients in some models. P&T members collaborate to develop processes and policies to support the safe selection, procurement, and appropriate use of medications. Often this is assessed through drug monographs or a medication-use safety committee. Pharmacy managers must be proactive with market surveillance, collaborate with purchasing staff, and communicate with drug manufacturers to manage the expectations of key customers, particularly during medication shortages (Ismail et al. 2018).

The ever-changing rules and complexities with major medical and pharmacy-benefit-management payers requires a close relationship with finance departments. The pharmacy finance team must optimize their knowledge of supply chain metrics, ensuring that the products purchased are cost effective while continuously identifying opportunities to reduce waste and improve inventory management, thus minimizing unnecessary holding costs. A close rapport with finance departments is necessary to ensure proper billing compliance for retail and ambulatory payers.

KEY PROCESS FLOWS

All disciplines of the care team are vital members of the medication use process; however, the Pharmacy Department plays multiple key roles to ensure medication safety and regulatory compliance. In many organizations, Pharmacy is the sponsor for medication management activities across the enterprise. Oversight of an effective medication-use process should include a balance of influential providers, pharmacists, and nursing representation. Formalizing medication-use process flows is strongly recommended for successfully maintaining delivery of quality patient care.

As medications are added to the drug formulary, a review of clinical efficacy, financial impact, and patient safety is required before allowing the Pharmacy Department to procure them. Once the medication is added and the drug is eligible for order, additional financial clearances may be required in both the inpatient and outpatient settings. Pharmacy along with Finance play key roles in ensuring the medication is therapeutically appropriate and covered by payers. To ensure the drug is appropriate for the patient, Pharmacy staff should perform medication order review and verification with intention. Order review and verification involve cognitive checks on the appropriateness of the therapy in relation to the patient's other treatments, disease conditions, lab values, drug interactions, food interactions, patient-specific pharmacokinetics, and patient physical characteristics (weight, absorption, body surface area). Clinical Decision Support Systems within electronic health records (EHRs) help Pharmacy team members obtain and share information with the healthcare team to optimize patient care. Some medications require additional attention and communication with the provider about coagulation values, electrolyte levels, documented pain scores, and microbiological identification. Additionally, some medication orders may require a review by pharmacists with specialized training, such as chemotherapy, investigational medication studies, targeted therapies, or immunotherapies. Exhibit 15.3 demonstrates this key process.

Since 2000 the preparation and dispensing phases of the medication use process have experienced several regulatory changes, particularly in regard to US Pharmacopeia (USP) Chapter 795: Nonsterile Compounding (USP<795>), US Pharmacopeia Chapter 797: Sterile Compounding (USP<797>), and US Pharmacopeia Chapter 800: Handling of Hazardous Drugs (USP <800>), requiring additional infrastructure and workflows. Some of these workflow solutions include using gravimetrics to verify proper preparations, single preparations to

Exhibit 15.3: Key Process Flow for Addition of Drug to Formulary Through Pharmacy and Therapeutics Committee

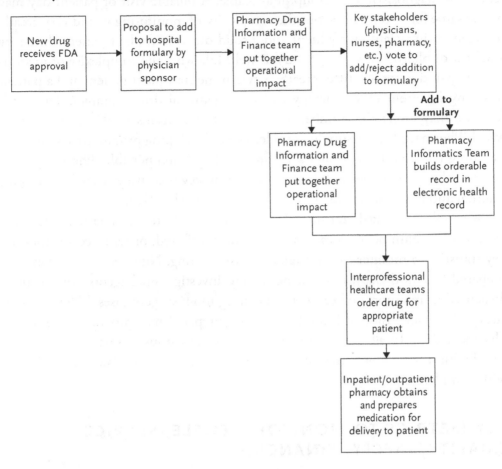

minimize mislabeling, and cameras to monitor preparation activities remotely. Along with process changes, regulatory requirements have added additional garbing requirements, and biological safety-cabinet- and room-cleaning workflows, that must be followed in specific sequencing to maximize cleanliness. These activities also dictate dedicated time and education to ensure they are completed properly.

KEY UNITS OF WORK AND VOLUME STATISTICS TO MONITOR

Healthcare organizations frequently report global volume metrics and statistics, and these should accurately reflect the intensity of work required by the referenced Pharmacy Department. Pharmacy leaders must understand their pharmacy's benchmarks and nuances. Metrics that Pharmacy leaders can easily understand include patient acuity information, length of stay, average cost, and charge per service or diagnosis-related group, if available. A billable visit or patient day may be the same for two patients, but the complexity of monitoring would vary greatly between an inpatient unit patient and a solid organ transplant patient. Intensity and cost of pharmacy work will vary as well. Likewise, the complexity of medication preparation would differ greatly between the transplant patient and a patient receiving inpatient chemotherapy and investigational drug therapies. These differences may affect the number and types of technicians working in the area, which Pharmacy leaders should consider when developing productivity standards, assigning tasks, and developing a staffing model. When possible, Pharmacy leaders should work with hospital leaders to identify key pharmacy-related metrics for internal and external benchmarking (Vermeulen et al. 2018).

Key volume-related statistics should relate clearly to the Pharmacy Department's work. Number of prescriptions filled, transferred, or returned to stock are key statistics to monitor in the retail pharmacy setting. Number of IV admixtures prepared (chemotherapy, non-chemotherapy, investigational agents), medications dispensed from automated cabinets, operating room surgery cases, billable ambulatory pharmacy visits, and number of doses prepared may provide vital hospital pharmacy data. In all cases these volume measures are just numbers unless compared with service-related metrics and financial measures so decisions can be made with complete data.

KEY METRICS TO MONITOR: PEOPLE, SERVICE, QUALITY/SAFETY, FINANCIAL

Several key metrics are continuously monitored in Pharmacy departments. Staff members' progress through developing key competencies should be tracked from the moment they are onboarded. Doing so develops a baseline of competency that can be monitored throughout an employee's service. Annual competencies should focus on high-risk, low-opportunity processes or regulatory required testing for key skills. Such competencies could include IV sterile processing, chemotherapy preparation, investigational drug preparation, malignant hyperthermia response, code blue response, and Risk Evaluation and Mitigation Strategy guidelines. Employees' everyday skills should be routinely reviewed as part of the annual evaluation but may warrant a periodic review after an event or changes to key workflows. Additional competencies may include practical order-validation testing, observing automated dispensing cabinet replenishment, or soft skills development (e.g., service excellence training, professionalism, handling difficult conversations). Monitoring staff turnover rate is important for identifying employee concerns that may need addressing. High turnover or first-year resignations may indicate a management issue, low employee morale, lack of a recognition system, or compensation inequalities in the marketplace.

Service-related metrics are as important as financial and productivity measures. Depending on the type of pharmacy operation, service metrics vary and should be developed for its most important aspects. Such metrics may include time from order generated to order verification, delivery turnaround time, automated dispensing cabinet stock-outs, or targeted interventions for special patients (e.g., those requiring anticoagulation counseling before discharge and at the point of service in retail pharmacy locations). For clinical pharmacy services, service metrics may be similar to those of other providers: number of new/return patients seen in a clinic hour, time to third next available appointment, chart documentation metrics, and patient satisfaction. Asking staff what service metrics are important will give leaders insight into staff's perception of the culture and Pharmacy leadership (O'Neal et al. 2018).

Medication-related errors are tracked and trended not only to identify service interruptions, but also to determine where processes have failed so systems can be improved. Errors may be classified by type and frequency, and certain events may be isolated for further investigation. Sentinel events may prompt a root cause analysis, or a step-by-step examination to discover where a system or workflow may have led to the error. Medication safety specialists and subject matter experts within the area of the error occurrence may be consulted to adjust processes and develop new safety steps to ensure the event does not recur. The Institution of Safe Medication Practices and the American Society of Health-System Pharmacists (ASHP) provide additional guidance to health systems for establishing safe medication use and workflows.

Defining national quality measures for pharmacy practice is a relatively new initiative to set consistent benchmarks for health system pharmacies. These measures are developed around specific leading measures demonstrated to provide improved lag outcomes for a particular disease state. Exhibit 15.4 describes some of these measures, taken from accountability measures recommended by the American Society of Health System Pharmacists (ASHP) Pharmacy Accountability Measures Work Group.

Along with personnel expenditures, medication procurement is a large expense for hospitals. The Pharmacy Department will have either one person or an entire service dedicated to medication expenses and ensuring that these purchases are the most cost efficient for the institution. Various metrics are used to justify the amount of each drug that needs to be purchased. These metrics can also be used to monitor how much daily waste is generated and how best to reduce it by optimizing workflow. These financial metrics are crucial in creating a Pharmacy Department budget in line with the whole hospital budget.

Exhibit 15.4: Accountability Measures

Measure title (measure description)	Setting of care	Numerator	Denominator	Measure developer/NQF endorsement status
Anticoagulation therapy for atrial fibrillation/ flutter	Inpatient	Ischemic stroke patients prescribed anticoagulation therapy at hospital discharge	Ischemic stroke patients with documented atrial fibrillation/flutter	The Joint Commission/ NQF Endorsed— Reserve: 0436
Preoperative beta blockade	Inpatient	% of patients aged 18 years and older undergoing isolated CABG who received beta blockers within 24 hours preceding surgery	Number of patients undergoing isolated CABG who received beta blockers within 24 hours preceding surgery	The Society of Thoracic Surgeons/NQF Endorsed: 0127
Patients treated with an opioid who are given a bowel regimen	Inpatient and outpatient	% of vulnerable adults treated with an opioid who are offered/prescribed a bowel regimen or documentation of why this was not needed	Patients who are given a bowel regimen or documentation of why this was not needed	RAND Corporation/ NQF Endorsed: 1617

Note: CABG = coronary artery bypass grafting; NQF = National Quality Forum.
Source: Adapted from ASHP Pharmacy Accountability Measures (Andrawis et al. 2019).

KEY INFORMATICS ISSUES

Pharmacy informatics is a growing practice area with the goal of improving the department's quality with information technology and medication-management systems (Johnson and Michael 2018). Pharmacy uses several key pieces of technology, such as EHRs, computerized physician order entry, automated dispensing cabinets, robotics for oral and IV medication orders, IV room workflow software, controlled-substance-diversion monitoring software, and medication barcode scanning. Although this and other technology is implemented for safety, efficiency, and optimization, technology and healthcare are constantly evolving. Each piece of technology implemented in the healthcare setting requires constant updates and maintenance, especially when new medications are added to the hospital's formulary.

Pharmacy departments are growing interested in machine-learning algorithms and artificial intelligence to aid in managing pharmacy data and running operations. Many retail pharmacies are also investigating telepharmacy use. Hospitals with an outpatient component have the opportunity to implement kiosk pharmacies and pharmacy services such as counseling. A few other areas where pharmacy informatics can improve operations include reducing the cognitive burden of clinicians, improving the accuracy of decision-support systems, reducing alert fatigue, and making patient health data more accessible.

STAFFING MODELS

Pharmacy Department staffing models vary with the type, size, and services an organization provides. These models may account for non–patient care activities such as drug information, EHR maintenance, regulatory monitoring, nursing unit inspections, purchasing, and inventory control activities (e.g., managing drug shortages or recalls, monitoring for expired medications, working with reverse distributors) should these functions exist in the department. The following summaries are examples of different pharmacy designs within healthcare organizations.

Centralized and Decentralized Practice Design

The centralized practice model is considered the traditional model of how pharmacies distribute medication, and is more typical in smaller hospitals. Although not recommended, smaller hospitals may have limited pharmacy hours, and pharmacists are available on call versus being on-site. In this model, pharmacy staff are centralized in one location to manage distribution. The pharmacy receives an order from a practitioner, a pharmacist verifies the order, either a pharmacist or pharmacy technician fills the order, a pharmacist verifies the medication, and the pharmacy sends the medication to the floor for the patient. The difference between centralized and decentralized practice is that decentralized practice uses automated dispensing cabinets throughout the hospitals, from which nurses procure medication orders after the pharmacist verifies them. In addition, a pharmacist may be present on the nursing units to perform their duties remotely and assist nursing staff with drug information or patient-care questions related to medications.

Specialist Model Design

This practice differentiates clinical activities from operational duties. Operational pharmacists verify orders and perform distributive duties as described earlier. In this model, operational pharmacists can be centralized in a pharmacy location or decentralized in strategic patient-care areas throughout the hospital. Clinical pharmacy specialists in this system have advanced training or experience and perform clinical activities with other members of the care team. Clinical pharmacists round with the teams, monitor patients' response to drug therapy (by using routine or specialized lab results), monitor for adverse reactions, provide patient-specific drug information, and make therapy recommendations. In some cases, they can be used in targeted programs for multiple patient populations such as antimicrobial stewardship interventions, total parenteral nutrition ordering and monitoring, and targeted drug interventions designed to reduce inappropriate use (e.g., anticoagulation, IV to PO programs, and dosing in patients with organ dysfunction).

Hybrid Model Design

In this model, all pharmacists are expected to assume the same clinical and operational responsibilities. The level of expectation may depend on the maturity of the model. Recent adopters of this model may have basic expectations for all staff to both verify orders and make targeted recommendations during a typical workday. Other models may have pharmacists rotate through rounding with the care team or operational areas according to a set schedule. The details of a particular hybrid model vary with organizational features and workforce skill set. Rotating pharmacists through different activities reduces burnout by providing variety, but also requires a dedicated workforce to maintain a consistent level of highly reliable service across all activities.

PRODUCTIVITY MODELS, INCLUDING WORK-TO-STAFF RATIOS AND INDUSTRY PERFORMANCE TARGETS

Most healthcare organizations require a global productivity measure that relies on measures easily obtained from monthly hospital-operations statistics. If new service lines are added, therapy modalities change, or the patient population changes, then the productivity metrics should be modified. Pharmacy leaders should monitor key workload statistics to track any changes and should reserve fixed full-time equivalents (FTEs) for predicted workload that is not volume dependent. For example, hood cleaning must occur every 30 minutes according to USP<797> requirements; the variability would come when the number of hoods in use changes. Other examples of fixed work may include infusion pump maintenance, crash cart replacement, and nursing unit inspections. Variable productivity calculations should be used in lieu of fixed FTEs when possible. An example of a variable productivity metric is the quantity of medication orders that Pharmacy verifies and prepares each day. Pharmacy leaders should periodically survey the work being completed and review the literature for any needed changes to metrics being monitored.

Internal and external benchmarks can be used to continuously evaluate department success. Internal benchmarks are monitored with data obtained from the Pharmacy Department itself. External benchmarking often involves multiple institutions sharing data for a specific metric and comparing their own department's performance against others'. Productivity workload ratios are often analyzed to determine if Pharmacy resources should be used for distributive medication purposes or clinical activities. Typical pharmacy productivity measures may include worked hours per adjusted patient day or doses; these are broad metrics, however, and can vary greatly. Characteristics such as hospital size, types of medications prepared, and structure of the pharmacy will influence the benchmarks used. Professional pharmacy organizations, hospital organizations, and group-purchasing organizations have implemented national performance benchmarks that can be used as an external resource when creating internal metrics and productivity models.

STRATEGIES TO IMPROVE RECRUITMENT AND RETENTION

Pharmacy Department recruitment follows a process similar to that of most other departments. Ensuring a candidate is competent and a good fit to help the pharmacy meet departmental and organizational goals is vital. The best strategy for reducing turnover starts with establishing a strong screening process. Current staff members can be part of the interview process through peer panels, where their input can be factored into hiring decisions. Incorporating job shadowing into the interview allows the candidate to experience what will be expected of them if hired. Hiring managers should choose candidates who understand the current culture and future direction of the department and organization.

Institutions can use career ladders to motivate individuals to continue working hard and move the pharmacy profession forward through advancement (exhibit 15.5). Career ladders for pharmacists may be based on residency training experience or research completed. For technicians, career ladders vary greatly and may be based on competencies or skill sets. During the hiring process, career ladders should be explained in detail with the goal of hiring and retaining pharmacy personnel who will grow within the department.

To improve retention of new hires, pharmacy managers can regularly interview the employee to ensure they are acclimating well and that their challenges are being addressed in a timely manner. Additional touch points throughout the individual's

Exhibit 15.5: Sample Pharmacy Technician Ladder

Key functions		
Pharmacy technician	Advanced pharmacy technician	Pharmacy technician supervisor
1. Accurately and efficiently fill unit dose carts and first doses 2. Accurately and efficiently deliver medications/supplies to designated areas 3. Accurately and efficiently prepare small- and large-volume parenteral sterile products (non-hazardous and non-investigational) 4. Restock medications/supplies	1. Accurately and efficiently prepare all types of sterile products including SVP, LVP, chemotherapy, biotherapy, and investigational agents 2. Demonstrate proficiency in two or more specialized areas of expertise, meeting accuracy and productivity standards 3. Accurately and efficiently order medications and supplies 4. Outdate expired or soon-to-expire medications in a timely manner	1. Supervise staff to ensure appropriate medication management (procurement, compounding/repackaging, and distribution) 2. Assist in interviewing new pharmacy technicians 3. Supervise training/competency of all pharmacy technicians 4. Monitor area workflow to ensure that all jobs are performed in a timely manner; adjust or shift staff as needed

Note: LVP = large-volume parenterals; SVP = small-volume parenterals.

employment will be established at the manager's discretion, to ensure the team member is progressing well and that leadership is meeting departmental growth and development needs as they relate to future plans for the team member. Successful departments will implement individualized opportunities for employee growth, such as educational programming, participation in department quality projects, and assistance with continuous professional development. An employee-led engagement committee can often help to obtain ideas from staff on new educational programming or retention. Never underestimate the value of a good employee engagement committee to help develop the staff's sense of culture and belonging.

KEY REGULATORY ISSUES

Federal and state regulatory bodies guide and direct pharmacy operations. The Centers for Medicare & Medicaid Services, The Joint Commission, Det Norske Veritas, and the Drug Enforcement Administration (DEA) are examples of federal regulatory bodies; each state is also monitored by its State Board of Pharmacy.

Even though these regulatory bodies focus on specific areas, the Pharmacy Department must follow each of them as it pertains to the institution. When the laws these agencies enforce conflict, the Pharmacy Department will abide by the strictest of multiple requirements.

Along with the federal and state regulatory bodies, the USP creates standards for safe handling of medications and compounds. Multiple chapters affect the practice of pharmacy within hospitals (USP <795>, USP<797>, USP<800>). In 2019, USP implemented revised guidance for all these chapters. Pharmacy leaders should be well versed in the standards and how hospital pharmacies or employees must modify infrastructure, practice standards, or quality standards.

Since 2015, there has been a tremendous spike in the abuse of opioids across the healthcare industry. As the DEA enforces new regulations, the Pharmacy Department has had to ensure institutional compliance. Pharmacy departments often work with other healthcare disciplines to create workflow to prevent drug diversion at the prescribing, transcribing, dispensing, and administering stages. Pharmacy staff are often assigned responsibilities that focus on diversion prevention and opioid stewardship.

KEY TERMS FOR PHARMACY

Drug diversion prevention: Implementation of processes, technologies, or committees to prevent drugs—often controlled substances—from being misused or redistributed from their original purpose or for illicit use.

Gravimetrics: A method of using an electronic balance and the density of a solution as quality-assurance checks to confirm the accuracy of compounded parenterals.

Medication order: Written directions provided by a prescribing practitioner for a specific medication to be administered to an individual in a hospital setting. Often contrasted with medication prescriptions, which are written directions provided by a prescribing practitioner for medications to be filled and dispensed to patients in an outpatient setting.

Pharmacists: Professionals who provide pharmaceutical care, which involves direct, responsible provision of medication-related care for the purpose of achieving definite outcomes that improve a patient's quality of life.

Pharmacy: The art, practice, or profession of preparing, preserving, compounding, and dispensing medical drugs.

Pharmacy technician: A pharmacy staff member who works closely with pharmacists in hospitals, standalone pharmacies and those based in retail outlets, and other medical settings to help prepare and distribute medicines to patients.

REFERENCES

Andrawis, M. A., C. Ellison, S. Riddle, K. Mahan, C. Collins, P. Brummon, and J. Carmichael. 2019. "Recommended Quality Measures for Health-System Pharmacy: 2019 Update from the Pharmacy Accountability Measures Work Group." *American Journal of Health-System Pharmacy* 76 (12): 874–87.

Ismail, S., M. Osman, R. Abulezz, H. Alhamdan, and K. H. Mujtaba Quadri. 2018. "Pharmacists as Interprofessional Collaborators and Leaders Through Clinical Pathways." *Pharmacy* 6 (1): 24.

Johnson, T. J., and J. B. Michael. 2018. "Development and Innovation of System Resources to Optimize Patient Care." *American Journal of Health-System Pharmacy* 75 (7): 465–72.

Learn How to Become. 2020a. "Pharmacy Schools & Pharmacist Careers: How to Become a Pharmacist." Accessed September 30. www.learnhowtobecome.org/pharmacist/.

———. 2020b. "Pharmacy Schools & Pharmacist Careers: How to Become a Pharmacy Technician." Accessed September 30. www.learnhowtobecome.org/pharmacy-technician/.

O'Neal, B. C., A. M. Friemel, J. E. Glowczewski, J. M. Coggins, M. Macchia, R. A. Forrey, K. R. Patel, and R. P. Granko. 2018. "Optimizing the Revenue Cycle to Promote Growth of the Pharmacy Enterprise." *American Journal of Health-System Pharmacy* 75 (12): 853–55.

Schneider, P. J., C. A. Pedersen, and D. J. Scheckelhoff. 2019. "ASHP National Survey of Pharmacy Practice in Hospital Settings: Prescribing and Transcribing—2019." *American Journal of Health-System Pharmacy* 75 (16): 1203–26.

———. 2018. "ASHP National Survey of Pharmacy Practice in Hospital Settings: Dispensing and Administration—2018." *American Journal of Health-System Pharmacy* 75 (16): 1203–26.

Vermeulen, L. C., J. Kolesar, M. L. Crismon, A. J. Flynn, J. G. Stevenson, P. J. Almeter, W. M. Heath, G. T. Short, S. Murphy Enright, P. Ploetz, M. D. Swarthout, W. A. Zellmer, R. Saenz, D. S. Devereaux, D. A. Zilz, J. M. Hoffman, W. E. Evans, S. J. Knoer, and M. D. Ray. 2018. "ASHP Foundation Pharmacy Forecast 2018: Strategic Planning Advice for Pharmacy Departments in Hospitals and Health Systems." *American Journal of Health-System Pharmacy* 75 (2): 23–54.

CHAPTER 16

Radiology and Imaging Services

Habib Tannir

DEPARTMENT DESCRIPTION

The discipline of radiology has its roots in the discovery of X-rays in 1895 by Wilhelm Roentgen, who won the Nobel Prize in Physics for doing so. Although the discovery of X-rays was accidental, within a decade several scientists had introduced them into medicine, including Marie and Pierre Curie, who used X-rays to peer into the human body without surgery.

Today, radiology is a much broader discipline that includes use of X-rays, ultrasonic waves, gamma rays, magnetic resonance, and radio waves to screen, diagnose, and treat disease. Because of the multitude of radiologic and non-radiologic technologies, numerous hospitals use the term *Imaging* for the departments that use these devices; for consistency and technical accuracy, this chapter will follow suit.

Imaging Services has two main components: technical and professional. In the technical component, technologists acquire images under direct or indirect supervision of a physician, depending on the imaging modality. Technologists may be categorized in three major categories: radiologic technologists, sonographers, and nuclear medicine technologists. Technologists may hold associate's or bachelor's degrees, obtained from allied health programs. The few master's degrees offered in these programs usually focus on management. These programs are increasingly offering undergraduate subspecialization with clinical internships as opposed to general studies. For example, radiologic technologists may specialize in computed tomography (CT) or magnetic resonance imaging (MRI). This educational background is an important consideration in hiring recent graduates when on-the-job training may not be available.

Technologists are required to be licensed in states where they work, especially if they are administering radiation (e.g., X-ray or nuclear medicine); however, these requirements are not universal. The professional societies governing the practice of imaging technologists offer subspecialty registries and certifications, which require a higher level of expertise and experience in those subspecialties to be demonstrated through testing. For example, the American Registry of Diagnostic Medical Sonography administers and awards certifications in medical, cardiac, vascular, and musculoskeletal sonography.

Staff involved with the professional component of Imaging Services provide the medical necessity, appropriateness criteria, acquisition-parameter protocol design, image interpretation, and result consultation and adjudication for procedures and patients. This component is primarily administered by a radiologist licensed in the state where images are made. A radiologist is a physician who receives four to six years of further training after graduating medical school. They may seek further subspecialization through fellowship training in neuroradiology, musculoskeletal radiology, thoracic radiology, emergency radiology, breast imaging, abdominal imaging, cardiac imaging, interventional radiology, and interventional neuroradiology. They may also seek board certification through the American Board of Radiology. An authorized user of radioactive materials, most commonly a licensed nuclear medicine physician, oversees the provision of nuclear medicine services. The nuclear medicine physician may seek board certification from the American Board of Nuclear Medicine.

When a new imaging modality is invented, fellowship programs commonly develop around it and sustain training in a modality-centric fashion. For example, fellowship programs in MRI and in ultrasound focus on the physics and on biomedical imaging properties and applications. As a technology matures and is integrated in the standard of care, the training on the modality is itself integrated in the fellowship training program for the system, body part, or organ, as in neuroradiology, abdominal imaging, or breast imaging. Eventually, the modality-centric fellowship program dissolves.

Other disciplines (e.g., cardiology, orthopedics, neurosurgery, emergency medicine) may use imaging or image guidance while providing services. Those disciplines increasingly include imaging in core physician training programs. Otherwise, they collaborate with radiologists to provide oversight of Imaging Services.

In most small and rural hospitals, technologists are the only professionals involved in image acquisition, under the supervision of a contracted radiology provider. In larger hospitals and academic medical centers, a host of other professionals may support the technical operations of an Imaging Department, including nurses, residents, fellows, and medical physicists. Nurses are an integral part of an Imaging Department, where they manage transition of care, conduct medication updates, respond to contrast-induced allergies, administer medication for patients with claustrophobia, and provide pre-, intra-, and postoperative patient management during invasive image-guided procedures. Medical physicists are professionals who contribute to the safe and effective delivery of care through such consultative services that include acquiring and installing equipment and facility shielding, initiating and commissioning services, optimizing acquisition parameters, calculating radiation doses, and setting radionuclide imaging parameters.

KEY DEPARTMENT SERVICES

Imaging departments serve inpatients and outpatients, including Emergency Center (EC) patients. In rural and smaller hospital settings, those are provided typically on the same equipment infrastructure; in larger settings, these services are best split into inpatient and outpatient facilities. Emergency Center patients are typically serviced with the inpatient equipment; larger settings and trauma centers may have dedicated or even co-located X-ray and CT machines as volumes and timeliness warrant. In larger settings, best practice is to have a set of equipment dedicated to the Ambulatory Services building, where outpatient schedules will not be disrupted by emergent cases from hospital inpatient floors or the Emergency Center. Outpatients may also benefit from convenient parking and proximity to the medical office building where they see their physician.

Services differ drastically by setting and, more important, by established service lines. If a hospital does not offer neuroscience services, for instance, it may not offer an interventional neuroradiology program. A list of common imaging services follows.

X-Ray

This service uses equipment that generates X-ray bursts and a digital detector to capture single images across the body part of interest. Studies are usually ordered in two views: anterior/posterior (referred to as A/P) and lateral. From these views, a radiologist can diagnose simple structural pathology such as bone fractures, confirm placement of an inserted tube, or detect a collapsed lung. X-ray equipment can be fixed in a dedicated room in the Imaging or Emergency departments, or can be mobile, where a portable X-ray unit can be pushed to wherever the patient may be on an inpatient unit or in the Operating Room.

Most hospitals have adopted digital radiology, where the X-ray generator and the detector are integrated in the same equipment and work in tandem to optimize image quality and dose. The images are stored on a Picture Archive and Communication System (PACS), which will be addressed in the Key Process Flows section. A few hospitals, however, continue to use film, capturing images physically and developing them with chemicals. These images are then interpreted over a light box and physically stored in a film library. Yet other hospitals are in the process of converting from film and are using a transitional technology called computerized radiography, where the X-ray is generated by old equipment and a plate inside a cassette captures the image. The plate is then scanned by a digital processor, and a digital image is produced and sent to PACS. The plate is then erased and prepared for another use.

Mammography

This service uses X-ray technology to image the breast for cancer screening and noninvasive diagnosis, and as image guidance for breast biopsies. The vast majority of hospitals have adopted digital mammography, and many offer tomosynthesis, also referred to as 3D mammography, as standard of care. Yet for economic reasons the adoption of these technologies has been gradual, and one still finds mammography performed on film. Because this modality is mostly used to screen otherwise healthy women, it is usually provided in highly consumer-centric, retail-like delivery channels. This setting usually manifests itself in aesthetically pleasing facilities with focused offerings. Hospitals regard women as the primary decision makers on healthcare matters for the household and have used mammography services as a gateway to guide patients' other family members into the healthcare system.

Fluoroscopy

This service is used in diagnostic and procedural exams. It produces continuous X-rays that travel through the body part of interest and onto a detector, which converts the X-ray into video. The equipment can be fixed in a room for a single use, such as an angiography suite for interventional radiology or cardiac catheterization, or for multiple purposes, such as lumbar punctures, and studies of swallowing and gastrointestinal disorders. Fluoroscopy equipment can also be mobile, such as a C-arm, which can be moved into a procedural area or the Operating Room. Depending on the application, fluoroscopy can be conducted with or without contrast enhancement. Contrasts are different types of radio-opaque fluids that can be ingested by mouth, injected rectally, or administered intravenously, depending on the area of interest and the pathology under examination.

Computed Tomography

CT is a cross-sectional imaging modality housed in a giant doughnut-shaped gantry with a patient table moving through its hole. An X-ray source and an array of small detectors rotate around the body part of interest while the patient on the table continuously moves into the machine. The images produced are axial cross-sectional slices, which can be further processed into coronal or sagittal projections and three-dimensional renderings. CT suites require lead shielding to prevent ionizing radiation from leaking into the environment and exposing workers. Such suites require qualified contractors; when they are completed, an independent physicist specializing in radiation safety should inspect the shielding before putting the suite into service.

CT has advanced in speed and diagnostic power since its inception and is now used in screening, diagnostic, and image-guided biopsy and therapeutic intervention. Advances include gating image acquisition, increasing the number of slices obtained in every revolution of the detector array, and using dual-energy X-ray capabilities. The ultimate aim of these advances is to enhance visualization of organs, better characterize normal and diseased tissue, account for motion or implant artifact, and improve diagnostic yield. Screening applications are dominated by lung-screening exams for high-risk populations and whole-body screening, primarily for retail or executive health. Diagnostic applications are numerous, can be done with or without use of contrast enhancement, and serve neurologic, oncologic, cardiac, and limited vascular angiography, among others. The technology is also useful for certain image-guided biopsies, where the correct placement of biopsy needles must be obtained to ensure adequate tissue sampling. Finally, CT can be used to accurately place ablation devices and then assess effects of ablation on tissue.

Ultrasound

In ultrasound machines, crystal transducers emit sonic waves above the audible spectrum into organs, then receive and process the reflected waves into images of these organs. Ultrasound machines also use Doppler technology to detect blood flow through vessels. Ultrasound is considered a low-end imaging modality because of its lower costs and comparatively lower diagnostic yield. Advances in miniaturization have produced handheld ultrasound devices that permit quick checks in Emergency Room settings. More recent advances allow the use of sheer waves to measure the elasticity of organ tissue, which can then be correlated to better characterize the tissue. Ultrasound is used to detect some vascular disease (e.g., deep venous thrombosis, carotid artery stenosis) and in oncologic settings (e.g., detecting breast and thyroid cancers). It can also be used to guide biopsies. Because of its known relative safety, ultrasound has become one of the cornerstone imaging modalities in women's imaging (gynecology, obstetrics, perinatology). In such specialty settings and in academic medical centers, dedicated ultrasound post-processing workstations and archive systems may be used for particular applications.

Magnetic Resonance Imaging

MRI is a high-end imaging modality with sophisticated technology. MRI uses a strong magnet (usually 1.5 or 3.0 teslas in gradient strength) to align water molecules in tissue. Then it alternates emission of radio frequency to excite these molecules out of alignment and receives the radio frequency they emit as they realign with the magnet. These radiofrequencies are then used to construct images of the organ of interest. Because normal tissue and disease tissue respond differently, the image processing can detect and characterize disease. MRI suites require copper shielding to prevent interference from radio frequency sources. Qualified contractors should be used to construct the shielding. Advances in MRI include the use of spectroscopy, a technique that identifies specific elements in tissue based on the profile of their magnetic resonance, which can help to diagnose disease. Another advance is called MR tractography, which is an advanced visualization technique that uses sophisticated post-processing algorithms to detect and trace vital neural tracts and pathways. These paths are represented on the anatomy so surgeons can avoid damaging them and preserve physiological functions as they remove or ablate tumors. Although CT is a great structural and anatomical imaging tool, MRI distinguishes itself in being a morphological and functional imaging tool.

Nuclear Medicine and Positron Emission Tomography

Nuclear medicine (NM) is a diagnostic and therapeutic discipline that uses radioactive pharmaceuticals as a source of radiation and gamma-ray detectors and a camera to image activity. The radiopharmaceutical is a compound containing a radionuclide formulated to find specific targets and then serve as a marker for the gamma camera to detect a given activity. NM provides diagnostic procedures for the endocrine, lymphatic, gastrointestinal, genitourinary, musculoskeletal, nervous, and cardiovascular systems. Although most NM procedures take place in the Imaging Department, more invasive diagnostics (e.g., lymphoscintigraphy-guided biopsies of lymph nodes) may start there and finish in the Operating Room.

Positron emission tomography (PET) is one application of NM principles that has found its most common use to date by measuring metabolism of tumors. More PET applications are being developed with the integration of CT technology on the same PET gantry and the advancement of digital detectors, which improve scanning time and location accuracy.

The therapeutic applications of NM involve the injection of a higher dose of radiopharmaceuticals than for measuring metabolism to target tumors and emit enough radiation into them to cause necrosis. Delivery can be through direct injections into the tumor, intravenous injections, or through a catheter as in the case of yttrium-90. These drugs tend to be very expensive, so preauthorization and cost recovery processes are paramount for keeping the service line financially viable.

Interventional Radiology and Interventional Neuroradiology

Interventional radiology is an image-guided discipline that engages mostly in minimally invasive and some noninvasive procedures. Such work may be vascular based, in which the interventional radiologist performs diagnostic angiography or venography, then optionally escalates to interventions such as angioplasty, stent or filter placement, embolization, or thrombectomy. Vasculature of interest may be cervico-cerebral, aortic (abdominal or thoracic), visceral (e.g., celiac, hepatic, splenic), renal, adrenal, or of the extremities. Nonvascular invasive procedures include biopsies, aspiration, fluid drainage, tumor ablation, vertebroplasty, kypho-plasty, and myelography.

Interventional neuroradiology is the application of vascular-based inter-ventions to the nervous system with greater focus on the brain than the spine. Although this discipline is rooted in interventional radiology and neuroradiology, neurologists and neurosurgeons have been joining training programs that would then allow them to obtain hospital privileges to perform these procedures. Endo-vascular interventions are increasingly becoming an integral part of neurosurgical training, and in some hospitals these suites may be placed in the Operating Room to accommodate combined endovascular and open surgical procedures. The rou-tine services offered include aneurysm coiling, vascular embolization of tumors and arteriovenous malformations, angioplasty, stenting, and infusing thrombo-lytic drugs for stroke therapy. Interventional neuroradiology is a critical service for stroke centers, as it provides more timely interventions to minimize the effect of stroke.

DEPARTMENT ORGANIZATIONAL STRUCTURES

Healthcare disciplines tend to value technical subject matter expertise in leader-ship. It is therefore not surprising that Imaging departments are typically organized by modality, where first-line leadership is a technologist trained and experienced in that modality. Depending on department size, an Imaging manager may handle a single modality and oversee multiple shift and location supervisors, or may manage the entire department with multiple modalities. In smaller hospitals, the flatter management footprint would put this manager at the top of the Imaging service line. In larger departments, a director of imaging would oversee the technical specialty managers and serve as the service line leader, reporting to the vice president of operations, a chief nursing officer, or a chief operating officer.

In larger academic medical centers, the service line leader, in addition to the reporting relationship just described, works in a dyad with the chair of radiology and may manage the director of technical operations, the director of the radiology physician practice, and the administrator of the academic components of the department. The larger the organization, the more complex and matrixed these relationships become. Nurses in Imaging departments tend to have a dual reporting relationship to the department director for operational management and to the nursing hierarchy for practice management and professional development.

As with all healthcare disciplines, there is a long-standing debate as to the managerial layer at which the formal technical training in radiologic technology would no longer be the required background, and a more general professional management and leadership training would be more relevant. The licensing requisites make this debate even more heated. There is no established regulatory requirement that would end this conversation, so the key is not to promote people to the level of incompetence. Rather, allow them to be the best practitioners they can be. Exhibit 16.1 depicts three organizational structures suitable to departments and organization scopes of various sizes.

KEY CUSTOMERS AND THEIR PERFORMANCE EXPECTATIONS

Customers of the Imaging Department can be internal or external to the organization. Routine check-ins through surveys, focus groups, and one-on-one visits are critical to keep the voice of the customer at the forefront of service delivery. Follow-up and follow-through on these surveys is critical to maintain customer engagement and loyalty. Key customers are listed next, with their respective performance expectations, starting with the expectations common to all.

Patients

Three categories of patients require imaging services: inpatients, outpatients, and emergency patients. All three share several expectations. For example, they expect an explanation of the procedure they are undergoing. They may want their loved

Exhibit 16.1: Three Different Organizational Structures

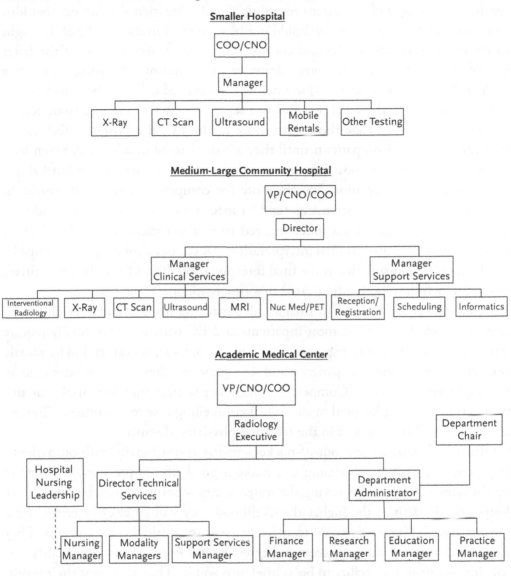

Smaller Hospital

COO/CNO → Manager → X-Ray, CT Scan, Ultrasound, Mobile Rentals, Other Testing

Medium-Large Community Hospital

VP/CNO/COO → Director → Manager Clinical Services, Manager Support Services

Under Manager Clinical Services: Interventional Radiology, X-Ray, CT Scan, Ultrasound, MRI, Nuc Med/PET

Under Manager Support Services: Reception/Registration, Scheduling, Informatics

Academic Medical Center

VP/CNO/COO → Radiology Executive; Department Chair

Under Radiology Executive: Hospital Nursing Leadership, Director Technical Services, Department Administrator

Under Director Technical Services: Nursing Manager, Modality Managers, Support Services Manager

Under Department Administrator: Finance Manager, Research Manager, Education Manager, Practice Manager

Note: CNO = chief nursing officer; COO = chief operating officer; CT = computed tomography; MRI = magnetic resonance imaging; PET = positron emission tomography.

one to be with them during lengthy procedures. Where their requirements vary, however, is by care setting.

Inpatients are admitted patients who require diagnostic or interventional imaging services and who are managed by their admitting physician, the attending specialist, or a hospitalist. Their studies are ordered as stat or routine. Although hospitals may have specific policies on timeliness expectations of studies, generally stat studies are expected to be completed and resulted within one to two hours. Routine studies are expected to be performed on the same day and resulted by the next morning before patient rounding occurs. Inpatients' other expectations concern comfort (e.g., patients should not be awakened in the middle of the night to complete a routine study) and coordination of care. An example of the latter is when patients need a laboratory draw for blood testing, and Imaging needs a glomerular filtration rate (GFR) test before a contrasted CT test, then the lab testing should include the GFR to avoid two separate draws and two separate tests.

Emergency patients are those who come to the EC of a hospital. Technically they are considered outpatients until they are discharged or admitted, when they become inpatients. In most hospitals, studies ordered in the EC are labeled *stat* by default. The expectations are therefore for completion and result within an hour. Many Imaging departments tend to meet these expectations by rendering a preliminary interpretation (once referred to as a *wet read*), followed within 24 hours by a more thorough final interpretation. Of course, a robust process must be implemented to ensure that if the final interpretation differs from the preliminary one, proper follow-up is adjudicated in a timely manner.

Outpatients are referred to Imaging departments from ambulatory clinics by referring providers. Unlike most inpatients and EC patients, who usually require stretcher or wheelchair transportation assistance, outpatients can ambulate mostly unassisted. Also unlike Inpatients and EC patients, they can choose where to receive imaging services. Competitive business practices therefore apply for this population, and the hospital must make a compelling case to customers. The case for quality will be reviewed in the referring physician discussion.

Patient experience and out-of-pocket expense count heavily with outpatients. For example, ease of scheduling can make a good first impression. Call center performance is critical for setting the tone. Access to services must be timely. The longer the lead time, the higher the likelihood they will go elsewhere. Anything greater than 72 hours is certain to drive patients to consider other options. They require convenient physical access and egress to and from the imaging facility and for time spent in the facility to be as brief as possible. They also want their results reported to their ordering physician by the follow-up visit at the latest—if they are in pain, they will expect results as soon as possible.

Referring physicians are those who order imaging services for their patient. Although patients ultimately choose where to go, they largely defer to the referring physician. Ensuring excellent relations with those physicians is critical to maintaining a referral stream. These relations are cultivated by a physician relations team who can address the reasons why their hospital is the best imaging provider: for example, proximity to physician offices, experience and training of the technologists, quality of equipment, and expedited test results. Historically, reports were faxed to referring physician offices, whose employees then filed them in the paper charts. In academic medical centers and many integrated delivery networks, the referring physicians are typically employees, or otherwise affiliated, and therefore now use the same information systems infrastructure as the hospital. However, in most other settings, where referring physicians are typically on several different platforms, information systems interoperability is playing an ever-increasing role. A hospital must solve the problem of interoperability to maintain referral streams, ensure proper follow-up, and improve quality of care.

Payers

Payers are broadly categorized as employers, health insurance companies, and government. These groups may have different primary interests, but their common goal is to lower the cost of care for the patients they cover. Payers have used several strategies to achieve these cost reductions. The most common is contracting with service providers for lower reimbursement in fee-for-service structures. Some reductions entailed reducing reimbursement when exams are being performed on contiguous body parts in a single encounter. Others involved bundling imaging with other services that typically occur in the same episode of care.

Benefits management, whether operated by the payers themselves or outsourced to intermediaries, is another form of cost reduction. Their tactics include directing the patients to providers in the payer's network who are contracted at a lower price. Such direction can occur by raising the patient's financial hurdle if they choose a more expensive provider by imposing higher out-of-pocket patient responsibilities (e.g., higher copays). Another disincentive is to raise the administrative burden, such as requiring patients to call the benefits management office for pre-authorization or to pay out-of-pocket and then file for reimbursement. A further cost reduction strategy is to deny payment for tests that do not meet the payer's chosen medical necessity criteria. These criteria are usually appropriate for the most common imaging tests, but may not be up to date with newer tests or new applications of existing tests.

KEY PROCESS FLOWS

Exhibit 16.2 shows a typical Imaging Department workflow. The process starts with a physician who needs further information to extract a diagnosis and thus places an order for an imaging procedure. The order must show the patient identifiers (name and date of birth), the reason for exam (best expressed as a diagnosis code), the exam to be performed (best expressed as a procedure code), and the physician's name and signature. The order can be in paper or electronic form.

Exhibit 16.2: Typical Imaging Department Workflow

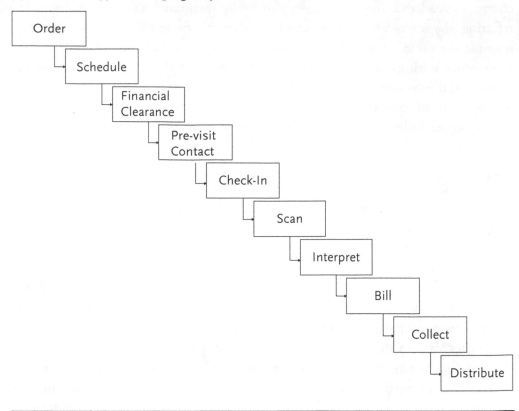

Starting in 2020, the Centers for Medicare & Medicaid Services (CMS) require that the ordering physician consult a Decision Support System, which matches the signs and symptoms of the patients and the exam ordered and checks them against appropriate use criteria. The criteria must be evidence based, generated by a professional society or a qualified provider-led entity.

The next step is to schedule the exam with the imaging service provider. This step is best performed with the patient to ensure convenience and therefore compliance with the appointment.

Next, for patients participating in payer plans managed by private insurance companies, the ordering physician's office or a central financial clearance department of the healthcare system (if the ordering physician is employed by the system) obtains authorization from the payer. This authorization is a two-step process of insurance participation verification and service coverage verification for the specific plan. Depending on the insurance company, a third-party benefits management intermediary could serve as the clearinghouse for such authorization. Authorization may be granted, denied, or require a peer-to-peer review, during which two clinicians, one working on the payer's behalf and one on the provider's behalf, discuss the appropriateness of the study. The end result of the peer-to-peer review would be an authorization of the exam, a recommendation of a different exam, or a denial, in which case the patient may be responsible to pay for the exam out-of-pocket.

The imaging service provider then contacts the patient before the visit to confirm the appointment and educate the patient on what to expect during the visit and on any preparation (e.g., fasting or drinking a laxative solution before the exam). Finally, the imaging provider may discuss financial obligations due at the time of service to avoid surprises upon arrival.

When the patient arrives at the imaging facility, they are checked in and registered in the facility's information system. A patient who is new to the facility takes longer to check in than an established patient because of the plethora of demographic, financial, and clinical information that must be entered anew into the system. By contrast, when an established patient returns, only changes since the last visit are entered. Most of this information can be obtained during the pre-visit call-in order, which expedites the check-in process and minimizes the patient's dwell time at the facility. Clinical information is verified at this point to ensure safety. For example, if the patient requires iodinated contrast for imaging, staff must verify kidney function against laboratory tests; if the patient is coming for an MRI exam, operators must verify that the patient does not have any ferromagnetic implants or on-body devices. Typically, the patient is given screening forms (paper or preferably electronic) to fill out before the exam. Also, a patient consent is obtained. Self-referred patients, typically for screening exams, provide contact information of their primary care provider (PCP) so that the imaging facility can provide the exam findings to the PCP for further follow-up when necessary. The patient may be asked to pay any financial obligations determined to be their responsibility at this time.

When the check-in process is complete, the patient is escorted into the clinical area for the procedure. Many exams require contrast injection through a peripheral venous catheter or an intravenous injection of radioactive pharmaceuticals. This step is usually performed in an anteroom in larger settings or in the scan room in smaller settings. In the scan room, the technologist positions the patient in accordance with protocols established by the supervising radiologists specific to the combination of patient diagnosis and procedure ordered. The scan is then conducted against parameters consistent with the specific protocol to optimize image quality, radiation dose, and organ of interest visualization. The protocol is usually predeveloped by the radiologist, an application specialist from the equipment manufacturer, and, optimally, a medical imaging physicist. The technologist performs a quality control step on the series of images obtained, reviews them, and either verifies or rejects them before archiving them in a PACS.

Once the images are verified, the radiologist chooses the study from a PACS work list for interpretation. The work list prioritizes which study to interpret first based on a predetermined algorithm, usually prescribed by the facility's policies. The algorithm takes into account whether the study is stat or routine, or from the EC, the inpatient floor, or the outpatient clinic. In some cases, the technologist can manually elevate the priority of a case because of a critical finding they may have detected during the scan or an administrative need, such as the patient is pending discharge or is waiting in the referring physician's office. The radiologist interprets the study and dictates their findings into the electronic health record (EHR), most commonly through an intermediary voice recognition system. The dictation follows a template that is best agreed upon with the ordering services. The template contains the patient identifiers, reason for exam, exam performed, any relevant patient history, the technique used to acquire and process the images, the impression, the finding, and any recommendation that the radiologist may have. If a critical finding is identified, the radiologist must report it to the ordering physician within a period usually determined by hospital policy and tracked as part of its quality assessment and performance improvement program.

Once the radiologist signs the final report, it is communicated to the ordering physician. This reporting occurs in an integrated EHR, through a secured electronic file transfer between two EHR systems, or (increasingly rarely) through older methods such as fax or certified letter. Meanwhile the final report is transmitted to the billing departments of the hospital and the radiologist practice, where a bill is generated from the information included in the report. The bill is electronically transmitted to the payer in accordance with contractual specifications of the bill itself and the contractually agreed-upon financial accountabilities of the patient, payer, and provider. Some hospitals and radiology practices outsource coding, billing, and collections to third-party companies.

KEY UNITS OF WORK AND VOLUME STATISTICS TO MONITOR

Imaging uses several standard units of work: number of exams and patients, ambulatory payment classification (APC) on the hospital services side, and worked relative value units (wRVUs) on the physician services side. The latter two are standardized values assigned by CMS to exams and services and are weighted according to complexity and time needed to complete the work. Although most administrators and radiologists disagree with the valuation of these classifications and units, they are indeed widely used—if not accepted—by the industry.

KEY METRICS TO MONITOR: PEOPLE, SERVICE, QUALITY/SAFETY, FINANCIAL

As with any service industry, successful administrators monitor several metrics that represent the totality of the work performed. Although they may focus periodically on improving one or two metrics during a low-performance period along the respective aspects of the service, all metrics must be managed concurrently to ensure that an improvement on one metric does not come at a detriment to another. This method is most commonly referred to as managing a Balanced Scorecard. The scorecard typically contains metrics to measure performance along pillars that support the mission of the organization. These pillars may include People, Service, Quality/Safety, and Financial.

Along the People pillar, Employee Engagement is a leading indicator of many other performance metrics. It is a composite metric of employees being able to perform at their best every day, having a sense of belonging with their colleagues and the institution, and having room to learn and grow. When a facility has high employee engagement, it usually performs well in all other aspects.

Along the Service pillar, patient satisfaction is measured through a battery of questions assessing facility comfort and wayfinding, perceived provider attitudes and competencies across the steps of the patient's journey, explanation of services, and service delivery. The questions are often punctuated with a satisfaction rating and whether a patient would recommend the service to others. Several accreditations, designations, and payer contracts require measurement and reporting of patient satisfaction, usually with benchmarking capabilities against peer groups. Several third parties offer variants of patient satisfaction surveys, processing, benchmarking, and even best practices.

The Quality and Safety pillar has a wide portfolio of metrics. Quality has two major categories: production quality and professional quality. Production quality measures indicators commonly found in any production system, primarily lead time to service access, turnaround time of service delivery, and typical service defects that may require repeat or recovery. Specific to a radiology operation, lead time is measured by time to next appointment—the sooner the better. Turnaround time can be segmented into multiple phases, but what matters the most to the patient and the ordering physician is the time it takes from ordering the exam to obtaining the final result—the shorter the better. Administratively, this time is parsed into the different phases of the service: for example, order to check-in, check-in to complete, and complete to result. Finally, service defects are measured in rates of the wrong exam being performed, unreasonable turnaround times, or misinterpreted studies.

Professional quality is more concerned with the practice of imaging. Issues under this category include the following:

- Was the appropriate imaging modality used?
- Were the image quality and diagnostic yield sufficient to answer the clinical question?
- Was the report structured to be helpful to the ordering clinician?
- Did the interpretation of the images account for the patient's family history?

Almost all Radiology operations are now preoccupied with production quality; increasingly, however, they are thinking about outcomes and value, which require management of professional quality.

Safety measures in Imaging operations share many metrics with other hospital departments, such as patient identification error rates, allergic reactions, and falls. In addition, Radiology-specific safety measures include unanticipated radiation exposure, contrast extravasation and reactions, laterality mistakes, MRI safety events, biopsies of the wrong lesions, and complications from interventional procedures.

Along the pillar of Finance, Radiology administrators follow absolute measures and ratios. Absolute measures include exam volumes, charges, collections, expenses (labor and non-labor), and contribution margins or net income. Ratio measures include volume per workday, collection rates, days in Accounts Receivable, percentage of fixed and variable expenses, percentage margins, asset utilizations, and productivity ratios (e.g., APC or wRVU per full-time equivalent).

To reiterate, successful long-term management of an Imaging operation heavily depends on managing the entirety of the Balanced Scorecard. Overemphasis of one pillar will inevitably harm performance on another even if it comes later in time. The operative word here is *balance*.

KEY INFORMATICS ISSUES

Imaging operations have been pioneers of healthcare informatics. They were among the first to communicate medical data across networks as a routine business practice in a healthcare setting, to use digital media to archive and timely retrieve historical clinical data, to use digital platforms to organize and execute routine clinical workflow, to use voice recognition as a mainstream clinical documentation aid, and to use computer-aided disease detection. As such, Imaging professionals have invested much time in optimizing digital tools to serve their needs for efficient patient turnover and effective integration of information at the point of image interpretation. As diagnosticians, radiologists rely on the availability of accurate, up-to-date clinical information to render a meaningful consultation. During the rise of a single EHR in the healthcare space, Imaging professionals promoted integrating best-of-breed systems into the EHR to maintain efficient operations and ensure availability of real-time, up-to-date clinical information. As EHRs became better at supporting high-turnover workflows, Imaging departments began adopting the technology as a primary driver. Imaging operations use information systems in the spaces of scheduling, clinical decision support, workflow management and prioritization, image communication and archiving, computer-aided lesion detection, voice recognition and dictation, result distribution and acknowledgment, and revenue cycle management. As with all other clinical operations, Radiology and Imaging Services increasingly rely on business intelligence, outcome analytics, and artificial intelligence systems.

STAFFING MODELS AND PRODUCTIVITY MODELS, INCLUDING WORK-TO-STAFF RATIOS AND INDUSTRY PERFORMANCE TARGETS

Imaging Services carries no regulatory requirements for specific staffing ratios. However, regulatory agencies do require that hospitals effectively manage staffing levels to care for the individual needs of patients. This overarching requirement applies to the provision of imaging services such that staffing levels conform to patient volumes. Several companies and professional organizations provide benchmarking services on a consulting or subscription basis. These usually require facilities to detail the imaging procedures performed at their facility and the staffing levels during the same period. Staffing ratios are then compared with a peer group, and a percentile rank placement is rendered. Hospitals may then target a specific staffing-ratio percentile rank among the peer group that can account for slight variation in the patient acuity and case mix. For example, a regional referral hospital or a cancer center may choose to have a richer staffing level and therefore a lower productivity percentile rank to account for its unique operation or their mission emphasis.

STRATEGIES FOR RECRUITMENT AND RETENTION

Imaging is highly dependent on technology. It is important for the technologist to know that they have the tools they need to perform their job. Therefore, having a healthy number of state-of-the-art imaging platforms and user-friendly information systems is a good attraction to potential hires. Knowing management's expectations and priorities is also most helpful.

People want to do a good job and live up to high standards, but they also need to feel that they are valued as individuals. Providing opportunities to participate on projects that elevate the practice is a major incentive for Imaging workers. Such projects include production management, performance improvement, or developing new imaging protocols. All make the technologist feel valued for their intellect.

Career progression is another important component of retention. As such, many departments have career ladder structures where technologists can learn and grow within their modality or learn new modalities. Other departments may offer incentives for obtaining registries and certification in imaging specific organ systems. The incentives can take the form of time allocated to study, mentoring to gain experience, or even a supplemental stipend for maintaining these registries. Although these tactics may improve short- and medium-term retention, a feeling of intrinsic connectedness to the mission of the organization is ultimately the highest level of loyalty.

KEY REGULATORY ISSUES

Several agencies and professional societies establish regulations and guidelines for the provision of imaging services. Some of these organizations include the Food and Drug Administration, CMS, the Environmental Protection Agency (EPA), the Occupational Health and Safety Administration, the American College of Radiology, the Radiological Society of North America, the American Society of Radiologic Technologists, the Alliance for Radiation Safety in Pediatric Imaging, the American College of Cardiology, the American College of Neurology, the American College of Physicians, the Society of Nuclear Medicine and Molecular Imaging, the American Society of Nuclear Cardiology, and the American Association of Physicists in Medicine. These bodies provide guidance on personnel qualifications, the practice of Radiology and Imaging, equipment manufacturing and maintenance, radioactive material transportation and handling, patient and personnel radiation protection, and facilities specifications. Some key regulatory issues include the following:

- Adopt the "as low as reasonably achievable" (ALARA) principle, as described by the EPA, as a standard of practice.
- Document clear protocols for scanning parameters that would optimize diagnostic quality and ALARA. These are to include provisions for the safety of patient populations at higher risk of adverse events, such as pediatric patients, pregnant women, patients with known allergies to contrast, and patients with ferromagnetic implants.

- Document MRI safety policies and procedures, including training of personnel; restrict access to MRI equipment and space; and provide for MRI-safe equipment needed for life safety (e.g., MRI-compatible fire extinguisher) and patient care (e.g., MRI-compatible stretchers and wheelchairs).
- Provide personal protective equipment such as shields and lead aprons, and monitor staff's cumulative exposure through the use of radiation badges. Ensure proper storage of radioactive material; walls must be lead shielded to contain radiation.
- Restrict use of radiation and radioactive material to qualified, trained personnel.
- Perform imaging procedures only in accordance with verified orders from qualified providers.
- Maintain records of reports and images for a period of no less than five years or in accordance with applicable state law.
- Comply with the Mammography Quality Standards Act, which provides for the periodic inspection of mammography facilities to ensure adherence to several standards. Among these standards are minimum qualifications for technologists and radiologists involved in the acquisition and interpretation of mammography exams, and for medical physicists charged with quality control of the mammography equipment.

KEY TERMS FOR RADIOLOGY AND IMAGING SERVICES

Diagnostic test: "A type of test used to help diagnose a disease or condition" (National Cancer Institute [NCI] 2020a).

Image-guided interventions: "The use of novel image-directed technologies for guidance, navigation, tissue differentiation, and disease identification for reaching specified targets during therapeutic procedures, which may range along the continuum from non-invasive to minimally invasive to open surgical interventions" (National Institute of Biomedical Imaging and Bioengineering 2020).

Radiation: "Energy released in the form of particle or electromagnetic waves. Common sources of radiation include radon gas, cosmic rays from outer space, medical x-rays, and energy given off by a radioisotope (unstable form of a chemical element that releases radiation as it breaks down and becomes more stable)" (NCI 2020b).

Radiologist: "Radiologists are medical doctors that specialize in diagnosing and treating injuries and diseases using medical imaging (radiology) procedures (exams/tests) such as X-rays, computed tomography (CT), magnetic resonance imaging (MRI), nuclear medicine, positron emission tomography (PET) and ultrasound" (American College of Radiology 2020).

Screening: "Checking for disease when there are no symptoms. Since screening may find diseases at an early stage, there may be a better chance of curing the disease" (NCI 2020c).

Technologist: "Radiologic technologists perform diagnostic imaging examinations on patients" (US Bureau of Labor Statistics 2020).

Therapy: "Treatment of a malady, an ailment, or a condition, local or systemic, with the intent to cure, arrest its progress or relieve pain resulting from it" (NCI 2020d).

REFERENCES

American College of Radiology. 2020. "What Is a Radiologist?" Accessed June 29. https://www.acr.org/Practice-Management-Quality-Informatics/Practice-Toolkit/Patient-Resources/About-Radiology.

National Cancer Institute (NCI). 2020a. "Diagnostic Test." Accessed September 18. https://www.cancer.gov/publications/dictionaries/cancer-terms/def/diagnostic-test.

———. 2020b. "Radiation." Accessed September 18. https://www.cancer.gov/publications/dictionaries/cancer-terms/def/radiation.

———. 2020c. "Screening." Accessed June 29. https://www.cancer.gov/publications/dictionaries/cancer-terms/def/screening.

———. 2020d. "Therapy." Accessed June 29. https://www.cancer.gov/publications/dictionaries/cancer-terms/def/therapy.

National Institute of Biomedical Imaging and Bioengineering. 2020. "Image Guided Interventions." Accessed September 18. https://www.nibib.nih.gov/research-funding/image-guided-interventions.

US Bureau of Labor Statistics. 2020. Occupational Outlook Handbook, Radiologic and MRI Technologists. Accessed September 18. https://www.bls.gov/ooh/healthcare/radiologic-technologists.htm.

CHAPTER 17

Rehabilitation Services

Brent Braveman

DEPARTMENT DESCRIPTION

Rehabilitation Services departments in hospital settings most often include the professions of occupational therapy, physical therapy, and speech language pathology. Each of these professions provides habilitative and rehabilitative services to promote patients' function and participation in everyday roles and in the contexts and environments in which they are performed. Although all three disciplines sometimes provide preventive services to populations not yet experiencing a functional deficit or disability, services provided to patients in hospitals are almost always provided in response to a medical condition that is impeding the performance of daily activities.

Occupational therapy practitioners include occupational therapists and occupational therapy assistants. Beginning in 2007, the entry-level educational requirement for the occupational therapist moved to the postbaccalaureate level; a master's degree or clinical doctoral degree is now required to enter the profession. Before 2007, occupational therapists could be educated at the baccalaureate or the postbaccalaureate levels. Occupational therapy assistants require education at the associate's degree level; beginning in 2020, educational programs for occupational therapy assistants may also be offered at the baccalaureate level.

Physical therapy practitioners include physical therapists and physical therapist assistants. The entry-level educational requirement for the physical therapist is a doctorate. Before 2017 physical therapists required a master's degree; before 2002 they could enter the profession at the baccalaureate level. Physical therapist assistants require an associate's degree.

Speech language pathology practitioners include speech language pathologists and support personnel who often hold the title of speech language pathology assistants. Speech language pathologists require a bachelor's degree. Requirements for speech language pathology assistants vary from state to state but are typically at the baccalaureate level (American Speech-Language-Hearing Association [ASHA] 2018a).

Occupational therapy, physical therapy, and speech language pathology are licensed professions in all 50 US states and the District of Columbia. Many jurisdictions allow therapists to evaluate patients without a physician order, but most require an order for ongoing intervention in a medical setting. In addition to physicians, mid-level providers such as physician assistants or advanced practice nurses may write therapy orders in most states.

KEY DEPARTMENT SERVICES

All Rehabilitation Services practitioners provide services to patients by following a plan of care developed as part of a comprehensive evaluation. Plans of care must be developed by the primary therapist, but portions of the intervention may be carried out by assistants under appropriate supervision. Plans of care include the therapeutic goals developed in collaboration with the patient and the strategies that will be used to achieve the goals. The duration and frequency recommended to achieve these goals are also identified. Progress toward goals is documented at every therapeutic session, and formal periodic reevaluations may be completed to assess progress, the need to alter the plan of care, or the appropriateness of continuing therapy.

The process that occupational therapists, physical therapists, and speech language pathologists follow includes these steps:

- Referral
- Evaluation
- Development of an intervention plan (plan of care) that includes goals, duration, and frequency of intervention
- Identification of targeted outcomes
- Intervention
- Reevaluation
- Recommendations for discharge, including durable medical or other equipment and the need for continued skilled therapy or follow-up
- Discharge, including discharge instructions

DEPARTMENT ORGANIZATIONAL STRUCTURES

The structure of a Rehabilitation Services Department can vary widely depending on the size of the organization, the volume of patient referrals, and the scope of services provided. Structures may also vary depending on the organization's approach to structuring oversight of services. As Braveman (2016, 113) noted:

> Although few large organizations perfectly fit the profile of any "named" organizational form or structure, there are a few basic structures commonly found in health care organizations that are useful for a new manager or practitioner to understand. These structures include the *dual pyramid* form of organizing, *product line* or *service line management* organizations, and *hybrid* or *matrix* organizations. The term *dual pyramid* has been used to describe the common structure found in many medical-model settings, such as acute and general hospitals. The symbol of a pyramid has been used to represent a typical organization of personnel, with upper management at the top of the pyramid and line staff at the bottom.

The dual pyramid form of organizing features two parallel structures of oversight for medical functions that physicians and mid-level providers fulfill and for administrative functions that administrators and managers provide. Exhibit 17.1 shows a simple dual pyramid structure. By contrast, in product-line or service-line forms of organizing, personnel are organized according to the service or product

Exhibit 17.1: Simple Dual Pyramid Structure

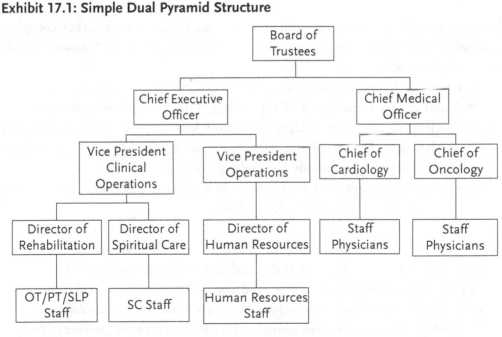

Note: OT = occupational therapist; PT = physical therapist; RN = registered nurse; SLP = speech language pathologist.

Exhibit 17.2: Simplified Product Line Organizational Structure

```
                        ┌──────────────┐
                        │  Board of    │
                        │  Trustees    │
                        └──────┬───────┘
            ┌──────────────────┴──────────────────┐
    ┌───────┴────────┐                    ┌────────┴───────┐
    │Chief Executive │                    │ Chief Medical  │
    │    Officer     │                    │    Officer     │
    └───────┬────────┘                    └────────┬───────┘
            └──────────────────┬──────────────────┘
    ┌───────────────┬──────────┴───────────┬───────────────┐
┌───┴────────┐  ┌───────────┐      ┌────────────┐
│Service Line│  │Service Line│      │Service Line│
│  Director  │  │  Director  │      │  Director  │
│ Orthopedic │  │ Behavioral │      │Rehabilitation│
│  Services  │  │   Health   │      │  Services   │
│            │  │  Services  │      │             │
└─────┬──────┘  └─────┬──────┘      └──────┬──────┘
```

| OT | PT | RN | OT | SW | RN | OT | PT | SLP |

Note: OT = occupational therapist; PT = physical therapist; RN = registered nurse; SLP = speech language pathologist; SW = social worker.

that they provide rather than according to the specific function that they complete or which departments provide education or training. Exhibit 17.2 shows a simple product line structure.

A matrix or hybrid organizational structure combines elements of the dual pyramid and product-line forms of organizing. These structures may be a function of having developed organically over time, but they can increase flexibility of service delivery. Because of the wide variation matrix/hybrid organizational structures, it is difficult to provide a sample of "typical" structure.

Regardless of organizational structure, Rehabilitation Services departments share some common professional roles and titles:

- The *director* will be responsible for managing the whole department or a product line and will perform the traditional management functions of planning, organizing, directing, and controlling (Businessdictionary. com 2020). These functions include elements of financial planning and budgeting; aspects of human resources including recruiting, training, and retaining employees; organizing daily work teams; and delivering clinical care to patients. The specific responsibilities of a director can vary widely between organizations. In large organizations, there may be an associate director to whom the director delegates some operational duties.

- *Supervisors* will be responsible for daily oversight of a group of employees and the work assigned to them. Their duties often focus on developing initial and ongoing competency of staff in their work roles. Supervisors are less likely to have administrative responsibilities such as budgeting or space planning; instead, they focus on the quality of the primary work product, which is typically the provision of occupational therapy or physical therapy services.

- A *senior therapist* or *senior therapy assistant* is often a practitioner with a minimum of three to five years of experience relevant to the specific therapy services an organization provides. "Seniors" typically carry a significant caseload of their own patients but may serve as a clinical resource for less experienced practitioners. They also may have responsibilities related to program development, oversight of student programming and training, or project-focused work such as continuous quality improvement projects or developing patient education materials.

- *Staff therapists or staff-level assistants* are therapy practitioners with the primary responsibility of delivering direct care to patients or clients. Although they may spend some of their time on projects focused on program development, quality improvement, or student programming, they typically carry a full caseload of patients and may have expectations for billable service that vary from 70 percent to 90 percent of their day, depending on the practice area.

KEY CUSTOMERS AND THEIR PERFORMANCE EXPECTATIONS

As with other clinically focused hospital services, key Rehabilitation Services customers include patients or clients (the term *patient* is most commonly used in medical settings, whereas *client* is more common in non-medical settings), families or caregivers, referrers to therapy including physicians and mid-level providers, payers, and other members of the interprofessional healthcare (e.g., nurses, social workers, case managers, nutritionists). Exhibit 17.3 identifies some of the key customers of Rehabilitation Services, with examples of performance metrics and how each metric is monitored.

Different customers commonly receive the same key service, but with varied expectations regarding performance characteristics. For example, as shown in exhibit 17.3, patients, physicians, and payers all expect a comprehensive therapy evaluation but have different expectations to measure quality performance. The development of metrics allows the director to examine how successfully the department is meeting the performance expectations of each key customer group.

Exhibit 17.3: Key Rehabilitation Services Customers, Services, and Requirements

Customer	Sample services	Sample requirements
Patient	• Evaluation	• Communicated in clear, easy-to-understand language with minimal medical terminology • Patient-centered, addressing patient's most important goals
	• DME recommendations	• Easy to use • Highest quality at lowest price (i.e., high value); covered by insurance if possible • Easily obtainable
	• Discharge recommendations	• Patient-centered and addressing functional problems
Physician	• Evaluation	• Provides clear rationale for therapeutic intervention • Facilitates communication with patient and caregivers
	• DME recommendations	• DME or recommendations provided before discharge (i.e., does not delay discharge) • Requirements for physician documentation; justification clearly communicated
	• Discharge recommendations	• Facilitates safe discharge
Payer	• Evaluation	• Comprehensive evaluation, including documentation that justifies plan of care (i.e., frequency and duration) • Provides measurable, obtainable goals
	• DME recommendations	• Medically necessary
	• Discharge recommendations	• Consistent with coverage limits • Medically necessary

Note: DME = durable medical equipment.

KEY PROCESS FLOWS

Process flows are graphic representations of the steps of an important work process and the order in which they should be completed. They can help standardize work processes and eliminate unnecessary and unwanted variation. They can also help to eliminate rework, bottlenecks, and other challenges to the efficient delivery of services. Process flows can be extremely useful for nonclinical work such as administrative functions (e.g., scheduling patients, entering patient charges). They are less useful and less commonly applied to the therapeutic process, because the need for clinical or professional reasoning is paramount to tailoring therapeutic services to the individual patient. Clinical algorithms, which might be considered similar to macro process flows, are sometimes used to identify common assessments used with particular diagnoses or other common clinical elements, such as screening for comorbidities or the application of specific medical or therapeutic precautions. Clinical guidelines, which are sometimes referred to as standards of care, are more comprehensive documents that include background information, clinical evidence, common assessments, and common approaches to therapeutic intervention (i.e., best practices). These guidelines may vary from a few pages to many pages in length and may include process work flows or clinical algorithms.

KEY UNITS OF WORK AND VOLUME STATISTICS TO MONITOR

A key unit of work for rehabilitative services is often one billed unit of care. Billed units are typically (but not universally) defined according to the Centers for Medicare & Medicaid (CMS) eight-minute rule (Kummer 2018). This rule states that therapy services provided in a period of seven minutes or less are not billable unless they are combined with another therapy session by the same discipline on the same day. Therapy provided in durations from 8 minutes to 22 minutes constitutes one unit of billable service; therapy provided from 23 minutes to 37 minutes constitutes two units of billable service.

Other key indicators and statistics often used to track the provision of rehabilitative services and finances related to these services include the following:

- Billed units per full-time equivalent (FTE) per business day (may include just therapy providers or support staff such as rehabilitation technicians or patient transporters)
- Revenue per billed unit (gross revenue or net revenue)
- Personnel expense per billed unit
- Non-personnel expense per billed unit
- Overall expense per billed unit

KEY METRICS TO MONITOR: PEOPLE, SERVICE, QUALITY/SAFETY, FINANCIAL

Key Rehabilitation Services metrics for monitoring people (e.g., therapy and support staff) typically relate to central aspects of quality and quantity. Quality can be a difficult concept to measure and define in Rehabilitation Services because of the complexity of service delivery and the necessary variation in work processes to customize service to each patient. However, quality often incorporates measuring clinical outcomes, stakeholder satisfaction, and achieving therapeutic goals. The quantity of service is typically measured by determining some percentage of productive or billable service and will be discussed in more depth later in this chapter.

Service outcome metrics measure aspects of care such as the timeliness and completeness of services rendered. Common metrics include wait time for evaluations or for the second appointment, missed visits caused by staffing or other operational issues, new referral volumes, and auditing of medical documentation and billing for completeness and compliance with regulatory standards.

Safety metrics relate to both patient and employee safety. Common issues that are monitored include patient falls (assisted and unassisted), skin integrity, patient injuries during therapy (e.g., burns from therapeutic modality use), exercise injuries, or injuries caused by poor patient handling. The most common staff injuries include strains and sprains of the back and extremities during patient transfers or other aspects of patient handling.

Finance metrics include those previously mentioned (e.g., key units of work) and are typically straightforward measures of income to expense after applying any discounts and anticipated unpaid debt.

Exhibit 17.4 shows a sample scorecard used to track and report metrics related to people, service, quality/safety, and finance.

KEY INFORMATICS ISSUES

Documentation of rehabilitative services is critical to ensure the efficient delivery of high-quality care and to meet or exceed mandatory accreditation standards such as those required by The Joint Commission (https://www.jointcommission.org). Most documentation in hospitals today occurs in some form of electronic health record (EHR). The primary reason to document rehabilitative services is to provide a record of care delivered as one form of interprofessional communication to promote effective care coordination. The EHR is the main mechanism for communicating information to physicians, mid-level providers, nurses, and other members of the interprofessional team. Other reasons for documentation include patient billing and compliance activities.

The focus of documentation can vary and can include medical data such as vital signs (e.g., heart rate, blood pressure, critical lab values) and plans of care developed by occupational therapists, physical therapists, and speech language pathologists. Plans of care are developed with data obtained during comprehensive evaluations. They identify the short-term and long-term goals for therapeutic intervention and the primary strategies to be used to obtain those goals.

Exhibit 17.4: Sample Scorecard for Tracking Rehabilitation Services Metrics

| | Instructions: Input monthly actual performance by the 15th of each month (effective 1/6/2020). | | | | | | |
	Metric	Under-performing	Threshold	Target	Stretch	Sept 2020	Oct 2020	Nov 2020
People								
P1	**Recognition Letters:** # of recognition letters sent	0		≥1				
P2	**Vacancies:** Total # of vacancies	*No performance ranges established*						
P3	**Vacancies:** Total # of CSS vacancies in Taleo and under recruitment >60 days	*No performance ranges established*						
P4	**Year-to-Date Turnover:** % of staff who (voluntarily and involuntarily) left the institution since 9/1/16	*No performance ranges established*						
P5	**First-Year Turnover:** % of staff who (voluntarily and involuntarily) left the institution <1 year from the date of hire	>14%	11%–14%	9%–10%	<9%			
Service								
S1	Medicare B Plans of Care: % of POC signed by MD within 30 days	≤89%	90%–95%	96%–98%	≥99%			
S2	**Customer Rounding:** % of customers responding "Very Good" to overall impression of service	<50%	50%–60%	61%–70%	>70%			
S3	**Customer Rounding:** Combined % of customers responding "Good" and "Very Good" to overall impression of service	<80%	80%–89%	90%–95%	>95%			
S4	**DME Award:** % of Patients whose DME orders go through the Case Management process to Complete Orders	100%	71%–99%	70%	<70%			

(continued)

Exhibit 17.4: Sample Scorecard for Tracking Rehabilitation Services Metrics (continued)

	Metric	Under-Performing	Threshold	Target	Stretch	Sept 2020	Oct 2020	Nov 2020
Quality								
Q1	**PNS Referral Response Time:** % of INPATIENT Patient Needs Screen responded to within 24 hours	<70%	70%–84%	85%–95%	>95%			
Q2	**PNS Referral Response Time:** % of OUTPATIENT Patient Needs Screen responded to within 24 hours	<70%	70%–84%	85%–95%	>95%			
Q3	**PNS Referral Response Time:** % of OVERALL Patient Needs Screen responded to within 24 hours	<70%	70%–84%	85%–95%	>95%			
Q4	% of PACU/CDU/EC patients evaluated within 4 hours of referral	≤95%	96%–97%	98%–99%	100%			
Finance								
F1	Revenue	> Budget	≤ Budget	≤ Budget				
F2	Personnel Expense	> Budget	≤ Budget	≤ Budget				
F3	**Other Operating Expense**	> Budget	≤ Budget	≤ Budget				
F4	**Total Operating Expense:** Personnel Expense + Other Operating Expense (Departmental Orders Financial Goal)	> Budget	≤ Budget	≤ Budget				
F5	**Operating Income/Loss:** % Variance Actual to Budget	Beyond ±5%	±5%	±4%	±3%			
F6	**Productivity:** Billed units per therapist per working day (refer to KUoW report)	Unfavorable	Neutral	Favorable				
F7	**Overtime:** Equal or below overtime target (refer to KUoW report)	> Target		< Target				

Note: CDU = Clinical Decision Unit; DME = durable medical equipment; EC = Emergency Center; KUoW = key units of work; PACU = Post-anesthesia Care Unit; PNS = Patient Needs Screen; POC = Plan of Care.

Documentation also provides a record for the clinical intervention provided, including therapeutic procedures and the patient response to care. Discrete data from individual assessments, the patient's progress toward goals, and alterations in the plan of care needed because of the lack of progress or complications are also included.

In addition to communicating with other members of the interprofessional team, data and information from the EHR is used for a range of managerial functions including program planning, program evaluation, and outcomes assessment. Most contemporary EHRs are designed to allow data to be mined for analysis. Data used by the rehabilitation manager might include trends in sources of referrals, staff productivity data, and trends in patient response to intervention such as length of stay or complications of care (e.g., falls, hospital-acquired pressure injuries).

STAFFING MODELS

Rehabilitation Services Department staffing models can vary greatly in the hospital setting. Choice of staffing model will be driven primarily by type of hospital environment and programming offered. For example, a small, community-based acute care hospital may have relatively few rehabilitative staff (e.g., two or three therapy practitioners from each discipline). In these cases, intervention is limited to patients with the most urgent needs related to patient safety or safe discharge. Services are often limited to six days per week, and it is rare for services to be available after the end of a standard business day. Services are often not available on Sundays or holidays. In contrast, large hospitals may offer services seven days a week, albeit at a lower level on the weekends. Services may be available to the highest-priority patients on holidays, and a few hospitals have therapy staff on call 24 hours per day, every day, to address emergencies such as evaluating a patient in the Emergency Department to help with an admission decision.

A key issue in developing a staffing model is that of generalization versus specialization. In small organizations, most staff are typically expected to practice as generalists. They may need to see patients with myriad diagnoses and rehabilitative problems, but with no single patient group in large enough volume to justify specialization. Staff must also be able to cover for each other during times of personal leave or when there is turnover or a vacant position. In larger organizations, some level of specialization may be more justifiable or advantageous. Although all therapy practitioners within a discipline share basic skills and knowledge, the skills and knowledge needed to treat a patient who has undergone, for instance, a coronary artery bypass graft are very different from those needed to treat a patient with complex cancer, a spinal cord injury, or a head injury. In settings with such a diverse patient census, it may be advantageous to have staff who specialize and develop advanced skills. These practitioners can then train other staff and students, become involved in performance improvement, and participate in program development and evaluation. Rotation between programs is also common in large organizations to promote the development of skills and knowledge in treating various patient groups. Rotation thus not only makes staffing easier but also is often seen as an advantage for staff because it broadens their experience and allows opportunities for skill development, which eases staff recruitment and retention. Exhibit 17.5 provides a sample staffing model for a large acute care hospital for outpatient and inpatient occupational therapy services.

Exhibit 17.5: Occupational Therapy Services Staffing Model, Large Hospital

1. **Using historical data for your organization, determine the number of expected paid and productive work days (or hours) for outpatient and inpatient services.**

   Exclude Nonproductive Time for All Practitioners

   - Exclude paid hours that are considered nonproductive such as paid time off, sick leave, jury duty, and FMLA.
     - Vacation average 120 hours per year
     - Holidays average 80 hours per year
     - Continuing education average 32 hours per year
     - Sick leave average 16 hours per year
     - FMLA average 8 hours per year
     - Mandatory training average 12 hours per year
     - Total: 268 hours
     - Time available for productive service is 2,080 − 268 = 1,812 hours or 226.5 worked days

2. **Using historical data for your organization and external benchmarks as available, determine the number of patients seen per day by each practitioner. Consider the following factors in addition to those demands identified in #1 (your time commitments may vary).**

   - 1 hour/day documentation time
   - 1 hour/week with committee work
   - 1 hour/week for supervision of physical therapist assistants/occupational therapy assistants by physical therapists and occupational therapists
   - Practitioners may be expected to see 7 patients on average per workday. Factoring in cancellation and no-show rates for your organization, you might consider scheduling 8 patients on some days for outpatient practitioners
   - Each practitioner has 7 appointment times per day (60-minute appointments) or 35 appointment slots per week or 1,585 appointment slots per year.

3. **Determine new patient demand from historical or expected data for your organization for the average number of new consults received each week.**

(continued)

4. Determine follow-up demand from historical or expected data for your organization for the average number of follow-up visits, considering the expected frequency and duration for plans of care.
5. Determine the expected number of FTEs by dividing total appointment demand by 1,585.

Example: Outpatient Occupational Therapy Staffing
Number of new consults per week = 52
Number of follow-up visits per week = 130

- 60% of consults (31 patients) seen 3 times per week or 93 visits per week
- 30% of consults (16 patients) seen 2 times per week or 32 visits per week
- 10% of consults (5 patients) seen 1 time per week or 5 visits per week

Total number of new consults and follow-up visits per week = 182
FTE needed for 182 visits per week is 182 visits/35 visits per practitioner = 5.2 FTE

Example: Inpatient Occupational Therapy Staffing (acute care services)
Number of new consults per week = 132
Number of follow-up visits per week = 853

- 80% of consults (106 patients) seen for 3 follow-up visits or 318 visits per week
- 15% of consults (20 patients) seen for 2 follow-up visits or 40 visits per week
- 5% of consults (6 patients) discharged at evaluation and no follow-up needed or 0 visits per week

Total number of new consults and follow-up visits per week = 490
FTE needed for 490 visits per week is 490 visits/35 visits per practitioners = 14 FTE

Note: FMLA = Family and Medical Leave Act; FTE = full-time equivalent.

PRODUCTIVITY MODELS, INCLUDING WORK-TO-STAFF RATIOS AND INDUSTRY PERFORMANCE TARGETS

In most hospital settings, productivity models arise from the definition of "productive" time, which can be more complicated than one might expect. Not all time that one might consider productive is billable. For example, patient care conferences are certainly productive for the process of coordinating care and planning discharge, but are typically not reimbursed by insurers and so often not billed. Setting productivity standards, measuring staff productivity, and using it as part of staff performance management can be a highly sensitive issue. In fact, productivity expectations and systems for measuring productivity are often the focus of discussions among rehabilitation managers and the topic of presentations at professional conferences (American Occupational Therapy Association 2017; Bender 2020; Swigert 2017).

Most often, productivity models focus on assessing the average percentage of time spent in productive or billable service during a standard work shift. The average is typically used because there can be both common-cause and special-cause variation in the amount of billable service provided on any given day. Common-cause variation can include time spent in documentation (which is nonbillable); discussions with physicians, nurses, or other members of the team; or things as simple as time spent waiting for elevators. Patient refusals are also a common cause of variation in productivity; time spent trying to convince a patient to participate in therapy is not billable. An example of special-cause variation that would affect productivity would be responding to a patient incident such as a fall. In this example, a practitioner might spend an hour or more attending to the patient that would not be billable. However, the practitioner should certainly spend whatever time is necessary attending to the patient to ensure their safety.

Performance targets for productive or billable time vary widely. Typical standards for hospitals range from 65 percent to 85 percent (Bennett et al. 2019; Tammany et al. 2019). Factors that affect expectations include issues such as the diagnostic groups treated, the geographic range each therapist must cover, expectations for participation in team or family meetings, and whether practitioners are expected to attend administrative meetings or perform administrative tasks such as supervising therapy assistants or support staff such as rehabilitation aides or technicians.

Exhibit 17.6 is an example of a control chart showing data for the key unit of work, billed units per total rehabilitation FTE per working day (includes support staff and rehabilitation technicians). The industry benchmark of treating seven patients per day was used to determine the expected mean of 9.062

Exhibit 17.6: Rehabilitation Services Key Units of Work: Billed Units per FTE per Business Day

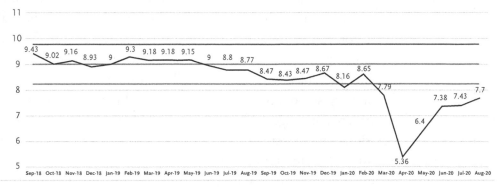

billed units per FTE per business day. The dramatic drop beginning in March 2020 reflects the impact of the COVID-19 pandemic on patient volumes and the slow recovery in activity.

STRATEGIES TO IMPROVE RECRUITMENT AND RETENTION

Successful recruitment and retention of high-quality rehabilitative staff is critical to the overall performance of a Rehabilitation department and to the delivery of highly effective and efficient care. Recruitment and retention can be time consuming and sometimes expensive. A high demand for rehabilitation professionals is projected to continue and possibly increase over the next decades as the US population ages (US Bureau of Labor Statistics 2020a, 2020b, 2020c; Vatwani and Hill 2018). The role of the rehabilitation manager in staff recruitment, screening, and hiring can vary between organizations. In some cases, the rehabilitation manager may be fully responsible for the process; in others, Human Resources may perform much of the process. Recruitment strategies may include advertising in professional magazines or journals, posting on popular job websites, attending recruitment fairs organized by professional associations or universities and educational programs, and exhibiting at professional conferences. These activities can be expensive, with the cost of job postings ranging from hundreds to thousands of dollars depending on the popularity of the website and the length of time the posting is up. Exhibiting at conferences likewise can cost several thousand dollars once the costs of travel are included. Free or low-cost strategies such as posting on social media sites can be effective if the rehabilitation manager or the organization has developed a wide network of followers. Training students is also a common and effective strategy to recruit staff. Although there is some risk (if students perform poorly), having a vibrant student program not only results in gaining exposure for an organization, but also provides the opportunity to assess a student's skills and fit in an organization before offering them a paid position.

Over time, staff recruitment and retention has gained some attention in professional literature, although there are few recent publications specific to the rehabilitation professions. Although research findings vary, common factors found to contribute to staff retention include the following (ASHA 2018b; Vatwani and Hill 2018).

- Continuing education
- Opportunities for development or promotion
- Involvement in projects and student programs
- Literature on retention
- Avoiding burnout

KEY REGULATORY ISSUES

Healthcare is highly regulated in the hospital setting. Many of the regulatory issues are related to accreditation by organizations such as The Joint Commission. Administrators from other staff functions such as Human Resources often take the lead on coordinating compliance activities. However, a limited number of key regulatory issues are the direct responsibility of the Rehabilitation Services manager, who must ensure that the department's employees meet all accreditation criteria. Examples of such criteria include annual fire and safety training, demonstrating age-specific competencies, maintaining CPR certification, documenting annual performance reviews, and reviewing each employee's job description annually. The Rehabilitation Services manager is also responsible for coordinating accreditation activities, including gathering and storing appropriate documentation (e.g., copies of CPR cards).

Another key regulatory issue is professional regulation and licensure. Occupational therapy, physical therapy, and speech language pathology are licensed professions in all 50 states and the District of Columbia (American Occupational Therapy Association 2018; SpeechPathologyGraduatePrograms.org 2020). The primary purpose of professional regulation and licensure is to reduce the risk of harm to the public by ensuring that healthcare practitioners are appropriately trained and have demonstrated at least entry-level competency for practice (Human Resources Professional Association 2017; Short 2016).

Other key regulatory issues relate to payment and third-party reimbursement for services rendered. The federal government is the largest single payer of healthcare in the United States, accounting for more than one-quarter of all US spending on healthcare (Pham 2019; Suddarth 2017; Ziaeian and Fonarow 2019). As such, the government plays a significant role in shaping regulatory requirements for third-party payment, including requirements for clinical documentation. Private insurers are not required to follow the lead of the government, but many do. In general, most rehabilitation managers choose to develop treatment and documentation policies and procedures to meet the requirements established by CMS, as these are viewed as the most stringent requirements. The assumption is that if CMS requirements are satisfied, then the requirements for most other insurers will be, too.

Other aspects of documentation that relate to regulatory affairs include medical coding and billing. According to Braveman (2016, 291), "Coding medical services including occupational therapy services is the first step in preparing the medical bill that will be sent to a third party payer such as Medicare, Medicaid or a private insurance. Various types of codes must be attached to the bill and supported in the documentation provided by the occupational therapy practitioner or other healthcare worker (i.e., physician, physical therapist, mid-level provider such as physician assistants or advanced practice nurses etc.)." Rehabilitation practitioners may be involved in the coding process by choosing the code that represents the rehabilitation diagnosis being treated (e.g., an ICD code) and the codes that indicate what service was provided (e.g., CPT codes).

Although the process of medical coding assigns particular numbers to the diagnoses and procedures found in documentation, the process of medical billing organizes and uses the codes and other information to submit medical claims to insurers or other payers. The billing process includes recording the medical codes on the claim forms sent to payers, providing examples of some of the medical documentation to support the claims, ensuring that accurate and complete patient insurance information is included, and appealing denials of billed services. Although it is common for rehabilitation practitioners to be involved in the coding process by selecting ICD and CPT codes that accurately reflect the patients' diagnosis or condition and the services provided, they are less frequently involved in the billing process. In larger hospitals, however, professionals with specialized training complete the billing and even much of the coding for Rehabilitation Services.

KEY TERMS FOR REHABILITATION SERVICES

Key customers: Patients or clients (the term *patient* is most commonly used in medical settings, whereas *client* is more common in nonmedical settings), families or caregivers, referrers to therapy including physicians and mid-level providers, payers, and other members of the interprofessional healthcare team (e.g., nurses, social workers, case managers, nutritionists).

Key unit of work: One billed unit of care for rehabilitative services. Billed units are typically (but not universally) defined according to the Centers for Medicare & Medicaid Services eight-minute rule.

Plans of care: The therapeutic goals that are developed in collaboration with the patient and the strategies that will be used to achieve the goals. The duration and frequency recommended to achieve the goals included in the plan of care are also identified.

Process flows: Graphic representations of the steps, and their order of completion, for an important work process.

Professional regulation and licensure: The primary purpose is to reduce the risk of harm to the public by ensuring that healthcare practitioners are appropriately trained and have demonstrated at least entry-level competency for practice.

REFERENCES

American Occupational Therapy Association. 2018. "Issues in Licensure." Accessed September 19, 2020. www.aota.org/Advocacy-Policy/State-Policy/Licensure.aspx.

———. 2017. "Dealing with Productivity Standards: Resources for Ethical Practice." Accessed September 19, 2020. www.aota.org/Practice/Ethics/Tools-for-Productivity-Requirements.aspx.

American Speech-Language-Hearing Association (ASHA). 2018a. "ASHA State-by-State." Accessed September 19, 2020. www.asha.org/advocacy/state/.

———. 2018b. "Retention and Recruitment Strategies." Accessed September 19, 2020. www.asha.org/careers/recruitment/healthcare/recruit_ret_strategies/.

Bender, J. C. 2020. "AC18 Maximize Your Time: Implementing Effective Productivity Principles in Your Practice." American Physical Therapy Association. Accessed September 19. http://learningcenter.apta.org/Student/MyCourse.aspx?id=fb9e548a-3952-4dae-9c1d-3a7811d3859f.

Bennett, L. E., V. D. Jewell, L. Scheirton, M. McCarthy, and B. C. Muir. 2019. "Productivity Standards and the Impact on Quality of Care: A National Survey of Inpatient Rehabilitation Professionals." *Open Journal of Occupational Therapy* 7 (4): 1–11.

Braveman, B. 2016. *Leading and Managing Occupational Therapy Services: An Evidence-Based Approach*. Philadelphia, PA: F. A. Davis.

Businessdictionary.com. 2020. "Four Functions of Management." Accessed September 19. www.businessdictionary.com/definition/four-functions-of-management.html.

Human Resources Professional Association. 2017. "HRPA's Regulatory Framework." www.hrpa.ca/Documents/Regulation/Regulatory-Framework.pdf.

Kummer, A. W. 2018. "Coding and Billing for Speech-Language Pathologists." *Perspectives of the ASHA Special Interest Groups* 3 (5): 36–47.

Pham, K. 2019. "Why Trump's Medicare Reforms Offer Superior Alternative to 'Medicare for All.'" Published October 4. www.heritage.org/medicare/commentary/why-trumps-medicare-reforms-offer-superior-alternative-medicare-all.

Short, S. D. 2016. "Regulating the Health Professions: Protecting Professionals or Protecting Patients?" In *Health Workforce Governance: Improved Access, Good Regulatory Practice, Safer Patients*, 227–44. Abingdon, UK: Taylor & Francis.

SpeechPathologyGraduatePrograms.org. 2020. "Speech Language Pathologist State Licensing and the Role of the CCC-SLP Credential." Accessed September 19. www.speechpathologygraduateprograms.org/state-licensing-overview/.

Suddarth, R. J. 2017. "The Burden of a Good Idea: Examining the Impact of Unfunded Federal Regulatory Mandates on Medicare Participating Hospitals." *Washington & Lee Journal of Civil Rights and Social Justice* 24: 463.

Swigert, N. 2017. "Balancing Documentation and Service Delivery Information." 2017 Convention of the American Speech-Language-Hearing Association, Los Angeles, California, November 9–11. www.nxtbook.com/nxtbooks/asha/conventionprogram2017/index.php#/p/122.

Tammany, J. E., J. K. O'Connell, B. S. Allen, and J. M. Brismée. 2019. "Are Productivity Goals in Rehabilitation Practice Associated with Unethical Behaviors?" *Archives of Rehabilitation Research and Clinical Translation* 1 (1–2): 100002.

US Bureau of Labor Statistics. 2020a. "Physical Therapists." *Occupational Outlook Handbook.* www.bls.gov/ooh/healthcare/physical-therapists.htm.

———. 2020b. "Occupational Therapists." *Occupational Outlook Handbook.* www.bls.gov/ooh/healthcare/occupational-therapists.htm.

———. 2020c. "Speech-Language Pathologists." *Occupational Outlook Handbook.* www.bls.gov/ooh/healthcare/speech-language-pathologists.htm.

Vatwani, A., and C. J. Hill. 2018. "Examining Factors, Strategies and Processes to Decrease Physical Therapy Turnover Rates in Acute Care Hospitals: A Review of the Literature." *Journal of Acute Care Physical Therapy* 9 (1): 11–18.

Ziaeian, B., and G. C. Fonarow. 2019. "When Payment Models Distort Perceptions and Care Delivery for Patients with Heart Failure." *Journal of Cardiac Failure* 25 (4): 227–29.

CHAPTER 18

Respiratory Care

Gautam H. Sachdev

DEPARTMENT DESCRIPTION

The American Association of Respiratory Care (AARC) describes respiratory care as the healthcare profession that specializes in the promotion of optimum cardiopulmonary function, health, and wellness. The practice of respiratory care is multifaceted and involves diagnostic evaluation, treatment, and education of patients and their families. Through education and clinical experience, respiratory therapists develop the expertise to help identify, treat, and prevent acute or chronic dysfunctions of the cardiopulmonary system. The knowledge and understanding they acquire through education and examinations enable respiratory therapists to apply the principles of respiratory physiology and pathophysiology (AARC 2020).

Respiratory therapists provide therapeutic care to inpatients in intensive care units, emergency rooms, general medical/surgical floors, neonatal units, and pediatric units. However, respiratory therapists are employed in outpatient settings too, where the role and responsibilities may differ. The care that respiratory therapists provide can be complex and may include initiation and management of life support systems such as mechanical ventilation, noninvasive positive pressure ventilation, or high-flow oxygen therapy. Additionally, respiratory therapists act as first responders to medical emergencies such as cardiac or respiratory arrests. Respiratory therapists also administer medications that help reduce excessive breathing efforts that result from airway constriction or inflammation. Other types of care that respiratory therapists routinely provide include airway management, bronchoscopy, lung protection and recruitment therapies, oxygen therapy, air and ground transports, and blood testing for assessing respiratory function.

Respiratory therapists require a minimum of a two-year associate's degree; however, bachelor's and master's degree programs are more common. These programs are accredited by the Commission on Accreditation for Respiratory Care (CoARC). At degree completion, respiratory therapists must pass a certification exam administered by the National Board of Respiratory Care (NBRC). Certification is required for being credentialed as a registered or certified respiratory therapist and is a prerequisite for earning additional credentials offered by NBRC such as Adult Critical Care Specialist (ACCS), Neonatal Pediatric Specialist (NPS), Registered Pulmonary Function Technologist (RPFT), and Sleep Disorders Specialist (SDS). Successfully completing the NBRC-administered examination requires exceptional knowledge and competency (NBRC 2020a). To earn the additional credentials, respiratory therapists must successfully complete each specialty's specific examination, which may include both written components and clinical simulations. The NBRC's examinations are written and developed by a committee of credentialed respiratory therapists and pulmonary function technologists, along with physicians who specialize in pulmonary and respiratory care. These examinations are accredited by the National Commission for Certifying Agencies (NCCA) (NBRC 2020c).

After earning their credential(s), respiratory therapists apply to their respective state licensing board and complete the necessary paperwork to become a licensed practitioner in that state. Each state may have different licensing requirements, including annual or biannual continuing education and license renewals. In addition to earning specialized credentials, respiratory therapists may be able to advance further in their careers by being promoted to a Respiratory Therapist III and Respiratory Therapist IV in organizations where career progression programs have been developed.

Credentialed respiratory therapists are also required to maintain professional knowledge and skills through lifelong learning. Since July 2002, the NBRC has required credentialed practitioners to participate in a Credential Maintenance Program to retain credentials for five years. Credentials awarded prior to July 1, 2002, are not subject to this requirement. Beginning January 1, 2020, credentialed practitioners who are subject to renew and maintain NBRC credentials for five years can do so by (1) completing quarterly assessments and, if needed, provide attestation of completion of up to 30 hours of continuing education based on assessment performance; (2) retake and pass respective credential examinations; or (3) pass one of the NBRC examinations not previously completed (NBRC 2020b).

KEY DEPARTMENT SERVICES

Respiratory therapists are healthcare professionals responsible for respiratory care of patients spanning neonatal through geriatric populations with cardiopulmonary system deficiencies and abnormalities (AARC 2018). A licensed provider based on state licensure laws directs the provision of respiratory care across the age spectrum. The practice of a respiratory therapist typically focuses on assessing patients directly and indirectly, implementing respiratory therapy procedures, educating patients and families, participating in human and animal research, assisting pulmonary rehabilitation, and facilitating student learning. Respiratory therapists participate in daily physician and interdisciplinary team rounds at the bedside, and practice respiratory care autonomously by using established protocols and clinical pathways. Respiratory therapists use critical thinking skills, patient assessment knowledge, and evidence-based clinical practice guidelines to develop and implement patient care plans, including the use of patient-care-driven protocols, disease-specific clinical pathways, and disease management programs. Respiratory therapists practice in a variety of clinical settings:

- Acute care hospitals
- Sleep diagnostic centers
- Long-term acute care facilities
- Rehabilitation hospitals
- Skilled nursing facilities
- Home care and home medical equipment companies
- Patient transportation services (air and ground transports)
- Ambulatory care centers, including physicians' offices and clinics
- Convalescent and retirement centers
- Educational institutions

Exhibit 18.1 lists key patient care services that respiratory therapists provide in various clinical settings.

Exhibit 18.1: Key Respiratory Patient Care Services

Mechanical ventilation	Noninvasive mechanical ventilation
High-flow oxygen therapy	Low-flow oxygen therapy
Blood testing	Respiratory patient air and ground transport
Lung recruitment therapy	Pulmonary function testing
Medical emergency response	Patient and family education
Airway clearance therapy	Metabolic studies
Sleep diagnostic studies	Bronchoscopy assist
Pulmonary rehabilitation	Neonatal and pediatric respiratory care

---

DEPARTMENT ORGANIZATIONAL STRUCTURES

Respiratory Care is usually an integrated service line within a large clinical division. The organizational structure and reporting responsibilities may differ depending on the type and size of the organization. In many academic medical centers, Respiratory Care is incorporated into a clinical department such as Critical Care, Pulmonary Medicine, or Anesthesiology. In nonacademic medical centers, Respiratory Care is often part of a professional service division that can include Physical, Occupational, and Speech Therapy; Pharmacy; and Laboratory Medicine. Acute care hospitals, long-term care hospitals, and skilled nursing facilities are staffed 24 hours by one or more respiratory therapists.

In many organizations, the Respiratory Care Department is led by a department director who supervises administrative and clinical operations. Many organizations usually require the director to be an experienced leader. It is not too uncommon for organizations to recruit a director with five to ten years of professional experience in a leadership role, along with advanced degrees in business or healthcare administration and credentials such as being an AARC fellow. The director usually reports to a vice president or department chair, depending on the type of healthcare system, and will also have a dotted-line reporting responsibility to the medical director of respiratory care. The Joint Commission's standards require healthcare facilities to have a physician medical director before practicing respiratory care. This director collaborates with the Respiratory Care Department on the clinical practices of respiratory therapists, use of therapist-driven clinical protocols, quality, and safety. The medical director also helps formulate clinical policies and procedures, provides continuing education, participates in purchase of new medical equipment, and performs clinical oversight of all Respiratory Care services.

Depending on the type and size of organization, the director role will be supported by managers, supervisors, and educators. To maintain clinical and administrative functions, the Respiratory Care Department needs to ensure that all required positions are recruited in a timely manner. Clinical functions include daily staffing, assigning workload to respiratory therapists, direct patient care, staff education, medical emergency response, patient rounding, service recovery on patient-care issues, and quality or safety initiatives. Administrative functions include performance evaluations, reconciling revenue and expense, supply and equipment management, scheduling, event planning, maintaining a database for respiratory therapist licenses and credentials, and correcting or processing payroll. Exhibit 18.2 depicts key positions and a typical organizational structure for Respiratory Care departments in academic medical centers. Nonacademic centers and community hospitals may have different key positions and structures.

Exhibit 18.2: Sample Respiratory Care Department Organizational Structure

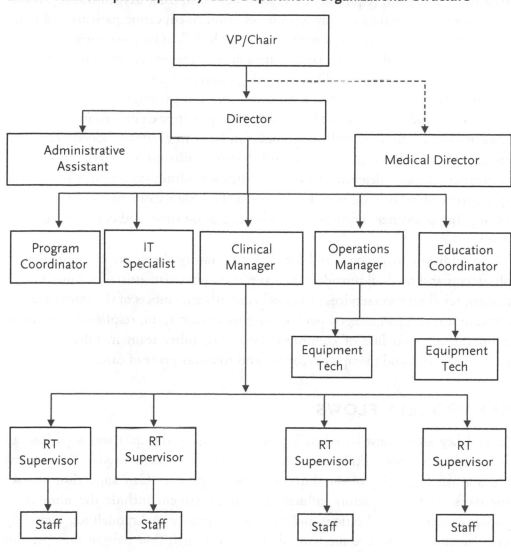

KEY CUSTOMERS AND THEIR PERFORMANCE EXPECTATIONS

As first responders to medical emergencies and experts in airway management and life support systems, respiratory therapists play a critical and vital role in both inpatient and outpatient areas. Because of this wide-ranging demand, respiratory therapists can be needed at any time. Breathing is inherently a passive bodily function and normally does not require significant effort. When a disease process disturbs this mechanism, breathing can become more difficult. Respiratory therapists help patients manage their disease process by helping to reduce breathing effort. To achieve this goal, respiratory therapists may administer oxygen therapy, medications, or lung recruitment therapy, in addition to educating patients and families on the disease process and ways to manage it. When patients' breathing effort becomes unsustainable, they may require a higher level of care in an intensive care unit, where they may receive life-supporting treatment through invasive mechanical ventilation and noninvasive positive-pressure ventilation.

Patients under the care of a respiratory therapist are seen on a routine, ongoing basis at defined time intervals (e.g., once an hour to every six hours). This care continues throughout their stay or until therapy is discontinued. As a measure of performance, many departments track medication administration times to ensure appropriate standards are met. For example, The Joint Commission may require an ongoing assessment of medication administration times and corrective actions, if any.

In addition to patients and families, respiratory therapists collaborate with physicians and medical providers such as nurses, physician assistants, nurse practitioners, rehabilitation services personnel, and other members of the interdisciplinary care team. As an integral part of the patient care team, respiratory therapists maintain an open line of communication with other team members to share patient progress and therapy outcomes, and to assess plans of care.

KEY PROCESS FLOWS

Several key steps must be taken before a respiratory therapist sees a patient, to ensure the therapist's skills align with the care the patient needs. This process starts at the beginning of the shift when the Respiratory Care supervisor assesses the day's workload. Factors influencing this assessment include the number of patients receiving medications and various respiratory care modalities, including invasive and noninvasive mechanical ventilation, high-flow oxygen therapy, and lung recruitment therapies. Once the Respiratory Care supervisor has made their assessments, they distribute staff assignments, calculated from the time needed to perform specific therapies. The supervisor then assesses the skill set needed in each area and allocates the appropriate amount of work accordingly. Many organizations also conduct a daily team huddle at shift change to review and highlight topics related to patient safety, quality of care, equipment and supplies, and information technology. After the team huddle, a hand-off report regarding patients takes place between respiratory therapists ending and beginning their shifts. Therapists use the information received during patient hand-off reports to understand patient acuity and to highlight and prioritize patients needing more timely care.

Before respiratory therapists treat patients, they require an order from a physician or licensed provider in the electronic health record (EHR). They also need orders for Pharmacy to dispense any needed medications, because therapists are not authorized to prescribe them. Respiratory therapists follow specific protocols, approved by assigned committees responsible for the efficiency of all facility protocols, that empower them to assess and adjust clinical pathways such as titrating oxygen therapy or adjusting medication frequency. Once at the bedside, respiratory therapists provide education on disease management to patients and families, and follow up with care teams on clinical updates. After completing patient care, respiratory therapists document it in the EHR. This documentation also captures billing charges and productivity. If there are any issues related to patient care or family concerns, respiratory therapists can escalate them to the shift supervisor for follow-up. Exhibit 18.3 identifies the key processes throughout respiratory care provision.

To allow Respiratory Care departments to assess and align process efficiencies, information systems must be able to track and provide up-to-date information on patient care plans. For example, metrics such as number of patients seen in one hour and contact time per patient can help assess efficiency, time management, or barriers to providing timely patient care. Focusing on barriers such as "patient not available at the scheduled treatment time" can help to revise the treatment plan and facilitate coordination of patient care with other disciplines. Another key Respiratory Care process flow metric is missed therapies. Therapies missed because of patient refusals, medication not dispensed from Pharmacy, or therapists' inability to see the patient at the scheduled time can offer insights into process issues, personnel matters, or supply and equipment concerns.

The Respiratory Care supply chain has its own key processes, which should be integrated into protocols to define how and when patient care supplies are ordered, stocked, and replenished. Processes such as Kanban and just-in-time supply management have proven effective. These processes should assess the availability of medical equipment while optimizing workflow to permit rapid turnaround of equipment after use. Tracking medical equipment and supply inventory electronically helps to streamline this workflow.

KEY UNITS OF WORK AND VOLUME STATISTICS TO MONITOR

Understanding key data drivers and related benchmarking is essential to optimizing clinical and administrative operations. These data points are important for assessing staffing, skills mix, productivity, supply and equipment needs, patient

Exhibit 18.3: Key Processes Before, During, and After a Patient Receives Respiratory Care

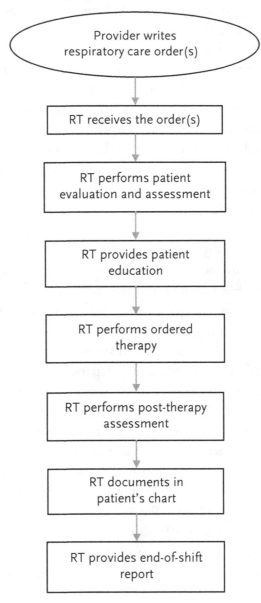

wait times, and turnaround times. With the help of the EHR, many of these data points can be customized and automated to provide hourly, daily, weekly, and monthly trends. In addition, many organizations use these data to forecast revenue, expenses, and full-time equivalent (FTE) budgets and to benchmark Respiratory Care departments with other organizations with similar size and services.

The specific work and volume data that a Respiratory Care Department generates can vary with the size and type of organization. The following are the most common and widely used statistics in most hospitals:

- Number of patients with treatment medication orders
- Number of patients on mechanical ventilation, noninvasive mechanical ventilation, and high-flow oxygen therapy
- Days on mechanical ventilation, noninvasive mechanical ventilation, and high-flow oxygen therapy
- Unplanned airway removal and reinsertion of airway
- Hospital-acquired conditions such as pneumonia and pressure injuries to tissue
- Disease-specific patient readmissions such as chronic obstructive pulmonary disease
- Total billed procedures as a percentage of budgeted procedures
- Productivity of respiratory therapists, as measured in worked relative value units (RVUs)
- Number of missed treatments as a percentage of total ordered treatments
- Total operating expense

KEY METRICS TO MONITOR: PEOPLE, SERVICE, QUALITY/SAFETY, FINANCIAL

Organizations use various data and benchmarks to assess operational effectiveness. Many of these metrics are cascaded at department or division levels and are incorporated into a department's operational scorecard, where they can provide focus and align priorities. The metrics are segmented into categories and benchmarked either internally or against national standards to assess performance. They also help formulate organizational strategies. For example, if an organization is interested in assessing workforce engagement, it must assess employee turnover and retention information along with employee satisfaction survey data. Similarly, if the organization wants to measure patient satisfaction, it can compare this metric to national measures by using benchmarks associated with patient satisfaction and their likelihood of recommending a facility to others. Metrics associated with quality of care can be measured by assessing internal and external benchmarks that reflect outcome of care metrics in different disease processes (e.g., pneumonia readmission rates, length of hospital stay for cardiac procedures). Safety of patients, families, and employees is paramount in every organization and should be the top-priority metric for all stakeholders. Safe patient care reduces complications during a patient's facility stay, which improves timely discharges and reduces readmissions. A safe enterprise also improves the bottom line by reducing operating costs.

As part of the patient care team, respiratory therapists are responsible for delivering safe and high-quality patient care. Exhibit 18.4 depicts sample key Respiratory Care metrics, including operational areas to assess performance and strategize goals for improvement. Some of these metrics are ongoing; others are assessed yearly and replaced by new metrics the organization believes are important to operational success.

Exhibit 18.4: Key Respiratory Care Department Metrics

Respiratory care key metrics	Previous FY	Goal	FY Q1	FY Q2	FY Q3	FY Q4	FYTD	Action plan
People								
RT turnover		<10%						
RT retention		>90%						
RT satisfaction		>80%						
Quality								
Ventilator Days Index		Better than average						
Missed therapy %		<5%						
Unplanned airway removal/100 airway days		Better than average						
Unplanned airway removal reintubation rate		Better than average						
Financial								
IP—respiratory Service revenue		At budget						
OP—respiratory Service revenue		At budget						
Supply expense		Within 5% of budget						
Overtime %		<10%						
Productivity (worked hours/unit)		>80%						
Operational expenses		Within 5% of budget						

(continued)

Respiratory care key metrics	Previous FY	Goal	FY Q1	FY Q2	FY Q3	FY Q4	FYTD	Action plan
Service								
ABG TAT routine (draw to analysis)		Better than average						
PFT TAT routine (complete to dictation)		<48 hours						
Patient satisfaction		>80%						
Growth								
IP revenue growth		2%						
OP revenue growth		5%						

Note: ABG = arterial blood gas; FY = fiscal year; FYTD = fiscal year to date; IP = inpatient; OP = out-patient; PFT = pulmonary function test; RT = respiratory therapist; TAT = turnaround time.

Many organizations enlist performance and quality improvement teams to help individual departments achieve their desired performance level. These teams may work on projects that focus on reducing variation and defects by aligning and hardwiring processes. The use of Six Sigma to reduce defects and improve quality is also becoming more common in healthcare. Even small quality improvement projects can reduce variation and defects in patient care processes. The first stage of an improvement project is to agree on a process that needs improvement and then assign ownership for it. Establishing a process owner is an effective strategy for achieving the desired outcomes. The next step is to establish a sample size, or "opportunities," and then assess how many "defects" are generated from these opportunities. Opportunities should be assessed routinely (daily or weekly), and the frequency of defects should be tracked. Next, the factors that contributed to creating the defects should be isolated and categorized into people, product, and process. The owner can use information from these categories to create an improvement plan.

KEY INFORMATICS ISSUES

New innovations and technical advances are continuously transforming medical informatics. The use of EHRs can be a challenge for Respiratory Care because the practice is not clearly defined in medical informatics language; Respiratory Care shares practice areas with many other disciplines such as physical therapy, nursing, occupational therapy, nutritional services, and laboratory medicine (Mussa 2008).

Regardless of these overlaps, respiratory therapists must engage in information systems design to ensure the systems are capable of meeting their information needs and those of the patients under their care. Many EHR vendors provide customization options that facilitate development of a robust health information platform. At minimum, the system should allow respiratory therapists to assess medical problems, review medical information, formulate and document a treatment plan, perform medical procedures, communicate medical information to patient care teams, and use built-in patient safety and quality tools.

As mentioned, Respiratory Care professionals can specialize to provide care to different-aged populations, such as neonatal pediatric specialists and adult critical care specialists. This specialization or subject-matter expertise means that respiratory therapists will have diverse information technology needs. Furthermore, respiratory therapists practice in various healthcare settings; their information technology requirements will thus depend on the adaptability of the EHR system. Respiratory Care leaders also play a key role in strategizing and prioritizing projects that focus on continuous enhancement of medical information systems. Designated personnel with experience in informatics systems and respiratory care delivery models may help Respiratory Care departments sustain ongoing improvements to information systems that involve their practice. Special attention must be given to designing and building operational reports that provide on-demand and routine data to assess patient care and administrative functions.

STAFFING MODELS

Respiratory therapists provide patient care 24 hours each day. Respiratory therapists mostly work 12.5-hour shifts three days a week. This schedule is designed to provide work–life balance while reducing employee burnout by permitting consecutive days off from work for a healthy lifestyle. In many organizations, respiratory therapists follow a regular, predictable work schedule; others base respiratory therapist scheduling on operational and patient care needs. Respiratory therapists may also work as needed, including for extra shifts.

When assessing staffing, Respiratory Care managers should review several key factors, including respiratory therapists' skill sets, patient volume and acuity, building and unit geography, special patient needs, and other responsibilities such as responding to patient care emergencies. Time standards are applied to calculate total worked minutes, which is used to assess staffing for the shift. Incentive-based scheduling programs may be necessary to staff more therapists on short notice. For example, respiratory therapists who are available to work on an "on-call" basis would receive additional pay. Staffing software can also help departments project worker needs from staff input, including day of the week, peak times for patient care, skills mix, and volume trends. All staffing models must comply with the Fair Labor Standards Act (29 USC §201, et seq.).

To ensure timely patient care, respiratory therapists must be able to escalate care issues and family concerns. One escalation method is to include implementing team leaders in a given geographical area who are responsible for addressing these issues. If the team lead is unable to respond or resolve the issue, the next person in charge is involved, such as a supervisor, manager, or director.

PRODUCTIVITY MODELS

In collaboration with Respiratory Care departments, AARC collects productivity survey data to analyze the time it takes for respiratory therapists to perform various procedures and clinical activities. This survey also takes into consideration the size, type, and location of the organization, the department's scope of service, the location of service, and the age groups served, among other parameters. Once the survey is validated, AARC offers this information for purchase as the *Uniform Reporting Manual*. This published manual helps to establish national time standards for respiratory therapy procedures and activities using RVUs to permit an accurate accounting of productivity. Many organizations could also have internal productivity benchmarks. However, metrics such as patient days, discharges, billed units, and revenue per respiratory therapist are poor indicators of workload because they do not use patient acuity to measure time resources (AARC 2011). Additionally, respiratory therapists' workload depends on types and frequencies of procedures that cannot be accurately measured by productivity metrics. For example, respiratory therapists often are on patient transport teams, and the time spent transporting a patient can vary. Because transport time is not a procedure, predicting and measuring the time for this activity is challenging.

Regardless, RVU time standards are a much more accurate representation of workload because they measure and benchmark actual time spent in completing different procedures. The unit used to measure RVU is "minutes per procedure," converted to hours. This time is then used to calculate productivity hours. For example, the maximum number of minutes that respiratory therapists can work in a 12.5-hour period is 750. To achieve 100 percent productivity, respiratory therapists would have to work all 750 minutes. This workload is unrealistic because nonproductive minutes spent on shift reports, daily safety huddles, gathering equipment and supplies, cleaning equipment, training and education, break and lunchtime, transit time to units, and other functions must be excluded from the total allowable worked minutes. The remaining minutes are then used to calculate respiratory therapists' productivity. Many Respiratory Care departments designate nonproductive minutes as a percentage of total allowable shift minutes. For example, if 20 percent

Exhibit 18.5: Productivity Calculations for Sample Respiratory Care Functions

Procedure	Procedure frequency	Minutes per procedure	Total minutes
Patient assessment	20	15	300
Setup	10	20	200
Monitor	5	15	45
Suction	2	11	22
Blood sampling	3	11	33
Total	40	N/A	600

of their time is deemed nonproductive in a 12.5-hour shift (or 750 minutes), the remaining 80 percent (10 hours or 600 minutes) is counted as total available worked time. Thus, working 10 hours or 600 minutes in a 12.5-hour shift amounts to 100 percent productivity for a respiratory therapist on that shift.

The productivity example in exhibit 18.5 shows a 600-workload-minutes calculation for a 12-hour shift that would require one FTE. Using this example, if there were 9,000 total minutes for all procedures in a given shift, then 15 FTEs would be needed to account for all the procedures at 100 percent productivity, excluding any additional procedures ordered or discontinued throughout the shift. At the end of the shift, the productivity could be higher or lower per each respiratory therapist depending on addition and deletion of procedures. Thus, assessing productivity at the beginning of the shift permits resources to be planned, whereas assessing productivity at the end of shift assesses whether those resources were effective.

Productivity data permit objective decision-making when assessing and reaffirming staffing requirements needed to meet daily workloads while optimizing labor expenses. The data can also bolster budget forecasting and justify requests for new or replacement staff. Furthermore, productivity tools can facilitate conversations regarding scope of service and expansion of service lines, patient safety, quality of care, and patient experience.

STRATEGIES TO IMPROVE RECRUITMENT AND RETENTION

Recruitment and retention of top talent is a challenge for almost every organization. Licensed professions such as respiratory care require a unique skill set that can be difficult to recruit depending on factors such as demand, reputation of the organization, advancement opportunities, location, job security, compensation, and benefits. Additional factors such as job satisfaction and work–life balance can also affect employee retention.

One of the most important strategies for improving recruitment is to develop a statement that conveys a recruitment message. This recruitment statement, which should focus on the mission and core values, can help to attract or influence applicants with similar values and goals to join the organization. Indeed, many candidates want to be part of an organization whose mission, values, and philosophy are closely aligned to their personal goals and values—a powerful tool that recruiters can leverage. In addition, aligning the knowledge, skills, and ability (KSA) inventory set with the position is crucial in identifying qualified applicants. If the KSA inventory is not defined appropriately, the position could need more than the average time to fill. Hiring managers also must ensure that the applicant screening questionnaire is not stringent to the point of impeding recruitment.

Among the more successful recruitment strategies is to establish an agreement with colleges and universities that offer undergraduate and graduate degrees in respiratory care. This agreement allows college students to rotate through Respiratory Care departments and complete their clinical training, where hospitals start their recruitment of top talent. Another strategy is to establish a robust referral program that incentivizes all staff to direct respiratory therapists to their facility from other institutions, which provides a flow of experienced therapists.

Data from Human Resources information systems are useful in developing recruitment efficiency. Data such as cost per recruitment, applicant rate, and recruitment time (time between job posting and offer acceptance) can help assess recruitment strategies. Costs associated with advertising, travel, referrals, staff time, processing, orientation and training, and sign-on bonuses can be used to develop and deploy sound business practices. Furthermore, the length of recruitment time can provide insights regarding the job market, compensation, or benefits. Recruiter effectiveness also plays an important role in successful recruitment.

The interview process also matters greatly for successful recruitment. Interviews provide an opportunity for both parties to assess the mutual fit and review the requirements of the position, along with the candidate's personal and organizational alignment with core values. When both parties can perceive this alignment, they will be more confident in the selection process. Interview panels and recruitment committees are also helpful for assessing personal and organizational fit while promoting equality in the hiring process. In most organizations, internal staff and the hiring manager form this committee. To limit personal and interview bias, ask interview questions strictly related to the workplace scenario. Such questions will better assess a candidate's ability to respond to specific situations and make decisions from their professional work experience. Use of standard interview questions allows for an objective assessment of the candidate to promote interview consistency and successful selection. Interview panels or recruitment committees also should use a standardized questionnaire to score the interview and make hiring recommendations. To assess applicants' clinical skills, these instruments should include questions that simulate clinical scenarios; this can also spotlight areas and resources for improvement if the applicant is offered a job.

Though recruitment planning is crucial to acquiring top talent in any job market, Respiratory Care leadership should also focus on employee turnover and retention. Factors affecting turnover include high demand, retirement, relocation, changing healthcare technology, job satisfaction, advancement opportunities, and compensation. The organization should benchmark internal data to assess staff turnover and develop a plan if turnover is consistently higher than 10 percent. Although some turnover is expected and, in some cases, healthy, organizations will need to establish protocols and guidelines to curb excessive turnover. Retention strategies include competitive benefits and compensation, flexible work schedules, workload ratio, and improving the work environment. Developing a career progression ladder and aligning pay with skills are also useful tools to reduce employee turnover. In addition, an outstanding leadership team is important for improving retention, because employees tend to leave their bosses rather than their actual work. The leadership team needs to be fully engaged with staff; rounding with respiratory therapists is a great way to build this engagement. Taking the pulse of daily operations, including staff concerns, allows leaders to address operational issues immediately. Leaders also need to pay special attention to employee satisfaction surveys, which provide insights on employee engagement and where satisfaction can be improved.

One effective tactic to assess recruitment, selection, and staff retention is to measure job-specific vacancy rates. A position with a high vacancy rate indicates a strategy is needed to reduce turnover while rethinking recruitment efforts. Organizations can also develop an employee engagement committee that focuses on staff retention activities and employee recognition.

KEY REGULATORY ISSUES

The respiratory care profession is regulated by various agencies, including state licensing bureaus and board certification authorities. Applicants for state licenses must go through a detailed application process that includes work and education history and a criminal background check. In addition, board certifications and state licenses require annual or biannual continuing education. Accrediting agencies such as The Joint Commission, the Healthcare Facilities Accreditation Program, and Det Norske Veritas require Respiratory Care departments to comply with accreditation standards. Regardless of the accrediting agency, they share common areas of regulatory interest such as patient safety, quality of patient care, documentation of patient care, environmental health and safety, and staff competency. For example, these regulatory bodies assign very high value to having a patient identification process before rendering patient care. Respiratory therapists therefore play a vital role in ensuring that the right patient receives the right care at the right time. Respiratory therapists need to maintain current and active licensure to practice respiratory care, and to pursue additional certifications and skills such as basic and advanced cardiac life support, knowledge of how to properly clean and disinfect equipment and devices, administration of respiratory care according to ordered time, use of approved protocols, and compliance with infection control standards.

Many organizations are now focusing their efforts on reducing patient safety defects with the goal of zero harm. One key area that continues to be reviewed is process alignment. When patient care processes are linked together without any variation, the likelihood of an unfavorable event nears zero. However, when events do occur, all parties must determine why they occurred and take steps to prevent future events from reaching patients. For example, when a respiratory therapist is unable to provide scheduled therapy, does the organization count this event as a patient safety issue? Tracking missed therapies can help the organization assess patient care processes, including therapy schedules, therapists' workloads and skill sets, and supply or equipment issues. Because Respiratory Care includes many activities governed by regulatory standards (e.g., infection prevention, medication management, patient identification, quality of care, patient privacy), monitoring compliance with these standards can uphold the role of the department as an integral part of patient care.

KEY TERMS FOR RESPIRATORY CARE

Benchmark: A metric for comparing business practices and processes with other similar organizations.

Interdisciplinary team: A cohort of medical professionals with various medical backgrounds and experiences collaborating to achieve a common goal.

Kanban: A Japanese term describing the use of Lean methods to improve efficiency.

Life support systems: Specialized medical equipment such as invasive and noninvasive mechanical ventilation used to sustain or support life by providing manual or automatic breathing assistance.

Registered Respiratory Therapist: A licensed and credentialed healthcare professional authorized to provide respiratory care to patients.

Relative value units: Time standards (usually in minutes) for respiratory procedures and activities.

Respiratory care: The healthcare profession that specializes in the promotion of optimum cardiopulmonary function, health, and wellness.

Six Sigma: A methodology used for reducing variation and defects by aligning and hardwiring processes.

REFERENCES

American Association for Respiratory Care (AARC). 2020. "Position Statement: Definition of Respiratory Care." Revised January. www.aarc.org/wp-content/uploads/2017/03/statement-of-definition-of-respiratory-care.pdf.

———. 2018. "Position Statement: Respiratory Care Scope of Practice." Revised November. www.aarc.org/wp-content/uploads/2017/03/statement-of-scope-of-practice.pdf.

———. 2011. "Productivity Systems—The Importance of Accurate Time Standards." Accessed October 26, 2020. www.aarc.org/wp-content/uploads/2013/07/time_standards.pdf.

Mussa, C. C. 2008. "Respiratory Care Informatics and the Practice of Respiratory Care." *Respiratory Care* 53 (4): 488–99.

National Board for Respiratory Care (NBRC). 2020a. "About Us." Accessed September 20. www.nbrc.org/about/.

———. 2020b. "Credential Maintenance Program." Accessed October 20. www.nbrc.org/credentialed-practitioners/#credential-maintenance.

———. 2020c. "Examinations." Accessed September 20. www.nbrc.org/examinations/.

CHAPTER 19

Social Work

Margaret W. Meyer

DEPARTMENT DESCRIPTION

The social work profession provides care to individuals to better the human condition. Patients in a healthcare setting receive excellent medical care, but their psychological and social needs (i.e., psychosocial) are often set aside and disregarded. When these needs go unaddressed, patients often require more time from physicians and nurses and end up back in the emergency room, which further consumes limited healthcare resources. For overall patient health and the best utilization of healthcare facilities' resources, social workers must recognize and address the patient's psychosocial needs to enhance a positive outcome.

Social workers are bachelor's- or master's-prepared professionals with training to specifically address patients' psychosocial needs (Barker 2003). The educational level a social worker will need depends on the service being rendered. Master's-prepared social workers are best equipped to provide in-depth psychosocial assessment and counseling. Many states require that the social worker be licensed by a state governing body.

Social workers work directly with patients and caregivers as part of multidisciplinary teams. In this context, a *caregiver* is an individual personally known to the patient who assists in the patient's care. Social workers are available to help patients and other caregivers cope with the impact and changes that result from a medical condition.

In some circumstances, social workers charge patients directly for counseling services; however, in most healthcare settings, services are free and can be provided in person or over the phone. The most common design is to allow patients open access to social workers by not requiring a written order from a physician or the medical team.

KEY DEPARTMENT SERVICES

Social workers provide comprehensive clinical services in the outpatient and inpatient settings by providing psychosocial assessments, counseling, crisis intervention, education, and linkage with hospital and community resources. In some settings, social workers also provide discharge planning services. As members of an interdisciplinary team, Social Work staff provide comprehensive psychosocial services to patients in their assigned service area.

Patients and their families needing social work services come to the attention of the social worker through screening, case finding, or referral. Referrals may be made to the Social Work Department by the patient, their family, the interdisciplinary team, or interested community agencies. Exhibit 19.1 outlines typical patient and family psychosocial needs and the services social workers provide.

Exhibit 19.1: Psychosocial Needs of Patients and Families, and Services Provided by Social Workers

Psychosocial needs	Services
Coping and emotional adjustment to diagnosis and plan of care	Psychosocial assessments
Distress management	Individual and family counseling
Suicide risk assessment	Education, support, and discussion groups
Patient protection concerns related to domestic violence, abuse, and neglect	Patient, caregiver, and family education
Advance care planning	Advance directive assistance
Caregiver and family issues	Advance care planning
Peer relationships	Resource linkage and education
Mental status issues	Discharge planning
Assistance with reintegration to a healthy living environment or work and educational settings	Special services and programs
Continuity of care	Psychosocial consultation with other healthcare professionals
Transitions in care	Triage to other mental health services
Safe discharge	
Cultural, ethical, financial, and legal support	
Assistance with troubleshooting issues related to disability and benefits	

Patients enter the healthcare setting with their own experiences and personal history. These experiences can affect the degree to which patients are managing the current healthcare episode. Engaging patients and their caregivers early in their care can keep potentially problematic issues from building up later in the healthcare continuum. Proactively screening for issues related to distress, depression, and suicide gives the healthcare provider and social worker the opportunity to counsel the patient on healthy coping mechanisms and recommend further psychiatric assessment if necessary. This screening should be conducted at significant points in the patient's care continuum for both outpatients and inpatients (e.g., office visit, change in treatment plan, relapse of disease, at Emergency Center visit or hospital admission). Early psychosocial assessment on arrival at an Emergency Center or hospital admission allows the social worker to identify any problematic issues that may arise during the stay, which can help minimize the patient's length of stay. Social workers also should assess for the patient's understanding of his or her illness, support systems, living arrangements, transportation options, and the like.

There will always be more patient needs than social workers available to address them. Social workers should ensure that the patients with the greatest needs are having them addressed. A solid screening process can help identify patients who need an in-depth psychosocial assessment. Typically, nurses have contact with all patients who come through the healthcare system. Incorporating the screening process into the nursing workflow streamlines the process and helps route patients with an identified psychosocial need to a social worker for assistance.

Identifying patients and caregivers in immediate need of social work services is imperative; this makes repeated prioritization of referrals in the social worker's daily caseload vital. Prioritization is a recurring process and happens with each additional identified need during a social worker's day. The type of need and acuity may change at different points in time and require reprioritization depending on the situation. High-risk indicators help identify patients or family members who may be in need of immediate psychosocial intervention. Such indicators may include but are not limited to suicide risk assessments, medical emergencies, codes, and anticipatory grief and bereavement. The presence of a single indicator may not be sufficient reason for immediate intervention, but indicators can be coupled together to identify potential need. A prioritization policy that outlines the process of identifying patients and their families for assessment will help ensure the appropriate provision of social work services.

DEPARTMENT ORGANIZATIONAL STRUCTURES

Department organization will depend on the size of the department and the healthcare facility or system. Selecting a social worker as the department lead is ideal when possible. This person would be best qualified to assess both the quality of psychosocial services delivered and the social workers' clinical competency. In facilities with only one social worker, a qualified outside social work practitioner should provide clinical and administrative supervision. Clinical supervision provides the social worker the opportunity to address specific issues that may arise in the course of providing clinical patient care (Barker 2003). Topics include how to manage difficult patient situations and issues of transference and the social worker's professional development. This supervision can be conducted one-on-one or in groups. In some states, the clinical supervisor must be approved by the state's professional licensing body if she or he is attempting to achieve a higher level of licensure.

In larger healthcare organizations, the organizational structure should include leadership, clinical supervision, and administrative functions. Exhibit 19.2 depicts a sample structure.

This example reflects a multi-tier design with both clinical and administrative functions. Separating clinical from administrative functions allows social workers to use their time to the highest level of their degree or license by giving the supervisory session focus and purpose. Evaluating how the social worker is using his or her time and redirecting tasks that do not require the social worker's specific educational degree enhances work satisfaction. The organizational structure should also be designed to foster succession planning by designing roles to provide professional growth and leadership in incumbents for positions. Key to the quality

Exhibit 19.2: Sample Social Work Department Organizational Structure

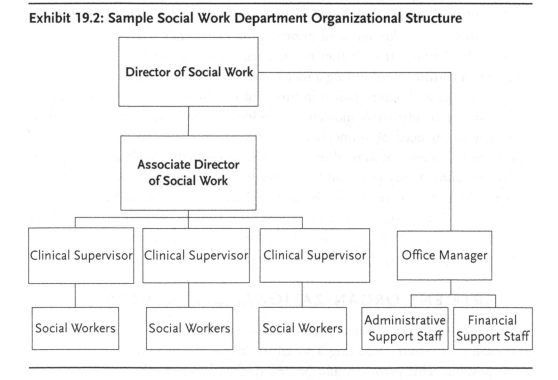

of services provided is ensuring the director, associate director, supervisors, and office manager have the necessary experience and qualifications.

KEY CUSTOMERS AND THEIR PERFORMANCE EXPECTATIONS

The reach of social work goes beyond the doors of the healthcare facility. Customers of a Social Work Department can include patients, families, caregivers, the interdisciplinary care team, members of the community, resource agencies, the institution, donors, and regulatory bodies. Exhibit 19.3 also includes how each customer metric is monitored and the key positions needed to provide the key services.

Narrowing the scope, the primary key customers for any social worker are the patient and caregiver. This customer is primarily seeking psychosocial services. They typically want their most pressing need addressed first, usually immediately. This need may be lodging, meals, safety from domestic violence, or counseling on how to adjust to a new diagnosis, to name a few. Addressing a patient's concrete need such as housing or transportation helps to develop rapport with the patient or caregiver and can be a springboard to a counseling-focused intervention.

Followed by the patient and caregiver, the next key customer would be the interdisciplinary care team. The expectation is that any issue the team identifies be addressed either immediately or within a specific period depending on the nature of the request.

Exhibit 19.3: Key Social Work Customers, Services, and Requirements

Key customer groups	Key customer requirements
1. Patients 2. Caregivers 3. Interdisciplinary team	1. Timely response to referrals 2. Recognition of right to self-determination and patient safety

Key services	How each key customer requirement will be measured and the time frame (e.g., weekly, monthly)
1. Responding to screening referrals as appropriate 2. Responding to advance directive referrals as appropriate 3. Providing assistance to patients/families through the patient assistance program (community resource linkage and distribution of donor funds)	1. Monthly chart reviews to ensure screening response time of 24 hours or less 2. Monthly chart reviews to ensure advance directive response time of 24 hours or less 3. Monthly adult and reconciliation of patient assistance funds

Current metric for each key customer requirement
1. 95%–100% compliance of screening responses 2. 95%–100% compliance of advance directive responses 3. 100% compliance with all applicable laws and policies

Key positions needed to provide: *Response to screening referral*	Key positions needed to provide: *Response to advance directive referral*	Key positions needed to provide: *Assistance through patient assistance program*
1. Social work counselor 2. Support staff 3. Nursing	1. Social work counselor 2. Support staff 3. Admissions	1. Social work counselor 2. Resource specialist 3. Support staff

KEY PROCESS FLOWS

Process flows can be vital for orienting new employees to ensure their practice is consistent, and for designing process-improvement initiatives to identify and eliminate wasteful steps and barriers to care processes. The key process flows in Social Work may include administrative functions such as triaging phone calls or incoming referrals and processing requests for patient assistance. Some clinical practices lend themselves to clinical care algorithms, such as responding to high-risk suicide referrals or advance care planning (ACP). These algorithms often include the interdisciplinary team and help clarify the process for all team members. Exhibit 19.4

Exhibit 19.4: Social Work Patient-Needs Screen Triage Process

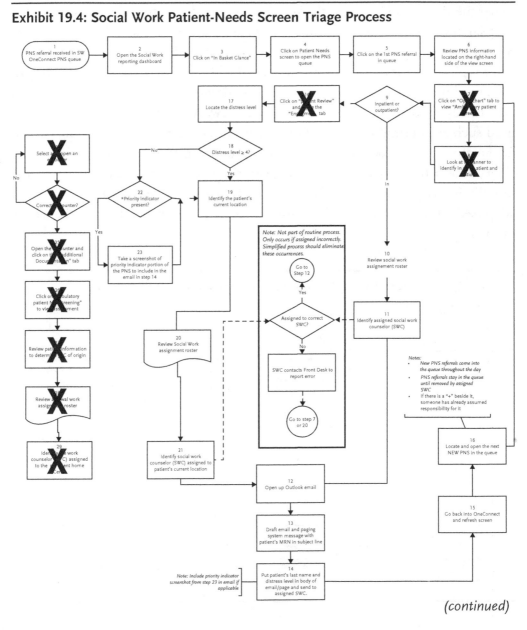

(continued)

<u>Types of Lean Waste</u>

Note: Not all waste is pure waste that can be eliminated. Some activities that are seen as waste from the customer's perspective are necessary.

<u>Overproduction</u>

Producing more than what is required

<u>Waiting</u>

Periods of inactivity that interrupt flow (waiting for the next process to occur)

<u>Underutilization</u>

Not fully using people's abilities

<u>Motion</u>

Any movement of people or material that does not add value to the product or service

<u>Defects</u>

Results that do not meet customer expectations or process standards (often leads to rework)

<u>Transport</u>

Any extra or unnecessary movement of products or services

<u>Extra Processing</u>

Extra operations such as rework, reprocessing, handling, or storage (typically a result of some other waste such as defects)

<u>Inventory</u>

Any material or resource that is not required for the current customer (information or products waiting in a queue)

<u>Waste Eliminated</u>

Overproduction: Box 27
Motion: Boxes 7, 8, 16, 23, 25, 26, 28, 29
Defects: Box 24

Note: PNS = patient-needs screen; MRN = medical record number; SW = social work; SWC = social work counselor.

shows the patient-needs screen triage process after a process improvement activity using Lean methodology reduced a 29-step process to 19 steps.

KEY UNITS OF WORK AND VOLUME STATISTICS TO MONITOR

Key units of work are the main activities performed by the Social Work staff that represent the services being provided. Many healthcare facilities now use an electronic health record (EHR), which makes obtaining data more convenient. In fact, one can easily get overwhelmed by all the data. The most important steps are to determine what data are needed and how to easily retrieve them. For example, is the information needed to assess staff productivity or to justify new positions? Is there a change in work volume caused by changes in numbers of patients seen by the Social Work Department or the institution?

The top data to track for managing a Social Work department are total patients seen, total full-time equivalent (FTE) positions available to provide patient care, and labor expenses. Collecting data over a long time allows the viewer to see where problem areas may exist or at least need further exploration. Using these three data streams, the graphs in exhibits 19.5 through 19.8 show a definite trend in increased activity for this department of Social Work.

Exhibit 19.5 provides a format for tracking key units of work. Exhibit 19.6 shows a consistent increase in total patients seen across four years.

Exhibit 19.5: Social Work Key Units of Work

	Measure	Month		Sept	Oct	Nov
1	# of patients seen (documented)	FY15				
		FY16				
		FY17				
		FY18				
		FY19				
		% change (FY17–FY18)				
2	FTE	FY19 FTE actual				
		FY19 FTE budget				
		FY19 FTE variance (actual vs. budget)				
		FY19 vacancies				
3	Personnel expense	FY19 personnel expense variance				
4	Overtime expense	FY19 actual YTD				
5	Total operating expense	FY15				
		FY16				
		FY17				
		FY18				
		FY19				
6	Total operating expense per patient seen	FY15				
		FY16				
		FY17				
		FY18				
		FY19				

Note: FTE = full-time equivalent.

Exhibit 19.6: Patients Seen per Month by Social Work Department

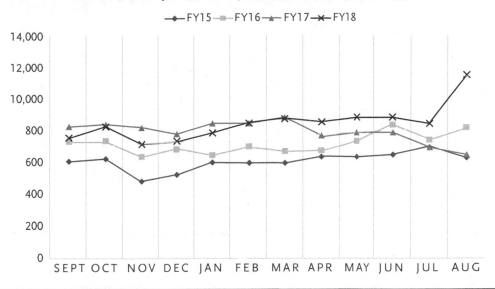

Exhibit 19.7 shows a trend of social workers treating more patients at less expense. Using a metric familiar with healthcare organizations, patients per working day, the graph in Exhibit 19.8 shows social worker productivity above the lower control limit (LCL) and below the upper control limit (UCL). Additionally,

Exhibit 19.7: Total Operating Expenses per Patient Seen by Social Work

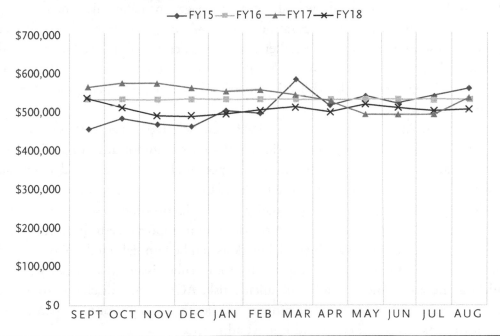

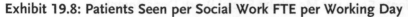

Exhibit 19.8: Patients Seen per Social Work FTE per Working Day

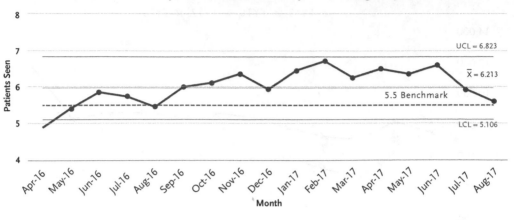

this graph documents an external benchmark of 5.5 patients seen exceeding productivity of a comparative external organization. Using comparative data from like organizations allows the director to think beyond his/her current setting and assess why the data is similar or different, which may require a reconsideration of work flow processes.

KEY METRICS TO MONITOR: PEOPLE, SERVICE, QUALITY/SAFETY, FINANCIAL

Monitoring metrics monthly will allow the manager to make adjustments along the way to improve care and operations. In *Hardwiring Excellence,* Quint Studer (2003) presents five pillars of excellence: People, Service, Quality, Finance, and Growth. This framework can help identify metrics to track. Exhibit 19.9 demonstrates a sample template for collecting metrics data that could help guide departmental improvements.

The metrics represented exhibit 19.9 were selected because they relate to specific initiatives. The People metrics emphasize the importance of staff recognition and inform the leadership team of potential recruitment and retention issues. The Service metrics monitor the staff-to-work ratios and productivity so leadership can act appropriately. Quality metrics incorporate response time and patient safety issues. Patient safety is of paramount importance to healthcare systems. Safety issues addressed by social workers can be familial, medical, or mental health related. All are equally important. Some safety issues that social workers address include domestic violence, suicide risk, ACP needs, discharge to a safe environment, and safe travel. The Finance metrics focus on personnel expense (the department's largest expense) and budget adherence.

Exhibit 19.9: Key Metrics to Monitor

Scorecard
SOCIAL WORK

	Under-performing	Threshold	Target	Stretch	Sept 2018	Oct 2018	Nov 2018
PEOPLE							
P1 **Recognition Letters:** # of recognition letters given	0		≥1				
P2 **Year-to-Date Turnover:** % of staff who (voluntarily + involuntarily) left the institution during the fiscal year	>20%	11%–20%	1%–10%	<1%			
P3 **First-Year Turnover:** % of staff who (voluntarily + involuntarily) left the institution less than 1 year from the date of hire	>14%	11%–14%	9%–10%	<9%			
SERVICE							
S1 **Outpatient Service Levels:** Ratio of outpatient social workers to 40% physician daily appointments	≥1:30	1:20–1:29	1:9–1:19	≤1:8			
S2 **Inpatient Service Levels:** Ratio of inpatient social workers to average daily census	≥1:55	1:44–1:54	1:26–1:43	≤1:25			
S3 **Abandoned Calls:** Reduce the average % of abandoned calls from 3.55% to 3%	≥3.55%	3.01%–3.54%	3.00%	<3.00%			
S4 **Productivity:** # of Key Units of Work metrics achieving productivity goals	<2		2				

(continued)

Exhibit 19.9: Key Metrics to Monitor (continued)

Scorecard
SOCIAL WORK

		Under-performing	Threshold	Target	Stretch	Sept 2018	Oct 2018	Nov 2018
QUALITY								
Q1	**Referral Response Time:** % of overall referrals responded to within 24 hours	<70%	70%–84%	85%–95%	>95%			
Q2	**Patient Safety:** Advance care planning notes per Social Work counselor	<10	10–12	13–15	>15			
FINANCE								
F1	**Personnel Expense**	>Budget		≤Budget				
F2	**Other Operating Expense**	>Budget		≤Budget				
F3	**Total Operating Expense:** Personnel Expense + Other Operating Expense	>Budget		≤Budget				
F4	**Operating Income/Loss:** % Variance Actual to Budget	>±5%	±5%	±4%	±3%			

Setting measurable targets for each metric helps to track the department's progress throughout the year. Metrics consistently underperforming indicate the need to evaluate practice, possibly through a quality improvement project.

KEY INFORMATICS ISSUES

Use of EHRs can make documenting patient care much less arduous. The critical step is to design the EHR with work processes and data needs in mind, making work functions more efficient for staff and data retrieval easy. Social Work departments should think strategically when designing EHR documentation tools. They should incorporate into one electronic template all pieces of data pertinent to patient care, including psychosocial assessment, suicide risk assessment, and mental status assessment fields. To avoid staff having to document their productivity separately, the template should be designed to collect productivity data such as time spent with the patient. Social work documentation in EHRs should only display fields containing data, so the reader does not see empty data fields. Productivity data, such as total patients seen by each social worker, can also be pulled into a report. Social Work managers should think about the data necessary to manage the Social Work Department while designing the documentation tool. See Exhibit 19.10 for possible metrics that Social Work EHRs can collect.

Some EHRs have additional packages that can be modified for creating and processing requests for patient assistance such as cash, taxi, and lodging vouchers. This electronic process allows data to be collected later for donor reports.

Exhibit 19.10: Sample Data Metrics for Social Work Electronic Health Records

Unique patients seen
Patient contacts
Non-patient contacts (e.g., interdisciplinary team, community resources)
Time spent with patients
Referrals
Referral source
Interventions
Resources used
Date service rendered

STAFFING MODELS

Social Work managers consider several indicators when developing patient care assignments, including hours of operation, patient volume, acuity, and unique patient needs. Psychosocial crises do not just happen between the hours of 8 a.m.

and 5 p.m; staff must be available after hours and on holidays. Depending on the volume and type of patient need, this work may require a staff member to be physically in the building or at least available by phone. Either way, staff needs to be compensated for time spent while on call.

Location of patients also needs to be considered when creating staffing assignments. For example, having the same social worker follow a patient in an ambulatory and inpatient setting is preferable but not always practical, because of the time required to travel between locations.

Two staffing models worth considering for the inpatient setting are staffing by geographic location versus staffing by medical team. Geographic staffing (assigning a social worker to a specific inpatient nursing unit) fosters a close working relationship between the social worker and bedside nurses. Medical team staffing allows the social worker to develop relationships with their team and affords him or her the opportunity to provide direct input to the physician regarding psychosocial barriers to care for an individual patient.

Exhibit 19.11 outlines a method for applying the preceding concepts into calculating total Social Work FTEs needed for nondirect and direct patient care

---

Exhibit 19.11: Social Work Staffing Model

Calculate how many FTE positions are needed to work an outpatient assignment

1. **Exclude Nonproductive Time**
   - Exclude paid hours that are considered nonproductive such as paid time off, sick leave, jury duty, or Family Medical Leave.
   - This is likely to range between 80%–90% of total paid hours
   - *Total = 4.5–8 hours/week per FTE is lost to nonproductive time*

2. **Exclude Time Spent on Nondirect Patient Care Activities**
   - 30 minutes/day to obtain and prioritize the patients to be seen that day and other organizational tasks, or 2.5 hours/week
   - 1 hour/week for committee work
   - 1 hour/week for continuing education
   - 1 hour/month or 0.25 hours/week in clinical supervision
   - *Total = 4.75 hours/week in nondirect patient care, or approximately 11% of the social worker's time per week, leaving 88% of their productive hours for direct patient care*

3. **Direct Patient Care Demand: Outpatient Care Assignment**
   A. 40% of outpatients need social work intervention
   B. Each intervention takes an average of 45 minutes (understanding that some patients take more time and some take less)

(continued)

Example: Clinic Staffing Model

Assumptions:
- *85% nonproductive time per Social Work counselor: 147.3 worked hours per month*
- *Deduct another 11% from productive hours to account for nondirect patient care time: 147.3 − 16.2 = 131.1*
- *Estimate that each intervention will take 45 minutes (0.75 hours)*

A	Total Patients Seen per Month	2,000
B	Total Patients in Need of Social Work Intervention per Month (40% of A)	800
C	Social Work Clinical Hours Needed per Month (B × 0.75)	600
D	Available Clinical Hours per Social Worker Per Month	131.1
E	Social Worker FTEs Needed (C / D)	4.6

Direct Inpatient Care Assignment

In an inpatient setting, a caseload of 1 social worker to 30 patient days is reasonable. Note this is filled beds and not an assignment based on a specific unit where there may be unoccupied beds. Caseloads for social workers assigned to intensive care units can be reduced depending on the acuity of the patient population.

Example:

Average Daily Census = 270
30 patient days per social worker
Divide A by C = # FTEs needed

As a general rule, a social worker can see 6–10 patients per day.

Note: FTE = full-time equivalent. Based on informal study conducted at a large academic cancer center.

activity. Time allotted to nondirect patient care activity can be adjusted according to the employee's professional commitments.

PRODUCTIVITY MODELS, INCLUDING WORK-TO-STAFF RATIOS AND INDUSTRY PERFORMANCE TARGETS

Productivity will vary by setting, patient acuity, and performance expectations of the position. Calculations should incorporate direct and nondirect patient care. In medical social work, the primary direct patient care productivity measures relate to total patients seen and support group activity. Nondirect care captures activities not related to a specific patient, such as time spent in committee meetings, clinical supervision, and continuing education.

For direct patient care, the setting must be considered. The number of patients expected to be seen in an ambulatory setting would be different from the number expected to be seen in an inpatient setting. On average, one can expect a social worker to see six to ten outpatients or inpatients per day. The range accounts for the acuity of the patient population and psychosocial activities conducted. In a setting that requires in-depth psychosocial assessments (e.g., transplant), the lower end of the range would be a reasonable expectation. If the activities are more related to housing and transportation, the upper end of the range could be expected. An unpublished study at a large academic cancer center using the National Comprehensive Cancer Network Distress Thermometer and Problem List for Patients showed that about 40 percent of all outpatients needed further social work assessment for distress-related psychosocial issues.

STRATEGIES TO IMPROVE RECRUITMENT AND RETENTION

Because the staff is the most valuable asset in a Social Work department, building and maintaining a talented workforce is well worth the time and effort. Successful staffing requires hiring managers to know exactly what the position entails. First, review the position description. Is it accurate? Next, review the key functions of the job, to ensure the educational and licensing requirements can support delivery of key functions. Does the work require a master's- or a bachelor's-prepared social worker? Modify the position description to reflect this. Hiring should follow the specifications outlined in the position description; do not settle for less than what is needed. Better to have a vacant position than one filled with the wrong person. Candidates who meet the job qualifications and have a calling to work with the specific patient population are preferable. Keep looking if the candidate is not interested in doing the specific type of social work needed.

There are multiple options for posting job openings. Graduate schools of social work often have job boards that new graduates and alumni frequent when seeking employment. Professional organizations such as the Society for Social Work Leadership in Healthcare also offer job boards. Graduate schools typically do not charge for job website postings. Professional organizations often charge a small fee but offer broader access.

Behavioral-based interviewing works well in social work. Questions are designed to solicit responses that can predict how the candidate would handle a situation. Sample questions might include:

1. What types of information do you look for when conducting a psychosocial assessment?

2. What theoretical modality do you tend to use most often? Tell me about a case where you used that modality.
3. Tell me about a time when you and a member of the medical team had a difference of opinion about what was in the best interest of a patient. How did you handle the situation? What was the outcome?

The next challenge is to retain staff. To continue working for an employer, social workers want:

- a clear understanding of what is expected of them,
- professional development,
- clinical supervision, and
- rewards and recognition.

To help an employee understand their job functions, start with a solid orientation to the institution (typically a two-week process), the Social Work Department, and the work assignment. Exhibit 19.12 provides a sample of topics to cover during orientation. Introducing teammates fosters the development of relationships. Shadowing other social workers in the field gives the new employee the opportunity to see their work in practice and how they manage workloads and

---

Exhibit 19.12: Social Work Orientation Content

Department orientation
Director welcome
Supervisor welcome
Review position description
Policies and procedures
Flow maps
Building a practice
Advance directives
Distress management
Suicide risk assessment
Documentation
Internal resources
Community resources
Tour areas within institution (e.g., Emergency Center, Intensive Care Unit, Radiotherapy, Clinic, Inpatient Unit)
Shadow team members
Accreditation readiness
Competency review

---

associated processes. Here's where the process flow maps discussed earlier can be helpful.

New employees will be eager to meet their supervisor's expectations. Provide clear expectations of these expectations and policies to be followed. Be sure the employee is fully competent before allowing her or him to deliver patient care by reviewing the orientation material together, observing a few sessions of the employee performing key job functions, and extending the orientation a few more days or weeks if the employee is not working fully independently yet.

Opportunities for professional development are important for engaging staff and ensuring high-quality care. A personal development plan with quantifiable goals allows the social worker and supervisor to measure progress, and a professional development plan should focus on the social worker's area of interest. Allow the social workers to explore facilitating support groups or test new theoretical modalities. Additionally, joining and becoming involved in a professional organization provides exposure to other professionals in the field, and attending professional conferences allows employees to refine their practice. Membership fees should be built into the department budget along with registration and travel expenses for conferences. Social workers should share what they learned at conferences with the rest of the department through brown-bag sessions, which help to reinforce the new material for the employee and provide professional development opportunities for other social workers in the department. Social Work departments have a lot of talent on their teams; creating a departmental staff development program and scheduling the social workers to present to each other continues that learning process and helps social workers hone their presentation skills.

One of the most important forms of staff development is the provision of clinical supervision, which can be offered one-on-one or in small groups. The process of clinical supervision provides the employee a safe place to work through challenging patient situations, delve into areas of transference, discuss issues with the multidisciplinary team, and explore opportunities to strengthen his or her clinical practice.

Delivering rewards and recognition is key to employee retention. Monetary rewards are always appreciated. Merit increases on top of a market-based salary send a message of support to the employee. However, not all rewards need to be monetary in nature; many employees want verbal recognition too. Telling a social worker that she or he has done an excellent job and why reinforces behavior and commitment. Take the opportunity at administrative staff meetings to describe what an employee has done well. Sharing the message with the entire department allows others to congratulate the employee and models the type of behavior Social Work leadership is seeking. Handwritten notes mailed to employees' homes bring the recognition right where they live and allow them to share the recognition with family. One special time that recognition must be provided is during National Social Work Month in March. Ideas for recognition during this period include continuing education events with special speakers, a luncheon, or social work service displays in public spaces throughout the institution.

KEY REGULATORY ISSUES

Federal and state regulatory bodies that guide and direct the practice of medical social work include The Joint Commission, the Quality Oncology Practice Initiative, the Commission on Cancer, and social work licensing boards. Some regulatory bodies focus on specific standards and elements of care; others direct ethical practice. All these expectations need to be balanced consistently so staff do not need to change practice when the regulatory body performs a site visit. Do what is needed and expected all the time so staff can respond accurately to surveyors.

The Joint Commission affects all healthcare organizations that seek its accreditation. It does not specify what discipline should perform functions; however, there are several standards for which the clinical social work skill set is a natural fit. Some pertinent to the practice of clinical social work in a healthcare setting are providing interdisciplinary care, treating patients for emotional disorders, identifying patients at risk for suicide, caring for victims of abuse and neglect, and making decisions about care and end-of-life support. (See The Joint Commission 2020 for a thorough review of the standards and elements of performance.)

Social workers play a key role in the implementation of ACP in most healthcare settings. Knowing the state regulations pertaining to Advance Directives is required. Additionally, other bodies such as the Quality Oncology Practice Initiative delineate expectations pertaining to ACP. Core Measure 25a from the Quality Oncology Practice Initiative requires documentation of Advance Directives or ACP discussions for patients with a diagnosis of advanced or metastatic disease by the third office visit (American Society of Clinical Oncology 2020).

Under the auspices of the American College of Surgeons (ACS), the Commission on Cancer has a standard regarding distress screening. This expectation also touches on social work practice and is the primary focus of many clinical social workers practicing in healthcare. The standards outline the time of screening, method, tools, assessment and referral, and documentation (ACS 2016).

Most important, social workers are obligated to adhere to the code of ethics outlined by the healthcare organization, the social work profession, and social work licensing boards. Such codes can be found in organizational documents and in state social work codes of ethics as part of licensing. Professional organizations such as the National Association of Social Workers (2017) also have ethical codes of conduct for their members.

KEY TERMS FOR SOCIAL WORK

Clinical social work: The professional application of social work theory and methods to the treatment and prevention of psychosocial dysfunction, disability, or impairment, including emotional and mental disorders. The term is considered a synonym for *social casework* or *psychiatric social work*. Most professional social workers agree that clinical social work practice includes emphasis on the person-in-environment perspective.

Distress: An unpleasant emotional state that may affect how a person feels, thinks, and acts. It can include feelings of unease, sadness, worry, anger, helplessness, and guilt (National Comprehensive Cancer Network 2018).

Ethics: A system of moral principles and perceptions about right versus wrong and the resulting philosophy of conduct that is practiced by an individual, group, profession, or culture (Barker 2003).

Psychosocial assessment: The social worker's summary judgment as to the problem to be solved; also referred to as the *psychosocial diagnosis*. This description may include diagnostic labels, results derived from psychological tests, legal status, brief descriptive expressions of the problem configuration, a description of existing assets and resources, the prognosis or prediction of the outcome, and the plan designed to resolve the problem (Barker 2003).

Suicide: The act of intentionally killing oneself (Barker 2003).

Supervision: An administrative and educational process used to help social workers develop and refine their skills, enhance staff morale, and provide quality assurance for clients. Social work supervisors assign cases to the most appropriate social worker, discuss the assessment and intervention plan, and review the social worker's ongoing contact with clients. Educationally, supervision is geared toward helping the social worker better understand social work philosophy and agency policy, become more self-aware, know the agency's and community's resources, establish activity priorities, and refine knowledge. Less experienced workers tend to be supervised according to a tutorial model, whereas more experienced workers use more case consultation, peer-group interactions, staff development, or social work teams.

REFERENCES

American College of Surgeons (ACS). 2016. *Cancer Program Standards: Ensuring Patient-Centered Care.* Chicago: ACS. https://www.facs.org/~/media/files/quality%20programs/cancer/coc/2016%20coc%20standards%20manual_interactive%20pdf.ashx.

American Society of Clinical Oncology. 2020. "QOPI-Related Measures." Accessed September 21. https://practice.asco.org/quality-improvement/quality-programs/quality-oncology-practice-initiative/qopi-related-measures.

Barker, R. L. 2003. *The Social Work Dictionary.* Washington, DC: NASW Press.

Joint Commission. 2020. "The Joint Commission E-dition." Accessed September 21. www.jointcommission.org/standards_information/edition.aspx.

National Association of Social Workers. 2017. "Read the Code of Ethics." Accessed September 21, 2020. www.socialworkers.org/About/Ethics/Code-of-Ethics/Code-of-Ethics-English.

National Comprehensive Cancer Network. 2018. "Distress Management." Accessed September 21, 2020. www.nccn.org/professionals/physician_gls/pdf/distress.pdf.

Studer, Q. 2003. *Hardwiring Excellence: Purpose, Worthwhile Work, Making a Difference.* Gulf Breeze, FL: Fire Starter Publishing.

CHAPTER 20

Spiritual Care

Gale Francine Kennebrew

DEPARTMENT DESCRIPTION

Professional Spiritual Care in a clinical context provides and supports the spiritual well-being and education of patients, their caregivers, the clinical team, employees, the healthcare organization, and the community. Quality healthcare addresses the whole person: body, mind, and spirit. The definition of spirituality this writer prefers is, "Spirituality is the aspect of humanity that refers to the way individuals seek and express meaning and purpose and the way they experience their connectedness to the moment, to self, to others, to nature, and to the significant or sacred" (Puchalski et al. 2014, 643). The definition was expanded to include the dynamic and community aspects of spirituality. Spirituality is the overarching umbrella that includes religion, but it is not limited to religion or its expression through a specific faith group or practice. All religions are spiritual, but spirituality is not limited to religion.

Historically, most hospitals were formed by religious groups. Professional chaplains were hired by Pastoral Care or Religious Services departments to meet the religious needs of patients and their family members. Hospital census reports reveal that although some people identify with a religion, increasing numbers indicate "none," "other," or "spiritual." In 2017, more than a quarter of US adults (27 percent) identified themselves as "spiritual" but not "religious," up from 19 percent in 2012 (Lipka and Gecewicz 2017).

In 1991, the World Health Organization (WHO) added spiritual as the fourth dimension of well-being along with physical, social, and mental. Holistic care strives to alleviate all manner of suffering, including spiritual suffering. Awareness that addressing spiritual needs improves patient-reported outcomes is growing (Dhar, Chaturvedi, and Nandan 2013; Hall, Hughes, and Handzo 2016).

Palliative care is an example of holistic care to individuals and families living with life-threatening illness. Such care strives to proactively prevent and diminish suffering through the early identification, assessment, and treatment of pain and other problems, whether physical, psychosocial, or spiritual (WHO 2020).

This chapter uses the term *spirituality* to include both religious and spiritual beliefs, values, and expressions. Additionally, the terms *chaplain* and *spiritual care practitioner* includes both chaplains and clinical mental health professionals, also known as pastoral counselors. Professional chaplains serve in a variety of settings: prisons, corporations, the military, academic institutions, first responders, government agencies, retirement communities, mental health centers, and hospitals. This chapter focuses on hospital chaplaincy for inpatient and outpatient settings. The following professional organizations established Common Qualifications for professional chaplaincy (exhibit 20.1) and Common Competencies, discussed in the next section (Association for Clinical Pastoral Education [ACPE] et al. 2018):

- Association for Clinical Pastoral Education
- Association of Professional Chaplains
- National Association of Catholic Chaplains
- Neshama: Association of Jewish Chaplains
- Canadian Association for Spiritual Care/Association canadienne de soins spirituels

---

Exhibit 20.1: General Qualifications for Hospital Chaplains

- A bachelor's and master's theological degree from an institution accredited by the Council for Higher Education Accreditation
- 1,600 hours of accredited clinical spiritual care education
- Letter of good standing from religious/spiritual judicatory and authorization to practice spiritual care
- 2,000 hours of professional chaplain experience
- Certification review by one of the certifying organizations
- Adherence to Association of Professional Chaplains Code of Ethics
- 50 hours of continuing education per year
- Periodic peer review

Demonstrated Competencies

A professional chaplain demonstrates competencies in four focus areas: Integration of Theory and Practice, Professional Identity and Conduct, Professional Practice Skills, and Organizational Leadership. Chaplains use these competencies along with knowledge gained from theological education that mirrors the education of academically trained clergy or laypersons. Most chaplains have also worked in a religious or community ministry setting. However, a professional chaplain continues to learn in a clinical setting through Clinical Pastoral Education (CPE). This experience helps chaplains engage and apply theological education in a healthcare organization as a member of the clinical team. Chaplains increase their knowledge by studying disease specialties, psychology, social science, ethics, group dynamics, and basic research from a holistic perspective that integrates the influence and impact of spirituality on care recipients and caregivers. CPE describes this as learning from what founder Anton Boisen called "living human documents" (Nouwen 1968). The term *clinical spiritual care practitioner* is helpful to describe the difference between a clinical chaplain and their theologically trained colleagues working in nonclinical settings.

Professional Identity and Conduct

Chaplains demonstrate the ability to be aware of their strengths and limitations as a spiritual care provider. This skill requires self-reflection and the ability to articulate and manage their feelings, attitudes, and assumptions that may influence their professional behavior or ability to provide care and function as a member of the care team. Chaplains demonstrate professional identity and conduct by engaging and applying their authority as spiritual care practitioners aptly and in a manner that respects multiple expressions of diversity while adhering to the boundaries of others. By virtue of specific religious and spiritual tasks, chaplains have the ability to communicate effectively in writing and verbally. Chaplains also advocate for individuals, families, and communities to influence the healthcare organization toward adhering to their mission and values during difficult times.

Professional Practice Skills

Chaplains functioning as clinical spiritual care practitioners demonstrate the following professional practice skills. They provide spiritual care to people from diverse religious and spiritual traditions, which requires the ability to establish, deepen, and conclude relationships with openness, sensitivity, respect, and compassion. Chaplains navigate and triage high volumes of crises and experiences of grief and loss. They also facilitate support groups, family meetings, staff debriefings after trauma, and employee or community educational seminars during a normal work schedule. Daily clinical practices include formulating and documenting spiritual assessments, interventions, outcomes, and care plans in the electronic health record (EHR). Effectively documenting spiritual care encounters provides their recipients an opportunity to voice the importance of spirituality as a vital resource to their well-being while living with illness. Documentation in the medical record is one way chaplains are distinct from local faith group leaders who may provide religious services to hospital patients and family members.

Organizational Leadership

Professional chaplains integrate spirituality into the culture and clinical practice of healthcare institutions whether they are faith based or publicly funded. Chaplains are able to navigate complex organizational cultures and systems and to use business practices to manage departments and complementary services. They help employees experience meaningful work and make connections to their spiritual values and the organization's mission. According to a joint report of leading spiritual care organizations (ACPE et al. 2018), chaplains demonstrate the ability to respect institutional diversity while creatively and proactively facilitating activities that recognize and honor the cultural, spiritual, and religious aspects of their organization's mission.

KEY DEPARTMENT SERVICES

Certified clinical spiritual care practitioners are guided by standards of practice for three domains: the care recipient, the healthcare organization, and the community. Chaplains educate about cultural and spiritual diversity and clinical spiritual care. Chaplains both initiate Spiritual Care encounters and receive referrals from such sources as admission screenings for spiritual needs, physician orders, and crisis care (trauma, code blues, rapid response, end of life). Key services include providing and documenting spiritual assessments, interventions, outcomes, and plans of care, along with education. Chaplains collaborate with clinical team members to achieve goals of care and enhance quality of life through spiritual well-being.

The Spiritual Care Department provides care to the healthcare organization by participating on institutional committees. The degree of involvement is determined by the organizational culture and governance. Professional chaplains may be members of the leadership team, governing council, mission and values integration committee, ethics council, community health programs, institutional review board, or diversity and inclusion council; in faith-based institutions they also may advise executive leadership. This author recommends inviting professional chaplains' participation on any clinical interprofessional committee that involves patient care or employee health and wellness. A few examples are medical and nursing education, psychosocial councils, survivorship, advance directives, employee orientation, critical incident management, safety committee, employee wellness and burnout interventions, education on spiritual diversity, patient experience, trauma or disaster management, and community health partnerships. Chaplains work closely with frontline staff and administrative leadership at all levels of the hospital and often serve as the moral compass of an organization's mission. They are also members of community organizations, faith groups, professional associations, and social service organizations. As such, chaplains have direct access to internal and external stakeholders, and often serve as a bridge between the competing interests of stakeholders and the healthcare institution. For example, during a union-organizing campaign at a faith-based healthcare system, chaplains provided crucial feedback during discussions with denominational sponsors.

The chaplain as educator is a foundational role that influences the care seeker, the organization, and the quality of care. Most people do not understand what a professional chaplain is or does. Chaplains regularly educate care seekers, clinical team members, other employees, and the institution about their role, function, and competencies that contribute to quality care. In a more formal educational role, chaplains may serve as faculty members at a school of health sciences. Other roles include providing lectures and grand rounds for medical students or medical divisions. In a practical role, chaplains educate the care team about how to accommodate patients' religious preferences and interpret requests that do not seem to have spiritual or religious significance.

Chaplains educate the institution about spiritual values inherent in its mission and how to articulate that mission in an inclusive and unifying way that can inspire employees. They help organizations by supporting the mission and values, facilitating spiritual integration, improving well-being, providing education and training, being a spiritual guide and consultant, and providing spiritual support and comfort. Chaplains' roles have been crucial to healthcare organizations during crises such as COVID-19, when those affected are experiencing grief, loss, and bereavement individually, locally, nationally, and globally. Chaplains provide support to caregivers who are isolated from their loved ones by using technology to connect virtually and providing special chapel or prayer services, support groups, sacraments or blessing of the hands rituals, memorial services, staff support, end-of-life rituals, and interfaith observances.

DEPARTMENT ORGANIZATIONAL STRUCTURES

The size and organizational structure of a Spiritual Care department varies according to the organization and the resources it devotes to spiritual care. This writer recommends aligning the Spiritual Care Department with a clinical division in the organization. Professional spiritual care provides direct clinical spiritual care to care recipients, caregivers, and the clinical team. To effectively and safely provide quality spiritual care, the chaplain needs to be part of the clinical team with access to clinical areas, while adhering to requirements for clinical documentation, infection control, credentialing, continuing education, clinical annual competencies, and safety (e.g., annual fit testing for personal protective equipment).

The scope of service for the department is also determined by the institution. This writer recommends staffing with board-certified chaplains to ensure the highest quality and competency level for a healthcare organization. If a department has multiple certified chaplains, a certified chaplain leader can facilitate chaplains' continued professional development and growth as subject matter experts. Some departments have long-established ACPE programs that train the next generation of professional spiritual care practitioners. Many departments recruit graduates of ACPE programs for open staff chaplain, palliative chaplain, emergency room, and on-call or part-time chaplain positions. Chaplain educators from quality ACPE training programs are often recruited for Spiritual Care leadership roles in healthcare systems.

A generic department organizational structure includes the positions of director, manager, chaplain, volunteer, and administrative professional. For departments with an accredited CPE program, the department might add positions such as chaplain educator and trainee. Positions that typically report to the director are manager, educator, chaplain, volunteer, and administrative professional; trainees report to the chaplain educator. The number of employees per position is determined by the institution size and scope of service. Exhibit 20.2 depicts a sample Spiritual Care department with a CPE program.

Exhibit 20.2: Sample Spiritual Care Department Organization

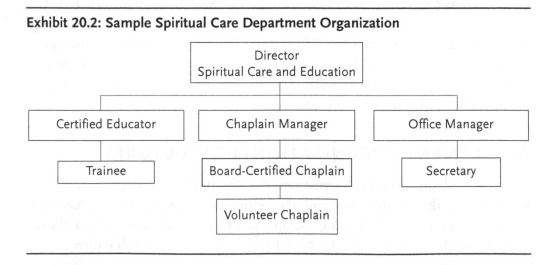

KEY CUSTOMERS AND THEIR PERFORMANCE EXPECTATIONS

The primary customers for spiritual care and education are patients and their care-givers. Professional chaplains are trained to recognize and treat the spiritual distress of patients and their caregivers. Chaplains also support the spiritual strength and resiliency of patients and families. Most patients want their spiritual beliefs and values included in their care and welcome a visit from a chaplain for prayer or ritual needs. Patients and their caregivers seek the presence of a chaplain when anxious about treatment, test or surgical results, or sudden crises, or when making difficult decisions and communicating them to loved ones.

Chaplains are members of the care team and also serve as chaplains to the care team. The interdisciplinary care team is also a key spiritual care customer. One example is a nurse who contacted a chaplain to provide end-of-life support for a dying patient. The nurse trusted the chaplain would promptly respond by being attentive, compassionate, and supportive, and would use spiritually appropriate resources to facilitate a peaceful transition. The chaplain joined the nurse at bedside so the patient would not die alone.

Chaplains spends the majority of their time providing Spiritual Care services to the patient and family, and the clinical care team. They devote their remaining time to nonclinical employees, serving the institution, representing the hospital in the community, and educating trainees. Each group of customers expects professional, compassionate, competent, ethical, and timely services and care from chaplains. They want privacy, confidentiality, and respect, and expect that chaplains will preserve their dignity and advocacy when they are unable to give voice themselves. They expect to be responded to without judgment and to be seen and experienced as a whole human being, not as a disease. Customers also expect to have their care team inquire about their spiritual and religious values and beliefs and eliminate any barriers to accessing them. Providing religious and spiritual rituals, and recognizing significant events and services, are two more key expectations.

Last, the care team expects chaplains to contribute to safe, high-quality care. They require 24-hour availability, concise documentation, and compliance with institutional policies and standards of practice, and that chaplains will consistently create and employ spiritual care best practices.

KEY PROCESS FLOWS

Key Spiritual Care Department process flows include (1) patient spiritual-needs screenings, (2) code blue, (3) death, (4) comprehensive spiritual assessment, (5) plan of care and education, (6) emergency preparedness, and (7) EHR documentation. Patient spiritual-needs screening consists of three short questions that any member of an institution's care team can administer. If needed, the care recipient's answers can trigger a referral for a professional chaplain to follow up within 24 hours. The questions are:

1. Are religion or spirituality important to you as you cope with your illness?
2. How much strength/comfort do you get from your religion/spirituality right now?
3. Would you like to see a chaplain? (Fitchett, Murphy, and King 2017)

Exhibit 20.3 depicts a sample chaplain-structured EHR note template. Key areas to note in this document are spiritual assessment, intervention, outcomes, and follow-up recommendations.

Exhibit 20.3: Downtime Documentation—Spiritual Care

Name/Medical Record Number: Location:

Date: Time:

Consult Information

Reason for Consult

Spiritual Care Visit at This Time

Spiritual Care Assessment

Meaning/Spirituality

Belief System

Initial Spiritual
Observation

Significant Spiritual Issues

Spiritual Peacefulness Scale

| 1—Strong | 2—Substantial | 3—Moderate | 4—Some | 5—None |

Current Spiritual Experience Rating Scales

Physical Suffering

| 1—No Pain | 2—Some Pain | 3—Moderate | 4—Substantial Pain | 5—Severe Pain |

(continued)

Spiritual Suffering				
1—No Suffering	2—Some Suffering	3—Moderate Suffering	4—Substantial Suffering	5—Severe Suffering

Relatedness/Connection				
1—Strong sense of connection	2—Substantial connections	3—Moderate connections	4—Little	5—Isolated

Forgiveness				
1—Strong sense of forgiveness	2—Substantial	3—Moderate, connections maintained	4—Some/ Minimal	5—Alienated from others/ things

Safety/Security				
1—Strong/secure and lovingly supported	2—Substantial/ secure and supported	3—Moderate, comfortable with support	4—Afraid	5—Fear and terror feelings

Coping with Spiritual Support				
1—Strong	2—Substantial	3—Moderate	4—Some	5—None

Spiritual Distress				
1—None	2—Some	3—Moderate	4—Substantial	5—Severe

Coping with Spiritual Distress				
1—Strong	2—Substantial	3—Moderate	4—Some	5—None

Meaning/Purpose				
1—Strong: Life filled with purpose/meaning	2—Substantial purpose/ meaning	3—Moderate: Maintaining purpose/ meaning	4—Some/ Minimal purpose/ meaning	5—None/Life is empty

Hope and confidence				
1—Strong: Filled with hope and confidence	2—Substantial sense of hope and confidence	3—Moderate: Maintaining sense of hope and confidence	4—Some/ Minimal sense of hope and confidence	5—None/ Deep despair/ hopelessness

Intervention

Intervention provided

Spiritual Care Outcome

Post-consult Spiritual Care Outcome

Follow-up

Patient is open to visit by spiritual community representative

Dashboard Collection Data

(continued)

Exhibit 20.3: Downtime Documentation—Spiritual Care *(continued)*

Present at Death within dashboard parameters	☐ Yes	☐ No
Present at Code within dashboard parameters	☐ Yes	☐ No
Patient Needs Screening within dashboard parameters	☐ Yes	☐ No

KEY UNITS OF WORK AND VOLUME STATISTICS TO MONITOR

Spiritual Care departments monitor metrics to manage operations and communicate their contributions to the hospital's mission, vision, and strategic goals. The key units of work in Spiritual Care are monthly number of spiritual care encounters, consults per chaplain full-time equivalent (FTE) per working day, and consults per total FTE per working day. These metrics provide department leadership a way to measure work volumes and monitor productivity. Using key units of work can help justify requests for new positions.

KEY METRICS TO MONITOR: PEOPLE, SERVICE, QUALITY/SAFETY, FINANCIAL

Similar to other entities in healthcare organizations today, twenty-first-century Spiritual Care has adopted the need to demonstrate its value to the operation. Measuring the quality of service provided to care recipients with an established customer service and satisfaction model has helped chaplains develop the business acumen to communicate with institutional leaders. Reviewing monthly scorecard metrics also communicates service expectations to staff. Exhibit 20.4 lists sample key metrics on a Spiritual Care Department scorecard.

STAFFING MODELS

Spiritual Care departments vary in size, qualifications, business and office hours, full-time or part-time hours, and in-hospital or on-call remote availability. Assessing the needs of patients, staff, and community is most helpful when determining a staffing model. Staffing models should be reviewed and revised according to the

Exhibit 20.4: Sample Spiritual Care Scorecard Metrics

People
- First-Year Turnover
- Overall Turnover

Service
- Customer Satisfaction Scores
- % Patient Encounters That Receive Spiritual Care
- % Ambulatory Consults
- % Patient-Needs Screening Responded to Within 24 hours
- % Completed Bereavement Packets

Quality and Safety
- % Completed Documentation for Key Spiritual Outcomes
- % Daily Safety Checklists Accurately Completed
- % Documentation of Spiritual Assessments
- % Abandoned Calls

Finance
- Personnel Expense
- Other Operating Expense
- Total Operating Expense
- Operating Income Loss: % Variance Actual to Budget
- Medicare Reimbursement for Clinical Pastoral Education

---

changing needs of internal and external stakeholders. Evaluating service outcomes, customer satisfaction, and community benefit will provide valuable information on how to adjust a staffing model.

It is important to receive feedback from the Spiritual Care staff when creating or adjusting staffing. Employee engagement and satisfaction should be consistently measured and supported. Important areas to consider when creating a staffing model include required hours of service to achieve key work processes, impact on staff and patient safety, service locations on and off campus, and effect on work–life balance. The staffing model depicted in exhibit 20.5 is a service-line model with five distinct spiritual care service lines: ambulatory, tele-chaplaincy, inpatient, weekend, and weekday evening/night. Each area has at least one dedicated chaplain. One ambulatory chaplain provides spiritual support to local hospital clinics. The tele-chaplaincy service line provides virtual response to ambulatory patient-needs screening requests, follow-up spiritual care consults with discharged patients, telephone requests, and scheduled appointments with a chaplain. This chaplain also provides in-person backup coverage as needed. The

Exhibit 20.5: Service Line Model

Service lines	Monday	Tuesday	Wednesday	Thursday	Friday	Saturday	Sunday	Total remote hours (weekly)
Ambulatory service	Ambulatory	Remote	Ambulatory	Remote	Ambulatory	OFF	OFF	16
Remote Service	Remote	Remote	Remote	Remote	Remote	OFF	OFF	40
Surgery	6 a.m.–4 p.m.	6 a.m.–4 p.m.	6 a.m.–4 p.m.	6 a.m.–4 p.m.	OFF	OFF	OFF	4
5th-floor Unit	OFF	9 a.m.–7 p.m.	9 a.m.–7 p.m.	9 a.m.–7 p.m.	9 a.m.–7 p.m.	OFF	OFF	4
7th-floor Unit	7 a.m.–5 p.m.	7 a.m.–5 p.m.	7 a.m.–5 p.m.	7 a.m.–5 p.m.	7 a.m.–5 p.m.	OFF	OFF	—
9th-floor Unit	8 a.m.–5 p.m.	8 a.m.–5 p.m.	8 a.m.–5 p.m.	8 a.m.–5 p.m.	OFF	OFF	OFF	—
ICU Unit	9 a.m.–6 p.m.	9 a.m.–6 p.m.	9 a.m.–6 p.m.	9 a.m.–6 p.m.	9 a.m.–6 p.m.	OFF	OFF	—
Weekend service	8 p.m.–8 a.m.	OFF	OFF	OFF	OFF	8 a.m.–8 p.m.	8 a.m.–8 p.m.	4
Weekend service	OFF	OFF	OFF	OFF	8 p.m.–8 a.m.	8 p.m.–8 a.m.	8 p.m.–8 a.m.	4
Evening service	OFF	8 p.m.–8 a.m.	8 p.m.–8 a.m.	8 p.m.–8 a.m.	OFF	OFF	OFF	4
Nights	1 p.m.–10 p.m.	1 p.m.–10 p.m.	1 p.m.–10 p.m.	1 p.m.–10 p.m.	1 p.m.–10 p.m.	—	—	—
								76

inpatient chaplains provide support to patients and clinical teams on units that have high acuity and volumes. Chaplains serving these units receive direct referrals from providers and have strong relationships with the medical service leadership. Chaplains provide staff education, round with the care team, attend grand rounds and family conferences, and help with discharge planning, ethics consultations, and goals-of-care discussions. The weekend chaplains work 12-hour shifts three days per week. Chaplains assigned to weekend service are high performers with advanced experience and competency in mentoring chaplain trainees. Weekend chaplains are autonomous and are able to make decisions quickly during crises. They form and maintain professional relationships with staff. Weekday evening and night chaplains provide after-hours spiritual care. These chaplains are responsible for completing referrals from colleagues, new patient consults, patient requests, crisis events, and staff support.

One strength of this model is that it provides 24-hour coverage, seven days a week. The model also addresses customer and staff needs in high-volume service areas by assigning a minimum of one chaplain to each area for a minimum of four weekday shifts. A second strength is that it provides a dedicated weekday-evening chaplain and overnight chaplain, and two weekend chaplains. Chaplains do not have to rotate covering day, evening, overnight, or weekend shifts, resulting in better work–life balance. A third strength is the opportunity for top-of-the-license chaplains to be known as integral team members in their clinical specialty. Last, this model provides in-person spiritual support to ambulatory services that did not have a chaplain. The weaknesses of this model are that only one chaplain provides backup for the department, and the weekend chaplains work 12-hour shifts that could disrupt work–life balance. The service line model is depicted in exhibit 20.5.

PRODUCTIVITY MODELS, INCLUDING WORK-TO-STAFF RATIOS AND INDUSTRY PERFORMANCE TARGETS

Spiritual Care productivity is as unique as the healthcare organization. Factors affecting productivity include size of the institution, number and type of staff, hours of operation, medical specialty, designation as a trauma center, and inpatient census volumes. Some productivity models for chaplains are based on the ratio of chaplains to inpatient beds, whereas others are based on the number of patient visits per day. Sue Wintz and George Handzo (2001) first introduced a chaplain ratio of one chaplain for every 50 hospital beds. Recent models from a joint publication of five professional chaplaincy associations recommend a staffing ratio between 1.5 to 2.3 chaplains per 100 patients (ACPE et al. 2018). An example of one productivity model is 9.5 patient encounters per working day for full-time chaplains and 4 patient encounters per clinical shift for trainees.

A productivity standard can be determined from peer-organization benchmark data and analyzing the department's historic productivity data.

STRATEGIES TO IMPROVE RECRUITMENT AND RETENTION

Recruiting and retaining certified professional chaplains is crucial to a quality Spiritual Care department. Hospitals with an accredited CPE program often employ their graduates. Spiritual Care leaders should encourage employees to participate in employee opinion surveys. Listening to the strengths and opportunities to improve engagement and employee satisfaction, and taking action to involve staff in implementing improvements, are some of the most important tasks for a leader. Professional chaplains are willing to assist with solutions when leaders demonstrate genuine concern for their well-being and professional development.

Examples of development opportunities helpful to chaplains include continuing education and development opportunities in research, coaching, advance practice chaplaincy, and postgraduate degree programs. Providing opportunities where chaplaincy skills can be used outside of the department is another growth option: for example, recommending a chaplain lead a quality improvement project. Giving chaplains the chance to educate staff about religious and spiritual diversity, lead service-excellence training, teach active listening skills and conflict resolution, provide feedback on group process, and host customer focus groups are further ways chaplain training can add value to a healthcare organization.

Spiritual Care leaders should ensure that certified professional chaplains are compensated appropriately by the healthcare organization when compared with peers on the interdisciplinary team. Also, chaplains are natural servant leaders. Acknowledging and recognizing their contribution to the overall caring environment of your organization is the best strategy for recruitment and retention.

KEY REGULATORY ISSUES

The Joint Commission (2018) recognizes the contributions professional chaplains make to healthcare institutions. Three areas where chaplains demonstrate compliance are (1) Patient Rights, (2) Part of the Interdisciplinary, Collaborative Team, and (3) Supporting Clinical Staff. First, professional chaplains are champions for Joint Commission Standard R1.01.01, respecting the cultural and personal values, belief, and preferences of patients, especially those most vulnerable (EP6). This standard includes the right to religious and other spiritual services (EP9). The second area where chaplains contribute is Provision of Care, Treatment, and Services (PC) Standard PC.02.01.05. As stated earlier in the chapter, chaplains have significant roles on the interdisciplinary care team because they provide direct spiritual care to patients and their caregivers. Chaplain assessments and interventions with patients are documented in the EHR and shared with the team. The Joint Commission looks at patient records for evidence of Spiritual Care involvement with patients to validate patient access to services that support their values and religious or spiritual beliefs. Last, Joint Commission Leadership Standard LD.04.04.05 requires healthcare leaders to provide staff support to mitigate the effects of adverse events on their well-being. Chaplains are attuned to stressors and can initiate intervention by meeting individually with staff, practicing active listening, and providing nonjudgmental support. They can use resources such as tranquility breaks, healthy snacks, tea for the soul, and blessing of the hands.

The Centers for Medicare & Medicaid Services reference spiritual care in the Conditions of Participation for Patient Rights, 42 CFR 418.52(c). Chaplains contribute to the Commission on Cancer standards through multidisciplinary cancer case conferences (2020 Standard 2.5) and addressing psychosocial distress for spiritual concerns (2020 Standard 5.2). The National Hospice and Palliative Care Organization is a membership association of providers and professionals dedicated to person-centered care, advocacy, education, and best practices for their patients. Though not a regulatory agency, it provides comprehensive Spiritual Care guidelines and resources that support patients with terminal diagnoses, and those wanting non-curative treatment. Spiritual Care focuses on the multidimensional needs of patients living with chronic and serious conditions such as cancer, renal failure, diabetes, heart failure, and pulmonary disease. Patients and their caregivers benefit from whole-person care that supports their physical, mental, emotional, social, and spiritual needs to help them experience better quality of life. Patients who have their spiritual needs addressed report higher satisfaction with their care.

KEY TERMS FOR SPIRITUAL CARE

Board-certified professional chaplain: A master's-educated spiritual care provider with qualifications and demonstrated competencies according to credentialing organizations' certification standards. They are employed by an agency or organization and serve in a variety of settings such as prisons, government, armed services, corporations, first responder organizations, the civil service, schools, hospitals, religious organizations, counseling centers, physician practices, and social service settings. Certified chaplains must renew their credentials annually through continuing education, adherence to professional ethics, peer review, and maintaining their faith group's endorsement.

Certified Educator: A chaplain certified by the Association for Clinical Pastoral Education (ACPE) who has completed postgraduate education in chaplaincy and education in a clinical setting. Certified Educators are faculty for ACPE-accredited Clinical Pastoral Education programs.

Clinical pastoral education: An interfaith or faith-specific chaplaincy training requirement for seminary graduation, certification with professional chaplaincy organizations, chaplain employment, or faith-group endorsement and ordination. The curriculum outcomes address three areas: pastoral formation, pastoral competency, and pastoral reflection. ACPE clinical pastoral education requires 400 hours of training per class.

Clinical spiritual care practitioner: Another term used for a professional chaplain hired by a healthcare organization who provides service in a clinical setting such as a hospital, mental health facility, hospice, or long-term care facility.

Interdisciplinary care team: A team of professionals who treat, care for, and support the care recipient and family from a holistic approach. Each team member provides services and support according to their professional discipline and area of expertise, and collaborates with others for the best health outcome.

Spiritual assessment: A primary assessment tool used by professional chaplains to understand and diagnose spiritual well-being. Spiritual assessment is the most comprehensive screening model and is best completed by a spiritual care practitioner.

Spiritual-needs screening: An initial, brief spiritual screening tool that can be completed by any member of the care team and that can trigger a chaplaincy consultation.

Spiritual well-being: Having spiritual health and spiritual balance. Experiencing spiritual connection, meaning, purpose, and peace regardless of external circumstances. The absence of spiritual distress.

Spirituality: The broad umbrella that expresses how a person experiences meaning and purpose, connection, and relationship with others, nature, or anything else that is important to them, including a divine being, if they believe in any. It includes religious belief and expression but is more inclusive than religion.

REFERENCES

Association for Clinical Pastoral Education (ACPE), Association of Professional Chaplains, Canadian Association for Spiritual Care, National Association of Catholic Chaplains, and Neshama: Association of Jewish Chaplains. 2018.

The Impact of Professional Spiritual Care. Hoffman Estates, IL: Association of Professional Chaplains.

Dhar, N., S. K. Chaturvedi, and D. Nandan. 2013. "Spiritual Health, the Fourth Dimension: A Public Health Perspective." *WHO South-East Asia Journal of Public Health* 2 (1): 3–5.

Fitchett, G., P. Murphy, and S. D. W. King. 2017. "Examining the Validity of the Rush Protocol to Screen for Religious/Spiritual Struggle." *Journal of Health Care Chaplaincy* 23 (3): 98–112.

Hall, E. J., B. P. Hughes, and G. H. Handzo. 2016. *Spiritual Care: What It Means, Why It Matters in Healthcare.* New York: Healthcare Chaplaincy Network.

Joint Commission. 2018. "Part 1. Body, Mind, Spirit: Hospital Chaplains Contribute to Patient Satisfaction and Well-Being." *The Source* 16 (1): 6–12.

Lipka, M., and C. Gecewicz. 2017. "More Americans Say They Are Spiritual but Not Religious." *Pew Research Center Fact Tank.* Published September 6. www.pewresearch.org/fact-tank/2017/09/06/more-americans-now-say-theyre-spiritual-but-not-religious/.

Nouwen, H. J. M. 1968. "Anton T. Boisen and Theology Through Living Human Documents." *Pastoral Psychology* 19: 49–63.

Puchalski, C. M., R. Vitillo, S. K. Hull, and N. Reller. 2014. "Improving the Spiritual Dimension of Whole Person Care: Reaching National and International Consensus." *Journal of Palliative Medicine* 17 (6): 642–56.

Wintz, S., and G. Handzo. 2001. "Pastoral Care Staffing and Productivity: More Than Ratios." *Chaplaincy Today* 21: 3–8.

World Health Organization (WHO). 2020. "Palliative Care." Published August 5. www.who.int/news-room/fact-sheets/detail/palliative-care.

Index

Note: Italicized page locators refer to exhibits.

Fishbone diagrams, 40, 42

Flowchart: definition of, 42, 161

Flow cytometry, 209, 211

Fluid analysis, 210

Fluoroscopy, 282

Focus groups, 23

Food and Nutrition Services Department, *5,* 99, 155–71; competitive compensation in, 167; description of, 155–56; employee engagement in, 167; hiring and onboarding process in, 167; key customers and their performance indicators in, 158, *160*; key informatics issues in, 163–64, *164*; key metrics to monitor in: people, service, quality/safety, financial, 162, *163*; key process flows in, 160–62, *161*; key regulatory issues in, 156, 169; key services in, 156–57; key terms for, 170–71; kitchen safety, cleaning, and sanitation metrics, sample, *170*; organizational structure of, 157–58, *159*; productivity models for, 165, *165, 166*; recruitment and retention strategies in, improving, 166–67, *168*; scorecard template example, 162, *163. See also* Clinical Nutrition Services Department

Foodborne illnesses: preventing, 169

Food insecurity: combating, 157

Food safety, 160

Foodservice care: components of, 157

Foodservice Director Magazine, 155

Formulary management, 265, 267

Fringe benefits: in healthcare food service, 165

Frozen sections, 209, 212

Full-time equivalents (FTEs): Admissions position control: budgeted positions, *64*; billed units for rehabilitative services and, 305, *312,* 312–13; in Case Management Department, *92*; in Clinical Nutrition Department, 112, *115, 116*; data tracking in Social Work Department and, 344, *346*; in Environmental Services Department, 130; in Facilities Department, 150; in Food and Nutrition Services, *165, 166*;

front-door registration requirements, *67–68*; in Health Information Management, 177, *180*; labor ratio: test per, 223–24; in Language Assistance Department, 201, *201–2*; pharmacy workloads and, 274; respiratory care productivity calculations, 332, *332*; revenue ratio, revenue per, 224; Social Work staffing model, calculations for, *350–51*; Spiritual Care Department consults and, 368; testing volumes in laboratories and, 217

Gamma rays, 279

Gating image acquisition, 283

Genetic markers: identification of, 211

Genetic testing, 227

Geographic staffing model: pros and cons of, 91; for Social Work Department, 350

Glomerular filtration rate test, 288

Goal alignment: brown-bag educational sessions on, 40

Governing body, 235; grievance process and, 244; key metrics to report to, 239, *239*; reporting complaint/grievance data to, 235

Gravimetrics, 268–69, 277

Grievance committee, 235, 244

Grievance Log: maintaining, 244

Grievance response, updating, and resolution: sample letters used for, 244, *245*

Grievances. *See* Patient grievances

Gross square footage, 128, 130, 144, 150

Growth scorecard measure: Baldrige framework and, 36, *36*

Handzo, George, 371

Hardwiring Excellence (Studer), 346

HCAHPS. *See* Hospital Consumer Assessment of Healthcare Providers and Systems

Healthcare delivery: value-based principles in, 232, *232*

Healthcare Facilities Accreditation Program, 117, 151, 335

Health Care Facilities Code (National Fire Protection Association), 149

Human leukocyte antigen: definition of, 228; testing, 209

Human Resources: regulatory issues in rehabilitation services and, 314; Respiratory Care Department and, 333

HVAC system performance: vivarium labs and, 152

Hybrid model design: in pharmacies, 274

Hybrid record: definition of, 189

ICD codes: for Rehabilitation Services Department, 315

Image-guided interventions: definition of, 297

Imaging Services: technical and professional components of, 279

Immunohistochemistry assays, 209–10

Important Message from Medicare, 71–72, 88, 90

Incentives: in Radiology and Imaging Services Department, 296

Industry performance targets: for Admissions Department, 68–70; for Case Management Department, 91–93; for Clinical Services Department, 115; for Environmental Services Department, 130; for Facilities Department, 150; for Food and Nutrition Services Department, 165, *165, 166*; for Health Information Management Department, 185; for Language Assistance Department, *202,* 202–3; for Pathology and Laboratory Medicine Department, 223–25; for Patient Advocacy Department, 242; for Patient Transportation Department, 259; for Pharmacy Department, 274–75; for Radiology and Imaging Services Department, 295; for Rehabilitation Services Department, 311–13; for Social Work Department, 351–52; for Spiritual Care Department, 371–72

Infection control: respiratory therapists and role in, 335; for transport equipment, 255

Infection Control departments/programs: Food and Nutrition Services Department and, 156; in healthcare organizations, Environmental Services partnerships with, 124

Informatics issues, key: in Admissions Department, 63; in Case Management Department, 89–90; in Clinical Nutrition Services Department, 112–13; in Food and Nutrition Services Department, 163, *164;* in Health Information Management Department, 180, 183–85; in Pathology and Laboratory Medicine Department, 220, *220–21;* in Patient Advocacy Department, 240; in Patient Transportation Department, 258; in Pharmacy Department, 272–73; in Radiology and Imaging services, 294–95; in Rehabilitation Services Department, 306, 309; in Respiratory Care Department, 329–30; in Social Work Department, 349, *349. See also* Electronic health records

Information systems: reliability and security of, 25. *See also* Electronic health records

Information technology: in Case Management Department, 90

Initial denials: addressing, in Case Management Department, 78

Initial time: definition of, 70

Inpatient pharmacies, 264

Inpatient Prospective Payment System, 87

Inpatients: imaging services for, 286, 287–88

Inpatient-to-inpatient hospital transfers: definition of, 74

Inpatient units: Admissions team and, 50

In-person interpretation, 192, *192,* 196, 197, 202, 204

Inputs: of Assess stage, 30, *31, 32,* 34; connection between outputs, processes, and, 35

Insourcing: definition of, 135; Environmental Services Department and, 131, 132; in Facilities Department, 148

Institute for Healthcare Improvement: Triple Aim Initiative, 113

monitor in, 217–18; organizational structure in, 212–14, *213*; productivity models for, 223–25, *225, 226*; recruitment and retention strategies in, improving, 225–26; staffing models for, 221–22, *222–23*

Pathology laboratories, 209–10

Patient Access Department, 47

Patient advocacy: definition of, 247

Patient Advocacy Department, *5,* 231–47; description of, 231–32; key customers and their performance expectations in, 235–36; key informatics issues in, 240; key metrics to monitor in: people, service, quality/safety, financial, 238–40, *239*; key process flows in, 236, *236–37*; key regulatory issues in, 244, *245,* 246; key services in, 233; key terms for, 247; key units of work and volume statistics to monitor in, 237–38; organizational structures in, 233–34, *234*; productivity models for, 242; purpose of, 231; recruitment and retention strategies in, improving, 242–44; staffing models for, 241–42

Patient advocates: benchmarking performance of, 239–40; burnout and, 234, 243; disclosure of medical errors and, 236; grievance process and, 235–36; role of, 231, 233; skills of, 243, 247; staffing ratios for, 241; work schedules for, 244

Patient- and family-centered care model: definition of, 247

Patient census levels: maintenance costs and, 147

Patient-centered care: Patient Advocacy program and, 231

Patient-centeredness: Institute of Medicine and focused improvement on, 29

Patient choice: Centers for Medicare & Medicaid Services Conditions of Participation and, 94

Patient complaints, 237–38; addressing, process for, 236, *236–37*; in ambulatory

settings, 241–42; definition of, 247; filing, 233; informatics issues and, 240; key metrics to monitor related to, 238–40; productivity metrics and, 242; regulatory issues and, 244, *245,* 246; tracking and trending, 235; voicing, 231

Patient experience: ancillary and support departments' role in, 7–9

Patient grievances, 237–38; addressing, process for, 236, *236–37*; in ambulatory settings, 241–42; definition of, 247; documenting, 233; filing, 235; informatics issues and, 240; key metrics to monitor related to, 238–40; presenting, 233; productivity metrics and, 242; regulatory issues and, 244, *245,* 246; review and resolution of, 234; tracking and trending, 235; voicing, 231

Patient health information: Health Insurance Portability and Accountability Act and, 188. *See also* Electronic health records; Medical records

Patient health records: protecting and preserving integrity of, 173. *See also* Electronic health records

Patient registration. *See* Consent and patient registration

Patient rights: protecting, 231

Patient Rights information: monitoring compliance with, 58

Patients: clients *vs.,* 315

Patient safety, 94, 233; admissions process and, 50; ancillary and support departments' roles in, 6; in Clinical Nutrition Department, 101, 118; International Standards Organization standards for enteral feeding connectors, *105*; in Patient Transportation Department, 251, 255, 261. *See also* Safety issues

Patient sample: definition of, 229

Patient satisfaction: in Radiology and Imaging Services Department, 293; room service programs and, 157; staff engagement and, 34; surveys, 129, 239

Patient services representative: definition of, 74

Patient-side testing, 208

Patient specimens, 207

Patient Transportation Department, *5,* 251–61; description of, 251; key customers and their performance expectations in, 253, *254*; key informatics issues in, 258; key metrics to monitor in: people, service, quality/safety, financial, 255, *256–57,* 258; key process flows in, 253–54; key regulatory issues in, 261; key services in, 251–52; key terms for, 261; key units of work and volume statistics to monitor in, 255; organizational structures in, 252–53; productivity models in, 259, *260*; recruitment and retention strategies for, improving, 259, 261; staffing models for, 258

Payers: cost reduction strategies and, 289

Peer-to-peer reviews: imaging services and, 290, 291

People metrics. *See specific departments, key metrics to monitor in*

People scorecard measure: Baldrige framework and, 36, *36*

Percentage Completion of Annual Mandatory Training, 145

Percentage Satisfactory on Routine Inspections, 147

Performance and quality improvement teams, 329

Performance dashboard: definition of, 261

Performance excellence: definition of, 26

Performance improvement, 4, 21; definition of, 42; education sessions, 38

Performance improvement, building culture of, 29–42; annual planning process, 30, *33*; assess current processes and results, 30, *30, 31–32,* 34; cycles of improvement in, 42; improve with Plan, Do, Study, Act approach, 30, *30, 31–32,* 36, *37–38*; infrastructure used for, *31–32*; integrated *vs.* add-on approach to, 41; people, knowledge, and skills in, 40; plan for short- and long-term success, 30, *30, 31–32,* 34–36; proactive *vs.* reactive approach to, 41; systems for performance management, 40; transparency and accountability in, 40–41; two examples of, 38–39

Performance improvement projects, examples of, 38–39; Case Management Department, 39; Health Information Management Department, 38–39

Performance management system: reviewing, 40

Personalized medicine, 211

Personal protective equipment, 124; definition of, 135; in Radiology and Imaging Services Department, 297

Person-centered care: eight principles of, 7–9, *8*

Personnel expense: in Clinical Nutrition Department, 115

Pharmacists, 266, *266*; career ladders for, 275; clinical, 274; definition of, 277; education and training for, 263; operational, 265, 273; postgraduate-trained, 265; role in patient experience, 9; roles of, categorizing, 265

Pharmacokinetics: patient-specific, 265, 268

Pharmacy-benefit-management payers, 267

Pharmacy Department, *5,* 263–77; centralized and decentralized practice design, 273; description of, 263–64; hybrid model design, 274; key customers and their performance expectations in, 267–68; key informatics issues in, 272–73; key metrics to monitor in: people, service, quality/safety, financial, 270–71, *272*; key process flows in, 268–69, *269*; key regulatory issues in, 276–77; key services in, 264–65; key terms for, 277; key units of work and volume statistics to monitor in, 269–70; organizational structure of, *266,* 266–67; productivity models for, 274–75; recruitment and retention strategies in, improving, 275–76, *276*; specialist model design, 273–74; staffing models for, 273–74

About the Contributors

Brent Braveman, PhD, OTR, FAOTA, is an occupational therapist and has worked as a manager and leader in multiple settings including graduate education, community-based organizations, and hospitals. He has presented and published extensively on management, work disability, and oncology rehabilitation, including three textbooks, multiple peer-reviewed journal articles, and 26 book chapters. He has served in various leadership and expert panel roles including those for the American Occupational Therapy Association, the National Quality Forum, and the National Institutes of Health. He is currently the director of the Department of Rehabilitation Services at The University of Texas MD Anderson Cancer Center in Houston.

Pamela E. Brooks, MSN, RN, is manager of Inpatient Admissions and the Discharge Center at The University of Texas MD Anderson Cancer Center. She holds a bachelor's degree in nursing, a master's degree in the science of nursing, and a post-master's certificate in nursing education from the University of Texas at Arlington. She has 27 years of nursing experience working with oncology patients at MD Anderson. For the past four years, her focus has been on patient throughput.

Leisa Bryant, RDA, MA, MBA, is a registered and licensed dietitian and the director of Food and Nutrition Services at The University of Texas MD Anderson Cancer Center. She holds a bachelor's degree in food and nutrition from Hunter College, a master's degree in community health education from Brooklyn College, and a master's in business administration from the University of Houston Downtown.

Elizabeth Comcowich Garcia, RN, MPA, NEA-BC, CPXP, has been a nursing and hospital administrator with a focus on safety, quality, and patient experience for over 30 years. She is currently vice president of Patient Experience at

The University of Texas MD Anderson Cancer Center, providing leadership for Patient Advocacy; Patient Education; askMDAnderson, a comprehensive call center; Food and Nutrition Services; the Patient and Family Advisor Program; and Spiritual Care and Education.

Pamela Douglas-Ntagha, DNP, JD, MSN, MBA, RN, is director of Patient Resources at The University of Texas MD Anderson Cancer Center, where she directs hospital patient flow and is responsible for Admissions, the Transfer Center, and the Discharge Center. Prior to this role, she served in numerous clinical nursing practice and hospital management roles within the Memorial Healthcare System and HCA System. She has served as immediate past president of the National Association of Healthcare Transport Management and an international speaker on patient flow. Dr. Douglas-Ntagha holds a doctor of nursing practice degree from Texas Tech University in Lubbock; a doctor of jurisprudence degree from Thurgood Marshall School of Law in Houston; a master of business administration degree from Our Lady of the Lake in San Antonio, Texas; a master of nursing degree from the University of Texas at Tyler; and a bachelor of nursing degree from Dillard University of New Orleans.

Lauren Goldberg, PharmD, is a PGY-2 Health-System Pharmacy Administration resident at The University of Texas MD Anderson Cancer Center. She graduated from the University of Houston College of Pharmacy in 2019 and completed her first year of residency at MD Anderson Cancer Center.

Elit Gonzalez, MBA, RHIA, is an assistant director in Health Information Management (HIM) at The University of Texas MD Anderson Cancer Center. She has over 20 years of leadership and project management experience in the HIM field. She earned a BS in health information management from the University of Cincinnati, summa cum laude, and an MBA from Texas Woman's University, summa cum laude. She is also an adjunct professor who enjoys teaching the next generation of health information technology students at Houston Community College.

Gayle Harper is the director of Patient Transportation & Clinical Support Services Administration at The University of Texas MD Anderson Cancer Center. She supports the vice president of Clinical Support Services, focusing on strategic planning, performance improvement, data management project consultation, and special projects. She has an MBA from Texas Woman's University and an MSW from the University of North Carolina, and has worked at MD Anderson for 30 years.

Ann-Marie Hedberg, DrPH, RD, LD, is associate director of Clinical Nutrition at The University of Texas MD Anderson Cancer Center, specializing in oncology care. She completed her dietetics training at the University of Delaware, earned an MS from the University of Texas (UT) Graduate School of Biomedical Sciences, and a doctorate of public health in health administration at UT School of Public Health, Houston. She has worked for 42 years in the areas of clinical dietetics, nutrition support, and healthcare management, and as an assistant professor/dietetic internship director.

Chris Hernandez, MBA, is executive director of Patient Services at The University of Texas MD Anderson Cancer Center. He is also a United States Air Force Medical Officer and Healthcare Administrator, Texas Air National Guard, Houston.

Gale Francine Kennebrew, DMin, MDiv, BCC, ACPE, is director of Spiritual Care and Education for The University of Texas MD Anderson Cancer Center. She received her MDiv from Chicago Theological Seminary and her DMin from United Theological Seminary in Dayton, Ohio. She is a Certified Chaplain with the Association of Professional Chaplains, a Certified Educator with the Association for Clinical Pastoral Education, and a United Church of Christ clergywoman. Dr. Kennebrew has worked as a chaplain leader in faith-based and not-for-profit healthcare settings for over 28 years.

Jenny Koetting, MS, RD, CSO, is a registered dietitian with expertise in clinical nutrition management, program development, and quality improvement. She has led clinical nutrition teams in the Texas Medical Center and at the academic healthcare institutions The University of Texas MD Anderson Cancer Center and Baylor St. Luke's Medical Center. She is passionately involved in training the next generation of registered dietitians through her work with dietetic internships and teaching nutrition courses at the University of Houston.

Megan McGugan, PharmD, MS, BCPS, received her PharmD from the Medical University of South Carolina College of Pharmacy in 2017 and completed residency training at The University of Texas MD Anderson Cancer Center in 2019 while also receiving a master of science degree from the University of Houston. She is currently the Specialty Pharmacy manager at MD Anderson Cancer Center.

Jermaine McMillan, PhD, is a former lobbyist in the areas of environmental health, telecommunications, and public health. He began a career in healthcare administration at The University of Texas MD Anderson Cancer over 12 years ago. During his time there, he has overseen implementation of mobile health programs, helped expand the tobacco cessation program, and served in several operational leadership positions. He now serves as the project director for the Division of Clinical Services, which houses the Department of Patient Transportation.

Margaret W. Meyer, MSSW, MBA, LCSW, received her MSSW from the University of Texas at Austin and her MBA from Texas Woman's University. She has enjoyed contributing to the psychosocial programming at The University of Texas MD Anderson Cancer Center for 35 years. For the past 25 years, she has led a stellar team of social work counselors as the director of the Department of Social Work. The work of these social work counselors is making a difference in the lives of patients and those who care for them.

Joyceann Musel-Winn, PhD, FACHE, MT(ASCP), has over 25 years of experience in varied leadership roles at multiple healthcare networks, including two progressive networks in New York State. She has executive responsibility for financial, strategic, and regulatory compliance in a dynamic and highly regulated industry. She completed her PhD in population health while employed as the administrator of the Division of Pathology and Laboratory Medicine at The University of Texas MD Anderson Cancer Center, Houston.

Judy Overton, MLA, is a program manager in the Office of the Chief Patient Experience Officer at The University of Texas MD Anderson Cancer Center. As a former caregiver, Judy's passion is for patients and their loved ones to be active participants in their care decisions, and for them to particularly be aware of the signs of the late stages of life.

César Palacio is director of the Language Assistance Department at The University of Texas MD Anderson Cancer Center. He has a BA in technical communications and Latin American studies.

Robert Ray, PE, MBA, has been in the healthcare industry for over 20 years and currently serves as the regional director of facilities and projects with Sutter Health at the California Pacific Medical Center in San Francisco. He has completed his comprehensive exams for his PhD in health services and systems research and is currently working on his dissertation. Over the last 20 years he has worked at major academic medical centers in Texas and Arkansas.

Ryan K. Roux, PharmD, MS, FTSHP, FASHP, currently serves as vice president for the Division of Pharmacy for The University of Texas MD Anderson

Cancer Center. Dr. Roux received his PharmD from the University of Houston in 1999 and his master of science degree from The Ohio State University in 2001, where he also completed an ASHP-accredited pharmacy practice residency with emphasis in health system pharmacy administration.

Gautam H. Sachdev, RRT, FACHE, CHFP, is a Fellow of the American College of Healthcare Executives (FACHE) and Certified Healthcare Financial Professional (CHFP) with experience in quality, safety, process reengineering, and business development. He holds graduate degrees in business and healthcare administration.

Cynthia St. John, PhD, is a professor of management and healthcare administration for The University of Texas at Arlington. Before transitioning into academia full-time, she was vice president and chief learning officer for Texas Health Resources and served in leadership roles for major academic medical centers, including The University of Texas MD Anderson Cancer Center. She specializes in leadership and organizational development, has been a member of the Baldrige community for over 15 years, served multiple terms on the board of examiners for national and state programs, and is currently a judge and fellow for the Quality Texas Foundation.

Habib Tannir, MS, FACHE, currently serves as the vice president of Diagnostic Operations at The University of Texas MD Anderson Cancer Center, working on institutional strategic initiatives under the direction of the chief operating officer. As he took on progressive leadership roles, he has continuously served as the division administrator of Diagnostic Imaging at MD Anderson for the last eight years. Previous employers are Emory Healthcare, Atlanta; University Community Health, Tampa, Florida; GE Medical Systems, Waukesha, Wisconsin; and William Beaumont Hospital, Royal Oak, Michigan. Habib received his undergraduate degree in chemistry from the American University of Beirut and his master of science degree in biomedical engineering from the University of Akron.

Donna Ukanowicz, MS, RN, ACM-RN, currently serves as director for case management at The University of Texas MD Anderson Cancer Center, with over 40 years of healthcare experience in nursing and case management. She is a founding member of the American Case Management Association (ACMA). During her years serving on the ACMA Board of Directors, she assisted with the development of the Accredited Case Manager (ACM) certification examination for nurses and social workers practicing in hospital and health system case management.

Michele Walker is associate director of Patient Advocacy & Patient Relations at The University of Texas MD Anderson Cancer Center.

Randal S. Weber, MD, is a professor in the Department of Head and Neck Surgery and chief patient experience officer at The University of Texas MD Anderson Cancer Center.

Sue Wilson DBA, BSN, ACM-RN, has 29 years of nursing experience and 23 years in case management. She currently works at The University of Texas MD Anderson Cancer Center as the associate director of case management. She is also a member of the US Army Reserves where she has served for the last 32 years.

About the Editor

Frank R. Tortorella, JD, FACHE, is vice president of accreditation and regulatory affairs at The University of Texas MD Anderson Cancer Center in Houston. In this role, he provides institutional strategic oversight and leadership for accreditation and regulatory matters. He previously served as vice president of clinical support services. Prior to joining MD Anderson, Tortorella served as vice president of finance and vice president of ambulatory care at Advocate Illinois Masonic Medical Center in Chicago. He holds a bachelor of arts degree from Harvard University, a master of business administration degree with a specialization in healthcare administration from the University of Chicago, and a law degree with a concentration in health law from Loyola University Chicago. Tortorella is also an adjunct professor at the Beazley Institute for Health Law and Policy at the Loyola University Chicago School of Law and at the Robert F. Wagner Graduate School of Public Service at New York University. He is a Fellow of the American College of Healthcare Executives and has served as a Baldrige examiner at the state and national levels.